THE AMERICAN CHALLENGE

The American Challenge

The World Resists US Liberalism

R. CATLEY
University of Newcastle, Australia
DAVID MOSLER
University of Adelaide, Australia

Routledge
Taylor & Francis Group
LONDON AND NEW YORK

First published 2007 by Ashgate Publishing

Reissued 2018 by Routledge
2 Park Square, Milton Park, Abingdon, Oxon OX14 4RN
711 Third Avenue, New York, NY 10017, USA

Routledge is an imprint of the Taylor & Francis Group, an informa business

First issued in paperback 2018

A Library of Congress record exists under LC control number: 2007025281

ISBN 13: 978-0-8153-9743-4 (hbk)
ISBN 13: 978-1-1386-2081-0 (pbk)
ISBN 13: 978-1-3511-4784-2 (ebk)

Contents

Preface

This is the third book we have written together on the theme of America's relationship with the world. Since we have both lived in Australia for some time, that country gets some prominence in our deliberations; but our principal focus is on the considerable impact that the US has had on the world during the period in which it has been the most powerful state – that is since about 1900.

The Universities that employ us – the University of Adelaide and the University of Newcastle – have been most generous with resources and we acknowledge their assistance. We would also like to thank Professor Marian Palley of the University of Delaware for reading some of the early draft and making some valuable suggestions, although of course she bears none of the blame for the resulting text.

We have also both been most fortunate to have supportive wives and acknowledge the help of Sharon and Pat.

David Mosler
(University of Adelaide)
R. Catley
(University of Newcastle)

Introduction

We wrote *Global America: Imposing Liberalism on a Recalcitrant World,* in 1999 and it was published in the closing days of the Clinton administration. Eight years later it is time for a re-evaluation of the impact of American power on the world order. In the preface to that book we wrote that the United States:

> Possesses supreme power [which] it has used … to assert its dominance over and to further liberalise the international system. It has also used force to pursue its interests, particularly in those three regions of greatest geo-strategic importance: the Middle East, Europe and East Asia. It has used its power over communications to persuade the world it is right. While liberals may support these ambitions, any reasonable person must wonder whether such ambitious plans are beyond even the capabilities of the United States and what portents they hold for the international order.

In the concluding paragraphs we suggested that:

> The United States, with its imperfect liberal model pursuing ideals and interests, may be, as Americans believe, the least worst hope for mankind. The world, however, may also be increasingly and steadily a less safe, hospitable, humane and democratic place for Americans to live in over the next half century.

Circumstances have changed under the administration of George W Bush.

It is tempting for Americans to take the view that they are in their fourth world war in a century. They should recall, however, that the First World War took 10–14 million deaths, the Second World War produced over fifty million fatalities, and in the Cold War perhaps ten million people were killed. Even if the Global War on Terror lasts forty years, as it well might, at the present rate of casualties it will not match even the Cold War. Nonetheless, for Americans the world was more dangerous during the Bush Presidency than under his predecessor.

Bill Clinton was elected President only because the right of centre vote was divided between George W H Bush and Ross Perot. The administration that he led struggled for several years with its reform program and declining public approval until it lurched to the centre in 1994 from which location it won the 1996 Presidential poll. The foundations of the Clinton regime were the democrat liberal reform coalition of coastal leftists from both sides of the continent. His coalition included intellectuals, the Universities, labour unions, most of Hollywood, the minorities of Blacks, Hispanics and recent migrants, the new south, the liberal media, most of the Jewish vote and some of corporate America. Its foreign policy was not militarily activist, but driven by the economic imperatives of globalisation from which it rightly thought the US would profit. Clinton presided over a period of prosperity that followed the winning of the Cold War and the onset of globalisation. By 2000, he had balanced the federal budget and largely overcome the massive debts accumulated during the Reagan/Bush administrations.

Clinton's foreign policy was dominated by globalisation. At first, he ran down military expenditure and took the 'post-Cold War peace dividend'. The administration chose to mothball much military equipment and one of the largest fleets in the world lay inactive, anchored off Newport, Virginia. A massive air force was grounded in Texas. The administration was also ardently multilateralist and tried to construct a new cooperative international regime to replace the bi-polarity of the Cold War. As a result, it was less committed to unqualified state sovereignty, which Clinton denounced at the UN when laying the ground for intervening against Serbia. But it largely ignored terrorism.

The Bush administration came to power in January 2001, after very narrowly winning the 2000 election against Clinton's Vice President, Al Gore, as a result of superior campaigning techniques combined with an overwhelming funding advantage. The Republicans had courted the heartland patriots, the big corporations, especially in the oil industry, the right wing media, including Foxtel and the radio shock jocks, the religious right, and the neo-conservatives. It was also assisted by the stench of sleaze that surrounded Clinton by 2000 after Monica Lewinsky and impeachment.

The Bush administration's foreign policy started with an ostentatiously unilateralist orientation. It had stated its intention to build up the US defence forces and later Vice President Dick Cheney and Defense Secretary Donald Rumsfeld had been instrumental in drawing up the program *Project for a New America*. The Revolution in Military Affairs, which was already underway under Clinton, was accelerated when the Republicans achieved power. They also saw China as the most likely main enemy and threat to the 'unipolar moment' of the US. But the Republicans also did not have much to say about terrorism until 11 September, which may partly account for President Bush's famous seven minutes of silence seen by the whole world on television on 11 September 2001.

In the current debate among intellectuals and academics about terrorism, the Iraq War, Israel, US power and the international order, a political polarisation has taken place. The political Left has insisted that a crisis has been created by the imperialist illusions and the excesses of the alliance of evangelical Christian and Jewish/Zionist neo-conservatives in the Bush administration. Often, it then continues that the UN (in spite of its clear incapacity or will) should take over in Iraq, or even Israel/Palestine as well, and bring peace and order to that region of the world. The Left in this context includes, among others, journalists such as the Australian John Pilger and Englishman Robert Fisk, the American satirist and filmmaker Mike Moore and academics like the old 1960s radical activist Pakistani, Tariq Ali, now a British academic, and the venerable American linguist and prolific social commentator from the Massachusetts Institute of Technology (retired) Noam Chomsky. The Right, in a recycling of its historical certainty from the Cold War, talks about reshaping the Middle East and the dominos of Arab states that will topple over following the process of democratisation begun by force of US arms in Iraq. This is the structure of debate in all the major English speaking countries which, whatever their differences over policy, share much of a common historical narrative and political culture.

In the US, the attacks of 9/11 at first produced a political class mostly united (including some major defections from the Left such as Christopher Hitchens and the *New Republic*) behind the Republican administration in its war against Islamist terrorists and prepared to define its supporters very loosely. In the UK, this pitted the majority of the Labour government elected in 1997 and led by Tony Blair against its Left critics who were often supported, ironically, by an opportunistic Conservative Party. In Australia, the Liberal/National Coalition government, in office since 1996, has wholeheartedly supported the US, despite the criticisms of the Labor Opposition and the shrill hostility of the predominantly leftist intelligentsia. The New Zealand Labour government, elected in 1999 on a largely leftist security agenda, veered towards the US after September 2001 and has since been re-elected twice with its National opposition promising even more rightist policies which served to keep the Left in line. A highly emotive and polarized debate of these issues was a feature of the federal election in Canada in 2006, which produced a Conservative victory for the first time in fourteen years. Both sides of this chasm can be somewhat apocalyptic and it is necessary to first provide some historical framework before any useful analysis can be made of any specific region of the world and the role of US power in it.

After the Second World War, global changes created some 150 new nation states through decolonisation and unleashed rampant forces of economic and social modernisation. Geopolitical crisis situations created by the Second World War, the Cold War and decolonisation also persisted: the division of the Korean Peninsula; the dispute between China and Taiwan over sovereignty; the festering and never-ending war in Palestine over conflicting territorial claims in the Levant; the struggle between India and Pakistan over Kashmir. These are crises which emerged in the 1940s and have not yet been resolved. The nation state system itself has also come under great strain in some regions, especially in the South and Western Pacific, the Caribbean and central Africa, and trans-national bodies such as the UN and the Commonwealth are often powerless to stop the process of failed nation state disintegration.

Perhaps even more far-reaching, however, is the impact of modernisation sweeping through the world as part of the economic forces of globalisation emanating from the US and Europe. As a consequence, the more fragile nation states are weakened by trans-national economic forces and organizations including the UN, IMF, World Bank, WTO, EU, APEC; weak local cultures and languages are swamped by dominant cultural forms from the West; religious-based belief systems are being challenged and sometimes obliterated by the scientific rationalism intrinsic to industrial society; anti-modernisation movements have emerged as a reaction to modernisation in the form of religious extremism including Islamic, Hindu, Jewish, Sikh and Christian, as well as reactionary cultural movements such as anti-Semitism, anti-scientism, alternative medicine and new age religious fads; and, the world hears at all levels of society and the arts, cries of anguish over loss of control, the crisis of belief structures and, amid unprecedented affluence and longer life expectancy in the West, increasing themes of despair from intellectuals. When one adds the fears of the consequences of global warming the future appears problematical at best.

Western leftist intellectuals now often see no place to hide: all problems are global whether they be environmental destruction, unequal distribution of income, energy shortages, overpopulation, crime, terrorism, disease, food production, water usage, labour movements, refugees, unemployment, transport, cultural exchange, intellectual property or privacy issues. These problems and their solutions seem overwhelming in complexity and require patterns of thought that are untried and mostly beyond the comprehension of technocrats or the capabilities of either the nation states system, the political elites who run them, or the trans-national bodies created during and after the Second World War.

Therefore, in examining the nature of US power this larger context should be kept in mind. The commitment of US-led Coalition forces (including Australia) to the Iraq war was one response to the Islamist/Jihadist movement that is one of several, and now the most consequential, anti-modernisation organisations in the world. Osama bin Laden and Al Qaeda are trying to revive the ninth century Caliphate in the Middle East. In the Pacific region, Abu Bakar Bashir, the spiritual leader of the Jemaah Islamiyah (JI) movement in Indonesia, advocates a new Islamic Caliphate in Southeast Asia which takes in Indonesia, Malaysia, Singapore, southern Thailand, southern Philippines and even northern Australia, as part of a new unified world Caliphate of Islamic peoples. Jihadist movements are active throughout many other regions and civil conflict has been a common result. These radical movements are profound and powerful reactions to modernisation and the extraordinary forces of destabilisation that were released by the geopolitical changes after 1945.

In the highly polarised debate on these issues – and the curiously symmetrical Manichaeism by Left and Right with, of course, different 'evil empires', the Left focusing on US imperialism, the Right on the forces of terrorism – these larger forces are often ignored. This study of the use of US power makes a sober analysis of these historical events within the context of the global changes in the international system that has dominated the world since the Second World War.

A common culture, history and geopolitical world view have often brought the US and the Anglo-sphere states together in alliance over the past century. In the aftermath of the Second World War, the British and Canadians joined the US in NATO (1948), and the US-Australian-New Zealand alliance was formalised with the ANZUS (1951) and SEATO (1954) treaties and these nations often fought side by side from 1917 to the Second Gulf War in numerous theatres of war around the world. In the early twenty first century, the foreign policies and military strategies of these five nations often coincided, and some would argue that the US has totally dominated the geo-strategic thinking of its subordinate allies in this asymmetrical alliance. But Britain, Australia and the Anglo-sphere continue to follow this course voluntarily although it has cost them much in terms of trade, men, matériel and perhaps national pride over the past century.

The presence of the US in the Pacific region dates from the late eighteenth century in the early years of the Republic, and early in the nineteenth century the Americans pushed west from their Eastern Seaboard foundation territory. With the Louisiana Purchase in 1803 by President Jefferson, and the Lewis and Clark Expedition into the new territories that he sanctioned (1804–1806), the US established territorial claims to the Pacific. Through war, treaties and territorial acquisition the US emerged as a major Pacific power with the Oregon Territory treaty with Britain (1846), seizing the now American southwest from Mexico in the Mexican War (Treaty of Guadalupe Hidalgo in 1848), purchase of Alaska from Russia (1867), the overthrow of the Polynesian monarchy and subsequent annexation of Hawaii (1898) and the victory in the Spanish-American War (1898) that placed them as a major East Asian imperial power with the taking of the Philippines. Subsequent to the intervention in China in the aftermath of the Boxer Rebellion and the Open Door Notes of Secretary of State Hay in 1899–1900, the US joined Russia, China and Japan in the competition for hegemony in the East Asian region. After the long world war of 1914–1945, the US emerged as the hegemon of the Western Pacific and the newly independent Australia played a minor role in power in the geopolitics in this sphere of the world now dominated by the US.

After the collapse of the British Empire in Asia after 1945, Australia would place its future in hands of its fellow Anglo-Sphere state, the US. During the past sixty years Australia has had a net gain from the US alliance. With a modest expenditure of men and arms in miscellaneous wars around the world, Australia has gained protection under the US nuclear umbrella and the savings in defence spending have been enormous. At present Australia's defence budget is a low 1.9% of GDP, although it is rising. The huge 2004 election victory for John Howard, giving him control of both houses of Parliament, was a strong endorsement of Australia's subordination to the US and the US alliance. In short, the US alliance makes strategic sense, is in the national interest of Australia and is accepted by the vast majority of the Australian people. But while the US alliance and a political and economic system of liberalism are acceptable to the Australian people, imposing a similar circumstance on the rest of the world proved much more difficult for Washington.

This, therefore, is the context of this study of the current state of America in the world and likely prospects for the future. The first decade of the twenty first century has been tumultuous indeed and the next few years will be fraught with geopolitical and environmental challenges which the US-led Western world may not be able to comprehend and act upon with efficacy and confidence.

Chapter 1

American Hegemony in the Twenty First Century

The dominant tradition for the examination of the foreign policy of states in the American academy has been that of the realists. But there is a deep seated reluctance to apply this method of analysis to the US itself. The most famous of the academic realist theorists was the late Hans J Morgenthau, whose classic realist textbook *Politics Among Nations, The Struggle for Power and Peace* educated the post-war generation of American students on the subject. It drew heavily on the intellectual foundations laid by Niccolo Machiavelli five hundred years earlier, and was put briefly into practice by the Harvard Professor and later Secretary for State, Henry Kissinger. Nonetheless, current US foreign policy is rarely analysed in such a manner and is chiefly judged by American academics and most commentators by the dominant liberal standards of the US academy itself, in which the overwhelming proportion of staff are Democrat voters (or further left). Perhaps making this even more difficult, is the intertwining of real American interests into these moral judgements.

Realists believe that all states pursue their own interests to the limits of the power that they possess. They usually believe, also, that the value systems or ideologies that states espouse are masks and/or excuses for the pursuit of those interests, sometimes merely designed to generate popular support at home or abroad. States will only be restrained from pursuing these interests by the limitations of their power or the application of countervailing power, usually by other states. These intellectual tools are as applicable to the US as to any other state, although this is often disputed, particularly by those prone to the 'American exceptionalist' mode of historical analysis.

The Nature of the Post-Cold War World

At the end of the Cold War there was a protracted debate among American intellectuals about the nature of power and interests in the post-Cold War world. Four basic positions evolved to describe the new structure of power.

The liberal strategists, associated with the journal *Foreign Policy,* argued about a condition described as the 'Unipolar Moment'.[1] Although it was recognised that the US had emerged dominant from its victory in the Cold War, this moment would not

1 Particularly, C Layne, 'The Unipolar Illusion: Why New Great Powers Will Rise', *International Security*, Spring 1993. See also, Charles Krauthammer, 'The Unipolar Moment', *Foreign Affairs*, No 70, 1990–91.

last long. It needed to be utilised by Americans to create a more durable world order, both more to the liking of the US and less susceptible to the rise of new dominant and aggressive powers. This could be seen as a call for the pursuit of multilateral policies to design multilateral institutions. By and large this was the main strand of the Clinton administration's foreign policy involving the creation of a multilateral order and a globalised international economy.

A second line of argument posited that the great ideological debates which had marked the international system for the previous century, and arguably much longer, had come to an end. In *The End of History and the Last Man,*[2] Francis Fukuyama suggested that the West's triumph in the Cold War heralded the final triumph of the liberal democratic state. In future all states would evolve to that condition and establish a largely war free international system in which disputes might be peacefully resolved. The role of US policy was to encourage that evolution – even if by intervention when necessary. Essentially this was the strategic posture adopted by the neo-conservatives who were influential in the Reagan administration and who re-emerged (as 'neo-cons') under George W Bush.

The third view believed that while the US had scored a victory over the Soviets and thereby ended the Cold War, this did not mark the end of traditional power politics. Usually accompanying this argument was the conclusion that the main rising new power was China, and that the US should retain a strong military posture in order to deal with the PRC if it proved too assertive. In the main this was the foreign policy posture of the early Bush administration in 2001.[3] It envisaged a new bipolarity of China and the US and some of its earlier concerns were with the defence of Taiwan, to whom it promised more, and more advanced weapons, and with the militarisation of North Korea (DPRK).

A final view was presented by the Harvard Professor, Samuel P Huntington in his *Clash of Civilisations*.[4] He argued that the world was divided into eight core civilisational groups, with most of them having a leading state apparatus. These were: the US-led West; the rather detached Latin America; the poor and inward looking Africa; the Orthodox Christian area under Russia, with declining power after its Cold War defeat; the Confucian world with China its leader; the Hindu world centred around India; the Japanese sphere; the Buddhist world from Thailand to Mongolia; and the Muslim world with a number of states contending for leadership. He identified the fringes of the Muslim world as being the most susceptible to armed conflict. This view corresponded to that of many in the Muslim world, and as the Global War on Terror (GWOT) progressed it became increasingly the view of many in the Anglo-Sphere that emerged as the core of the West.

---

2 Francis Fukuyama, *The End of History and the Last Man* (New York, 1992).

3 Bob Catley, 'The Bush Administration and Changing Geo-Politics in the Asia Pacific Region', *Contemporary Southeast Asia*, April 2001.

4 Samuel P Huntington, *The Clash of Civilisations and the Remaking of World Order* (New York, 1996).

A Realist Approach to American Power

In considering America as a post-Second World War global power, it is useful to examine the theoretical and historical background inherited by those who were charged with making its state policy. Theories on the practice of statecraft in the modern era date back at least to the writings of Machiavelli in Renaissance Europe that, in turn, drew on a long tradition of advice to rulers on the nature and principles of foreign policy and war. In the post-industrial modern era, however, paradigms of geo-strategic theory grew chiefly out of inter-state diplomacy and war in nineteenth century Europe. The practitioners of *Realpolitik,* such as Prince von Metternich of Austria in the post-Napoleonic European world, about whose work Kissinger wrote his doctoral dissertation, and later in the century, Germany's Otto von Bismarck, elaborated state policy strategies in foreign affairs that emphasized actions based upon national self-interest, but exercised with reason and caution. These views were dubbed realist and came to be associated with conservative diplomacy and the cautious use of military power applied decisively (some would say amorally) when exercised. Henry Kissinger is associated most prominently with this historical legacy of conservatism and the realist school of state foreign policy formation.[5]

Geopolitical theorists in the nineteenth century elaborated on the necessity for the state to exercise military power in order to further the aims of state interests and diplomacy. The European state, which had emerged in the early modern period after the Treaty of Westphalia in 1648, was designed essentially as an entity to make war and collect taxes in order to make war. Later, it evolved into an entity structured to make mass warfare employing the new technology of the industrial era. These military strategies, however, had to be clearly focused on purpose; and in both autocratic and democratic states they had to be employed with popular support and close ties maintained between ruling elites, the mass of the people and the military. These views were expressed by the greatest theorist of land warfare, Carl von Clausewitz (1780–1831) in his *On War* in 1832, who pointed out the delicate balance that must be maintained in warfare in order to maintain domestic political support: pick the right war, at the right time and in the right place. These were views of which George W Bush undoubtedly was unaware when he launched his crusade in Iraq.

The 'Clausewitz of the Sea', the American Admiral Alfred Thayer Mahan (1840–1914), in his seminal *The Influence of Sea Power upon History, 1600–1783,* published in 1890, argued that state power – and he meant the US – must also be exercised at sea by a powerful navy, and that this would give a state access to economic power as well controlling the lines of commerce. The US, rapidly

5 The former National Security Adviser and Secretary of State (1973–1977) Henry Kissinger's statecraft is, of course, extremely controversial and described empirically in his three volumes of memoirs and more theoretically in *Diplomacy.* It has been subjected to liberal, Left and Right critiques; for liberal see William Shawcross, *Sideshow* (New York, 1979); for the Left, see the highly polemical but interesting analysis in *The Trial of Henry Kissinger* (New York, 2001) by Christopher Hitchens, the former English Trotskyite, recent neo-conservative and rumoured model for the journalist character, Peter Fallows, in Tom Wolfe's wonderful satire, *Bonfire of the Vanities* (1987). The Reagan administration foreign policy was a Right repudiation of Kissinger's realism.

expanding into the Pacific in the nineteenth century, closely followed this strategy in securing territory roughly twenty degrees of latitude north and south of the equator across the Pacific to guarantee the security of its trade routes to East and South Asian markets. American society would, therefore, evolve by the mid-twentieth century with as strong commercial and geopolitical ties with East Asia and the Pacific, as those with the old Atlantic world from whence it came.

President Benjamin Harrison (1889–1893), a former Union Brigadier General, took Mahan's views into account, substantially expanded the US naval fleet and also began the process of expanding the American presence in the Pacific, subjecting Hawaii to a 'popular' revolution in 1893 which led to annexation in 1898. Both Clausewitz and Mahan perceived the link between military power and extending and protecting economic power; these links would guide US policy through its period of late nineteenth century regional imperial expansion, its rise to global power status after the First World War, and its late twentieth century Cold War strategy of the protection of Western global economic interests. Similarly, it underpinned the need to secure oil supplies and reserves concentrated in the Middle East, especially in Iraq and the Gulf region, in the twenty first century Global War on Terror.[6]

From the Civil War to the early twentieth century, the rapidly expanding US state acquired a new empire in the Philippines after the Spanish-American War (1898), and intervened militarily, especially in the Caribbean and Central America, to protect and extend American trade and commercial interests. It was never an isolationist power in the western hemisphere. Republican Presidents William McKinley (1897–1901) and Theodore Roosevelt (1901–1909) vigorously pursued American imperial interests with a much stronger naval force and, especially under Roosevelt, a far greater impact on the world. Teddy Roosevelt extended Harrison's policies on expanding the naval fleet as Assistant Secretary of the Navy under McKinley (1897–1901) before he went to Cuba to become a national hero in the Spanish-American War in 1898. Roosevelt was an admirer of Mahan, and as President, Roosevelt expanded the US Navy and established a battleship-based fleet that he proudly sent into the Pacific in 1907–1908 to show the flag and impress the region with the power of the 'Great White Fleet'. It auspiciously visited Sydney. Roosevelt led a nation enthralled with its newly won Empire and sense of national unity that indicated it had finally evolved beyond the divisions of the Civil War. It was a unity built upon jingoism, visions of imperial greatness and a propensity, when America's strategic and economic interests were threatened, to send in US forces.

Roosevelt's doctrine of intervention adumbrated the Bush Doctrine of Pre-emption and was expressed in 1904 in his annual address to Congress as the 'Roosevelt Corollary' to the Monroe Doctrine (1823): 'Chronic wrongdoing…may in America, as elsewhere, ultimately require intervention by some civilized nation, and in the Western Hemisphere the adherence of the United States to the Monroe Doctrine may force the United States, however reluctantly, in flagrant cases of

---

6 See the editions of *On War* (Princeton, NJ, 1989), and *The Influence of Sea Power upon History* (Boston, 1898). For a general overview see Brian Downing, *The Military Revolution and Political Change* (Princeton, NJ, 1991), and Geoffrey Parker, *The Military Revolution: Military Innovation and the Rise of West* (New York, 1996).

such wrongdoing or impotence, to the exercise of *an international police power*'. The doctrine was put into practice almost immediately with the intervention in the Dominican Republic in 1905 after which America installed a collector of customs in order to guarantee debt repayments to American creditors and made it a Protectorate until 1941. Swinging the big stick in Central America, Roosevelt then supported the creation of the state of Panama which he carved out of Colombia in 1903 with another 'popular revolution' in order to facilitate the building of the Panama Canal for US inter-coastal shipping. He asserted American diplomatic power globally and under Roosevelt the emergence of the hegemonic power of America was well under way.[7]

Roosevelt's Republican successor and former first American civil Governor of the Philippines (1901–1904), President William Howard Taft (1909–1913), continued the linkage between American commercial interests and diplomatic activity with his 'dollar diplomacy' and interventions to protect US economic interests. The normally lethargic President attempted some heavy-handed but unsuccessful interference in northeast Asia, challenging Russia and Japan on building and financing the Manchurian railroads. He also continued the American tradition of policing the Caribbean with additional armed interventions by US forces in Cuba, Honduras and the Dominican Republic.

The Democratic President Woodrow Wilson (1913–1921), was a former Princeton Professor who after the cataclysm of the First World War, which America belatedly entered in 1917, took his Fourteen Points to the Versailles Peace Conference and proposed interventionist idealism. He advocated an American policy of activism to promote democracy in Europe and around the world in order to avoid the civil and inter-state conflicts which led to the First World War. But the US failed to adopt the Versailles Treaty, including the League of Nations, since the US Senate, led by isolationist Republicans and, in spite of their interventionist and imperialist past, rejected them. The resultant relative absence of US power in world geopolitics in the 1930s, with the exception of continued interventions by America in the Western Hemisphere, contributed to the rise of fascist regimes in Italy and Germany and, when coupled with the Great Depression, the international instability which led directly to the Second World War.[8]

This diplomatic history could easily be seen as merely the development of a new state avoiding the conflicts of Europe. But Americans have often chosen to view it as the development of a unique form of society and political entity. The concept of the unique historical mission of America to spread democracy and civilisation has deep roots in the American psyche dating back to the chiliastic ideology of American Puritanism and its millenarianism. This drew, in turn, on ancient Near Eastern Manichean ideas and Christian Patristic sources such as St Augustine, and fuelled their hopes for the creation of a New Jerusalem in America as the 'city upon a

7 Roosevelt's speech is quoted in George Tindall and David Shi, *America* (New York, 1992), pp. 929–930 [emphasis added]; Edmund Morris, *Theodore Rex* (London, 2002), pp. 493–495.

8 For the legacy of interventionism and the impact on George W Bush, see David M Kennedy, "What 'W' Owes to 'WW'", *The Atlantic Monthly*, V. 295, No. 2 (March, 2005), pp. 12–20.

hill', suggested by the Governor of Massachusetts, John Winthrop. In the nineteenth century, this 'exceptionalist', as it is now called, view of American destiny and history was expressed in the concept of its Manifest Destiny proclaimed by the journalist John Lewis O'Sullivan in 1845 and a fully conscious part of the writings of American historians such George Bancroft in the nineteenth century and Samuel Flagg Bemis in the twentieth century. Whether or not this paradigm for American history and its mission is the most appropriate mode of analysis is, in the early twenty first century, still hotly debated.[9] This stands in sharp contrast to the almost universal acceptance of the realist tradition in the analysis of foreign policy behaviour of all other states.

One of the most important twentieth century interpreters of American character, Seymour Martin Lipset, has written an influential volume on the subject entitled, *American Exceptionalism: a Double-Edged Sword*,[10] and the Global War on Terror has again stimulated the debate about America's allegedly God-given mission to democratise the world. One of the curiosities of this debate, Lipset points out, is the congruence of the Left and Right on the issue of American uniqueness, in which they seem to agree on the existence of 'American exceptionalism'. The Right sees America as founded by God's historical intervention and given a unique Mission; the Left sees America as a unique bastion of liberty whose behaviour must meet legal and ethical standards not required or expected from other nations and empires. Both sides of the political spectrum believe America is, and should be, special; both believe America is, and should be, a beacon to the world. Americans embrace the tensions inherent in simultaneously accepting religious collective values *and* the libertarian tradition of individual freedom from state coercion. The Right wants central government intervention on moral issues but not on guns or capitalism; the Left wants economic interventionism from the central government but liberty protected in the areas of personal freedom. Lipset summarizes these apparent contradictions when he states that America 'is the most religious, optimistic, patriotic, rights-oriented and individualistic' nation on earth and a *unique* combination of values.[11]

9 See the views of Ian Tyrrell, 'American Exceptionalism in an Age of International History', *The American Historical Review*, Vol. 96, No. 4 (1991), pp. 1031–72; and the review essays on exceptionalism in Volume 102, No. 3, in *The American Historical Review* (1997), pp. 748–774, which continue the argument on whether it is more appropriate to consider American history in the context of international patterns, rather than the national US context of the exceptionalist paradigm (or indeed whether it is valid to charge US historians with being exceptionalist at all).

10 Seymour Martin Lipset, *American Exceptionalism: a Double-Edged Sword* (New York, 1996).

11 Lipset, quoted from Roy Eccleston, 'American dreams and nightmares', *The Australian,* 21 March 2005. See also Edward Rothstein, 'Touring an America Tocqueville Could Fathom', *New York Times*, 11 April 2005; and also the French philosopher Bernard-Henri Lévy, commissioned by *The Atlantic Monthly* in 2005 to retrace the steps of Tocqueville's famous journey through America in 1831 that was published as *Democracy in America,* and in which he stills finds America to be an exceptional culture. This paradigm continues to exercise a powerful influence on American scholars, especially of the colonial period: for a recent example see Richard Francis, *Judge Sewall's Apology: the Salem Witch Trials and the Forming of an American Conscience* (New York, 2005).

With the collapse of diplomacy at the end of the 1930s, exemplified by the failure of the Munich Agreement, the outbreak of War was seen by the Americans as the consequence of weakness of the Western powers in general, and the Americans in particular, in the face of threats from an expansionist dictator. The next two generations, who fought the Cold War from the late 1940s to the early 1990s, were deeply imbued with a belief that US security must never again be jeopardized by weakness and what was perceived as relative inaction by Franklin Delano Roosevelt in the 1930s. Thus, not only did the Democrats, starting with Harry Truman (1945–1953) the architect of the Cold War and the interventionist Doctrine of Containment, embrace the old Wilsonian interventionist ideals in the Holy War against Communism; but the Republicans did as well. Many Republicans, the ideological descendants of the isolationists from the 1920s, joined the Democrats in global and interventionist opposition to Communism. This produced bi-partisan support for decades of intervention to support anti-Communist causes, organizations and regimes around the world, whether democratic or not, as long as the regimes subscribed to the dual American policies of anti-Communism and facilitating capital investment from the West. This geo-political strategy overlooked the practices of illiberal regimes as long as they opposed Communism. This Doctrine of Containment, as defined by George Kennan in his pseudononimous 'X' article in 1947, established anti-Communism as a global geopolitical strategy. Virtually any regime that met its tests received covert and/or overt support from the US.[12]

The Cold War debates, launched by Paul Nitze (who drafted NSC-68) and George Kennan (in the 'X' article), adumbrated the geopolitical ideas and controversy surrounding the neo-conservatives in the present time. This original Cold War generation, that grew out of government service and the intelligence community of the Second World War, particularly in the OSS, the precursor to the CIA, had extraordinary longevity and an intense anti-Munich mentality and included key figures such as Kennan,[13] the Dulles brothers and Dean Acheson, among others, who influenced US policy for decades. Douglas Brinkley's biography of *Dean Acheson* provides many insights into this generation and the atmosphere of Washington in the early Cold War years, when the relatively small foreign policy-making elite concentrated in and around the Washington suburb of Georgetown and discussed foreign policy objectives very much in the light of the failed practice of appeasement in the late 1930s.[14] The next generation of policy makers in the Departments of State and Defense, such as the brothers William and McGeorge Bundy, Dean Rusk, Robert McNamara, Zbigniew Brzezinski and Henry Kissinger, were deeply influenced by the same analysis of historical forces as their mentors.

---

12 See also Gaddis Smith, *The Last Years of the Monroe Doctrine, 1945–1993* (New York, 1994).

13 Kennan's article appeared as 'The Sources of Soviet Conduct', *Foreign Affairs*, July 1947, pp.566–582.

14 See also Robert Merry, *Taking on the World, Joseph and Stewart Alsop – Guardians of the American Century* (New York, 1996).

The current Wilsonian neo-conservatives were strongly influenced by the hawkishness of this generation, but wished to greatly and probably imprudently extend American interventionism. Many of them, such as Richard Perle, who was Assistant Secretary of Defense under Reagan and former Chairman of the powerful civilian advisory Defense Policy Board to Bush, Secretary of Defense, Donald Rumsfeld, and the Deputy Secretary of Defense and key generator of neo-conservative ideas, Paul Wolfowitz, actually initially worked for Democrats and were formerly to the left of governmental debates. Both Perle and Wolfowitz worked for Democrat Cold Warriors such as the US Senator from Washington State and sometime presidential candidate Henry 'Scoop' Jackson (1972 and 1976 and died in 1983) in the 1960s and 1970s (Perle from 1969–1980 and Wolfowitz for a shorter period in the late 1960s and early 1970s). These two American architects of US late Cold War geopolitical strategy of offensive containment or 'rollback', advocated a muscular and interventionist strategy to impose US 'moral' and 'democratic' values on the world and oppose Communism (and, of course, protect US economic interests). The opposition to their views at the time was similar, if not exactly parallel, to the critique of the neo-conservatives today.

In early twenty first century debates, the Left views the neo-conservatives as militaristic and imperialist, whereas the Right, whether called conservative or realist, views Bush's Iraq policy as adventurist and his hopes for democracy in the general Middle East as wildly optimistic at best and dangerously naïve as worst. Kennan and Nitze were subjected to an attack by the Left and Right, then and now, of a similar vein. The Australian researcher, Josh Ushay, concluded that the neo-conservatives' strategy, as with that of the seminal Cold War theorists, must stand the test of time to determine the efficacy of their ideas and geopolitical strategies.[15]

The Revival of the Right in the 1980s

During the administrations of Ronald Reagan (1981–1989) in the US, and Margaret Thatcher (Prime Minister, 1979–1990) in the UK, a shift to the right began in politics and culture in those states, in the Anglo-Sphere in general, and then globally, and this continued and deepened into the 1990s. This sprang from a number of sources. The old Keynesian style of economic management had been unable to deal with the stagflation crisis of the late 1970s. There was widespread disillusionment with the leftish governments of Jim Callaghan in the UK and Jimmy Carter in the US. At that time the Soviet Union appeared to be making uncontested gains in the international system. Some of these problems were resolved by the move to the Right, and economic growth rose, inflation fell and the Soviet Union disintegrated. These victories gave the Right renewed strength and prestige, particularly in the US which had long been more right wing than other developed countries.[16]

---

15 Josh Ushay, 'Cold War wise men saw strength in containment', *The Australian,* 23 March 2005, p. 15.

16 John Micklethwait and Adrian Wooldridge, *The Right Nation: Why America is Different* (New York, 2005).

The inauguration of Clinton's apparently centrist Democrat administration in 1992, did not entirely offset this shift to the Right as Clinton himself then moved to the Right also in 1994 to accommodate it. In the new century the George W Bush (2001–) presidency added a strong evangelical Christian Right dimension to the conservative movement, along with the increased influence of the neo-conservatives in foreign policy who gave a more interventionist and unilateral edge especially in foreign policy. Thus the trend toward the Right in American culture, always a politically conservative society, begun sharply in the 1950s, was moderated in the late 1960s and 1970s in response to the defeat in Indo-China, and then continued to develop in the twenty first century into the dominant paradigm in US politics and society. In the race for the White House in 2007–2008, however, the power of the Christian Right has waned and some of them have even planned for a third party candidate so alienated are they from the mainstream parties including Bush's Republicans.[17]

The neo-conservative movement began in New York in the late 1970s when a group of intellectuals, many of them Jewish and clustered around the *Commentary* magazine, moved from the Left to the Right. The impetus appears to have been the ineffectiveness of President Carter's policy towards what they viewed as Soviet aggression and expansion. They then provided substantial intellectual underpinnings for President Reagan's foreign policy of assertiveness, but their influence waned after the collapse of the Soviet Union. In the early twenty first century the neo-conservative movement revived and became again influential in the George W Bush administration. They also became more influential in the flow of information in the Anglo-Sphere societies more generally, particularly through the NewsCorp media. The neo-liberal policies pursued by many, but not all of the neo-conservatives for deregulation of the economy, continued to be hotly debated inside and outside the academy. The neo-liberal agenda was resisted by critics in the universities, the media and the labour unions, thus drawing fierce criticism from the neo-conservatives and their allies in the media and government. Increasingly, their tactic was to employ the populist cry of 'anti-elitism' under which the neo-conservatives present themselves as the defenders of the masses, democracy and egalitarianism, against the elitists, especially in the universities, who allegedly sit idly by drinking foreign coffee and wine (in the US), or latte and chardonnay (in Australia), while attacking the integrity of the 'true patriotic masses'. In the US this means the mid-West; in Australia, the suburbs and regional areas.

This neo-liberal crusade may be depicted, therefore, as intended to reduce the pockets of Left resistance remaining from the Cold War in order to impose a cultural hegemony for the neo-liberal society to be established in peace and quiet without noisy and disrupting dissenting opinion. In achieving these objectives, the neo-liberals have been so far extraordinarily successful and on the issues of national security and the economic policy there was less dissent in the early years of the George W Bush administration. In other areas, however, consensus was not so well established and the Christian Right tried unsuccessfully to add Creationism/ID, stem

17 Kevin Kallaugher, 'Is James Dobson's legendary power starting to wane?', *The Economist*, 1 March 2007.

cell research, abortion, flag-burning, school prayer, gay marriage and other issues to this list.[18]

At first, the Global War on Terror only accentuated this process of the tightening up of the range of opinion permissible both in the media and the public at large with legislation such as the 2001 Patriot Act. But later, the pressures of the Iraq war created serious rifts in the conservative ranks in all the Anglo-Sphere countries. Some traditional conservatives broke ranks with the Republicans, including, in the US, William Buckley, Pat Buchanan and George Will. Also, one of the key figures in neo-conservative thought Francis Fukuyama came out against not just the war in Iraq, but the whole neo-conservative paradigm of global interventionism. The mainline conservatives in Congress became alarmed by the deficit spending of President Bush and envisaged decades of red ink building up in federal budget deficits and a national debt of one trillion dollars. Similarly, in the UK many traditional conservatives were so hostile to Prime Minister Blair that they opposed his joining the war in Iraq, and the conservative magazine *The Spectator* usually reflected this perspective. Conservative opposition to the manner of the fight against terrorism has been less extensive in Australia, but has nonetheless included the former Liberal prime Minister, Malcolm Fraser, and his one time national security advisor and influential intellectual, Owen Harries.

Many neo-conservatives, on the other hand, moved to a more bellicose position and were influential in persuading the Bush administration to invade Iraq in 2003 and supported Israel's invasion of Lebanon in 2006, and in 2006, William Kristol of the *Weekly Standard* and Charles Krauthammer of the *Washington Post* called for the bombing of Syria and Iran. These views have been more widely disseminated including by the Canadian resident Mark Steyn, British neo-conservative, MP and editor of the *Spectator*, Boris Johnson, and the Australian NewsCorp columnist, Andrew Bolt.

The Clinton Administration and Globalisation

The Republicans have generally dominated the White House since 1953. Dwight Eisenhower (1953–61) represented a patriotic, low taxation, low key foreign policy administration that was good for business and the economy. He ended the Democrats' Korean War and generally stayed out of other conflicts. The Kennedy-Johnson administration then got the US into the War in Vietnam and was destroyed by it. Richard Nixon was also badly wounded by an over ambitious foreign policy, although his mortal wound was struck at the Watergate Hotel. Jimmy Carter (1977–81) won the Presidency amid revulsion at Washington insiders, and when his amateurish shortcomings were revealed he lost the 1980 election. The first full two-term President since Eisenhower was Ronald Reagan (1981–89) who proceeded to win the Cold War.

In 1991 Bill Clinton broke this mould and was elected President largely because the majority right vote was divided between George H W Bush and the independent

18 For Australia, Marian Sawer and Barry Hindess, eds, *Us and Them: Anti-elitism in Australia* (Perth, 2004).

Texan billionaire, Ross Perot. The Cold War had ended and security issues gave way to the urgency of the early 1990s recession – 'It's the economy, stupid'. The administration, nonetheless, struggled for several years largely due to Clinton's quite ambitious, by American standards, policies of social reform, until it lurched to the centre in 1994. From that location it won the 1996 Presidential poll in a period of post-Cold War peace dividend prosperity.

The foundations of the Clinton regime were the old Democrat alliance of labour unions, the more left wing, cosmopolitan coastal states, particularly in California and New York, the intellectual elites, including in Hollywood, the Universities and the liberal media, a majority vote among minorities including blacks and Hispanics, and 75 per cent of the Jewish vote. By 1996 corporate America was sufficiently settled into prosperity to give Clinton funding levels to match the Republicans, with which he won a majority over an ageing Bob Dole. Clinton himself was a domestic reformer who had created a career in the domestic politics of Arkansas, rather than the strategic debates of Washington or the international corporate world of New York and Wall Street. His foreign policy was not unduly activist but driven by the economic imperatives of globalisation from which he rightly thought the US would profit. This ensured that the period was dominated by multilateral arrangements designed to remake the post-Cold War world into one of integrated prosperity. This was the purpose for which the unipolar moment of American dominance was to be used.[19]

Clinton's foreign policy was dominated by the globalisation project. The administration ran down military expenditure with the end of Cold War and mothballed much military equipment. This had a short term impact on the military production regions of the country while their economies were restructured – particularly the Washington-Boston corridor, Virginia and southern California – although that pain was short lived. But the US still clearly remained the strongest military state in the world. Yet, under Clinton it was reluctant to use force, particularly after the deaths of eighteen US military personnel in Somalia left public opinion unwilling to act. Nonetheless, Clinton later was personally regretful that he had not intervened to prevent the dreadful massacres in Rwanda/Burundi. This influenced his eventual decision to intervene belatedly against Serbia in the wars in the Balkans that followed the break up of the communist state of Yugoslavia. In justifying this activity he launched a substantial critique of national sovereignty at the UN which the Russian veto had prevented from acting.

Clinton's record on terrorism will likely be the main criticism launched against him by historians. The organisation of the Islamic terrorist network centred on Al Qaeda was in its early phases and Clinton's response was not to take it as an urgent matter. Nonetheless, as the attacks mounted to include the first attack on the Twin Towers, the killings in Somalia, the bombing of two US embassies in Africa, the attack on the US base in Saudi Arabia, and then the murderous assault on the *USS Cole*, more attention might have been given to this growing menace. It was not, other than a number of Cruise missiles being launched at Al Qaeda training camps in Afghanistan. Indeed, it was later reported that the Sudanese government, anxious

19 Mosler and Catley, *Global America,* as above.

to avoid further missile strikes, had offered to hand over Osama bin Laden but that the US had declined the offer. Bin Laden then moved to Afghanistan. But although the Clinton administration's approach to terrorism was weak and thereby appeared to confirm bin Laden's allegation that the US, like the Soviet Union before it, could not withstand a spirited Muslim assault, he came under only scant criticism from the Republicans for this posture.

Years later, Clinton strongly defended his handling of the threat posed by bin Laden, saying he tried to have the Al Qaeda leader killed and was attacked for his efforts by the same people who later criticised him for not doing enough: 'That's the difference in me and some, including all of the right-wingers who are attacking me now. They ridiculed me for trying. They had eight months to try – they did not try ... We contracted with people to kill him. I got closer to killing him than anybody's gotten since'.[20]

In opposition, nonetheless, the Republicans were classical realists. They said little about terrorism in making their critique of the Clinton administration in the run up to the 2000 Presidential election. Clinton's failure to hand over the White House to Al Gore stemmed more from his personal behaviour than foreign policy failings. The economy was booming, the fiscal deficit was turning around quite rapidly, the US had only intervened, and then successfully and briefly, in the Balkans, and the Republicans offered little by way of clearly articulated alternative policy. But Clinton had been impeached, had been the subject of a number of misconduct allegations, and in 1999–2000 was embroiled in the fallout from his affair with and misrepresentations about Monica Lewinski. This was quite enough to lose Al Gore the election, if only by the narrowest of margins.

Clinton did successfully advance globalisation. Historically the pattern of lowering tariff barriers and deregulation of labour and capital markets, the heart of globalisation, first took place in the mid-nineteenth century and continued until interrupted by the First World War and the Great Depression. In the current, second great wave of globalisation, growing out of the architecture of international trade established by the Bretton Woods Conference in New Hampshire in 1944, the world has seen greater global homogeneity of social objectives, labour deregulation, privatisation and a decline in the authority of the social democratic model for social services and as an agency to achieve greater social equity. Some aspects of the sovereignty of the modern nation state system have also been eroded by transnational trends and organisations such as the IMF and the WTO who challenge state sovereignty by the policies emanating from global financial structures.[21] The Left alleges that globalisation has transferred wealth from the poor nations of the world to the developed West and that within societies wealth has been shifted upwards away from the middle and lower classes to a small and increasingly super rich elite. The

20 'I tried my best to kill bin Laden: Clinton', *The Australian*, 26 Sept 2006.

21 See Herman M. Schwartz, *States Versus Markets: History, Geography and the Development of the International Political Economy* (New York, 1994) for historical trends; and for the nation-state see John Dunn, 'Introduction: Crisis of the Nation State?', *Political Studies*, 42, 1994, pp. 3–15; and Peter F Drucker, 'The Global Economy and the Nation-State', *Foreign Affairs*, 107, Sept/Oct 1997, pp. 159–171.

Right scoffs at these allegations and argues that globalisation has been good for all classes of people, including the world's poor, and points to countries like China in which some 150 million people have been shifted from the bottom to the middle of income structures in the last ten years.[22]

Closely associated with the debate on income distribution and globalisation, has been the debate about its consequences for the environment. The environmental issue debate dates back to the nineteenth century but the modern debate dates from the 1960s and the publication of seminal books like Rachel Carson's *Silent Spring* (1962) and Paul Erhlich's *Population Bomb* (1968) on the destruction of the environment by pollution and the effects of overpopulation. In the twenty first century globalisation debate, the issues have become global warming, water usage, air quality, epidemic disease and the pressures of population density around the globe. The Left alleges that global warming and general environmental destruction has accelerated with globalisation; whereas the Right counters that much of the data for this is exaggerated and/or fabricated by the Left who cannot accept that they have lost the argument on the historical project of industrialisation and modernisation. Both sides tend toward alarmist positions, with the Left postulating the imminent collapse of the earth's ecology and the Right predicting economic catastrophe if the environment policies of the Left, such as the Kyoto Agreement, are implemented.

This opposition to the impact of globalising policies on income distribution and the environment by the Left is matched by unease about the concomitant drift of world culture to an American model, especially in the arts and entertainment. The homogenisation of world culture has provoked a reaction by traditional social forces on the Left *and* the Right against the trend toward Americanized social forms. The convergence of both ends of the political spectrum on this issue has increasingly been characteristic of anti-globalisation protest and discourse. In Indonesia cinemas have been torched by Jihadist Muslims; in India McDonalds restaurants have been invaded and trashed by right-wing Hindus; in Australia American films are attacked by Left nationalists for drawing away 99 per cent of revenues from film receipts; and throughout the Middle East American culture is viewed by the majority as the evil and dark force of the infidel and idolatry. Globalisation has sparked protests at the meetings of international bodies such as the WTO with a diverse opposition from environmental, cultural and political groups from all ends of the political spectrum.[23]

The globalising trend, however, seems inexorable and world problems such as AIDS, poverty, overpopulation, crime, migration, water usage, global warming, terrorism, nuclear weapons, pollution, democratisation, land mines, labor rights, child labor, to name a few, all demand global approaches, financing and solutions. Globalisation, therefore, is proceding and future strategies must be elaborated in that

22 For the Right view extolling the virtues of globalisation see Thomas Friedman, *The Lexus and the Olive Tree* (London, 1999), and *The World is Flat: a Brief History of the Twenty-First Century* (New York, 2005); for the Left view emphasising the problems of poverty and environmental damage allegedly exacerbated by globalisation see Joseph Wayne Smith, *Global* Meltdown (New York, 1998).

23 See George Ritzer, *The McDonaldization of Society* (Thousand Oaks, CA, 2004).

contextual framework.[24] A major World Bank report made it clear that globalisation has engendered faster rates of development. It has also been beneficial for the US economy and corporations, one reason the US state has encouraged the process. But while globalisation has reduced the proportion of the world's people living in poverty, largely as a result of economic growth in its two largest countries, India and China,[25] it has also made the wealthy countries, including the US, even more dependent on international trade and finance.

George W Bush and the Neo-conservatives

In his election campaign of 2000, George W Bush was, like his opponents, heavily dependent on corporate donations. His political power base had developed in Texas and his family connections were rooted in the largest industry of that region, oil.[26] The new Vice President, Dick Cheney, was a former CEO of the Halliburton Corporation, a major oil field services firm, and had strong links with the oil and energy sector. The Army Secretary had been vice chairman of Enron Energy Services and others had similar backgrounds. The big oil companies like Chevron, Exxon and Enron, had been major Republican campaign donors and were quickly and extensively consulted on policy.[27] Continuing access to sufficient oil to drive the US and global economy, was never far from the policy planning of the new Republican administration.

The election of George W Bush also brought to prominence a number of advisors, senior government officials and prominent commentators lumped together as the 'neo-conservatives'.[28] These included, Wolfowitz, Perle and Douglas Feith, Under-Secretary of Defense. In the press corps the key supporting figures included William Kristol of *The Weekly Standard* and Charles Krauthammer of the *Washington Post,* and outside the establishment commentators such as James Woolsey, the former Director of the Central Intelligence Agency (1993–1995) and Zalmay Khalilzad, in 2006 US Ambassador to Iraq. These neo-conservatives drew upon a tradition that had its origins in the ideas of an obscure but distinguished University of Chicago philosopher Leo Strauss (1899–1973); the journalist, commentator, former Trotskyite and one time editor of *The Public Interest,* Irving Kristol (father of William); and polemicist Norman Podhoretz (b.1930) earlier editor of *Commentary* magazine. Underwriting this trend was the major media company NewsCorp, owned by Rupert Murdoch and including the Fox TV network, 180 newspapers around the world, the *Weekly Standard*, and the Fox movie production company.

---

24 A thoughtful overview on the subject is John Micklethwait and Adrian Woolridge, *A Future Perfect: the Challenge and Hidden Promise of Globalisation* (New York, 2000).

25 Paul Collier and David Dollar, *Globalisation, Growth, and Poverty: Building an Inclusive World Economy*, World Bank, 2001.

26 See particularly, Kevin Phillips, *American Dynasty, Aristocracy, Fortune and the Politics of Deceit on the House of Bush* (New York, 2004), chapter 8, 'Indiana Bush and the Axis of Evil'.

27 Michael Klare, *Blood and Oil* (New York, 2004); and *New York Times*, 1 March 2001 and 27 March 2001.

28 See Irwin Stelzer, ed, *The Neo-Con Reader* (New York, 2004).

Several of this group espoused a muscular and interventionist American foreign policy, taking over both the Wilsonian interventionist position to spread democracy and the Cold War activist policies to protect American economic interests. After the attack of 9/11 their foreign policy model became the dominant paradigm for the Bush administration. Bush, under the more traditional conservative influence of Dick Cheney, and Donald Rumsfeld, pursued these objectives with the Global War on Terror, the military invasion of Iraq and an activist support for Israel in the Lebanon war in July-August 2006, thereby implementing the precepts of the Bush Doctrine on intervention around the world in pursuit of democracy and American interests.

The pressures of the Iraq and Lebanon wars, however, caused serious rifts in the conservative ranks with some old conservatives breaking ranks, such as William Buckley (*The National Review*), Pat Buchanan (journalist and commentator) and George Will (*Newsweek*). A most important defection has been by the superstar historian Francis Fukuyama (now at Johns Hopkins), who came out against not just the war in Iraq but the whole neo-conservative paradigm of global interventionism. Furthermore, mainline conservatives in Congress became alarmed by the deficit spending of the President and saw decades of federal budget deficits and a national debt inching toward one trillion dollars.

Some of the neo-conservatives, on the other hand, moved to an even more bellicose position with the Israel-Lebanon war in which Kristol and Krauthammer called for the bombing of Syria and Iran, and an even more direct confrontation with the Jihadist forces and their Syrian and Iranian backers. Edward Luttwak, often close to the neo-conservative camp, also advocated pre-emptive strikes against Iran in late 2006. The Christian conservatives were also energized by the Lebanon war and some, such as the televangelist John Hagee, from his position as founder of 'Christians United for Israel', believed it was a 'biblical imperative' for the US to give strong support for Israel. This was based on the commonly held evangelical apocalyptic belief that the 'final days' are presently being acted out in Palestine and that the Jews must be protected in anticipation the Second Coming.[29]

When Saddam Hussein, with his eye on the oil reserves on his southern flank to which he believed Iraq had a legitimate irredentist claim, attacked and occupied Kuwait in 1990, a chain of events started that would lead to a new phase of US interventionism in global politics. After the Gulf War in 1990–91 the US greatly increased its presence in the Middle East including with troops in Saudi Arabia, and gave the forces of Jihadism, led by Osama bin Laden, greater cause for anti-American action against what they perceived as a world-wide attack on Islam and its territory. The Jihadist forces were especially agitated by the presence of infidels in their holy space of Islam in the Arabian Peninsula. Even though the US led a

---

29 See Norman Podhoretz, 'World War IV: how it started, what it means, and why we have to win', *Commentary*, Sept 2004; Franklin Foer, 'Death of the neo-cons', *The Australian,* 16 Dec 2004; Eric Alterman, 'A short history of neoconservatives', *The Australian Financial Review,* 29 April 2005; Francis Fukuyama, 'Confessions of a former neocon', *The Australian Financial Review*, 21 April 2006; and *The Economist*, 9 Aug 2006, online edition.

broadly based coalition in 1991, the bulk of the firepower was American and the ire of Islamists was directed at the US.

Increasingly, as a result of the failure of the US to overthrow Saddam in the First Gulf War as coordinated by Bush Senior, the conservative forces in America who again came to power under Bush Junior in 2001, adopted the view that it was the mission of America to 'spread democracy'. They were the heirs of Wilsonian idealism in a crusade against radical Islam whether in the Arab nationalist form in Ba'athist Iraq or the Islamist form as espoused by bin Laden.[30] The neo-conservatives in the Bush administration extended this Wilsonian interventionist position to a *reductio ad absurdum* with the Bush Doctrine of Pre-emption. Not only should the US intervene to extend democracy, including by regime change, but it should also strike first if democracy and/or American interests were perceived to be under some future *theoretical* threat. The Bush administration, emotionally charged by 9/11, abandoned the conservative realist caution of Nixon and Kissinger, and entered into costly, poorly planned and dangerous overseas adventures against Jihadist forces in first Afghanistan and then Iraq.

This neo-conservative strategy, whose supporters in the administration by then included the more traditional conservatives like Cheney and Rumsfeld, was to employ rapid strike forces to take advantage of the technological superiority of the US and quickly press home victory. Rumsfeld was a radical force in strategic military thinking and attempted to reorganise American armed forces along the lines of what he calls the policy of 'Transformation'. This rather ambiguous term was applied to a wide variety of changes, but included a reduction of troop levels, greater reliance on high-technology war-fighting equipment, closing many bases around the world, and having a command structure more fully under the control of the civilians, especially the Secretary and Deputy Secretary of Defense. It corresponded to what others have termed the Revolution in Military Affairs (RMA). His then Deputy, Paul Wolfowitz, the former Johns Hopkins academic, was very influential in elaborating and implementing these strategies. In March 2005, Bush took everyone by surprise by announcing that Wolfowitz, in spite of being one of the key men running the US Iraq policy, was the US choice to succeed the Australian, James Wolfensohn, as head of the World Bank.

The Democrats at first supported the Iraq war. Then during John Kerry's candidacy for president in 2004, in which Iraq and the Global War on Terror became major campaign issues, the Democrats cast themselves as quasi-isolationist with a strategy to protect American society by multilateral alliances and international actions under the legal umbrella of the UN. In the twenty first century, therefore, the liberals (Left) tried to become the cautious conservative realists, while the conservatives had become the radical neo-conservative interventionists. This almost turned on its head the ideological and foreign policy line-up from the 1920s between the forces of the Left (interventionist) and Right (isolationist) in the American political spectrum. 'Bushism', as it became known by both critics and supporters, had become a radical force, rejecting the traditional conservative inheritance of the Republican Party of sometime isolationism (1920s), America First-ism (late 1930s) and the cautious

30 Dilip Hiro, *Desert Shield to Desert Storm* (London, 1992).

interventionism of Kissingerian balance of power realism (1960s–1970s). It also embraced some of the New Deal domestic policies, such as using Keynesian deficit spending and supporting a high level of central government involvement in welfare and education.[31] The anti-New Deal Republicans would have turned over in their graves.

This Bush radicalism was opposed by many traditional conservatives who believed that his support for massive spending on education and the military, large-scale immigration, tax cuts and big deficits when coupled with foreign policy adventurism would lead to the 'discrediting [of] any sort of conservatism for generations'.[32] Other conservatives voiced grave disquiet about Bush's damage to traditional conservatism, including: Robert George of the *New York Post* who wrote in the *New Republic* that, 'he endangers the long-term health of the Republic'; former Reagan adviser and head of the Economic Strategy Institute, Clyde Prestowitz, who said 'country on the wrong track'; conservative commentator Andrew Sullivan who referred to Bush's 'glaring failures, his fundamental weakness as a leader'; and conservative Christian Right writer Paul Weyrich who was, 'shocked by the vehemence' of many dissident conservatives. They were joined in 2004 by editorial opinions in the conservative *Detroit News,* that Bush 'failed to deliver on…promises', and *The Tampa Tribune*'s reference to 'failed promises'; both papers reversed their endorsement of Bush in 2000 for the 2004 election.[33] Some conservatives pronounced conservatism to be dead as Bush assaulted old neo-isolationist and Kissinergerian concepts abroad, and spent into deficits at home.[34]

Nonetheless, the Presidential election in 2004 re-affirmed public support for the Global War on Terror and the Iraq War strategy of Bush and his neo-conservative advisers. Bush won a majority in the popular vote of 51 to 48 per cent, with a record majority of around 3.5 million, and with a solid (34) electoral college margin (286-252) he could implement his mandate with an increased majority in the House (30: 232 Republicans to 201 Democrats, 2 Independents) and Senate (10: 55 Republicans to 45 Democrats). Illness and retirements, furthermore, gave him an opportunity to control the Supreme Court as well, giving him power in all three branches of government. In 2005 this gave Bush a position of presidential authority not seen since Franklin Roosevelt's massive win in 1932. This was replicated in the states, with Republicans winning clear majorities in state legislative and gubernatorial elections.

The interventionist shift in American foreign policy could continue, therefore, with little domestic constraint, and the second term Cabinet was even more hawkish.

---

31 Nonsense, thundered Norman Podhoretz, who saw Bush as the true conservative: 'World War IV: How it Started, What it Means, and Why We Have to Win', *Commentary,* Sept 2004. See also Eric Alterman, 'A short history of the neoconservatives', *The Australian Financial Review,* 29 April 2005.

32 So wrote Scott McConnell, director of *The American Conservative,* a right-wing magazine run by Bush antagonist and opponent for the presidency in 2000, Pat Buchanan: 'Betrayal of the Right', *The Australian,* 26 Oct 2004.

33 *The Australian,* 1 Nov 2004.

34 See Doug Bandow, senior fellow at the Cato Institute and former assistant to Ronald Reagan, in 'Modern Liberalism takes hold', *The Australian,* 8 Nov 2004.

The moderate former General Colin Powell was replaced by the more hard-line and interventionist neo-conservative National Security Adviser, Condoleezza Rice, as Secretary for State. As her Deputy, the equally conservative former trade negotiator, Robert Zoellick, replaced the more 'moderate' Richard Armitage. Not only could Bush continue to press for a favourable result in Iraq and Afghanistan, but could seemingly increase pressure on Iran, including contemplating an air strike on its nuclear facilities. A firm position could also be maintained on China over the Taiwan issue and on North Korea to conform to American demands on nuclear weapons programs. The Bush Doctrine, therefore, could hardly have received a stronger endorsement by the American electorate than it did in 2004. But it soon faced other obstacles.

The Bush administration's neo-conservatives had more difficulty in coming to a consensus over Iran than they did about intervention against the Taliban or against Saddam Hussein. Prominent neo-conservatives in the State Department, led by Under Secretary of State, John Bolton, who was appointed US Ambassador to the UN in 2005, in spite of being a long-time and fierce critic, like his fellow neo-cons, of that institution,[35] and in Defense, led by (retiring) Under Secretary of Defense Douglas Feith, the editors of the important neo-conservative *The Weekly Standard,* and other neo-conservatives in the Washington think-tanks, split over whether intervention or diplomacy should be employed in dealing with Iran's nuclear program. But by 2006 Bush had his hands full in Iraq and Afghanistan and the capacity of the US armed forces was severely stretched. Bombing Iran's nuclear facilities would be a high-risk strategy and one not guaranteed to succeed. This issue, therefore, challenged the neo-cons' policy of US interventionism that had characterized the Bush administration's foreign policy since 9/11.[36] Foer's prediction of the death of the neo-conservatives in late 2004, however, was somewhat but barely premature.[37]

George W Bush's Second Inaugural Address in January 2005 pronounced a radical extension of the Bush Doctrine of Pre-emption and re-affirmed the most interventionist dimensions of the neo-conservative geopolitical strategy. He said: 'It is the policy of the United States to seek and support the growth of democratic movements and institutions in *every nation and culture, with the ultimate goal of ending tyranny in our world'*. Bush reiterated America's historical sense of mission, and combined it with national security objectives when he asserted further that, 'America's vital interests and our deepest beliefs are now one'. America would fulfill its allegedly God-given historical destiny to democratise the world and come to the aid of democratic forces around the globe; the promises of a New Jerusalem, so central in the cosmology of the Puritan settlers in Massachusetts in the second and third decades of the seventeenth century, still rang true in the consciousness of some

---

35 *The New York Times*, 8 March 2005.

36 See Franklin Foer, 'Death of the neo-cons', *The Australian,* 16 Dec 2004, reprinted from the *New Republic.*

37 'Philosophers and Kings', *The Economist,* 21–27 June 2003.

Americans nearly four centuries later.[38] The Religious Right component of the Bush electoral alliance was being given its space.

But Bush's push for democratization in the Middle East came under fire from some of his own supporters who warned that the result might be to push the region into the arms of the Islamists. Middle Eastern scholar, neo-conservative guru and Director of the Middle East Forum, Daniel Pipes, pointed out that the electorates of Iraq, Lebanon, Egypt and Syria might vote for Islamist governments. They had done so in Algeria and Turkey, although both results were subsequently overthrown by military intervention. The Islamists were well organized politically and in many countries of the Arab-Muslim region have well-armed militias capable of backing up political victories. In 2006 the Hamas won control of the Palestinian Authority even when the PLO was much better placed to rig the election. Pipes urged Bush to go slow and cautioned his fellow neo-conservatives in the US Departments of Defense and State to show prudence on the pace of reform in the Middle East.[39] In one sense the Iraq war produced another round in the older debate of whether or not the US was/is an imperial power, and how its own self-perception, generally as not having an Empire, had evolved over time. Most realist historians dismiss the general historical American self-perception that the US has not been imperial and that it does not aspire to that status, a position still argued by President Bush, as essentially a self-delusion. The only remaining argument is whether the American Empire has been benign or malignant over the past two centuries.[40]

The Bush Regime and Unilateralism

In contrast to the Clintons, the Bush family is one of the wealthiest and best connected in the US. The Bush family has been closely tied to the oil industry since Prescott Bush made steel to sustain the original Pennsylvania oil boom of the 1860s. It then shifted to more direct involvement with the Rockefeller oil corporations, and to the finance industry particularly with Harrimans. In the 1940s Prescott Bush became a Senator. George H W Bush, who had moved to Texas and made money in oil, lost two senatorial races, before becoming a Congressman from Texas, CIA Director, head of the US mission to China, Vice President and then President. George H W Bush's first term marked the end of the Cold War although his predecessor, Reagan, got most of the credit for this. Bush foundered in making his 'vision thing' for the post-Cold War world and then ran into the early 1990s recession just in time for

38 Emphasis added. This extravagant vision frightened even conservatives such as Michael Desch from the George H W Bush School of Government and Public Service at Texas A & M University: 'Folly in exporting 'liberty'', *The Australian,* 25 Jan 2005.

39 'Neo-con caution', *The Australian,* 9 March 2005. See also Eric Foner, 'The Lie that Empire Tells Itself', *London Review of Books,* 19 May 2005, pp. 15–17.

40 The former view has been taken by, among others, the English historian Niall Ferguson in his, *Colossus: the Price of America's Empire* (New York, 2004); whereas the latter view has recently been forcefully argued by Fred Anderson and Andrew Clayton in, *The Dominion of War: Empire and Conflict in North America, 1500–2000* (New York, 2005).

his re-election run. He would probably still have won this against the little known Clinton, had not Ross Perrot split the right wing vote.

The new George W Bush regime was very different to that of Clinton. It came to power after very narrowly winning the 2000 election as a result of superior techniques combined with overwhelming funding. It was backed by a corporate America that expected and got substantial tax cuts which, together with the 2001 recession that the collapse of the dot.com boom developed, produced a turnaround in the American fiscal position and a descent into a new round of deficits, both external and internal, and renewed growing debt. This was only exacerbated by an increase in military spending, which was itself then accelerated by the onset of the Global War on Terror.

The new administration was very close to corporate America, particularly the oil industry. In addition, many of its personnel had served with Reagan and Bush Snr, then sat out politics under Clinton in the corporate sector, and returned to Washington in 2001. Its ideological backbone was provided by a patriotic position on national security. Essentially the Republicans argued that Clinton had run the US military down too far. The *Project for a New America* argued that the US should maintain its hegemonic power by increasing its defence expenditure and capacity to project power. But it did not argue that terrorism was the most serious threat to US interests, and to the extent that it identified one at all, it was China. The conduit of this message of the need for patriotic rearmament to the American people was the right wing media. It was to provide a narrow majority in 2000 based on the so-called red states of the mid-west and south where heartland patriots and the religious right were more common and who swung even further to Bush in 2004. Important in this process was the right wing media, notably NewsCorp and the radio 'shock jocks'.

Rupert Murdoch, the CEO of NewsCorp, was an Australian who had inherited a small Melbourne-based newspaper company in 1953, while still a student at Oxford. He then took over the management of its masthead paper, the Adelaide *News,* where he developed his left wing opinions and honed his journalistic skills. In the 1960s he extended into the Sydney market and then to the UK where he acquired newspapers and later a television operation and moved to the right. He used the considerable profits from his British operations to acquire US media in the 1970s while expanding further in the UK and Australia.

In the 1980s Murdoch used his by now vast media company to develop political power throughout the Anglo-Sphere and beyond. And by that time his opinions and that of his company, now called NewsCorp, had shifted much to the right. In 1983 Murdoch became a US citizen to enable him to own US media, but remained an Australia resident to retain his interests there and indeed expand heavily into the New Zealand market. In the early 1990s NewsCorp suffered near insolvency but recovered to finance a new round of expansion. This involved the creation of a new US television network, Foxtel, under the direction of former Nixon staffer, Roger Ailes. This purposefully took a rightist posture to give it that market segment against the three established networks that were more liberal in orientation. NewsCorp also expanded into communist China with a television presence and ownership of the Hong Kong daily, *South China Morning Post*. In order to do this, voluntary censorship arrangements were undertaken to ensure the PRC regime escaped criticism. Key PRC regime personnel were also rewarded with lucrative publishing contracts.

By the early twenty first century News Corp was a major political influence in the key Anglo-Sphere countries. Its general orientation followed the direction given by the CEO and there were rarely any great divergences of opinion between NewsCorp outlets. By then they included a global television system, about 180 newspapers scattered throughout the world, the Fox motion picture company, several book publishing houses and, more recently, internet technologies. It also had a deep involvement in the most popular sports organisations, particularly the various football codes. It espoused free market principles, except where they interfered with oligopolies that included NewsCorp, supported rightist government of any friendly party including Thatcher and Blair in the UK, Hawke and then Howard in Australia, and Bush in the US, and promoted a neo-liberal and neo-conservative agenda.

In the US this took the form of establishing and owning the *Weekly Standard,* edited by William Kristol in Washington, the leading publication of neo-conservative ideas. The views advanced in it were then given wider circulation in the Foxtel television network and affiliated newspaper outlets, both in the US and in the wider Anglo-Sphere. In international affairs it was supportive of Israel, hostile to the anti-western Arab states, accepting of the friendly oil exporting states' indiscretions, laudatory of China's (and then India's) economic performance but quiet about its political structure and human rights record. It was very supportive of Bush and its network was the first to call his victory in 2000, thereby possibly influencing the electoral outcome in western state time zones.

The Global War on Terror (GWOT)

On 11 September 2001, 19 Arab terrorists from the Islamic extremist organisation, Al Qaeda, high-jacked four planes flying from the East to the West Coast, and so carrying a full fuel payload. They crashed two into the Twin Towers at the World Trade Centre in New York, thereby collapsing them and killing nearly three thousand people. They crashed a third plane onto the Pentagon building, headquarters of the US military forces in Virginia, adjacent to Washington DC. In the fourth plane passengers fought with the terrorists and it was brought down in a field in Pennsylvania.

The Bush administration responded to this attack by declaring a Global War on Terror, or GWOT, which quickly became the principal focus of the administration and the chief mission of the US armed forces. During the following year, the US tightened its domestic security arrangements, set up a Department of Homeland Security, passed the Patriot Act, and began co-ordinating its international search for the terrorists and their organisations with other allied and friendly states of which there were initially many. In late 2001, the US and allied forces attacked the Taliban regime in Afghanistan and, after a ground invasion, overthrew it. Islamic terrorists then threatened retaliatory activities against both the US and other participating states and they planned or actually undertook such terrorist attacks, including against Britain, Australia, Spain, India, the Philippines, Canada, Indonesia, Egypt, and others. At that time there was much international sympathy and even support for US policy.

In March 2003 the US then undertook the invasion of Iraq. It was opposed in this venture by many of the world's governments and popular opinion, and by many of its own citizens who by 2006 had come to form a majority. This invasion and occupation was to prove a turning point not only in the GWOT but also in the history of US modern foreign relations. Although initially successful, the invasion produced a series of failures in 2004–07 that had a profound impact in the standing of the US as a relatively benign, hegemonic power.

Chapter 2

The Anglo-Sphere Nations

During the Global War on Terror, the US received no stronger support than from the group of nations often called the Anglo-Sphere[1] but which Winston Churchill would have recognised as the core English speaking peoples.[2] Following the perspective of the 'clash of civilisations', this is a group of states which mostly share a core set of values and language, have a liberal economy and democratic state, and who are among the richest and most developed in the world. Their clash with Islamic terrorism is not only geopolitical, but also a conflict between the most advanced states and modernised societies in the world, with some of the least developed. But while their governments have remained staunch popular support for US policies has ebbed, including among the American people.

These nations are clearly not merely those states that share a common history as British domains. The imperial British state made some effort to establish such a group of countries. In the early twentieth century its largest self-governing, settler colonies, including Canada, Australia, New Zealand and South Africa, were brought into some aspects of the decision making of the British Empire and called the British Commonwealth. In some ways the Irish colonial domain, that also periodically had a separate Parliament, enjoyed a similar status. Later, this usage was extended to British Empire and Commonwealth to incorporate the non-self governing colonies. Then, as those colonies acquired independence, starting with India in 1947, many of these states joined what became known as the Commonwealth of Nations. Some, like Ireland and Burma, chose not to join; others again that had not been British colonies, like Angola, chose to do so; and others, like Hong Kong, joined other states.

The utility of this organisation came into question in the late twentieth century as the most important foreign policy relationships for many of the Commonwealth countries were outside the Commonwealth. For Britain, itself, the most important strategic links were with the US, and economic ones with the EU. For Canada, the relationship with the US was paramount. Australia has its strongest strategic relationship with the US, while economic linkages with Asia were extremely important. New Zealand's most important ties were with Australia. The US held a pivotal position as the hegemonic power that linked these states together, economically, strategically, culturally and, in some measure, as the centre of their unique Anglophone civilisation.

---

1 James C Bennett, *The Anglosphere Challenge: Why the English Speaking Nations will lead the way in the Twenty-First Century* (Maryland, 2004); see also Andrew Roberts, *A History of the English-Speaking Peoples Since 1900* (New York, 2006).

2 Winston Churchill, *A History of the English Speaking Peoples* (New York, 1965).

These Anglo-Sphere Commonwealth countries, of course, had more in common with each other, and with the US, than they had with many other members of the Commonwealth of Nations. Their major features in common were: an English language used by the overwhelming majority of their populations; a commitment to a combination of common and statute law; a majority European derived ethnicity; similar systems of representative government; a common culture derived from Christianity, but with religious toleration; a civil society in which voluntary association was permitted and encouraged; and a liberal capitalist economy on which basis they had created some of the materially most wealthy societies on earth. Many Commonwealth countries were, in contrast, quite poor.

The Commonwealth of Nations

Created out of the British Statute of Westminster (1931) the Commonwealth comprises some fifty four nations with a population of over two billion people, thirty percent of the world's population. Its nominal head is Queen Elizabeth II of the House of Saxe-Coburg Gotha/Windsor, and it has a large and expensive secretariat. It has a diverse membership in cultural, ethnic, and economic terms ranging from Britain, Australia and Canada, to Kiribati, Lesotho, and the Seychelles. It runs the Commonwealth Games every four years, pursues a variety of educational, legal, cultural and human rights functions, and holds an annual meeting of the heads of government (CHOGM). It has no power, little cohesion and is without strategic value. Many of its states are not democratic, including Pakistan, Zimbabwe, Fiji, Brunei, Mozambique, Nigeria, Tonga, and Zambia, but the Commonwealth has never expelled any state permanently and only Nigeria (1995–99), Pakistan (1999–), Fiji (left in disgrace in 1987 and rejoined in 1997), and Zimbabwe (2002–) have been suspended. At least one-half of the member nations have serious human rights deficiencies including the absence of trial by jury, the use of torture and the suppression of free speech, assembly and press, including Zimbabwe, Nigeria, Pakistan and Sierra Leone. Extending democracy may be an admirable objective of the Commonwealth of Nations, but in practice its success has been limited.

For the Anglo-Sphere the Commonwealth has limited worth. Until the 1950s, Australia (and New Zealand) retained strong economic relations with Britain and the Commonwealth. More recently, however, its trading relations have been revolutionized towards Asia and America. Today over seventy percent of Australia's exports go to Asia and America, with less than ten percent going to the entire European Union, including Britain.[3] The UK is tied politically and economically to the European Union, and no longer looks for identity in the Commonwealth. Canada's primary economic relationship is with the US, particularly since the conclusion of NAFTA in 1994. New Zealand's interests are tied to those of Australia, and beyond them to those states that Australia values. The Commonwealth perpetuates the illusion that the British Empire still exists in some form but is a rather pathetic atavism of the old *Raj* and might be better replaced by a more formal Anglo-sphere.

3 Mosler, *Australia, op cit*, pp. 42–44.

British Origins of the Anglo-Sphere

There is a grouping of recognisably similar states and societies that did originate in the expansion of Britain between the sixteenth and nineteenth centuries and these comprise the Anglo-Sphere. The real origin of the Anglo-Sphere was, of course, British imperialism. This originated in the British state that was itself a creation of the Normans after the conquest of 1066. With the collapse of Romano-Celtic hegemony in the British Isles, the north German and Danish tribes moved across the English Channel to settle in the British Isles in the fifth and sixth centuries. The later Scandinavian invasions, and then conquest of Britain by the Normans, added to the Anglo-Saxon syncretistic mix of culture that from the sixteenth to the eighteenth centuries evolved into a great European power.

The English explored, traded and expanded into the north Atlantic, North America, Asia and the southern Pacific. The people of England were searching for land and markets and, backed by maritime power, created the greatest empire in world history. From that beginning it detached itself from continental Europe and consolidated its unique social and political form on the British islands.[4] England was joined by Wales by conquest, Scotland by more or less voluntary union, and Ireland with reluctance. This United Kingdom then began a process of expansion outside Europe to create the first British Empire in the seventeenth and eighteenth centuries and then, after some setbacks, the second British Empire during and following the defeat of Revolutionary and Napoleonic France in 1815.

The first British Empire was essentially confined to the Atlantic littoral. At first, it was concentrated in North America and the Caribbean, but then extended to southern Africa and South Asia with the victory in the Seven Years War (1756–63). But despite the often brilliant means by which this empire was created, its rulers deeply offended their American colonial subjects and were evicted in the war of American Independence (1776–83) by a combination of the colonial militias and the intervention of other powers, such as France. Even the most powerful imperial government with popular domestic support cannot guarantee victory in an imperial war.

The second British Empire was created shortly thereafter. A revolution begun (1789) in France for liberty, quickly became an imperial dictatorship and seized most of Europe. It was defeated by 1815 by a combination of powers, often led by Britain. For the next century the British mostly ruled the high seas and fashioned a new system of freer international commerce based on the British Empire and naval power. The Empire was extended to Africa, Asia and the Pacific and many societies brought under British rule. Ancient empires, like India and China, were subdued in the process. Some of the legacy of this system, in the form of shipping routes, commercial laws, stock exchanges, navigational systems, time zones and so forth, remain in place to this day. Although the British thought they were bringing this system of civilisation to a welcoming world, it actually rested on British military and particularly naval power. The British were a hegemonic power and stimulated the first wave of globalisation.

4 Norman Davies, *The Isles* (Oxford, 1999).

The British had devised two great social institutions which enabled a small nation off the coast of the European peninsula to become the strongest state in the world with only three per cent of the world's population. They were the liberal representative state and the capitalist economy.

The liberal state has its origins in the thirteenth century, but its first proponents appeared in the seventeenth century, notably Oliver Cromwell and John Locke. It started by challenging regal despotism, developed representative characteristics of government in the eighteenth century, and became a liberal democracy in the nineteenth and twentieth centuries. This enabled people increasingly to pursue their own interests and generated enormous popular energies in the arts, commerce, warfare and science. A bi-product was the capitalist economy.[5]

The capitalist economy sprang from the defeat of statism and the deregulation of commerce. When Adam Smith published *An Inquiry into the nature and causes of the Wealth of Nations* in 1776, he was describing what largely already existed – a prosperous market economy in England. Scientific inquiry followed curiosity, but technology often followed commercial and military requirements. Despite its small population, Britain was soon the major world power as a result of leading in these developments and channelling them into its supreme achievements: the stock exchange and joint stock company; the pound sterling as an international currency; and the Royal Navy.

Nonetheless, other powers observed and emulated these processes and by the early twentieth century Britain was hard pressed to maintain its superiority. It then made this more difficult by heavily regulating its own domestic economy to a degree that diluted its previously successful liberal impulses. By the same historical structures that had led to the decline of other imperial systems, British imperial power was dismantled during the twentieth century. The colonies were granted the independence they would in any case have seized. After 1945, the British economy declined relatively since it had been structured as the centre of an empire that no longer existed and it undertook a series of rearguard actions to ensure an orderly downgrading of its status which varied in character from the forlorn in Suez (1956), through the fruitless in Rhodesia (1979), to the heroic in the Falklands (1982) and the devious in Hong Kong (1997).

This British decline was only arrested when it became clear to the British state that a new role, other than that of the imperial power which it had pursued for four hundred years, was required. Two British governments undertook this transformation. The Conservative government of Prime Minister Edward Heath (1970–74) made Britain a member of (what became) the European Union in 1973. And another Conservative government under Prime Minister Margaret Thatcher (1979–90) deregulated the British economy with the effect that, after a lag, it became once more among the strongest in Europe and, relatively, the world. By that stage the US had, as it were, assumed Britain's earlier place as hegemonic power.

But in the process of imperial decline, Britain had been socially transformed. In 1948 the Labour government (1945–51) passed legislation permitting unrestricted Commonwealth immigration to Britain. Millions of citizens from former colonies –

5 The first actual British settlement was 400 years ago in 1607 in Jamestown, Virginia.

including several hundred thousand Muslims – migrated to Britain and the relatively homogeneous, secular Christian nation was changed substantially ethnically and culturally. The British attempted some re-regulation of immigration in the 1960s and 1970s but the process did not slow until the 1980s. Then changes to the EU enabled European immigration and by the twenty first century up to half a million people were migrating to Britain annually including over 100,000 migrants from outside Europe, 300,000 from the EU and an unknown but substantial number of illegal entrants – all drawn by the booming liberal British economy and residual welfare services.

The British state remained a quite powerful middle power of sixty million people with substantial military forces and the financial strength from the world's fifth largest economy to support them. But those sociological and cultural changes made its society less willing to participate in an activist external strategy. It joined the EU but not its currency union in order to foster the independent City of London and Pound Sterling – with considerable success. But the capacity for unified popular will and social mobilisation had been severely eroded by two generations of imperial defeat and the rise of a multicultural ideology which made the identification of enemies problematic. In 1997 a Labour government was elected, committed to the end of traditional Britain and the beginning of a new country under the non-satirical slogan, 'Cool Britannia'. Ironically, it was the leader of this government, Prime Minister Tony Blair (1997–2007), who later tried to reverse these processes.

The origin of the Anglo-Sphere, then, was British imperial expansion coupled with mass migration from the UK since the Mayflower left Plymouth for New England in 1620. For 400 years, Britain was an emigrant country. One third of the millions of Europeans who migrated from Europe to America in the nineteenth century were from Britain and Ireland. Between 1853 and 1913, 13 million British citizens left, bound mainly for North America, Australia, South Africa and New Zealand. Some came back, but cumulative net emigration was equivalent to 13 per cent of the population, mostly those aged between 18 and 45. These flows are continuing and in 2004 207,000 British nationals left the country. This was the highest number since before 1914 when the outflow was running at 300,000 per annum and more young men were leaving the country every year than died on the battlefields of Europe.[6] Cumulatively from 1997 to 2007, 1.6 million British nationals left the country and 806,000 have returned. At the same time, three million foreign nationals arrived and 1.41 million left. In 1998, the net annual outflow from the UK of British nationals had dwindled to 22,000. By 2004, this had risen to 120,000. Over the same period, the net inflow of non-Britons grew from 106,000 to 342,000 a year. Most of the overseas nationals who stayed were from the Commonwealth or described as 'other foreign'. EU nationals tended not to stay. Between 1997 and 2004, 594,000 EU nationals came, but 412,000 left.

This migration from the UK over four hundred years laid the basis for the Anglo-Sphere; the recent immigration to the UK has modified the UK commitment to this Anglo-Sphere. By the onset of the twentieth century the largest of the Anglo-Sphere countries was already the USA.

---

6 A J P Taylor, *English History 1914-45* (Oxford, 1965).

The Anglo-Sphere in North America

The United States entered the global power contest in 1917 with a unique combination of advantages. It was a large democratic state, practising a form of the separation of powers which gave its executive almost untrammelled executive authority, combined with popular support to be an expansionist nationalist state, practicing high productivity corporate capitalism, and pursuing a free trade order which it could dominate[7] and which Canada joined with the North American Free Trade Agreement of 1994.

The United States of America declared its independence in 1776 and enforced it by 1783 by successful revolt against Britain. But the new Republic rested on weak economic and political foundations in 1783 provided by the new Constitution, the Articles of Confederation. These did not give adequate taxing powers, nor enough political power in the executive branch of government to give the nation stability and power to deal with geopolitical threats from the great European powers surrounding it – notably Britain, France, Spain and Russia. This intrinsic weakness in the power of the executive reflected the use of ideas of the state derived from Locke and Montesquieu, whose concepts of limited authority of the central state and separation of powers was employed in drafting the Articles of Confederation. In 1787, after a constitutional convention, this deficiency was largely corrected with a new constitution permitting stronger executive powers to allow the expansion of the central state. This constitutional structure with the powers of the head of state, head of government and commander in chief all vested in the President would remain, together with the diffusion of powers to the states, as one of the central features of the constitutional power arrangements in America. Although the power to declare war was given to Congress, by the late twentieth century the President, through his executive authority, had effectively usurped it and become the dominant agent in determining whether American forces go to war.[8]

These stronger executive powers were soon exercised by President Thomas Jefferson (1801–1809) when undertaking the Louisiana Purchase in 1803, which nearly doubled the size of the United States. The purchase of the vast territory from Napoleonic France, then in desperate need of funds for the war in Europe, launched America into a cycle of expansion and empire which took its frontiers to the Pacific Rim and then beyond. The challenge of European powers in the Americas, however, did not cease with the Louisiana Purchase. With the Lewis and Clark Expedition (1804–1806) to the Pacific coast, the US extended its territorial ambitions, staked its claim to be an Atlantic and Pacific power, and challenged the old European Imperial powers. In 1812 war erupted again between the US and Britain as a collateral result of Britain's naval campaign against France. After this, the United States was then determined to secure its own continent. This prompted President James Monroe (1817–1825) to enunciate his Monroe Doctrine in his message to Congress in 1823 which declared that the Americas were off limits to colonization by outside powers

7 We explored this theme more extensively in *Global America,* as above.

8 R C Simmons, *The American Colonies, From Settlement to Independence* (London, 1976).

and warned off the Europeans. He vowed, in return, not to interfere in European quarrels. To enforce his doctrine, Monroe counted on support from the British, with their vast naval power, who wished to preclude their European rivals from any further expansion in the Western hemisphere.

The Monroe Doctrine was refined and expanded throughout the nineteenth century and became the cornerstone of US policy in its region and the basis for vastly increasing US power and interference in the Americas. President James K. Polk (1845–1849), worried about Britain in Oregon and California, announced in 1845 that Monroe's principles were 'our settled policy, that no future European colony or dominion shall, without our consent, be planted or established on any part of the North American continent'. Polk also exercised US power in a successful and expansionist war against Mexico from 1846–1848 that ended with the Treaty of Guadalupe Hidalgo which added almost the entire modern Southwest to the emerging imperial domain of the United States.[9]

The Americans were also energised by an ideology of expansion that blended a Puritan sense of eschatology, Anglo-Saxon ethnicism, Social Darwinism and American jingoism into a quasi-religious ideology of Americanism. This eclectic theory was pulled together in the Doctrine of Manifest Destiny that was first enunciated in 1845 by the journalist John Lewis O'Sullivan as editor of the *United States Magazine and Democratic Review*. He stated, 'Our manifest destiny is to overspread the continent allotted by Providence for the free development of our yearly multiplying millions'. This gave a pseudo-moral substratum to imperial ambition for the young and ambitious nation from the early heady days of occupying the American continent through to two recent Gulf Wars. Although nineteenth century US policy makers often pursued isolation from the affairs of Europe, America also perceived itself as a nation whose destiny was sanctioned by God to spread democracy and civilization to the entire globe if possible. With the collapse of the British and other European empires, and the economic destruction to America's competitors caused by the Second World War, the American behemoth, and its foreign policy practitioners, saw the twenty first century as an opportunity to fulfil this ancient dream for America's divinely sanctioned destiny.[10]

With this happy coincidence of ideology, space and resources, provided by God or chance, the US continued to expand into the Pacific Rim. In 1848 the conflict with Britain over the Pacific Northwest and the boundary with Canada was settled. The purchase of Alaska in 1867 by the Secretary of State William Seward (1861–1869) for $US7.2 million (roughly 2 cents per acre) from the cash-strapped Tsar Alexander II (1855–1881), was to be an extraordinarily perspicacious move and must be viewed as the bargain of the century. Building on Commodore Matthew Perry's opening of Japan to trade with his visits in 1853–54, the American presence in the Central and Western Pacific expanded enormously including in the Polynesian Kingdom of Hawaii and throughout the Western Pacific. Trade and economic activity was soon matched with military power as the US pressed its claims to be a Pacific power along

9 Sam W Haynes, *James K Polk and the Expansionist Impulse* (New York, 2002).

10 O'Sullivan, quoted in George Tindall and David Shi, *America* (New York, 1984) p. 527.

with the British, Germans, Russians, Chinese and the Japanese. Conflict would seem, in this great power context, inevitable.

In 1895 President Grover Cleveland (1885–1889, 1893–1897) reiterated Monroe's point and declared, again in the original form intended by Monroe, that the prohibition on European interference applied to all of the Americas. Cleveland pursued a robust policy in the Pacific and established the foundations that led to the annexation of Hawaii in 1898 and the Spanish-American War (under President McKinley) in the same year. The administration of Theodore Roosevelt (1901–1909), the hero of the Spanish-American War, extended the Monroe Doctrine with his Roosevelt Corollary (1904) in the context of an imperial American power that now had the force, the Empire and the intent to enforce not only its dominance in the Americas but, in one generation, around the globe.[11]

The US became the world's greatest industrial power by 1900; was among the leading military powers from then until 1945; from then until 1990 was one of two superpowers; and, by the twenty-first century, had become the world's sole superpower. Among the most important factors leading to this rapid development were: abundant natural resources (especially initially water and water power, then coal and iron, and finally oil); ready maritime access to foreign and domestic markets; national/ethnic unity among a diverse and energetic population; territorial space for expansion; a strong work ethic and/or ideology of efficient work; ease of internal transportation; the strong growth of literacy and educational institutions; democratic and representational government including equal rights for women; strong family structures; the maintenance of law and order; sound financial and banking structures; good national savings rates; the sanctity and transaction/portability of property; and the social strength of religious traditionalism combined with the separation of Church and State. Many of these structures are central to the differential development patterns of the developed and underdeveloped world, but many also apply commonly to all Anglo-Sphere countries and most particularly to the US, Canada and Australia.[12]

The first permanent European settlements in Canada were established by the French at Port Royal in 1605 and Quebec City in 1608, and then by the English in Newfoundland, around 1610. Introduced European diseases spread rapidly through native trade routes and decimated the native population. For much of the seventeenth century, the English and French colonies in North America developed in isolation from each other as French colonists settled the St Lawrence River Valley, while English colonists concentrated in the southern Thirteen Colonies. However, as competition for territory and resources escalated, several wars broke out between the French and English which culminated with a complete British victory in the Seven Years War (1756–63). Britain gained control of all of France's North American

---

11 Robert Ferrell, *American Diplomacy, a History* (New York, 1969) p. 183.

12 Some historians argue that 'the acquisition of landed property' was the basis of the 'American spirit' and that Americans became a nation of enterprising small property owners whose primary social objective was the accumulation of wealth: Andro Linklater, *Measuring America, How the United States was Shaped by the Greatest Land Sale in History* (London, 2002) p.190.

territory east of the Mississippi River, except for the remote islands of St. Pierre and Miquelon.

The British gained possession of a large territory, whose mostly French-speaking, Roman Catholic inhabitants had recently taken up arms against Britain. To avert conflict, Britain passed the Quebec Act of 1774, re-establishing the French language, Catholic faith, and French civil law in Quebec. But this helped to fuel the American Revolution. Following the independence of the United States, approximately 50,000 United Empire Loyalists moved to British North America. Canada was a major front in the War of 1812 between the United States and the British Empire and its successful defence had important long-term effects on Canada, including the building of a sense of unity and nationalism among British North Americans. Large-scale immigration to Canada began in 1815 from Britain and Ireland. A series of agreements led to long-term peace between Canada and the United States and a demilitarised border.

Following the mostly French and failed Rebellions of 1837, which demanded responsible government, colonial officials issued the Durham Report in 1839. One goal was to assimilate the French Canadians into British culture. The Canadas were merged into a single, quasi-federal colony, the United Province of Canada, with the Act of Union (1840). The Canadian population grew rapidly due to high birth rates, although high European immigration was offset by emigration to the United States, especially by French Canadians moving to New England. Following the Great Coalition, the Charlottetown Conference the Quebec Conference of 1864, and the London Conference of 1866, the three colonies – Canada, Nova Scotia, and New Brunswick – undertook the process of Confederation. The British North America Act created 'one dominion under the name of Canada', with four provinces: Ontario, Quebec, Nova Scotia, and New Brunswick. After Canada assumed control of Rupert's Land and the North-Western Territory, which together formed the Northwest Territories in 1870, inattention to the Métis led to the Red River Rebellion and ultimately to the creation of the province of Manitoba and its entry into Confederation in July 1870. British Columbia and Vancouver Island (which had united in 1866) and the colony of Prince Edward Island joined the Confederation in 1871 and 1873, respectively.

Despite this sovereign status, Canada automatically entered the First World War in 1914 with Britain's declaration of war, and sent formed divisions, composed almost entirely of volunteers, to the Western Front to fight as a national contingent. Casualties were so high that Prime Minister Robert Borden was forced to bring in conscription in 1917 a move that was extremely unpopular in Quebec. In 1919, Canada joined the League of Nations in its own right, and in 1931 the Statute of Westminster confirmed that no act of the British Parliament would extend to Canada without its consent. After supporting appeasement of Germany in the late 1930s, Liberal Prime Minister William Lyon Mackenzie King secured Parliament's approval for entry into the Second World War in 1939, mobilising the military even before Germany invaded Poland. The economy boomed during the war mainly due to the amount of military materiel being produced for Canada, Britain and the Soviet Union. Canada finished the war with one of the largest military forces in the world. In 1949, the formerly independent Dominion of Newfoundland joined the Confederation as Canada's tenth province.

By Canada's centennial in 1967, heavy post-war immigration from European countries had changed the country's demographics. Increased immigration, combined with the baby boom, an economic strength paralleling that of the 1960s United States, and reaction to the Quiet Revolution in Quebec, initiated a new type of Canadian nationalism. At a meeting of First Ministers in November 1981, the federal and provincial governments agreed to the patriation of the constitution, with procedures for amending it. Despite the fact that the Quebec government did not agree to the changes, on 17 April 1982, Canada patriated its Constitution from Britain, thereby making Canada wholly sovereign, though the two countries continue to share the same monarch.

After French speaking Quebec underwent profound social and economic changes during the Quiet Revolution of the 1960s, some Québécois began pressing for greater provincial autonomy, or even independence from Canada. Alienation between English-speaking Canadians and the Québécois over the linguistic, cultural and social divide had also been exacerbated by other things. While a referendum on sovereignty-association in 1980 was rejected by a solid majority of the population, a second referendum in 1995 was rejected by a margin of just 50.6 per cent to 49.4. In 1997, the Canadian Supreme Court ruled unilateral secession by a province to be unconstitutional, but Quebec's sovereignty movement has continued. Economic integration with the US increased significantly after 1945 and accelerated after the Canada-United States Free Trade Agreement of 1987. In recent decades, Canadians have worried about their cultural autonomy as American television shows, movies and corporations became omnipresent. Canadians take special pride in their unique multiculturalism.

By the 1970s, Canada was sufficiently significant to become a member of the Group of Seven – now G8. Canada's total land area is nearly 10 million square kilometres, a bit larger than the US and second only to Russia. It has vast natural resources including: iron ore, nickel, zinc, copper, gold, lead, molybdenum, potash, diamonds, silver, fish, timber, wildlife, coal, petroleum, natural gas, and hydropower. The Canadian population is 33 million with a growth rate of 0.9 per cent. Approximately 90 per cent of the population is concentrated within 160 km of the US border. Their origins are claimed to be British 28 per cent, French 23, other European 15, Amerindian 2, and other, mostly Asian, African, Arab 6, mixed background 26. This underestimates its Anglo-sphere characteristics, which are better described in linguistic affiliations, which comprise English 59.3 per cent, French 23.2 per cent, and 'other', who are mostly Anglophone, 17.5 per cent. It is mostly Christian, except for a Muslim minority of 1.9 per cent.

Canada most resembles the US in its market-oriented economic system, pattern of production, and affluent living standards. After the Second World War the growth of manufacturing, mining, and service sectors transformed the nation from a largely rural economy into one primarily industrial and urban. The 1989 US-Canada Free Trade Agreement (FTA) and the 1994 North American Free Trade Agreement (NAFTA) (which also includes Mexico) produced a dramatic increase in economic integration with the US. Exports account for a third of GDP and

Canada enjoys a substantial trade surplus with its principal trading partner, the US, which absorbs more than 85% of Canadian exports. Canada is America's largest foreign supplier of energy, including oil, gas, uranium, and electric power. It has a large GDP of over $US1.1 trillion and a GDP PPP per capita of $US 35,000. But more recently wealthy Canada has grappled with the multiculturalism, the collapse of its external power after the Cold War, and concerns about loss of identity and state authority.

Canada's four major political parties were the Conservative Party of Canada, Liberal Party of Canada, New Democratic Party (NDP), and the Bloc Québécois. The current government is led by the Conservative Party of Canada under Prime Minister Norman Harper. Canada has a close relationship with the US: they share the world's longest undefended border, co-operate on some military campaigns and exercises, and are each other's largest trading partners. But Canada also shares a history and long relationship with both the UK and France, the two imperial powers most important in its founding. These relations extend to other former members of the British and French empires, through Canada's membership in both the Commonwealth of Nations and La Francophonie.

For the past sixty years, Canada has been a major advocate for multilateralism. During the Suez Crisis of 1956, Lester B Pearson proposed peacekeeping efforts which led to the inception of the United Nations Peacekeeping Force. Later, Canada tried to maintain a leading role in UN peacekeeping efforts and served in fifty peacekeeping missions, including every UN peacekeeping effort until 1989, although Canada's UN peacekeeping contributions diminished into the twenty first century. A founding member of NATO, Canada currently employs about 62,000 regular and 26,000 reserve military personnel, 1,400 armoured fighting vehicles, 34 combat vessels, and 861 aircraft. Canada supported coalition forces in the First Gulf War of 1991, contributed forces to the wars over former Yugoslavia in the 1990s, and since 2001 Canada has had troops deployed in Afghanistan as part of the US stabilisation force and the UN-authorized, NATO-commanded International Security Assistance Force. But it did not contribute to the US-led invasion of Iraq in 2003.

The election in Canada in January 2006, brought to power a conservative in the Bush mould, Stephen Harper, who restored the fortunes of the conservatives that had suffered one of the worst defeats in Anglo-Sphere history in 1993 under Prime Minister Kim Campbell. Harper represents, like Bush and the Australian Prime Minister John Howard, a blend of economic neo-liberalism and social conservatism. The distribution of Harper's support is also a classic red state-blue state split with Harper winning virtually no seats in the main urban centers of Toronto, Vancouver and Montreal, where seats were won by the opposition leftish parties: the Liberals, the social democratic NDP and the Parti Québécois. The Conservatives polled strongly in the provincial areas especially the western Provinces. The acceptance of the US alliance was clearly endorsed by Canadian voters, a result which was also an election issue in an earlier victory by John Howard in the Australian election of 2004 and Angela Merkel in Germany in 2005.

The Anglo-Sphere on the Pacific Rim

The Pacific Rim embraces the littoral of the largest ocean and is inhabited by diverse peoples of Asian, European and Malay-Polynesian origin. Humans migrated into the Pacific Basin from southern China and Southeast Asia about 40,000 years ago. They employed rafts or canoes and by island hopping colonised the vast Pacific Ocean and its land masses. These people were skilled navigators and developed farming techniques that allowed them to transport livestock, seeds and agricultural goods to the next island or land mass. By these methods ancient cultures were shifted from mainland Asia to Australasia, America and beyond.[13] Migration to Australia from the Asian mainland also occurred about 40,000 years ago, beginning habitation by the Australian Aborigines on the Australian mainland.[14]

Four main culture modes dominated East Asia and the Pacific: Indian, Chinese, Muslim and Pacific Islander (Malay-Polynesian). Chinese culture, dating from 3000 BC, spread to Korea, Japan and south to Vietnam including with it the Buddhist religion. Indian culture, dating from 1500 BC and originating in the Ganges and Indus River Valleys of northern India, spread east to Burma, Laos, Malaysia and Indonesia, and Hindu culture still exists, despite the Islamisation of much of Indonesia, on the island of Bali. Islam spread east from its seventh century origins in the Arabian Peninsula, to Asia in the fourteenth century; reached India in the early part of that century and spread south and east to Indonesia (then Buddhist and Hindu), Malaysia and the southern islands of Mindanao and Sulu in the Philippines by the mid-fifteenth century. Pacific Islanders, originally Malay-Polynesian peoples from Southeast and East Asia, dominated the routes east and south across the Pacific to Hawaii, reaching and as far south as New Zealand and in the other direction the southeast coast of Africa in modern Madagascar.

Asian trade and commercial routes, especially along the coastal regions, took these ancient cultures throughout the Indian and Pacific Oceans. Chinese sea voyagers covered the Pacific south to probably the northern coast of Australia and west to South Asia and the Arab world. Indians frequented trade routes to China and the Middle East for centuries before the arrival of the Europeans. When the Europeans arrived, therefore, they challenged established ancient Hindu, Muslim, Buddhist and Pacific Island cultures, for supremacy in Asia and the Pacific. The military technology of the Europeans gave them a physical advantage, and the ideology of expansionist and muscular Christianity, provided a bureaucratic and powerful rationale for dominance. Commercial gains also beckoned. The old traditional modes of culture in Asia came under siege and the battle for hegemony in Asia between European structures and those of traditional societies provides a leitmotif for the history of the Asia-Pacific region to the present phase of Jihadist confrontation with and resistance to modernity and the West.

---

13 Donald Denoon, *et al*, *A History of Australia, New Zealand and the Pacific* (Oxford, 2000) pp. 38–39; Andrew Sharp, *Ancient Voyagers in the Pacific* (Mitcham, Victoria, 1957).

14 Alan Thorne, 'Australia's Oldest Human Remains: Age of the Lake Mungo 3 Skeleton', *Journal of Human Evolution,* Vol. 36, pp. 591–612.

The Europeans expanded out of the Old World through advances in navigational technology, arms and boat building techniques. These changes gave them the edge over their Arab, Indian and Chinese competitors in the global race for resources in general, and in the Pacific in particular. Marco Polo brought back knowledge of China to Europe from his travels from 1271 to1295. Bartholomew Dias discovered the sea route to India in his1486–1488 voyages down the west coast of Africa; Vasco da Gama sailed the length of the west coast of Africa, to map out the route to India in his voyages from 1497 to 1499; Columbus reached the New World from Spain in 1492; and, the Spaniard Ferdinand Magellan circumnavigated the globe (1519–1522) and claimed the Philippines for Spain in 1521. The Dutch United East India Company (VOC) took control of Batavia (Island of Java, Indonesia) after it was formed as an aggressive trading company in 1621. Over the next two centuries the French, Portuguese, Spanish, Germans and British established colonies in and about the Pacific Basin. But the English gained hegemony in South Asia after defeating the French in a series of successful and brazen actions by Robert Clive for the East India Company in the mid 1760s which constituted a theatre of the Seven Years War. With the addition of the Russians in Siberia and Alaska, and the Americans joining the race for colonies in the nineteenth century and the European domination of territory in the Pacific which unleashed the forces of modernisation was completed.[15]

The United States, Canada, Australia and New Zealand evolved as products of the expansion of British civilisation. The US and Australia both occupied continental space and were established as settler societies with a great wealth of resources and room for territorial aggrandizement at the expense of aboriginal peoples. In the early nineteenth century, however, the US had gained independence as a new Republic with great potential power, while Australia, Canada and New Zealand were still in their colonial infancies.

The epic voyages of discovery by Captain Cook on the *Endeavour* from 1768 until his murder in Hawaii in 1779 set the stage for the English peoples to expand to the southern hemisphere. Australian settlement began with the landing of Captain Arthur Phillip at Port Jackson (Sydney) on 18 January 1788 on the ship *Supply*. Almost from the beginnings of the Australian colonies interaction took place between the US and Australia in trade, culture and strategic policy. American clipper ships soon sailed into Sydney harbour and sealing and whaling opportunities quickly attracted Yankee entrepreneurs. In the nineteenth century, Americans pressed their claims for a major commercial and strategic position in the Pacific region and Admiral Perry's visit to Japan in 1853–54 inaugurated a period of US expansion that culminated in the Spanish-American War in 1898. With victory over Spain, America established itself as an imperial power in the Pacific and the intertwining of Australian and American destinies began.

The race for colonial possessions in the Pacific was as fierce and complex as in nineteenth century Africa, and the geopolitical issues surrounding trade and military competition between the great European powers were similar. The global struggle between Britain and France lasted for centuries: from the late medieval dynastic wars for the control of France and England, to English opposition to the ambitions

15 Teodoro Agoncillo, *A Short History of the Philippines* (New York, 1969).

of Louis XIV in the seventeenth century, to the mid-to-late eighteenth century wars in Europe, North America and Asia and through the Napoleonic Wars. These two early superpowers had battled for European and world hegemony on land and at sea. After 1815, the British with superior naval power emerged as the world's greatest imperial power.

In the Pacific Basin this global struggle was also acted out. The British outflanked the French in the southern Pacific and gained Australasia in the late eighteenth century while France was consumed by its attempt to control Europe. They then established themselves throughout the Western and Southern Pacific in New Guinea, Fiji, Tonga and New Hebrides (now Vanuatu) with some additional smaller outposts of the British Empire. The French colonised French Polynesia, with their headquarters in Tahiti, from 1842 onwards and, after defeating a resistance war by Tahitians, expanded to control a large swath of the central Pacific covering 4200 square kilometres. They ruled the New Hebrides jointly with Britain after 1887, and annexed New Caledonia in 1853 and used it as a penal colony.

Germany came into the colonial race late and established colonies in the northeast of the island of New Guinea in 1884 while Britain annexed the southeast in 1888. In 1906 the British gave its Territory of Papua to Australia and German New Guinea became a League of Nations Mandate under Australia in 1920, although the Dutch controlled the western half of the island. The German territory in the Solomon Islands was ceded to Britain by treaty in 1900. New Zealand annexed German (western) Samoa and with the outbreak of war in 1914 was made the League of Nations Mandate power after 1919. This was extended to the UN until 1962 and the colony is now the nation of Manu Samoa, while the eastern part is still American since the US navy took control in 1900.[16]

Germany declared a protectorate over the Marshall Islands in 1885 (from Spain) but after the First World War they were given to Japan as a mandate power in 1920 as part of their Micronesian responsibilities. The Republic of the Marshall Islands became independent in 1979. The Carolines were purchased by Germany in 1899 from Spain and included also in the mandate with the Japanese in 1920. Germany acquired Palau from Spain after its defeat in 1898 and in 1921 it also passed to Japan under its mandate in the northern Pacific. After the Americans assumed control after 1945 it went through a series of constitutional changes culminating in membership of the UN in 1994 as the Republic of Palau which also joined the South Pacific Forum in 1995. After the Second World War the US controlled part of Micronesia (Carolines) and in 1982 they became the Federated Republic of Micronesia (FRM) and joined the South Pacific Forum in 1987. The northern Marianas were also given to the Japanese as a mandate after 1919 from the German Empire, came under US control, after 1945, originally as a UN trusteeship in 1947, and were designated after 1986 as the self-governing Commonwealth of the Northern Mariana Islands.

16 New Zealand annexed the Cook Islands and Niue in 1901, and took control of the Tokelau Islands in 1925 making it a micro-imperial power in its region. All of the islanders in these groups have New Zealand citizenship and as a consequence large numbers have migrated to New Zealand. New Zealand's most populous city of Auckland now has the largest number of Polynesian peoples of any city in the world.

The Spaniards maintained their colonial rule in the Philippines until war with the US in 1898, after which it ceded the colony to Washington. The Portuguese maintained a presence in East Timor; the Russians were positioned in Siberia and Alaska (until 1867); and the Dutch consolidated their rule in Indonesia, finally seizing Bali in 1903. The Americans moved west from Hawaii into the Western Pacific: Midway was occupied in 1867, Guam taken as spoils in the Spanish-American War in 1898, Johnston Island taken in 1898, Wake Island occupied in 1899, and Samoa shared (the eastern part or American Samoa) with Germany and Britain in 1899 (Britain renounced all claims in 1900). After the Meiji restoration in 1868, the Japanese positioned themselves in East Asia and especially China, with their own imperial ambitions to match the old powers of Europe.

This colonisation of the entire Pacific and its littoral, as in Africa and Latin America, produced the traumatic and dramatic patterns of modernisation as it did in the rest of the world's non-Western nations and cultures. The colonisation of the Pacific by the Europeans, notably the British and Americans, initially did not have the global geo-strategic importance of South Asia or Africa. Nor did it initially have such economic value; but for the peoples of the region the social impact was just as great. Rapid modernisation and Westernisation dramatically altered the social order. The integration of these regional and localised economies into global markets often turned them into vulnerable monocultures, producing tradable commodities from agricultural, forestry or mining. Also, Christianity took root extensively as Methodists, Mormons, Catholics and Pentecostals alike flooded the Pacific Basin challenging indigenous world views and suppressing the customs and practices of the traditional cultures of the Pacific Rim. Modernity had come late, but then with a rush after which no Asian or Pacific culture would easily survive in its traditional historical form.

The Commonwealth of Australia

The Australian colonies were, like the American colonies, initially developed as parts of the British Empire. Australians then fought around the globe in defence of the Empire. From 1860 to 1872 they journeyed to New Zealand to help their fellow Anglo-Saxons defeat the resisting Maori population in the New Zealand Wars (1860–72). When the British were securing their position in East Africa, Australians helped in the Sudan War (1885). As the British consolidated their hold on southern Africa by defeating the Dutch-speaking Afrikaans population in the Boer War (1899–1902), the Australians fought with the Empire.

In 1901 the six British colonies of the Australian continent federated to form the Commonwealth of Australia. At first the citizens of Australia appeared ambivalent about being an independent nation state. They sought strategic protection from the British imperial navy and Britain retained effective control over Australian external affairs and diplomatic representation in most parts of the world. The build up of tensions around the world between Federation and the outbreak of war in 1914, especially in Europe, did not alter the perceptions of Australians that their destiny was in the Empire. Australia was a white dominion in the Empire and if duty called to serve overseas Australians would do so. With the assassination of Archduke Ferdinand in 1914 they were given their opportunity, and Australia, along with the rest of the Empire, was at war.[17]

The British Empire at the turn of the twentieth century might have appeared to its supporters in England and around the globe in the dominions to be unconquerable and permanent. The British navy and British culture appeared to still reign supreme in the world and the Empire inspired loyalty and power everywhere. But the ruling circles were already concerned that rivals were eroding its lead, and, particularly with historical hindsight, the early indications of the weaknesses in the imperial edifice were there for the perceptive observer although they did not become manifest until the Second World War: the British economy was in serious trouble with its balance of trade deeply in the red after the 1880s and only income from overseas investments kept the economy overall in the black; the British army and its navy, were overstretched as the ignominious collapse of British naval power in the Far East in 1941–1942 would reveal; nationalism in the Empire grew leading to independence movements, especially in the Ireland and then India, that could not be contained; and the moral and intellectual bankruptcy of European imperialism was close at hand for Europe in general and Britain in particular. As Europe was about to engage in probably the most insane and self-destructive war in its history in 1914, the viability of Imperial Europe and its overseas possessions was already in jeopardy. Although the British monarchy would at least survive the internecine, long European War (1914–1945) the Russian, German, Austrian and Ottoman monarchies did not. Empire loyalists in Australia and New Zealand appeared blind to most, if not all, of these historical realities.

New Zealand

New Zealand was settled by Polynesian Maoris from the Cook Islands about 1200 CE and they established a notably unique culture within a Polynesian framework. The islands were then populated by Europeans mostly from the Australian colonies from the early nineteenth century. In 1840 the Maori chiefs ceded sovereignty under the Treaty of Waitangi to the British Crown under conditions which remain controversial. The Dominion then achieved self government in 1909 and assumed full sovereignty at about the same pace as the six federated Australian colonies which it declined to join in 1901. In 1909 it became a separate almost sovereign state but fought with Australia in the joint ANZAC force during the First World War.[18]

New Zealand retained close links with the UK, but drifted away from the Australian Commonwealth as both developed protected and state directed economies. This separation may have been sharpened during the Second World War, when New Zealand kept its forces in Europe when Australians returned to defend their own country. Nonetheless, the two retained a similar strategic perspective on the Cold War, signed the ANZAC mutual defence pact in 1944 and joined the US together

17 Helen Irving, *To Constitute a Nation* (Cambridge,1999).

18 See Bob Catley, *Waltzing with Matilda: Should New Zealand Join Australia?* (Wellington, 2001).

in the ANZUS Treaty of 1951. But this relationship unravelled in the mid 1980s when the New Zealand Labour Government opposed Reagan's successful strategic confrontation with the Soviet Union and was turned out of the ANZUS Treaty but remained in ANZAC. This anti-nuclear posture proved popular and was retained by the Nationals when they regained power in 1990.

This adoption of near neutrality was matched by an interpretation of the Treaty of Waitangi by the Labour government that was very favourable to the Maoris enduring rights and claims. Together with the influx of Pacific Islander immigrants, this diluted the British nature of New Zealand culture and developed a uniquely bi-cultural society of Anglo-Polynesian character. While it did not entirely remove the country from the Anglo-Sphere, it did raise countervailing forces. But in other respects, including sports, media, laws, and religion, New Zealand remained a core Anglo-Sphere society.

But at the end of the Cold War, New Zealand believed it was in a secure, benign environment, particularly since Australia lay across any likely route for invasion. It ran down defence expenditure and kept its distance from the US. When Labour was re-elected under Prime Minister Helen Clark in 1999, it set about running down the defence forces even further and effectively abolished the air force and withdrew from joint strategic defence planning with Australia. In early 2000 the Prime Minister declared that the country was in 'an incredibly benign strategic environment' and it seemed unlikely it would project its power any further than neighbouring Pacific islands.

Anglo-phone Abstainers

Not all states that had historically qualified for the Anglo-Sphere wanted to be members, just as not all states that qualified for membership of the Commonwealth of Nations wanted to join.

The first successful war of independence against the second British Empire was fought by the Irish. In the middle of Britain's imperial war with Germany the Irish staged a popular rebellion in Easter 1916. The British repressed this savagely but in the longer term acquiesced to Irish nationalism and conceded independence in 1923. This produced a civil war in Ireland chiefly because the terms involved the northern Protestant provinces remaining in the United Kingdom. Irish nationalism was heavily interwoven with the Catholic religion and although the partition was not entirely inappropriate, the Irish had little reason to remain within British institutions. Indeed, in both the Second World War and the Cold War, Ireland remained neutral.

The Republic of South Africa also exited from the Anglo-Sphere for not dissimilar reasons. The British conquered the whole of South Africa – chiefly for gold – in the Boer War of 1899–1902. It then ruled the Union against the hostility of the Boers and the passivity of the Black Africans. In 1948 the Boers took power in an election and used it to serve their interests through an apartheid state – which was in the 1980s close to Israel. Its racism led to its exclusion from many international activities until sanctions and an internal Black revolt led to the collapse of Boer power in the early 1990s. As the communist supported African National Congress had little reason to sympathise with the British, the state it then controlled moved away from the Anglo-Sphere and towards a regional and African identity. Although it remained in the Commonwealth – which imposed no burden – it had only loose links with the West and on many issues indeed sympathised with the Arab countries, particularly with those that had supported the ANC against the Boers.

Other Anglo-phone countries are not part of the Anglo-Sphere because of ethnic concerns such as the West Indian nations, cultural distinctiveness such as India, or cultural divergence as in Malta. But the core states as identified did exhibit some of the characteristics of a core civilisation as identified by Huntington in his path breaking study. They had a similar culture, political configuration and reacted similarly to the events of 9/11.[19]

19 Samuel P Huntington, *Clash, op cit.*

Chapter 3

The Great Wars and Cold War, 1914–1991

The US became a potential Great Power at the turn of the nineteenth to twentieth centuries; it participated in the international system as a Great Power 1917–1921; it lapsed into isolationism from the affairs of Europe, 1921–41; and then re-emerged as the most powerful single state in the world during its participation in the Second World War, 1941–45. From 1945 to 1991, the US was one of the two superpowers contending for global domination in the Cold War, which it finally won. Throughout this period the US espoused a liberal agenda and ideology, which was always self-serving but often simultaneously beneficial for the world at large.

During this evolving encounter with the wider world, the US continually engaged with traditional societies experiencing the processes of development and the problems of modernisation. As a relatively new society and even newer state, the US had been modern from its foundation and crafted a flexible form of liberalism that, whatever its other difficulties, made adjustment to new technologies, economic processes and social structures not only possible but often exhilaratingly stimulating. For more traditional societies this was not the case, and one of the recurring themes of US foreign relations is the difficulty of mutual understanding this often generated. But for a long period, America's optimism about progress and modernisation was shared by the European powers.

After 1815, and with the exception of the Crimean War (1854–1856), Europe enjoyed a century of relative peace and unprecedented prosperity and optimism about the ultimate achievements of industrial society. In Britain, the Crystal Palace Exhibition in 1851 was intended to extol the great achievements of the British Empire and industrial society in general and to present the limitless possibilities open to human progress. Across the spectrum of European cultural life brilliant achievement was visible: in art, music and literature, and scientific discovery and technological innovation, European culture not only dazzled itself but dominated the world. The European, then American, model of urban industrial society was becoming the model for all the world's civilizations. Europe controlled virtually all continents, directly or indirectly, although the new expansionist societies in America and Japan were making their bids to join the old European great powers. In 1914 Europe plunged into the most brutal and costly war in its history ending the balance of power in Europe. Empires disappeared as war spread around the globe.

From 1914 to 1945 the world was, almost without a break, engulfed in global war. The collapse of the old imperial monarchies of Europe, particularly the German, Austrian, Russian and the Eurasian Ottoman empires, set off global forces of conflict and change. These were matched on the other side of Eurasia with the end of Imperial Manchu rule in China, and the rise and fall of Imperial Japan as an East Asian power that also produced decades of war in Asia. The resulting disorder was further complicated by the dislocation of the Great Depression to make this period one of unprecedented misery, death, genocide and destruction, which set off cycles of socio-political change the final consequences of which have not yet been seen.

Modernisation involves substantial and rapid change for traditional societies in Asia, Africa and the Middle East, made all the more disruptive when initiated by foreign conquest rather than organic evolution. The dominance of traditional cultures is challenged by scientific outlook; agricultural production displaced by urban activities; labour replaced by technology; the pre-existing order of precedence and power displaced by representation and commercial wealth; religion and superstition by a rationalist outlook; and the native system of political authority is displaced by foreigners and then new patterns of hierarchy. These were all very disruptive experiences. In the first decade of the twenty first century we are living under the long shadow of the 1914 to 1945 war and the long rippling effects of social and political change it set off around the world.

Great Powers on the Pacific Rim

For centuries the struggle for power in the Pacific Rim revolved around the history of peoples and empires expanding into the vast Pacific region. The Americans pushed west after independence and throughout the nineteenth century, by the final decades of which they were poised for superpower status. The Russians expanded east to the Pacific and claimed territory in Siberia and from China even while the Tsarist state crumbled domestically under increasing pressure for radical change. Japan, almost uniquely in Asia at that time, overcame the challenge of the modernisation of feudalism when confronted by the more powerful West, and emerged in East Asia by the turn of the twentieth century searching for its own empire to match that of the old great powers of Europe. China, the 'sick man of Asia', was carved up by the European imperial powers and took until the end of the twentieth century to consolidate its reaction to modernisation and regain its place as a great power.

From the mid-nineteenth to the late twentieth century, in a quadrilateral contest for power, wars occurred between China and Japan (1894–1895), Russia and Japan (1904–1905), China and Japan (1937–45), Japan and the US/Russia (1941–1945), and China and the US (1950–1953). The Cold War then emerged as a long confrontation between the US and China and Russia that dominated the geo-strategic environment in the region for decades. After the end of the Cold War, the politics of the region became more complex. China, Japan, South Korea, the DPRK, Taiwan, Russia and the US were pitted against each other in a series of bilateral and multilateral conflicts over trade, military threats, nuclear weapons, irredentism and nationalist ambitions. Yet they shared a common interest in the development of cooperative globalisation and the realisation of its benefits.

The West first encountered Japan in the modern era from contacts made by the Portuguese in 1543, but it was several centuries before modernisation really challenged traditional Japanese political and social structures.[1] From the late nineteenth century to the 1930s, Japan made the extraordinary transition from a xenophobic, isolationist and pre-industrial feudal society at the time of the Meiji Restoration (1867) to become the major power in East Asia. The European powers ended imperial expansion at the end of the nineteenth century but Japanese nationalist forces by then saw their rightful place as an imperial power in East Asia. In war with China in 1895, Japan gained power over Taiwan, Korea and Pescadores from the ailing Manchus. Seizing opportunities to expand, an industrialising Japan asserted itself with an easy victory in the Sino-Japanese War (1894–95), intervened along with the European powers in the Boxer Rebellion in China (1900), achieved a stunning victory over the European, Tsarist Russia in the Russo-Japanese War (1904–05), became the colonial power by annexing Korea (1910) and then, by seizing Manchuria (1931–1932). By this expansion Japan fatefully upset the balance of power in China, East Asia and the Pacific in general and became the dominant East Asian power. The drift to war between the imperial challenger Japan and the US had begun, for the US would not allow China to be conquered by imperial Japan and so closed to US commerce. In this quadrilateral contest for power between Japan, China, Russia and the US, the battle for hegemony of the Pacific had begun.[2]

China had abandoned external relations in the fifteenth century and assumed an isolationist strategy of high income stagnation. In the nineteenth century it then struggled to meet the strategic challenge of the Europeans and the social difficulties of modernisation with very little success. The last Chinese Manchu Dynasty (1644–1911) was unable to deal with the challenge of the West and was humiliated and defeated in the Opium War (1839–1842)) by the British who became the dominant commercial power in South China with bases in Hong Kong and Shanghai. The humiliation was compounded by defeats by other European powers, including France and Russia, and the Boxer Rebellion (1900) when several European powers (including the Americans and Japanese) defeated the rebellious Boxers supported by the moribund Manchus and further divided the Chinese among themselves.

The Chinese Revolution in 1911 ended dynastic rule and the revolutionary forces led by Sun Yat-sen (1866–1925) set off a civil war between the Nationalists (Kuomintang) led by Chiang Kai-shek, and the Communists led by Mao Ze Dung which ended in Communist victory in 1949. This conflict for domination in China coincided with the Japanese invasion and occupation of much of the country (1937–45). As a result, building a modern Chinese nation had to take place simultaneously with war, civil war, the establishment of the Taiwan government by the defeated Kuomintang, distorted modernisation under the Communists, the great upheavals of the Cultural Revolution, the conflicts of the Cold War and liberal reform of the

---

1 Donald F Lach, *Japan in the Eyes of Europe* (Chicago, 1968).

2 See Michael Barnhart, *Japan in the World Since 1868* (London, 1995); W G Beasley, *Japanese Imperialism, 1894–1945* (Oxford, 1987); Walter LaFeber, *The Clash: a History of US-Japanese Relations* (New York, 1997); and the excellent recent overview of East Asian geopolitics of the past century by Robyn Lim, *The Geopolitics of East Asia: Search for Equilibrium* (New York, 2003). Edwin O Reischauer, *Japan, the Story of a Nation* (New York, 1981), remains a classic.

Chinese economy in the 1990s.[3] Only then did Chinese modernisation seriously begin and China emerged as a potential superpower challenger to America.

Russia also struggled with modernisation throughout the nineteenth century, but nonetheless continued its expansion as a state into East and Central Asia. The political pressures for change, starting with the abortive revolution of the Decembrists in 1825, produced reactions from the Tsarist state that alternated between cycles of reform and repression, with some political freedoms extended including the emancipation of the serfs in 1861. In the Far East, after a century of expansion, the Russians secured from China the lower course of the Amur River and the right bank of the Ussuri River to the Pacific in the 1860s. Although Alaska was sold to the Americans in 1867, Russian power was firmly established in Islamic Central Asia as it captured Tashkent in 1865 and Samarkand in 1868, thus giving it control over the Uzbek, Tajik, Kazakh, Kyrgyz and Turkmen peoples until the collapse of the Soviet Union in 1991.

Russian expansion in East Asia led to the unsuccessful war against the Japanese in 1904–1905 and that humiliating defeat was partly responsible for the abortive Revolution of 1905. The First World War was a disaster for the monarchy, with Russian forces in retreat from the Germans almost from their entry into the war in 1914 until the Bolsheviks under Lenin seized power in the 1917 Revolution and pulled Russia out of the war with the Treaty of Brest-Litovsk in 1918. The resulting communist regime in the Soviet Union, after the forced industrialisation of the Stalinist economy, secured a victory against the Nazis. After its acquisition of nuclear weapons in 1949, it became a superpower, until the demise of the Soviet Union in the 1991 again brought Russian influence to a low ebb.

The First World War

When war broke out in Europe in 1914, the colonial and ex-colonial settler nations of the British Empire rallied. For Australians an attack on the Empire was an attack upon the national security and integrity of Australia and they volunteered by the thousands to protect the old Hanoverian monarchy of King George V of Saxe-Coburg Gotha, which was quickly renamed 'Windsor' because of wartime Germo-phobia. Australians, like Canadians and New Zealanders, also hoped to demonstrate their national and military virility on the battlefield. In the trenches of the Western Front, in the deserts of the Middle East, and, above all in terms of future Australian national identity, on the barren cliffs of Gallipoli in Turkey, there was ample opportunity for Australians to fulfil their destiny as a fighting nation with massive blood sacrifice.

In the US, however, the political environment was very different. Taking office in 1913 President Woodrow Wilson faced no public clamour for an American interventionist policy in the European war. America had become enmeshed in Mexico as a consequence of the Mexican Revolution (1911) and, in 1916, when Pancho Villa, part revolutionary-nationalist and part bandit, killed American citizens

3 See Jung Chang and Jon Halliday, *Mao: the Unknown Story* (London, 2006) for a perceptive account of these processes.

in northern Mexico and in the new state of New Mexico, the US sent in a military force under General Pershing to capture Villa. The expedition did not achieve its objective and this intervention in Mexico proved to be both embarrassing and costly. The American voting public, therefore, was not in a mood for additional overseas military activity.

Although the majority of Americans were pro-British, there was substantial pressure from the Irish and German immigrant communities against intervention. Neutrality made sense to many business interests trading with belligerent states on both sides. Wilson, however, had a profound bias toward Britain and found neutrality increasingly difficult to maintain with his growing anger at interference by German naval forces, especially their U-boats, with US and allied shipping. In 1915 the nation was outraged at the sinking of the *Lusitania* with 128 American lives lost, and Wilson's strong response prompted his less hawkish Secretary of State, William Jennings Bryan, to resign. These issues led America to declare war on Germany on 6 April 1917 after the sinking of three American ships. The US was no longer detached from European politics and its climb toward the position of a major world power, and eventually a global hegemon, had seriously begun.

In the aftermath of the First World War, Japan was militarist and expansionist, China wracked by warlord-ism, the Soviet Union struggling with civil war and economic chaos, and America was evolving into a superpower with hegemonic ambitions. It was a geopolitical recipe for a major conflagration in the Asia Pacific.

Japan allied with Britain and the US in the First World War, but revealed its expansionist aims in its final stages. Japanese troops occupied Vladivostok in 1918 and after negotiations with the Russians only evacuated in 1922. Japan then set its sights on Manchuria and after the Mukden Incident in 1931 occupied the region and created the puppet state of Manchukuo in 1932. Its intentions for a full-scale dominance of the Chinese mainland became increasing apparent in the next few years. In 1937 the Japanese bombed Shanghai, began the Sino-Japanese War and confronted US interests. Hostilities also broke out with the Russians in Manchuria and Mongolia in 1938–1939, and in 1940 Japan moved its forces into French Indochina. In October, 1941, General Tojo Hideki became Prime Minister and, faced with American attempts through diplomacy and economic boycotts to stop Japanese expansionism, the Imperial Cabinet decided war was unavoidable and started planning for it. The US would not allow Japanese control of China which it believed would threaten the commercial interests and then the national security of the US.

Degraded by Revolution, Civil War and economic dislocation from 1917 to the mid-1920s, the position of Russia/Soviet Union was greatly weakened in the Far East. Japanese expansion, especially in China, threatened the Soviet state and it bolstered its defensive positions in the region. Japan agreed to evacuate its positions in Russian Siberia and the northern half of the Island of Sakhalin in 1922 and 1925 respectively. With the creation of the Soviet-backed Mongolian People's Republic (MPR) in 1924 the Soviets moved to strengthen further their position in the region against Japanese expansionism. In 1934 Soviet troops were moved to Mongolia, and with the outbreak of the Sino-Japanese War in 1937 conflict with Japan seemed likely. Localised hostilities broke out between Soviet and Japanese forces in 1938 in Manchuria and in 1939 in Mongolia but the Japanese government, not wishing to be sidetracked at this crucial point by a war with the Soviets, made peace with the Soviet commander Marshall Zhukov. When war broke out in Europe in August 1939 and the Japanese moved south into Indochina and beyond in 1940–1942, both powers had more urgent strategic military requirements than in the Russo-Japanese theatre.

In the first five decades of the twentieth century China was beset by civil war and invasion as the ancient civilisation struggled to cope with modernisation and to maintain its political independence. Sun Yat-sen's creation of the Chinese Republic in 1911, however, could not mask the massive problems faced by the new and very weak national government. The Republic could not exercise effective national authority and was confronted by geopolitical threats from Japan and Russia. Already humiliated by the extra-territoriality agreements with the European powers, the new government was unable to gain control of its own territory.

Although China entered the First World War on the allied side in March 1917, its main foreign policy focus was to establish sovereignty within its existing boundaries. This was to prove impossible. The centrifugal forces were strong: Mongolia and Tibet were pulling away from Chinese authority and Japan, having imposed its Twenty-one Demands in 1919, wanted to gain Chinese territory, beginning in northeast China with Manchuria. China had some success in reducing the extra-territoriality agreements by 1930 and regained some authority in Shanghai, but this was offset by the Japanese seizing Mukden in 1931 and then occupying Manchuria. This led to full-scale war with the Kuomintang government in 1937, a war that found the ineffectual and corrupt Chinese government hopelessly ill-prepared.

The foundation of the Communist Party by Mao Ze Dung and others, in Shanghai in 1920, prepared the way for simultaneous war and civil war in China between the two contenders for power in China, and the collateral international war with Japan. Chiang Kai-shek, having outmanoeuvred the Communists in the late 1920s and early 1930s, faced both the Japanese and the Communists by the end of that decade. Mao took his forces north in the Long March in 1935 to Shensi Province, from where he could consolidate his army, organise for an ideological and strategic campaign to defeat the Nationalists and simultaneously attack the Japanese forces. The civil war for control of China began in the 1920s, continued through the Second World War and lasted until the Communist victory in 1949.

The USA – Emerging Hegemon

A Great Power can successfully pursue its interests against other Great Powers; but a Hegemonic Power is a rule setting Power. The US became a Great Power after the First World War and a Hegemonic Power after the Second World War.

The ineffectual Republican administrations of Warren Harding, Calvin Coolidge and Herbert Clark Hoover (1921–1933) failed to stabilize the growing threats to world order, and maintained a broad policy of neutrality and isolation. The major exception was the Washington Naval Conference of 1921–22 between nine nations designed to limit naval armaments to ensure peaceful relations between the great powers, especially the US, Britain and Japan. In effect, the world was divided into naval spheres of influence with Japan dominating the Far East, the US the Western Hemisphere, and Britain from the North Sea east to Singapore. Japanese naval power was checked more than that of US or Britain by the Conference agreement which allocated allowable battleship tonnage in a ratio of 5, 5, 3, 1.75 and 1.75 between the US, Britain, Japan, Italy and France respectively. The Japanese were further humiliated by the banning of immigration to the US in 1924. Nonetheless, in the 1930s a naval arms race took place with little inhibition by treaty obligations which did not prevent the drift to the Second World War.

After the Great Economic Depression started in 1929, the global environment was plagued by domestic political crises and international economic relations became more competitive with states seeking markets and resources. Many of the nations of Europe adopted more assertive regimes, notably Fascism, first in Italy under Mussolini (Prime Minister, 1922) in the early-to-mid-1920s, which then spread to Portugal (António Salazar, 1932), Germany (Adolf Hitler, 1933) and Spain (Francisco Franco, 1939). The Depression overwhelmed the US economy from 1929 to 1933 and it turned inwards for a successful solution which nonetheless proved to be disastrous for the long-term stability of the European and then the world order. After the early 1930s no serious international attempts were made at arms limitations and the nations of the world were embroiled in economic crises and civil unrest, as they increasingly turned to jingoism, rearmament and authoritarianism in the hope of creating national political and social order and winning a better place in the international economy.

In pursuit of an economic zone, the Japanese bombed the US into the status of belligerency in December 1941. Thereafter Americans believed it was vital to maintain a decisive military capability in the Western Pacific, not only to prevent a repeat of Pearl Harbor, but to counter the power of the Communist states of the Soviet Union and, after 1949, the PRC.

The Second World War in the Pacific

The interwar period marked a watershed for the Pacific region in geopolitical terms and transformed the dynamics of modernisation. In the Pacific basin and throughout Asia, the old European Empires of the British, Dutch and French and others, were now faced with potent nationalist opposition to colonisation.

Fascism in Europe grew out of a sense of betrayal after the First World War in Germany and Italy who wanted equality of access to economic empires with the old imperial powers of Europe, Britain, France and Holland in particular. Resentment was heightened enormously by the impact of the Great Depression during which the political system of parliamentary democracy in Germany and in Italy failed to deal with the economic crisis. In much of Europe – notably Germany, Italy and the Iberian Peninsula – the crisis of modernisation could not be resolved effectively by democratic political structures faced with the strain of post-war adjustment, economic depression and political chaos. Instead these fostered aggressive, violent and well organized Fascist forces which also mobilised hatred against minorities and blamed them for the general ills, past and present, of their societies. The fascist states then wanted to create their own imperial systems to aid economic recovery and undertook aggressive expansion by military means.

Many of these elements were also present in Japan. The society was humiliated by the Western challenge to the power and authority of the traditional Japanese society and state. Japanese nationalism fostered a desperate desire to match the West by developing an expansionist state and powerful military machine with Western technology and use it to regain dignity for Japan with its own empire in East Asia. Japan overcame the crisis of modernisation with an aggressive xenophobia and rapid industrialisation, but without wholly destroying traditional Japanese authority structures, including the Emperor. For Japan, its expansion that led to the Second World War was necessary to survive in a hostile world.

Yet the extreme rightist movements in Europe and Japan in the 1930s also shared some elements of anti-modernisation. Modernity was, for them, associated with secular, urban, and ('Jew infested') multicultural society, and both the Fascists and the Japanese nativists targeted these minority cultures as indicating a breakdown of traditional social values. They both required female subordination and the hegemony of male dominated warrior classes in which women were mainly procreators and carers. In Germany and Japan, racial purity was pursued and bestial treatment was administered to 'inferior' races and groups, including Jews, Gypsies (Romany), Koreans, homosexuals, mentally handicapped or other assorted 'undesirables' such as socialists, intellectuals and trade unionists. The 'other' was to be removed from the body politic in order to 'save' the purity and integrity of the 'superior' races and their traditional social order from contamination. Thus, even though these were political movements that employed the technology and bureaucratic methods of modern industrial society, characteristics that run counter to the anti-modernisation paradigm, they both contained within them deep strains of rejection and hatred of modernity as it existed in the societies of Western Europe and North America.

Japan's attacks on Pearl Harbor in December 1941, on Singapore on 15 February 1942, and on Darwin in February 1942, were the most dramatic manifestations of the shift of the power balance in the Asia-Pacific region. When Britain went to war against Germany in 1939, the Australian Prime Minister immediately declared, 'as a consequence, Australia is also at war'. But with the fall of Singapore, the final blow was struck against the continuing Australian dependence on the British Empire for its security in the Asia-Pacific region. In the words of historian/journalist Paul Kelly, 'Singapore was the grand illusion on which Australia's strategic policy was based in the inter-war period'.[4] The dynamic of power in the Pacific was then further changed by the intervention of the US.[5]

The modern evolution of America's position to that of world hegemonic power can be dated from the attack on Pearl Harbor in 1941. After that war, the US could no longer withdraw from world affairs as it did from most regions of the world after 1919. The bombing of US military installations in Hawaii was the first strike on US territory by foreign forces since the War of 1812. The nation and American policy makers were shocked that the US was vulnerable to direct attack; and the lessons

4 Paul Kelly, '100 Years – the Australian Story', (Australian) ABC TV, 5 Sept 2004.
5 Robyn Lim, *East Asia, op. cit.*, p. 34.

from that experience are still in the consciousness of geo-strategic thinkers, including the neo-conservatives in the Bush Administration. In any case, the war also marked the transition of the US economy to one dependent on imported commodities and access to foreign investment opportunities.

Japan also occupied some American territory in the far west of the Aleutian Islands in Alaska in 1942, and seized the two westernmost islands of the chain, Attu and Kiska. But after many US attacks by air on the islands, American forces took them back at the end of May 1943, after the Japanese suffered 3,200 casualties in fierce fighting. It was the last time in the War that the Japanese occupied US territory. The mainland of America did not come under direct attack again until the 9/11 terrorist attacks on New York and Washington.[6]

Although the US quickly subscribed to the doctrine of its British allies to win the war in Europe first, the US in fact fought most of its Second World War in the Pacific where it took two-thirds of its nearly 300,000 battle deaths. The Pacific War was the theater where its own territory had to be defended and where the bulk of its wealth was expended. Through the very bloody and difficult strategy of MacArthur's island-hopping, the Americans fought their way toward Japan for three years culminating in the use of two Atomic bombs in August 1945. This technological leap ended the Pacific War but the legacy of the Second World War – including a divided Korea, pacifist Japanese military policy, conflict over China and Taiwan – continued to be major international issues in the geopolitics of East Asia. The old empires of Europe in the Asia Pacific were destroyed by the War and the rise of Asian nationalism. The US sometimes tried fill the vacuum left by the British, French, Spanish, Portuguese, Dutch and Japanese empires, but this was a gigantic task and proved to be too much for one nation to maintain, even one as strong as the US.[7] Its efforts to replace France led it into Vietnam and to replace Britain eventually led it into Iraq.

In September 1939 Robert Menzies declared that as Britain was at war with Germany then so was Australia. But the loss of support for his war policies led to his resignation as Prime Minister in August 1941 and the formation of a government under the Country Party leader Arthur Fadden that only lasted forty days. The Leader of the Australian Labor Party (ALP), John Curtin, then took over in October 1941. After the attack on Pearl Harbor, Curtin had to prepare his nation to fight a possible Japanese invasion. Australia was in the line of attack from Japanese forces sweeping south after victories in Malaya and Singapore towards northern Australia. The capital of the Northern Territory, Darwin, was bombed in February 1942 with the loss of eight ships in Darwin harbour and the deaths of 250 people. The war in that region then persisted for eighteen months.

---

6 For the Russo-Japanese front see John Stephan, *Sakhalin: a History* (Oxford, 1971), *The Kurile Islands: Russo-Japanese Frontier in the* Pacific (Oxford, 1974), and *The Russian Far East: a History* (Oxford, 1994).

7 For a Pulitzer prize-winning overview of the key period in the rise of the US to the status of a hegemonic power see David M. Kennedy, *Freedom from Fear, the American People in Depression and War, 1929*–1945 (New York, 1999).

Following the British defeat in Southeast Asia, Curtin broke with Imperial defence strategy and brought Australian troops from the Middle East and the Mediterranean back to Australia. Churchill, supported by Roosevelt, wanted to keep them in the European war and used the example of the 'loyal' New Zealanders who stayed in Europe and fought in Italy. That failed, so he then pressured Curtin to divert the returning troops to Burma. But Curtin also resisted that redeployment and stuck to his plan to defend Australia first. In March 1942 General MacArthur was evacuated from the Philippines and arrived in Australia to launch the campaign to defeat the Japanese Empire in the Pacific using Australia as his base of operations.

The Australians assisted the Americans to drive the Japanese Empire back to its homeland. In 1942, fierce fighting took place in the New Guinea campaign along the Kokoda trail that Australian forces captured from the Japanese by November. With the crucial American naval victories in the Southwest Pacific, at Coral Sea and Midway (in May and June of 1942), the Japanese threat to Australia was stopped and the allied forces began pushing the Japanese lines back to their home islands. The bulk of the fighting in the Pacific after the New Guinea campaign, however, was carried out by the more numerous Americans with Australian forces playing an ancillary role.[8]

But there was, nonetheless, some notable friction between MacArthur and the Australian high command over tactics and strategy. There were also some fights between Australian and American troops that were kept secret during the war including the 'Battle of Brisbane' in November, 1942, in which one Australian was shot and killed by an American MP, eight were wounded and at least 100 injured. For three years the Yanks and the Diggers forged relationships that would see not only the part Americanisation of Australian culture, but the strengthening of personal ties between the two nations, and marriages growing out of the war would provide lasting ties between the two countries. With victory in August 1945 the wartime alliance would turn into the peacetime partnership that would persist to the next century. Australia continued to fight alongside its Pacific ally from Korea to Vietnam and through both Gulf Wars and Afghanistan. It was ironic that in February 2005, the Liberal Prime Minister, John Howard, announced that Australia was sending additional forces of 450 troops to protect non-combatant *Japanese* forces in southern Iraq and Howard would sign a new security pact with Japan in March 2007.[9]

The Second World War changed the world fundamentally. The huge expenditure of material, deaths of over fifty million people and widespread destruction were only some of the immediate consequences of the war. The trauma of failed diplomacy at Munich, the vileness of the Holocaust, the smashing of all human social norms

8 For the New Guinea campaign see Peter Brune, *A Bastard of a Place, the Australians in Papua* (Sydney, 2003), and Paul Ham, *Kokoda* (Sydney, 2004); for the Pacific campaign in general see John Costello, *The Pacific War, 1941*–1945 (New York, 2002).

9 For US-Australian relations in the Second World War see E Daniel and Annette Potts, *Yanks Down Under, 1941–1945: the American Impact on Australia* (Melbourne, 1984); Barry Ralph, *They Passed this Way: the United States of America, the States of Australia and World War II* (East Roseville, NSW, 2000); and Peter Thompson and Robert Macklin, *The Battle of Brisbane* (Sydney, 2000).

of behaviour by the combatants, haunted the nations of the world and impacted greatly on their geopolitical calculations. The simultaneous collapse of empires, the decolonisation of the globe, creation of failed states, neo-colonisation, re-colonisation and massive problems of governance in new states have affected the capacity of nation states to deal with poverty, disease and basic law and order. The war unleashed the forces of modernisation, which swept through the cultures of the world, devastating centuries-old religions, ideas and social patterns, the consequences of which are still emerging. This process of rapid change is often extremely difficult to manage. Ironically the bi-polar stability of the Cold War allowed these processes of war and modernisation to be contained by two superpower-led political blocs. But that era is truly over. Perhaps no nation was more willing to embrace the *Pax Americana* than Australia. This was in spite of some opposition from the Right, by old Anglo-Australian Tories, and from the Left by self styled anti-imperialist forces in Australian culture incensed at the abandonment of old cultural forms and values. There was no going back for Australia: the American behemoth was in the southern Pacific for the long-term.[10]

The bombing of Hiroshima and Nagasaki at the end of the Second World War, and the subsequent spread of nuclear weapons capability to Russia in 1949, Britain in 1955, France in 1960, and China in 1964, created a new balance of power in the world, nuclear deterrence, within which the Cold War would be fought. The doctrine of Mutually Assured Destruction created both the terms of conflict as well as limited its consequences. However, the introduction of nuclear weapons into world geopolitics, created long term instability and new threats to world peace. By the first decade of the twenty first century the development of nuclear capabilities by states such as Israel and Iran in the Middle East, Pakistan and India in South Asia, and the DPRK in East Asia, presented stresses in the world order to which the great powers had no answer. In contrast, the Cold War stand off involved a kind of benign stability for several decades, 1948–91.

Wars in Korea and Indochina

After 1945 Australia faced a changed world as a fully independent nation state. The British Empire was being dismantled. Canada, Australia, New Zealand and miscellaneous Caribbean and Pacific states, would cling to some of their imperial identity even into the twenty first century in an attempt to maintain an Anglo-Saxon sense of stability. The legal, political and cultural ties between the former colonies and the Mother Country were maintained in the post-war decades and sporting links grew and prospered into national obsessions, with constant contests in the British international sports of cricket, rugby, netball and others between the old imperial nations. But after 1970 the growth of British ties with Europe shocked loyalists in the South Pacific, as Britain abandoned preferential treatment for the Australian and New Zealand economies. Simultaneously, therefore, Australia shifted its alliance

10 See John Moore, *Over-sexed, Over-paid and Over Here, Americans in Australia, 1941–45* (St. Lucia, Queensland, 1981).

system and strategic thinking towards the US. Throughout the twentieth century, this attachment to the old Empire combined with subservience militarily and culturally to America, was a double resentment for the Left in Australia and New Zealand. But for the dominant conservative political and business elites this was business as usual.

America had been moving westward towards and then into the Pacific, for virtually all its four hundred years of history. For its culture and history it looked east to Europe, but increasingly after 1945 the US looked west for trade and economic expansion. In the Second World War two-thirds of American casualties were in the Pacific War and its geo-strategic future concentrated as much energy and commitment to the Pacific world as to the old Atlantic world. The emergence of the economic giants of Japan and then China, and then the lesser but considerable economies of India and Korea, as well the Southeast Asian economies of ASEAN, created a huge market in Southeast and East Asia. The projection of US power into the region, therefore, had to take into account the new realities of the post-war world: the implications of the spread of nuclear weapons; new and powerful economic forces and military threats from Asia; and, later, the future of a world redefined by the global technological revolution in travel, communications and cultural dispersal.

The Cold War had its origins in the division of Europe in the dying days of the Second World War as the victorious Allied armies moved into Germany, the Anglo-American forces from the west and the Soviets from the east. The Americans and Russians had conflicting economic ideologies complicated by geopolitical rivalries in Europe. President Truman and Stalin escalated their differences into a bi-polar conflict that dominated the world for the next four decades. The competition between the capitalist West and the socialist East produced a complex web of military conflicts and economic warfare. This global contest needed their respective societies to fight the opposing 'Evil Empire' and required mass mobilization of human and economic resources.

The Cold War and decolonisation, which coincided in space and time, rippled around the world and few nations were exempt from the implications of the conflict; all aspects of culture and society in every nation of the world would be partly shaped into this bi-polar world of Cold War competition between the US and Soviet Union. Australia was, of course, well within the Asian-Pacific orbit of the Cold War as it spread to the region with the victory of the Chinese Communist Party in 1949 and it was not exempt from this global process. It helped shape the conflict between left and right which has dominated modern Australian politics.

No ally would be more reliable (or obsequious) to the US in the Cold War, than Australia. Australia generally followed the prescriptions of American foreign policy in the war against communism. As in Imperial defence strategy, Australians shed blood on foreign soil at the bidding of its Great Power protector, in order to meet its imperial military and treaty obligations, but this time with the US. In the frozen wastes of the Korean Peninsula and in the jungles of Vietnam, Australians demonstrated their value as an ally in the understanding that, in exchange, the US nuclear umbrella would protect it from foreign invasion and/or threats. Australians believed that loyalty to the US alliance was a small price to pay for the security and territorial integrity of their homeland. The Australian military strategy of 'defence in depth' during the Cold War also required putting US forces between Australia and the communist bloc when the opportunity occurred.

The Cold War included major hot wars in Korea, Vietnam and Afghanistan, directly involving the two superpowers. Dozens of other minor conflicts were fought with great power influence and/or with surrogates for the bi-polar antagonists. The US in Vietnam and the Soviets in Afghanistan both fought long, costly and in the end unsuccessful wars to support their Cold War surrogates in Southeast and Central Asia respectively. This series of conflicts ended with the fall of the Soviet Union and gave way to a new type of global warfare between the US and several entities operating under the global umbrella of Jihadist forces.

Korea was the first opportunity for the Australians to demonstrate their value to the US which was then dominant throughout the Pacific Basin. The Soviet Union and the US had both established their geopolitical interests on the Korean Peninsula in the aftermath of the Second World War. Attempts to create a unified Korean state failed and in May 1947 the Americans set up a separate South Korean interim government south of the thirty eighth parallel. In September 1947, the Democratic People's Republic of Korea (DPRK) was proclaimed north of the parallel, thus creating the formal division of Korea that stands today. On 24 June 1950 (US time), DPRK forces crossed the thirty eighth parallel and began the first large-scale hot war between the two superpowers and/or their surrogates of the Cold War period. It ended in stalemate in 1953.

America's involvement in Vietnam began during the French Indochina War (1950–54) and the decision of the Eisenhower administration to back an anti-communist government in South Vietnam, under the Catholic Ngo Dinh Diem, after the Geneva Accords of 1954 ended French colonial rule. The Americans attempted to fill the post-colonial power vacuum left by the French and pledged to defend the integrity of the southern state of a Vietnam divided at the seventeenth parallel. Throughout the 1950s and 1960s, the US became increasingly bogged down in the politics of first Vietnam, then the Indochinese Peninsula, and finally Southeast Asia in general. When Eisenhower left office and handed power over to the new Democratic President, John F Kennedy, in early 1961, the strategic context for a much greater entanglement had been established.

The escalating US commitment from 1960 led to the final and ignominious Communist victory over America and its Vietnamese allies in 1975. Some of the same errors that led to that defeat have been made by the neo-conservative influenced Bush administration in Iraq early in the new century, with another ill-fated intervention based on Wilsonian idealism landing them in the middle of a civil war – in Iraq essentially between Shi'ite and Sunni forces by 2007. It is especially ironic that the Bush administration is still obsessed with dominoes falling, only this time the dominoes are in the Middle East, and beginning with Iraq, are supposed to fall smoothly in the other direction after democracy has been established as an attractive model in Iraq. At the end of 2007, this result seems most unlikely.

Kennedy narrowly won the 1960 election over the Republican Richard Nixon and pledged to bridge the alleged missile gap with the Soviet Union. The Kennedy family, headed by the family patriarch, Cold Warrior and extreme right sympathizer in the 1930s, Joseph P Kennedy, had always been hawkish on the bi-polar conflict with the Soviet Union. The new President, with his equally hawkish brother Robert in the cabinet as Attorney General, both the new heroes of Democratic liberalism, was not about to back down to the forces of Communism in Asia, Europe or in Cuba. Out of this historical dynamic of Cold War ideology and confrontation, Kennedy deepened the military engagement in Vietnam in order to prevent the 'dominoes' falling from the Chinese border with Vietnam to the south and embracing Laos, Cambodia, Thailand and Malaysia in the orbit of Communism. In his inauguration address he pledged to pay any price to defend freedom anywhere in the world that it was threatened. This was a Wilsonian blank cheque. Kennedy's assassination in 1963 enabled sympathetic historians to disguise his responsibility for the US commitment in Vietnam. Nonetheless, it was his war. His successor, Vice President and then President, elected in his own right in 1964, Lyndon Johnson, paid his political price.

This was the logic and historical circumstances that led to the great Vietnam fiasco, which would force Johnson to retire in 1968 rather than seek a second full term. The Vietnam War also contributed greatly to the downfall of his Republican successor, Richard Nixon, brought on by illegal activities to suppress opposition to his Vietnam policies. These were revealed especially after the publication of the *Pentagon Papers,* leaked by Daniel Ellsberg, in June 1971, by the *New York Times,* that were confirmed in the Watergate scandal and Congressional investigations leading to Nixon's ignominious resignation in August 1974. As well as contributing to the downfall of two Presidents, the Vietnam War greatly destabilised the American and world economies which resulted in the global pattern of debilitating stagflation in the mid-1970s.[11] The US was able to hold the line in Korea, with United Nations authorisation, clear war aims, superior air power and domestic support. It lost in Indo-China with the international community divided, its war aims confused, the Vietnamese communists able to hold on with foreign support, and with US domestic support collapsing. There should have been a lesson there for the GWOT.

The polarisation of American society during the Cold War led to a dramatic shift in the body politic of America after twenty years (1933–1953) of Democrat control of the White House and domestic policy in America. In the heat of the Cold War the opposition to the New Deal coalesced with anti-Communism to form a syncretistic mix with a potent and long-lasting effect as a cohesive ideology for Americans. With the enormous pressure of McCarthyism on the Left in the universities, unions, public entertainment, the arts and all essential institutions in the political arena, a giant pall descended on the exchange of views in American culture. This essentially emasculated the Left in American society and permanently shifted the central fulcrum of the media and public discourse to the right. The Reaganite and Thatcherite movements toward neo-liberal hegemony and the Bush-ite quasi-religious crusade of the neo-conservatives, have reaped the benefits of the quashing of Left liberalism during the Cold War period.[12]

11 Milton Osborne, *Southeast Asia, an Introductory History* (St Leonards, NSW, 2000).

12 Ellen Schrecker, *Many are the Crimes: McCarthyism in America* (Princeton, NJ, 1999).

For thirty years after its defeat in Vietnam, recognised at the Paris Peace of 1973, the US (and its allies) gave very careful consideration before committing ground troops to war. This was the 'Vietnam Syndrome'. One result was that troops were not so committed. The major exception was the war to evict Iraq from Kuwait in 1990–91. In that war, the US and its allies had UN authorisation, a clear defensive objective, massive international and domestic support, a battle plan to produce a short successful war, and a sound exit strategy. These were lessons learnt in the defeat in Vietnam. The US entered the Vietnam War with no clear objective, an unlimited time frame, divided international opinion and a vague military strategy. These elements conspired to produce its defeat. They were circumstances a generation of US policy makers vowed not to repeat. Nonetheless, they did so with the invasion of Iraq and once again they found themselves in the middle of a civil war and what appeared in 2007 to be a lose-lose situation.

The End of the Bi-Polar World

Despite the victory of its Vietnamese allies, the Soviet Union later collapsed for two central reasons: it could not generate an innovative growth economy and it failed in the strategic competition with the US.

The Soviet Union was managed by a communist dictatorship from the early 1930s. Its economy was centrally controlled by the state that tried to direct production and distribution through five year plans. These were imposed by a parallel state apparatus of the Communist Party operating as a *nomenklatura,* not unlike an inducted priesthood. This system generated a form of economic growth until the mid-1970s when stagnation and then decay set in under Leonid Brezhnev. In any case, Brezhnev over-extended the Soviet state by his costly expansionist policies. Gorbachev took over in 1985 and tried to reform the system. This failed because, when the ordinary people were given the choice they did not want communism, and it was voted out and the anti-communist, Boris Yeltsin, was elected President of the largest successor state, the Russian Federation. By that stage the managers of the system had decided they could do better by privatising its assets and liberalising its market. During the early 1990s they systematically looted former Soviet assets and formed a new ruling class in the Russian Federation around the super-rich 'oligarchs'. US advisors were deeply involved in this process and it delivered a better outcome for the US.

As the Soviet economy faltered, and with it the popular base of the regime, so the US confronted it by electing the Reagan administration. The US intensified its strategic competition with the Soviets by outspending it in strategic weaponry, notably with 'Star Wars', challenging its conventional forces in Europe in particular, undermining its allies and clients, and waging a propaganda war of considerable skill. In the late 1980s, Gorbachev succumbed to these pressures, progressively withdrew Soviet power and concluded agreements with the US that eventually amounted to surrender in the strategic competition. This withdrawal seriously damaged many of the allies and clients of the Soviets.

But the collapse of the Soviet Union also brought a world of uncertainty rather than heralding a new era of peace and the benefits of the 'peace dividend'. Hopes had been raised that the end of bi-polar conflict between the United States and the Soviet Union would usher in democracy throughout Eastern Europe and that the two superpowers would convert savings in defence spending to solve the problems of world population, maldistribution of income and uneven economic development. Democratisation in the 1990s did come to Eastern Europe and to some lesser extent to the former Soviet republics in the Caucasus and Central Asia, but a peaceful and equitable world proved to be a chimera. Russian itself became a debtor nation beset with complex problems of political instability and a deadly, seemingly unending war against Muslim/Jihadist separatist forces in Chechnya.

Opposition to modernisation in much of the world throughout the modern era has taken many forms, from legitimate political varieties to groups that embrace terrorism and violence to prevent their traditional cultures from being overtaken by what they perceive as alien modes of modern culture threatening to swamp their societies. Perhaps the greatest resistance has, in the late twentieth and early twenty first centuries, come from Islamic societies. But there are also active and often violent reactions by Hindus, Christians and Jews to modernisation which impinges on sensitive areas such as the rights of women, abortion, gay marriage, allegedly salacious cultural behaviour, some forms of free speech and democratic political processes that threaten the power of entrenched traditional bureaucratic (especially religious) elites. For over two decades the clash between Islamic extremism, particularly in its Jihadist/Islamist variety, had been building against the forces of Western modernisation.

The rise of Islamism has stimulated many scholars to examine the roots and evolution of anti-Western thought and the source of antagonism to the West both from within and outside the West. Some see the origins of Jihadist thought in many strains of nineteenth century European Romantic thought[13] hostile to industrial, materialist, free market, multicultural, pluralist (tolerant of Jews), urban society. It is both a critique of modernism as well as an assertive Islamic antagonism toward the 'mongrel' culture of the urban West with its breakdown of family structures, equal rights for woman, pervasive idolatry and collapsed traditional social controls. This anti-modernisation, and concomitant anti-Semitism, was found in Fascist, Nazi, and Stalinist Communist states as well as in the nativist romanticism of Japanese militarism. They all saw the West as decadent, bourgeois, democracies attempting to pollute the purity of traditional societies. In the nineteenth century the British Empire was viewed as the source of social breakdown for the non-Western world; and after the Second World War the British were progressively replaced by the Americans.

Even the US Left, harbouring anti-Americanism, attacks the decadence of materialist culture, and evangelical Right Christian conservatives like the Protestant Ministers Jerry Falwell and Pat Robertson, suggested 9/11 was a punishment on America for its sins of idolatry and rampant homosexuality. For Islamists, the West has been the enemy for centuries and, drawing on Persian concepts of Manichaeism,

---

13 Ian Buruma and Avishai Margalit, *Occidentalism: the West in the Eyes of its Enemies* (New York, 2004) which was composed in opposition to Edward Said's concept of *Orientalism.*

they see threat from the West involving a conflict between good and evil.[14] Throughout the nineteenth century Arab Muslim thinkers struggled to come to terms with the challenges of modernisation asking whether the Arab world could accommodate the ideas of secularism, democracy and modernity with traditional Muslim society without the implosion of the religious and social order. The Egyptian, Muhammad Abduh, struggled with the dilemmas of Western penetration of Middle Eastern culture and initially offered some philosophical solutions, but eventually drifted into xenophobia and hostility to the West in general and the British in particular. After a century of speculation Arab thinkers reached a near consensus, 'a determination to rid themselves, first and foremost, of the economic and military power of Europe and the West – and, perhaps, the cultural influences that went with it'. Although the Jihadism of the twenty first century also has more modern causes, the intellectual foundations for it were already set down in previous centuries.[15]

An instructive historical prototype for the current phase of anti-modernisation was the Boxer Rebellion in China in the final years of the Manchu Dynasty in 1900. This quasi-mystical society of Boxers attempted to eject the 'foreign devils' from China in 1900 by attacks on Europeans. This failed miserably and accelerated the carving up of China by the Western powers. The Boxer Rebellion heralded the coming of age of the US and Japan as imperial powers in the Western Pacific and indicated the great price the US would have to pay when it later took over the role of the world's policeman from Britain. The 'flowering flag devils', as the Americans were called by the Boxers, inherited not only the mantle of world imperial hegemon, but also faced the wrath of the world's anti-modernisation forces. The Americans then bore the costs of being the dominant Western nation not just in Asia but throughout the world, and these costs would be high indeed. The highest costs, however, of the Boxer Rebellion were borne by the 100,000 Chinese Christians who were slaughtered by the Boxer forces.[16]

When the Shah of Iran was overthrown in 1979 and replaced by a government of radical Shi'ite Muslims, the main target was the 'Great Satan' of America, but they also had moderate Muslim states and their leaders in the Islamist pantheon of enemies. In 1981 the President of Egypt, Anwar Sadat, was assassinated by a radical Islamist organisation, the Muslim Brotherhood. In 1983 the intervention of the

14 Buruma and Margalit, *Occidentalism.* The Jihadist thought of Islamists like Osama bin Laden and the late Abu Musab al-Zarqawi, the former commander of the insurgency in Fallujah and the so-called Sunni Triangle in Iraq (2004–2006), stems from a particularly violent opposition to infidels and the justification of the use of violence against all infidel forces inspired by the Salafi movement in Islam (a variant of Wahhabism). Zarqawi also had ties to the Jihadist Ansar al-Islam group of 600–800 Kurds living in the northeast of Iraq who are hostile to the American occupation of Iraq as well as the Kurdish parties in Iraqi Kurdistan. For the issue of Islam and modernisation see Bernard Lewis, *What Went Wrong?, the Clash between Islam and Modernity in the Middle East* (London, 2002). For al-Zarqawi, see Loretta Napoleoni, 'The most wanted man in Iraq', *Foreign Policy,* No. 151.

15 Peter Manning, 'Shifting sands of democracy, on how the West was lost in the Middle East', *The Weekend Australian Financial Review,* 29 Dec–3 Jan 2004–05.

16 Diana Preston, *A Brief History of the Boxer Rebellion, China's War on Foreigners, 1900* (London, 2002), pp. xvi, 13, 364–66; Van Alstyne, *East Asia, op cit ,* pp. 63–65.

Reagan administration in Beirut was ended by a suicide bomb attack on American Marines that killed 241 troops and prompted the President to withdraw US forces. In 1986 Palestinian extremists seized the Italian cruise ship the *Achille Lauro* and threw overboard a wheelchair-bound American tourist. The confrontation in all these instances wove together antagonisms from the Arab-Israeli conflict in Palestine, the hatred of US influence in the Middle East, and the opposition to modernisation, especially where it threatened the hegemony of Islam. The terrorism of the late 1990s was clearly adumbrated in the 1980s; and the Wahhabi form of Islam in Saudi Arabia espoused by the Saudi, Osama bin Laden, as the ideological underpinning of global terrorism by Al Qaeda/Jihadist movements, had clear anti-modernisation foundations.

Chapter 4

End of the Cold War and the Middle East

The Cold War was, in some respects, a conflict between two great powers over which should dominate the world order. But it also involved a dispute about the nature of a modern society and how the countries of the world should re-shape themselves – and be re-shaped by great powers. The Soviet vision derived from Marxist theory and proposed an authoritarian political regime, planning a state owned economy, imposing financial equality on the mass citizenry, and severely limiting the freedom of an individual. The US ideal was for a state with limited and separated powers, permitting a privately owned and managed corporate economy, with citizens living in a civil society that accepted economic inequalities as the price for considerable liberty for the individual.

The collapse of the Soviet bloc suggested that the US vision would triumph, at least for the time being, particularly after Communist China moved to adopt the US model for its economy even if not for its political structure. The US then moved to pursue this agenda through its globalisation proposals of the 1990s.[1] Many states found this a difficult program to adopt: for the European Social Charter states because of their statist economies; for many of the ASEAN states because of their authoritarian political regimes; in the former Soviet bloc, because of their communist legacy; or in much of Africa with fragile economies. In the Islamic Middle East, the reaction to globalisation involved several problems.

After 1956 socialist – and other authoritarian ideas – had become quite strong in the Middle East, and were generally supported by the Soviet Union with aid and arms. With the Soviet collapse, many Islamic states and political organisations were left with economies unable to cope with the challenges of open international market competition, with regimes that had been nurtured by the losing side in the Cold War, and facing a US that they had confronted when powerful allies had been available for this task. The world order became more difficult for them.

Further, Islam and the different varieties of Arab socialism, made it difficult for these societies to construct the central requirements of modernisation: a representative political structure, an incorruptible state, a secular civil society, and a commitment to rational and scientific production processes and conflict resolution. But the region contained much oil, indeed, the most plentiful supply of the most important single commodity for the world economy. Many of the region's economies, therefore, acquired financial resources almost entirely by rent seeking through the price of

1 David Mosler and Bob Catley, *Global America, Imposing Liberalism on a Recalcitrant World,* as above.

oil. Yet none of them was able to translate these riches into the modernisation of their economies and societies. The economies of Saudi Arabia, Iran, Ba'athist Iraq and the Gulf states depended almost entirely on oil revenues. Egypt's much poorer economy rested on Suez Canal charges, tourism and US aid. Jordan depended on worker remittances and US aid. These societies were not modernising; indeed, most resisted the process with great success.

For over two decades the clash between Islamic extremism, now particularly in its Jihadist/Islamist variety, has been building against the forces of Western modernisation.

US Policy in the Middle East

The Middle East was controlled by the Ottoman Empire until its defeat by the British, French and allied forces in the First World War. This mostly Arab and Islamic region was then divided into British and French spheres of influence. These two powers, acting ostensibly through the League of Nations, redrew the political map of the region to correspond to their own interests, rewarding their allies, punishing their opponents, and ensuring their access to oil as it became the most important commercial opportunity in the area.[2] The French created then Christian-dominated Lebanon out of the Syrian mandate, thereby ensuring that Damascus would harbour irredentist claims to it. The British installed their various First World War dynastic allies into ruling houses in Saudi Arabia, Jordan, and the smaller oil-rich states of the Gulf. British forces from India occupied Mesopotamia and created 'Iraq' from the three Ottoman Provinces of Basra, Baghdad and Mosel by conquest, fiat and diplomacy.[3] Arabs resisted these processes but were defeated by a French army outside Damascus in 1920 and the British subdued an insurgency in Iraq with massive use of air power in 1921 and installed King Feisal. Zionist Jews defied the British authorities to settle in the Palestinian mandate, and then with armed force created the state of Israel in 1948.

The US progressively replaced the British and the French as the dominant external power in the region after 1945. It did this in pursuit of oil. In 1928 its companies had been party to the Red Line Agreement which divided Middle East oil among the allies, but after 1945 its companies progressively superseded those from Europe and began to control production and distribution.[4] From the late 1950s, the US also emerged as the principal external guarantor of Israeli security against the surrounding Arab states. The US military and political role in the Middle East progressively expanded, until by the 1990s its power in the region appeared near hegemonic. By that time, one key US interest in the region was the flow of oil through the sea lanes of the Persian Gulf; another was the protection of the state of Israel. After September 2001 the pursuit of the Global War on Terror became the third.

2 Daniel Yergin, *The Prize: The Epic Quest for Oil, Money and Power* (New York, 1991) pp. 200 ff.

3 See Edwin Black, *Banking on Baghdad: Inside Iraq's 7,000-Year History of War, Profit and Conflict* (Hoboken New Jersey, 2004).

4 Yergin, *The Prize*, chapter 23, 'Old Mossy and the Struggle for Iran'.

Bruce Riedel, special assistant to President Clinton, said in 1998 that,

> The Gulf region has been recognized by every American President since Franklin Delano Roosevelt as an area of absolute vital strategic importance for the United States. Not only is it the energy storehouse of the world – home to two-thirds of the proven oil reserves of the globe – but it is also the nexus where three continents come together. Nowhere else in the world have US military forces been more actively engaged in the last quarter-century than here. … this is where the vital interests of the United States have been defended most vigorously in the last two decades.[5]

Also, nowhere else in the world was the disjunction between the liberal principles and geopolitical interests of the US so clearly demonstrated as in the Middle East. Indeed, in this region these two objectives could not be easily simultaneously and jointly pursued. The pro-Israeli lobby[6] and the oil industry,[7] have both continually urged the use of US power in the region, although in somewhat different manners. It should be stressed that remarks similar to Riedel's could be cited from every US administration since 1945. The paramountcy of maintaining the flow of oil in US strategy does not result merely from the lobbying of oil interests in the US Congress and White House. It transcends this day to day activity as a long term and settled national interest and objective. All major parties and all Presidential candidates have recognised this fact and need little reminder of it.

The modern history of the Middle East has been shaped by externally imposed colonialism, first by the Arabs themselves, who brought a religion, language, and culture, then by the Ottoman Turks, who created administrative regions, and more recently by the West Europeans, who created many of the present state boundaries.[8] The regimes of the immediately post-independence period were mostly traditional and autocratic, as they remain in Saudi Arabia, Jordan and the Gulf states, and were often installed by the British or French to protect their commercial interests. Some of these were overthrown by Arab nationalists and gave way to revolutionary regimes with socialist rhetoric and often a military disposition, as in Egypt, Syria, Iraq, Yemen, and Libya. In the non-Arab state of Iran, a friendly regime under the Shah was protected from revolutionary impulses by the US after the late 1950s. This dynasty collapsed when President Carter refused to continue such US support in 1979, and it was replaced by a revolutionary Islamic Republic.

---

5 Bruce O Riedel, Special Assistant to the President and Senior Director Near East and South Asian Affairs, National Security Council: 'Remarks at the Washington Institute for Near East Policy', Washington, 6 May 1998.

6 David Howard Goldberg, *Foreign Policy and Ethnic Interest Groups: American and Canadian Jews Lobby For Israel* (New York, 1990); Edward Tivnan, *The Lobby: Jewish Political Power and American Foreign Policy* (New York, 1987); John Mearsheimer and Stephen Walt, 'The Israel Lobby and U.S. Foreign Policy', *London Review of Books*, 23 March 2006 (the 'Harvard Paper').

7 Anthony Sampson, *The Seven Sisters: The Great Oil Companies and the World They Made* (London, 1975).

8 See Bernard Lewis, *The Middle East: Two Thousand Years of History from the Rise of Christianity to the Present Day* (London, 1996).

The Oil Economy

The principal US strategic interest in the Middle East was initially oil. Access to the regional countries' oil reserves is the reason the US has guaranteed the security of illiberal regimes in the Middle East, including initially Iran, and then Saudi Arabia and the Gulf States, for the last half century. Oil is the most internationally traded resource in the global economy, whether measured by volume or value. About two thirds of the world's known oil reserves are located in states adjacent to the Persian Gulf, and some forty per cent of internationally traded oil passes through the Straits of Hormuz at the mouth of the Gulf. The US has been a net importer of oil for over fifty years, and most of its major trading partners in Europe and East Asia are even more heavily dependent on imported oil as a source of energy. The price of oil is now set on world markets by the interaction of a supply side dominated by state owned oil companies, many in the OPEC states, and a demand side dominated by four large oil companies, two of them American, with refining and distribution systems throughout particularly the major developed country markets. The world economy and American primacy within it, rests on oil. The Bush family grew rich partly through four generations being in the oil business. The bin Laden family also grew rich in the construction industry during the Saudi oil boom. The Global War on Terror makes no sense unless related to oil.

Crude oil is a liquid found in porous rock formations, composed mainly of carbon and hydrogen.[9] For this reason, it is, like coal, often called a hydro-carbon energy source. Most oil extracted is used for producing fuel oil and petrol, both important 'primary energy' sources. Oil is easy to transport and is used to fire the internal combustion engine which now provides the most common form of private transportation in developed urban economies. It also provides the feedstock for the textile, aerospace, agricultural fertiliser and computer sectors. As the most influential history of oil development put it: 'At the end of the twentieth century, oil was still central to security, prosperity, and the very nature of civilisation'.[10] In terms of primary commercial energy usage world wide, the OECD estimated that in 2003 it was: oil 35.4 per cent; natural gas, 23.7 percent and liquid products from gas, 2.7 per cent; coal 23.7 per cent; hydro-electricity, 6.5 per cent; nuclear electricity, 6.4 per cent; and renewables, 1.4 per cent. Fossil fuels provided about 86 per cent of the world's commercial energy. About 65 per cent of known world oil reserves are in the Middle East, in Islamic states most of which are Arab. Perhaps another five per cent of world reserves are located in states that are partly Islamic, like Malaysia, Indonesia and Nigeria and the states of Central Asia.

The US economy is heavily dependent on oil and has been a net importer of it for at least fifty years. Although the US has diversified its electricity production away from oil fired power stations, its transportation system remains very heavily dependent on oil. It is also a vital feedstock for industries as diverse as artificial fibres, agricultural fertiliser, plastics, road surfacing and aerospace materials. In

9 For the technology of the industry see, Matthew R Simmons, *Twilight in the Desert: The Coming Saudi Oil Shock and the World Economy* (Hoboken, New Jersey, 2005).

10 Yergin, *The Prize,* p.13.

the late 1940s the US began to import oil and the proportion of imports to total consumption has been rising ever since. In the 1950s, imported oil accounted for ten per cent; in the 1960s around 18 per cent, and in the 1970s about 35 per cent of US consumption. Domestic production then rose somewhat and checked this trend, but this peaked in 1972 and thereafter declined. The share of imports in the US supply then rose again from 42 per cent in 1990 to 49 per cent in 1997. In April 1998, US dependence on imported oil exceeded fifty per cent and it has risen since then as consumption has increased and domestic production has fallen.

By 2010 it is estimated the US will consume 23 million barrels a day and produce around eight million barrels per day.[11] Its dependence on foreign oil will rise from 55 per cent in 2001, to 58 per cent in 2010, to 66 per cent in 2020, and 70 per cent in 2025. Some of that oil will be located in countries that are unstable, unfriendly or located in dangerous areas.[12] In some cases, like Saudi Arabia, the presence of US forces to defend oil supply may worsen these conditions by generating local resentments of the kind that alienated Osama bin Laden and Al Qaeda.[13] After the 1991 Gulf War, the US military stationed 5,000 personnel in Saudi Arabia to protect the House of Saud and its oil, and between 1991 and 2000 they conducted 240,000 sorties to enforce the no-fly zone in southern Iraq and sold $40 billion in military equipment to the Saudis.[14]

The world economy is dependent on oil. Most of the EU economies are heavily dependent on imported oil and the same is true of the East Asian market economies, Japan, Taiwan and South Korea, who import all of their oil. China, which is now emerging as a major trading partner of the US, also imports increasing quantities of oil and has been a net importer since 1995. This trend will accelerate as China moves towards private motor vehicles.

The price of oil is now determined by supply and demand on the world market and prices are posted daily. OPEC can still have a significant impact on short term supply, and so price, but things have changed massively since the 1974 oil crisis which was largely caused by OPEC activities. OPEC now has a lower proportion of total output and therefore has less control over supply and price. Also, many more substitutes for oil have emerged although it would still be difficult to find total substitutes, especially in the short term. The task of ensuring that this flow is maintained has fallen since the 1970s to the current hegemonic power, the US, and it is finding it increasingly difficult to sustain. From the late 1970s, the US has maintained a naval force including 25,000 personnel on permanent station adjacent to the Persian Gulf as a deterrent, as a shield, as an enforcer of UN sanctions against Iraq, and in 2001 as a support for the invasion of Afghanistan and since 2003 as the reserve for the army of occupation in Iraq.

---

11 Michael Klare, *Blood and Oil*, quoting US Department of Energy, *International Energy Outlook* (New York, 2003).

12 Klare, as above, p. 18.

13 Gunaratna, *Inside Al Qaeda,* as above, pp. 46 ff.

14 Klare, as above, p. 53.

The American oil industry began with the discovery of oil in 1859, near Titusville, Pennsylvania. The industry grew slowly in the late nineteenth century, driven by the demand for kerosene and oil lamps. It became a major national industry in the early part of the twentieth century with the invention and spread of the internal combustion engine, which provided most of the demand that produced the growth of the industry into the twenty first century. This led to the development of the first giant oil corporations, of which the Standard Oil Company controlled by John D Rockefeller was the most prominent. Standard Oil was developed into a 'trust', or monopoly, and became the subject of much hostile commentary and was broken up by Congress.[15]

Until the mid-1950s, coal was still the world's most common fuel, but thereafter oil quickly took over. The 1974 and then the 1979 energy crisis showed that oil is a limited resource, that none is now being formed, and that it will eventually run out, at least as an energy source. At the time of the 1974 OPEC-induced price rises, many popular predictions, like those associated with the Club of Rome[16] and Paul Erhlich,[17] were usually quite dire and anticipated total depletion. When catastrophic shortages did not eventuate, such predictions were dismissed. But the future of oil as a fuel remains limited, although the date of exhaustion may be later than earlier predictions. For example, in 2004 some experts reported that there were 40 years of oil left in the ground.[18] As a result, some therefore argued that because the total amount of oil is obviously finite, the dire predictions of the 1970s have merely been postponed.

But other analysts, often economists, argue that technology will continue to improve and allow for the production of other cheap hydrocarbons. For example, there are vast sources of now unconventional oil reserves in the form of tar sands, bitumen fields and oil shale that will enable petrol to be used in transport into the medium future. The Canadian tar sands and US shale oil deposits represent potential reserves that almost match existing liquid oil deposits worldwide. Further, other presently unknown substitutes will be developed if financial incentives are created by the market. But in 2007 about ninety per cent of vehicle fuel needs were met by oil. Oil also makes up forty per cent of total energy consumption in the US, although it is responsible for only two per cent of electricity generation. The Hubbert peak theory, also known as 'peak oil', predicts that future world oil production must inevitably reach a peak and then decline as reserves are exhausted.[19] The major issue it raises concerns when the global 'peak' will actually take place, since logically oil must at some future point be exhausted. Proponents have previously (and incorrectly) predicted the peak for world oil to be in years 1989, 1995, or 1995–2000.

---

15 Yergin, *The Prize*, chapter two, 'John D Rockefeller and the Combination of American Oil'.

16 Dennis L Meadows, *et al*, *The Limits to Growth* (New York, 1972).

17 Paul R Ehrlich, *Population, Resources, Environments: Issues in Human Ecology* (San Francisco, 1972).

18 David R Francis, 'Has global oil production peaked?', *The Christian Science Monitor, 29 Jan 2004.*

19 See http://www.peak-oil-news.info/hubbert-peak-oil-predictions/

During and after the Second World War the US made extensive plans[20] to ensure access to raw materials necessary for both its own economy and those with which it would be integrated. Oil figured prominently in these calculations, just as it had in the war time strategies of all other major powers.[21] In February 1945 when victory over Nazi Germany seemed assured, Stalin, Churchill and Roosevelt met at Yalta to divide the European continent. Roosevelt then left and met King Saud of Saudi Arabia on the *USS Quincy,* on the Great Bitter Lake in the Suez Canal system. They essentially agreed that US companies should develop Saudi oil and that, in exchange, the US would guarantee the House of Saud. In succeeding decades the Saudi state emerged as the site of the world's largest oil fields, holder of one quarter of world oil reserves and, with its small population, the largest single exporter of oil. It did this with US oil companies undertaking the exploration and production functions. This arrangement was essentially still in place in 2007 although the Saudis had nationalised production. It became apparent by the 1950s that the Saudi fields were the largest in the world, with one, Ghawar, near the Kuwait region of the Gulf, being the largest ever discovered.

Since 1945 the US has thus been committed to the defence of the feudalist, repressive and incompetent Saudi regime.[22] The House of Saud had seized much of the peninsula in the eighteenth century and then in 1902, Abd Al-Aziz bin Abd al-Rahman Al Saud captured Riyadh and in a 30-year campaign unified the Arabian Peninsula by force. The country's Basic Law stipulates that the throne shall remain in the hands of the male descendents of the kingdom's founder. But the presence of foreign troops on Saudi soil after Operation Desert Storm, created tensions between the royal family and the Saudi public – and Al Qaeda – until the US military's nearly complete withdrawal to neighbouring Qatar and Iraq in 2003. The first major terrorist attacks in Saudi Arabia in several years occurred in May and November 2003, and prompted renewed efforts on the part of the Saudi government to counter domestic terrorism and extremism. It permitted a slight improvement in media freedom and announced plans to phase in very limited political representation. As part of this effort, the government permitted elections for half the members of 179 municipal councils.

Saudi Arabia is nearly two million square kilometres of harsh, mostly dry desert with a population of 27 million growing at over 2 per cent annually, but that includes 5.5 million non-national workers. It is governed according to Sharia law, and the Basic Law that states the government's rights and responsibilities was only introduced in 1993. In theory, adult male citizens age 21 or older may vote, but voter registration only began in November 2004 for partial municipal council elections held in early 2005. The King, Prime Minister, chief of state and head of government has been Abdallah bin Abd al-Aziz Al Saud since 1 August 2005. The Heir Apparent is the half brother of the monarch. A Council of Ministers is appointed by the monarch and includes many royal family members, but there are no elections to it.

20 Gabriel Kolko, *The Politics of War: The World and United States Foreign Policy, 1943–1945* (New York, 1968) Chapter 11 'Planning for Peace, I, General Principles'.

21 See Yergin, *The Prize,* Chapter 20, 'The New Centre of Gravity'.

22 David E Long, *The United States and Saudi Arabia* (Boulder, 1985).

The state's ideology is Salafi and the Saudi government has spread this by funding the construction of mosques and Koranic schools around the world. In the 2005 succession, the leading members of the royal family chose the king from among themselves with the subsequent approval of the *ulema* (senior Muslim clergy). A significant contraction of oil revenues combined with the high rate of population growth to produce a fall in its per capita income from $25,000 in 1980 to $8,000 in 2003, one of the worst suffered by any nation-state in peace time history until Zimbabwe 2002–7. It may be ironic, but it is also understandable, that this regime, protected by the US, nurtured one of the most effective terrorist organisations in the world – Al Qaeda.

The International Trade in Oil

The total world production/consumption of oil in 2005 was approximately 84 million barrels per day (MMbbl/d).[23] The major producers of oil, in order, with output figures were:

Saudi Arabia (OPEC)	10.37	MMbbl/d
Russia	9.27	MMbbl/d
United States	8.69	MMbbl/d
Iran (OPEC)	4.09	MMbbl/d
Mexico	3.83	MMbbl/d
China	3.62	MMbbl/d
Norway	3.18	MMbbl/d
Canada	3.14	MMbbl/d
Venezuela (OPEC)	2.86	MMbbl/d
United Arab Emirates (OPEC)	2.76	MMbbl/d
Kuwait (OPEC)	2.51	MMbbl/d
Nigeria (OPEC)	2.51	MMbbl/d
United Kingdom (Scotland)	2.08	MMbbl/d
Iraq (OPEC)	2.03	MMbbl/d

But many of these producers were also heavy consumers and therefore net importers of oil. Taking the amount of oil *exported* in 2005 in millions of barrels per day, the order of countries is a little different, reflecting their different levels of economic development and different population sizes:

Saudi Arabia (OPEC)	8.73
Russia	6.67
Norway	2.91
Iran (OPEC)	2.55
Venezuela (OPEC)	2.36

23 The statistical basis for this analysis can be found at the US Department of Energy, Energy Information Administration, web site: http://www.eia.doe.gov/emeu/international/contents.html

United Arab Emirates (OPEC)	2.33
Kuwait (OPEC)	2.20
Nigeria (OPEC)	2.19
Mexico	1.80
Algeria (OPEC)	1.68
Libya (OPEC)	1.34

The Middle East dominates inter-regional export flows, despite the strong growth in production in other areas in recent years. The three large oil consuming regions of North America, Europe and the Asia-Pacific, are all net importers of oil. The US is the largest individual importer, both net and gross. But North America is not the largest regional importer, because Canada and Mexico are two of the three top oil suppliers to the US. The largest regional importer is the Asia-Pacific region which includes rapid growth and oil deficient Korea, Japan, Taiwan and the PRC. These basic factors explain the two major ‘choke points’ of the world oil trade being the Straits of Hormuz and the Straits of Malacca.

Recently, there has been strong growth in the supply of oil from Latin American countries, particularly Mexico and Venezuela, whose governments are committed to nationally owned oil companies. On the other hand, there has been a strong growth in demand for oil with the long Asian boom in countries deficient in oil and in a region with only a few exporters like Indonesia, Malaysia and Brunei, although Vietnam may soon be joining them. As a result, regional self-sufficiency has actually increased within the Atlantic area, US imports notwithstanding, but declined in East Asia and around the Pacific Rim. This has meant fewer Middle East barrels moving west, and very many more moving east to Asia. The Atlantic Basin markets in the US and Europe have been increasingly supplied from the North Sea, West Africa and Latin America.

The rapid growth in US crude imports in the 1990s was accompanied by a swing toward crude oil from Western Hemisphere sources which now form the majority of US imports. At the same time, the proportion of crude imports from the Middle East has dropped from 30 per cent to 20 per cent. Although this has reduced US dependence on Middle East oil, the US is still vulnerable to price shocks. Since oil trades on a global market, the impact of a disruption in supply on US prices is determined by world price and not US dependency on a particular region’s supply. But US dependency has become increasingly concentrated with nearly two thirds of all US crude imports coming from just four countries: Mexico, Venezuela, Saudi Arabia and Canada.

As a commodity of great strategic importance, oil has long been the object of geopolitical competition since the decision in 1912 by the British Admiralty to convert its warships from coal to oil propulsion because of speed and range advantages. Britain then had no oil resources and it nationalized the Anglo-Persian Oil Company and committed itself to the protection of this resource in Persia (Iran after 1934). In the 1920s civilian demand for oil grew rapidly as the automobile became a significant mode of private transportation.[24]

24 Yergin, *The Prize*, as above.

Oligopolistic control of the price and production of oil was first established in 1928 by the Achnacarry Agreements between the 'seven sisters', the major oil companies of the time.[25] These Seven Sisters by the early twentieth century had achieved dominance over the industry. Five of them were American including Exxon (Standard Oil of New Jersey), Mobil (Standard Oil of New York), and Socal (Standard Oil of California which later became Chevron), which were the result of the forced break up of the Standard Oil Trust in 1911.[26] The Gulf and Texaco companies were created after the discovery of oil in Texas in 1901. The two British companies were Royal Dutch Shell (a joint venture with the Netherlands) and British Petroleum (BP), whose interest in world oil expanded with the discovery of oil fields the Dutch East Indies (Indonesia) and in Persia (Iran) respectively. Since then through mergers and acquisitions the 'Seven Sisters' have now become essentially four 'super-majors' or giant, vertically integrated private, oil, natural gas, and petrol companies: ExxonMobil, Chevron-Texaco, BP and Royal Dutch Shell.

Exxon Mobil Corporation is also the world's largest and most profitable company formed on 30 November 1999 by the merger of Exxon and Mobil. It is the largest of the four oil 'super-majors' that have displaced the seven sisters. Chevron Corporation, also one of the world's largest global energy companies, was originally Standard Oil of California, or Socal. In 1984, the merger between Chevron and Gulf Oil was the largest corporate merger in world history at the time. In 2001, Chevron merged with Texaco to form ChevronTexaco. In August 1998 British Petroleum took over Amoco. Royal Dutch Shell[27] was initially conceived and served as a British rival to Standard Oil. Shell also has a significant petrochemicals business and is incorporated in the UK but has its corporate headquarters in The Hague.

Already by the 1920s, the seven large oil corporations had invested massively in extraction infrastructures, especially in the Middle East and Latin America, and distribution outlets in richer countries. They were then a cartel effectively in control of the world's oil supply and demand, with a set of strategies for fixing quotas, prices and production. But a nationalization trend had started in Russia in 1917, and in 1938 Mexico also expropriated its entire oil industry. This undermined Mexico's access to foreign markets that the seven sisters controlled, but it also triggered sympathy in many other oil- rich countries and set an example for them.

OPEC, the US and the Geopolitics of Oil

In view of the economic control of oil production by Western multinational corporations, several producing countries, some in the Middle East, developed the idea of acquiring a greater share of oil revenues by directly controlling supply.

25 Anthony Sampson, *The Seven Sisters* (London, 1975).

26 Yergin, *The Prize*, as above, pp 101 ff. Standard Oil became: Standard Oil of New Jersey (Exxon); Standard Oil of New York (Mobil); Standard Oil of California (Chevron); Standard Oil of Ohio (Sohio and then BP); Standard Oil of Indiana (Amoco); Continental Oil (Conoco); and Atlantic (ARCO).

27 Yergin, *The Prize*, as above, Chapter eight, 'The Oil Wars: The Rise of Royal Dutch'.

Venezuela, Iran, Iraq, Saudi Arabia and Kuwait founded OPEC in 1960 at the Baghdad Conference. But at first OPEC was unable to use its cartel power to increase oil prices because non-OPEC member countries were still important producers and exporters and OPEC members could not agree on a common policy. This situation, however, changed quickly in the early 1970s. OPEC achieved control over more than 55 per cent of the global oil supply as new members joined, and the cartel started to fix production quotas based on the declared oil reserves of each of its members. OPEC member states also began to nationalise their oil industries: Libya, 1971; Iraq, 1972; Iran, 1973; Saudi Arabia, 1975; Venezuela, 1975. OPEC also tried to avoid supply competition that would bring the down the price of oil. As a result, between 1970 and 1973, oil prices increased modestly from $1.80 to $3.29 per barrel.

The Yom Kippur War in 1973 gave OPEC political impetus to intervene by nationalising production facilities, reducing production by 25 per cent, and imposing export quotas. The immediate goal was to undermine support for Israel, mainly by the US. The price of oil climbed to $12 per barrel by late 1973. OPEC had the ability to control the price of oil and thereby produced the first 'oil shock'. Under the control of OPEC, the price of oil remained higher but stable from 1974 to 1978, at around $12 per barrel. The developed countries started to worry about the exhaustion of oil reserves and unreliable supply sources. The Iranian revolution of 1979 and the ensuing Iran-Iraq War (1980–1988) then caused the second 'oil shock' where the price of oil surged to over $35 per barrel, and several developed countries imposed administrative measures to lower oil consumption and diversify energy production. Coupled with the Soviet invasion of Afghanistan and the Iranian revolution, this shock also led to the 'Carter Doctrine'.

President Carter said in 1980 that the US would intervene militarily if its oil supply was threatened. The US military presence in the Middle East was increased, as the flow of oil through the Persian Gulf was clearly perceived as critically important to US national security. From that time, the US has in fact been prepared to use military force to protect the supply of Middle East oil to the US and world economy.

Nonetheless, during the late 1980s and early 1990s, the OPEC countries gradually lost their price-fixing power because of disagreements within OPEC including particularly the Iran-Iraq war. Also new producers developed outside OPEC including: Russia after the Soviet collapse; Mexico, that discovered new fields; Norway and the UK with the North Sea fields; and Colombia. Latin American countries, such as Columbia and Brazil, also tried to boost their oil production, as did others in Africa and Southeast Asian.[28] After 1982, disagreements also occurred between OPEC members about how to fix quotas and prices. Furthermore, the share of OPEC again dropped from 55 per cent of all oil exported in the 1970s, to 42 per cent in 2000, with a low of 30 per cent in 1985. Saudi Arabia sometimes lowered its oil price to increase its market share and OPEC members competed with each other to be allotted larger quotas. OPEC then allocated quotas to members in proportion to their proven oil reserves, which were often realigned: Kuwait's reserves suddenly climbed from 64 billion to 92 billion barrels and those of the UAE were also increased unilaterally from 31 billion to 92 billion barrels. Iran announced that its

28 Bob Catley and Makmur Keliat, *Spratlys* (Aldershot, 1997).

'real' reserves were 93 billion barrels, up from a previous 47 billion barrels. The most significant 'increase' in oil reserves in 1985 was from Iraq, with its reserves going up to 100 billion barrels, from the previous figure of 47 billions. Those reserve figures remain in the twenty first century, further increasing the difficulty of evaluating the 'peak oil' theory. The result was an oil 'counter-shock' that lowered the price to $20 a barrel, with a low of $15 in 1988.

Iraq then invaded Kuwait in 1990 and the price of oil again jumped to $23 per barrel. The US then applied the Carter Doctrine and ousted Iraqi forces from Kuwait. An oil embargo was then established on Iraq by the UN. However, other oil-exporting countries expanded their production to replace the shortfalls of Iraq and Kuwait, and the price of oil again fell to $15 per barrel by the end of the 1990s. By then OPEC countries only controlled about forty per cent of global production and could only influence oil prices. The oil market had again become a market mostly controlled by the laws of supply and demand. The ability of the OPEC cartel to control supply, allocate quotas among member states, and thereby run the world oil output, had been greatly diluted. But the twenty first century then brought other insecurities in oil supply, political pressures and military interventions. The Second Gulf War, waged to fight terrorism and secure WMDs, produced the American occupation of Iraq. One intended outcome was a greater US control of long term oil supply sources.

The oil industry is thus partly oligopolistic: in its supply, demand, control, and in its functional and geographical concentration. Demand is partly controlled by the large multinational conglomerates, 'super-majors', each with a production and distribution system comprising refineries, storage facilities, distribution centres and, at the end of the supply chain, petrol stations. Supply is heavily influenced by a few countries where the oil industry is often nationalized and/or by the OPEC umbrella, which still regulates about thirty seven per cent of global oil production. The US military attempts to ensure protection. Oil is produced into this semi-regulated market.[29]

In 2004, an average of 80.2 million barrels of crude oil were produced each day, 32 per cent of it in the Middle East. About 60 per cent of all the oil being produced was already committed under contracts, and around forty per cent was sold on open markets. These are the spot prices openly quoted. More significantly, this 'excess' oil production is limited both in capacity and in its geographical origin. About ninety per cent of this 'excess' oil production was located in the Persian Gulf with Saudi Arabia believed to be the only major supplier able to provide instant additional production. In 2004 an average of 80.7 million barrels of oil per day were also consumed, sixty per cent of it in the developed OECD countries. The US was the leading global consumer of oil at 20.1 Mb/d, but the rapid growth of the Chinese economy has taken China to second place of oil consumers at 5.5 Mb/d, surpassing Japan at 5.3 Mb/d. China has accounted for around forty per cent of the global growth in oil demand in recent years and is the world's most rapidly growing automobile market. Fifty two per cent of all oil produced was consumed by transportation activities

29 See, Energy Information Administration, Official Energy Statistics from the US Government, 'World Oil Transit Chokepoints, General Background', November 2005.

and the internal combustion engine remains one of the driving forces behind the increasing consumption of oil.

Oil is extensively traded internationally because oil is mainly produced in poor, underdeveloped countries but consumed in wealthy developed countries. Each year, about 1.9 billion tons of oil are shipped by maritime transportation, about sixty per cent of all oil produced. The remaining forty per cent is transported by pipelines, trains or trucks. The maritime trade in oil follows maritime routes from producing to consuming regions. About half the oil shipped is loaded in the Middle East and then shipped through the Straits of Hormuz to Japan, the US and Europe. Tankers bound for Japan then use the Strait of Malacca, while tankers bound for Europe and the US either use the Suez Canal or the Cape of Good Hope. There are roughly 3,500 tankers in the international oil transportation market. In general, tankers have got much larger over time in order to reduce the unit costs of transporting a barrel of oil. About 435 Very Large Crude Carriers (VLCCs) account for a third of the oil being carried. Transportation costs account for only a small percentage of the total cost of petrol at the bowser and account for only about 5 to 10 per cent of the added value of oil. The Persian Gulf is a major region of oil production for export, and much of this first goes through the Straits of Hormuz; from there maritime routes reach Europe through the Suez Canal, Japan through the Strait of Malacca, and North America around the Cape of Good Hope. These routes require protection from hostile activities and the US military is the major provider.

The US has several interests in oil.[30] The US economy remains heavily dependent on imported oil and is interested to see that sufficient supply is maintained. Its major trading partners throughout the world are in a similar position, and the US is, therefore, also concerned to maintain their supply. The US oil companies still dominate the distribution of much of the oil, the exploration for more oil, and, at a reduced but still significant level, the extraction of oil. Much of the oil supplied by state owned companies is also pre-sold to the four super-majors and other large 'independent' oil corporations, many of which are US owned. These companies have a limited interest in conservation and substitution policies designed to lessen US dependence on oil. These companies are also extremely well represented in the US political system, particularly in the Bush administration.[31] The Bush family has for generations worked for or with the major oil corporations.

The US made itself the hegemonic power of the world political and economic system[32] by fighting a victory in three world conflicts – the First and Second World Wars and the Cold War – and by enforcing it in literally hundreds of lesser conflicts, including, recently, in Afghanistan and Iraq. During this process, the US became and remains the richest country in the world. Largely, this is because its domestic economy is the most productive per capita and in total, of any substantial country. But it is also because the US has been able to shape the global economy to suit its own ends. These include the flow of oil – and it will fight to preserve it. In 2000 the

30 David S Painter, 'Oil', in A DeConde, R D Burns and F Logevall, eds, *Encyclopedia of American Foreign Policy* (New York, 2002).

31 Craig Unger, *House of Bush, House of Saud* (New York, 2004).

32 David Mosler and Bob Catley, *Global America*, as above.

US intended to protect its access to oil in the Gulf by defending the House of Saud, by removing Saddam Hussein, and by trying to get a change in the policy of Iran by encouraging its then more moderate government or if necessary by regime change. In late 2001 it added the GWOT to its oil strategy, with far reaching results.

Wars and Instability in the Middle East

The other major US asset in the Middle East is the state of Israel. In 1948 the Zionist Jewish settlers defeated the local Arab population, supported by the neighbouring Arab states, as the British retreated from the mandated territory of Palestine, and created the new Jewish state of Israel. Neighbouring Arab states refused to recognise Israel, although the UN and both the superpowers, the US and the Soviet Union did so. Most of the Palestinian Arab refugees settled in the Gaza strip under Egyptian control, the West Bank under Jordanian control, in Lebanon, or dispersed throughout the wider Arab world.

In 1954 the Egyptian monarchy was overthrown and the country came under the control of Colonel Nasser who adopted a more belligerent attitude towards Israel. He also nationalised the Suez Canal and the British and French secretly plotted with Israel to seize back the Canal and possibly overthrow Nasser. In the Suez War of 1956 these three powers invaded Egypt but America intervened on Nasser's behalf, in order to prevent the Soviets from making inroads into the Arab world.

Nonetheless, Nasser continued to threaten Israel and in 1967, together with Syria and Jordan prepared for war. Israel launched a pre-emptive strike, destroyed much of the opposing air forces on the ground, and in six days imposed another humiliating defeat on the neighbouring Arab regimes. Israel then occupied the Golan Heights of Syria, the Gaza Strip and the Sinai Desert to the Suez Canal from Egypt, and the West Bank from Jordan. For the next six years the Arabs waged sporadic guerrilla war against Israel. The Palestinian Arabs also firmed up their complex political formations into the umbrella Palestine Liberation Organisation, led by Yasser Arafat of the Al Fatah faction. The PLO instigated much violence against Israel and was evicted from Jordan in 1970, to prevent Israeli retaliation. In the same year Nasser died and his successor Anwar Sadat determined that only a change in the military balance could break this deadly stalemate.

In 1973 the Egyptian and Syrian forces again attacked Israel during the Yom Kippur festival with initial success. The Egyptian forces crossed the Suez Canal and pushed the Israelis back. The Syrians also had some initial successes to the north. The other Arab states supported these actions by imposing an oil embargo on states supporting Israel, including the US. The US moved from near neutrality in 1956, to strong support for Israel in 1973–74, rearmed the depleted Israeli forces, and enabled them to snatch victory from near-defeat.[33] The US then tried to engineer a peaceful settlement to the Arab-Israeli conflict.

Under Nasser Egypt had developed a secular model for Arab socialist states with an extensive public sector, suppression of Islamic religious extremism, good

---

33 Ian Lustik, ed, *Arab-Israeli Relations in World Politics* (New York, 1994).

relations with the Soviet bloc and an anti-Western foreign policy. Sadat saw this as a dead end with economic stagnation the result. In 1979 Sadat made peace with Israel at Camp David and the Israelis withdrew from Egyptian territory, Egypt recognised Israel and the US gave both sides large sums of money. This became the model for some future Arab settlements with Israel, but also led to the assassination of Sadat by militant Islamist army personnel in 1981. But his successor, Hosni Mubarak, stuck to the deal. Syria had been unable to regain the Golan Heights and continued to harbour hostile intent towards Israel which it then started to pursue through Lebanon.

Evicted from Jordan in 1970 the PLO moved to Lebanon where it stimulated the fragmentation of the country into religious based mini-states and maintained its guerrilla war on Israel from southern Lebanon. The Syrians took the opportunity to encroach on Lebanon and effectively occupied much of it from the late 1970s. In 1982, to offset this threat to its northern borders the Israelis invaded Lebanon, evicted the PLO to Tunis and occupied the south of the country as a buffer zone. The Iranians created a Shi'ite militia of resistance there which became Hezbollah.

The most destructive war in the region, however, was that fought for eight years between radical Shi'ite Iran and Arab Ba'athist Iraq (1980–88). In 1979 an Islamic revolution overthrew the Shah and the country was disorganised while establishing a new Caliphate-style state structure. Baghdad attacked Iran to wrest some territory, resources, and oil from the weakened regime. At first, the Iraqis made advances, but the Iranians eventually held the line and seemed likely even to force a successful outcome which the US supported Iraq to prevent. The war generated a million fatalities, resulted in a stalemate and further militarized both regimes.

In 1975 the PLO was recognised by the UN as the legitimate/sole representative of the Palestinian people and continued to pursue the destruction of Israel. By 1988 this was becoming a futile endeavour for which Soviet support was no longer available. In a sharp turn, Arafat announced the PLO would recognise Israel in return for a broader settlement and started negotiations during which Jordan dropped its claim on the West Bank, Israel moved towards a 'two state solution', the PLO recognised Israel and the US provided aid to the Palestinian Authority. This settlement was delayed, however, by the First Gulf War, 1990–91.

Gorbachev's withdrawal of subsides and arms to allies and clients, had a profound impact on the Middle East. Soviet client states rethought their strategic ambitions and, in the first instance anyway, opposition to US power in the region diminished. The Iraqi regime misread this change. In July 1990 Iraq invaded and annexed Kuwait. Its larger ambition was to advance its power throughout the Arabian peninsula and with Yemen, the PLO and Jordan, gain control of around half the world's oil reserves, and become leader of the Arab world. Saddam misconstrued US signals and policy. George H W Bush organised a coalition of forty states who were then authorised by the UN to evict Iraqi forces from Kuwait. This task was accomplished in a week long ground war – Desert Shield/Desert Storm campaigns – involving mostly US forces but with some British and French support.[34] The war ended when Iraqi forces were defeated and fell back along the road to Baghdad. The

34 L Freedman and E Karsh, *The Gulf Conflict 1990–1991: Diplomacy and War in the New World Order* (London, 1993).

US then accepted their surrender and a peace settlement was concluded. Saddam remained in power, because Bush Senior did not believe he could get a mandate from the UN to remove him. Bush did publicly suggest, however, that the Iraqi people should remove him themselves and implied the US would support them. There were revolts in the country, but the US offered no support and the Ba'athist regime put them down with great ferocity.

But the US did insist on reductions in Iraqi military forces and a UN sponsored agreement allowed for inspection of Iraqi compliance. In addition, Iraqi trade was controlled to prevent its gaining the finance for re-armament. Saddam claimed to have won this war against the US and periodically pushed the sanctions regime to its limits by various transgressions, including bribing UN officials, repressing dissidents and seemingly building up his military forces, including by acquiring weapons of mass destruction (WMDs).

By 1982 the Palestinian Arabs had established their major military force around the PLO in southern Lebanon and launched raids against Israel. In 1982 the ruling Israeli Likud government invaded and occupied southern Lebanon to evict the guerrillas and prevent further attacks. The Israeli forces reached Beirut from where the PLO leadership by agreement embarked for Tunis. Israel then occupied southern Lebanon from 1982 to 2000, but despite the Israeli occupation with the help of local Christian militias, guerrillas continued to attack northern Israel. A new Islamic movement, Hezbollah, was formed with Iranian and Syrian encouragement and Israeli casualties mounted. In 2000, when there were some prospects of a negotiated settlement between the Palestinians and the Israeli state, the Israeli forces were withdrawn from Lebanon entirely. But this strategy also proved to be unsuccessful.

By the late twentieth century the Middle East contained five of the world's most vociferously anti-US states: Iran, Iraq, Libya, Sudan and Syria. These states pursued anti-US policies and articulated them in ideologies that were partly Islamist, anti-West, anti-liberal, and anti-globalisation. Iran depicted the US as the Great Satan that had maintained the dictatorial Shah. Iraq's neo-fascist Ba'athist government overthrew the monarchy in 1969 and then bloody infighting brought Saddam Hussein to power in the late 1970s. Libya, under the dictator Gaddafi from 1969, initiated the early OPEC oil price rises and used some of the proceeds to finance anti-US campaigns, including the use of terror. The Sudanese Islamic regime was bankrolled by oil-rich Arab states, and waged war on its southern, Christian population. The Syrian Ba'athist regime, a rival of Iraq, was principally concerned to reduce US and Israeli power to regain Lebanon, which it already informally dominated by the early twenty first century.

Oil shocks from the Middle East severely disrupted the liberal world economy twice in the late twentieth century. In 1973–4 OPEC raised the price of oil by 400 per cent helping to induce the then deepest world recession since 1945. The disruption to the flow of oil from the Gulf, and the accompanying increase in price caused by the Iraqi attack on Iran in 1980, helped to create the global economic depression of 1981–82.[35] After these two disruptions were dealt with, stable oil prices contributed

35 Simon Bromley, *American Hegemony and World Oil: The Industry, the State System, and the World Economy* (University Park, PA, 1991); P R Odell, *Oil and World Power*, 8th ed. (New York, 1986).

to the economic boom of the 1990s. But by then US armed forces were committed to directly defending the energy-rich illiberal Gulf oil states. As well as wanting to avoid another oil price shock, the US worried about rogue regimes using oil income to acquire WMDs.

US policy to maintain the flow of oil from the region involved it in wars against states that obstructed its flow, as in the 1990–91 Gulf War; in the maintenance of illiberal regimes that were prepared to give the US access to oil, notably that of the Saudi dynasty since 1945 and that of the Shah of Iran until the 1979 revolution; and in the subversion of regimes, like that of Mossadegh in Iran in 1954, that were not consistent with these objectives. At these times US policy was inconsistent with liberal principles of sovereignty, national self-determination, and democracy. Geopolitics and the well-being of an industry dominated by US companies took precedence. From 1991 to 2003, oil production was predictable, at high levels, and prices were mostly low. The Middle East share of world oil output indeed rose from the historic low of 27 per cent in 1986 to 32 per cent in 1991 and then to 35 per cent in 1996.

Nonetheless, because of the volatility of the Middle East, the US has encouraged the development of oil fields in other parts of the world. The Caspian basin, for example, became accessible to Western capital and corporations after the collapse of the Soviets and then rose in importance compared to the Middle East. The cost of producing oil dropped due to improved technology, resulting in more output from other oil fields – for example, in Norway, Nigeria, Venezuela and Canada. The Middle East did become marginally less significant to the liberal world economy as a source of energy and oil, although it was nonetheless still sufficiently important for the US to rate its protection from hostile encroachment as one of its key strategic objectives.

Dual Containment: Iran and Policing US Interests in the Middle East

During the height of the Cold War there was some concern about Soviet geopolitical penetration of the region, which was termed in the early 1980s 'the Arc of Crisis'.[36] The collapse of the Soviet Union greatly reduced this concern. Nonetheless, both Iran and Iraq remained committed to evicting US power. Iran maintained a revolutionary Islamic regime, with an ideology that justifies intervening in other countries, destroying Arab states with regimes linked to the US, like members of the Gulf Cooperation Council (GCC), and disrupting the Israeli-PLO peace process. Iraq's ruler, Saddam Hussein, had invaded two of his neighbours – Iran in 1980 and Kuwait in 1990 – and the US feared he might well try again. After the Cold War ended and it had evicted Iraqi forces from Kuwait, the US adopted a policy of 'dual containment' towards Iran and Iraq.

Dual containment, according to then US Assistant Secretary of State for Near Eastern Affairs, Martin Indyk,

36 Fred Halliday, *Soviet Policy in the Arc of Crisis* (Washington DC, 1981).

> was premised on the notion that the United States needed to shift away from our earlier policy of relying on one of these regional powers to balance the other, a policy we had followed throughout the previous decade with disastrous results. Rather, we would now focus our efforts on containing Saddam Hussein's threats to his neighbours and his own people, while at the same time pursuing multilateral efforts to prevent Iran from acquiring and developing weapons of mass destruction and the ballistic missiles necessary to deliver them.[37]

This policy at first succeeded in containing Iran and Iraq and maintaining the flow of Gulf oil, but at some cost.[38] It was also not always supported by US allies, particularly in Europe, and at the start of the twenty first century the two hostile regimes appeared secure.

Saddam Hussein's hold on power appeared strong.[39] The Iraqi opposition in exile was divided and ineffective, despite support from the US. Using this opposition to overthrow the Iraqi regime, as was advocated in the US in 1998, was a pipe-dream. The opportunity easily to depose Saddam was lost in 1991, when he was allowed to regroup after his army's military defeat. Despite the constraints which that agreement imposed on Iraqi rearmament and the military patrolling of some of its own territory, Saddam refused to cooperate fully with the UN Special Commission on Iraq (UNSCOM), which was responsible for ensuring that Iraq did not produce WMDs.[40] The UN Security Council initially supported UNSCOM, but later it reduced its commitment as France edged towards commercial deals with Baghdad, China and Russia became disenchanted with US hegemony, and China began looking for additional energy supplies. Only the US use or threat of force, with some British, Australian and French assistance and without much support from regional powers, had resulted in Iraqi cooperation with the UN.

The Islamic regime in Teheran steadily consolidated its power. The US hoped that change might come as the generation of 1979 lost its revolutionary impetus. There was a struggle over foreign policy but Iran remained anti-American[41] and the US had only limited success in isolating Iran. Russia started building a nuclear power capacity and continued arms deliveries, and China sold arms to Iran. EU members, India and Japan expanded their economic relations with Iran. GCC states regarded Iran as a security threat, but maintained dialogue with it. But Iranian sponsored radical Shi'ite Islam also appeared to be doing poorly in the mostly Sunni Arab Middle East. In May 1997 the Iranian presidential election was won by the underdog

37 Martin S Indyk, Assistant Secretary for Near Eastern Affairs: remarks at the Council on Foreign Relations New York City, NY, 22 April 1999.

38 Z Brzezinski, Brent Scowcroft, and Richard Murphy, 'Differentiated Containment', *Foreign Affairs,* 76, May/June 1997, pp. 20–30.

39 Daniel Byman, Kenneth Pollack, and Gideon Rose, 'The Rollback Fantasy', *Foreign Affairs,* 78, Jan/Feb 1999, pp. 24–41.

40 Andrew Cockburn and Patrick Cockburn, *Out of the Ashes: The Resurrection of Saddam Hussein* (New York, 1999).

41 Martin S Indyk, Assistant Secretary for Near Eastern Affairs: remarks at the Council on Foreign Relations New York City, 22 April 1999.

moderate candidate, Khatarni, and in 1999 he undertook a state visit to Italy. But in the 2005 election the reform impetus was dramatically reversed.

Iran was also trying to develop nuclear weapons. It already had a substantial inventory of missiles, including 400 SCUDs and SS-8s. It was also developing missiles with the 1,000-km range needed to reach Israel. Iran had also upgraded its naval and air capabilities, including Russian KILO-class submarines, fast-attack craft and patrol boats with missiles, a number of frigates, and had around 300 combat aircraft, of which about 175 were operational. In a conflict with the US, although clearly outmatched, Iran could block shipping through the Strait of Hormuz, interrupt the flow of oil and severely affect world oil markets. It might also arm and activate terrorist groups.

Iraq also remained a potential military threat to US interests. Although reduced by its defeat in the Gulf War and sanctions subsequently imposed by the UN under US direction, Iraq still had an army of over 350,000 with reserves of 650,000, over 2,000 battle tanks, and 4,500 armoured vehicles. Iraq was the dominant land power of the Gulf, although the Saudi Air Force may have been comparable.

The US had an overwhelming ability to win a conventional war with these rogue states, but this might well push them to adopt asymmetric strategies, including WMDs and terrorism. The US wanted these two hostile states to accept US regional hegemony, and to this end it used sanctions and threats against both Iraq and Iran. UNSCOM, therefore, established a monitoring programme to stop Iraq developing WMDs. The US military carried out strikes against Iraq to enforce compliance with UNSCOM demands. In December 1998 it did so amidst allegations that UNSCOM was being used by US intelligence to assist in targeting Iraqi facilities. To slow down the development of Iranian WMDs, the US tried to limit the transfer of technology to Iran, but Iran was able to access Chinese weapons sales.

The US tried to stop state-sponsored terrorism, but this had not stopped attacks on US territory and on US missions, including those in Africa and the Middle East. Many of these were sponsored by Islamic organisations or by rogue states that had developed asymmetric war fighting strategies to oppose US policy in the Middle East. The retaliatory aerial bombardments of Afghanistan and Sudan, ordered by President Clinton in late 1998, were widely viewed outside the US (and by Hollywood[42]) as essentially futile, illiberal and indiscriminate. Sanctions, too, had limited success in persuading these regimes to change policy, although they may have served to reduce the resources Iran and Iraq had with which to purchase modern weapons.

The US tried in the Middle East, particularly under Clinton, to act multilaterally and get allies to support its policies, preferably with military force. But the small GCC states were mostly oil-rich, small population illiberal oligarchies. The Saudi regime was dynastic and feudal and would not pass any liberal human rights test. But these countries contain the richest oil fields in the world. The friendly regional states included, possibly, Egypt, effectively a dictatorship; occasionally Syria, a military regime that supported Desert Storm against Iraq, but would not work with the US; and Israel, which is unacceptable to other regional states.

---

42 See the satirical movie, *Wag the Dog*, 1998.

As a result, the US was particularly keen to get the NATO states to make a contribution to Gulf oil security, but had limited success. French and British forces were involved in the first Gulf War and then undertook over-flights, policing Iraq from Saudi bases. Other European states were more reluctant, hence US urging for a change in NATO's role to a more interventionist posture during the Kosovo War in 1999. US policy in the Middle East, therefore, tended to become more unilateral, even under the Clinton administration, and this habit formed the basis of its regional policy under the more interest-oriented Bush Presidency.

The Protection of Israel

After 1956, the US developed a close strategic relationship with Israel[43] and then underwrote Israeli security. This support often complicated US oil policy in the region. While Israel was a liberal democracy itself, it occupied territory once populated by expelled Palestinian Arabs. Partly as a result, the surrounding Arab states – both those friendly and those opposed to the US – which often hosted large Palestinian refugee communities, were to varying degrees hostile to Israel. The US tried to overcome this dilemma by supporting any and all moves towards peace and reconciliation between Israel and neighbouring Arab states and the PLO. Israel was not, however, a US puppet state and pursued its own interests. When a rightist coalition is in power, Israeli policies are often too strident for US policies of accommodation. Nonetheless, US policy was also to maintain Israel's military advantage over its Arab neighbours. As a result of this policy, threats to Israel's survival have been reduced, but at the cost of allowing Israel to escape other liberal dictates, ethnically cleanse Palestinians, and periodically wage aggressive pre-emptive war against Arab neighbours as it did in 1956, 1967, 1982, and 2006. During the 1973 war between Israel and Egypt, US support enabled Israel to recover after some early defeats.

Yet Israel is the only country in the region that can be considered, even with qualifications, a liberal democracy. Some analysts argue that while the US has provided considerable financial assistance to Israel, this has provided Washington with a reliable ally in the region.[44] But the US commitment to Israel is often in conflict with its other interests in the Middle East, notably the cultivation of friendly Arab regimes to facilitate access to oil. US support for Israel can be explained, therefore, partly by domestic US politics and the pro-Israeli concentration of six million Jewish Americans in the politically vital states of New York, California, and Florida, in the US media and film industry,[45] within the foreign-policy-making elite (at perhaps an all-time record level in Clinton's second administration), and among US university social scientists. Many Jews among the neo-cons only added to this already impressive list.

---

43 D Schoenbaum, *The United States and the State of Israel* (Oxford, 1993).

44 A Organsky, *The $36 Billion Bargain: Strategy and Politics in US Assistance to Israel* (New York, 1991).

45 Neal Gabler, *An Empire of Their Own: How the Jews Invented Hollywood* (New York, 1989).

The US has also developed close relations with several Arab states, especially Saudi Arabia since the 1940s, Egypt since 1979, Jordan since 1995, when it reversed its choice of the losing side in the 1991 Gulf War, and the smaller GCC countries in the 1990s. It wants these quite undemocratic but pro-Western states to be more fully integrated into the liberal world order and has some interest in the political reform of these Middle East regimes. This liberalisation has not, however, been very strongly pursued.

The strongest ideological challenge to liberal democracy – and Israel – in the region comes from radical Islam, which provides a religious basis for opposition to US interests. Since 1979 the Iranian regime has provided succour for regional anti-US and anti-Israeli Shi'ite movements. Radical Arab nationalism was also potent and the Ba'athist Iraqi regime tried to mobilize it in its support. Sunni radicalism was stimulated by the activities of Al Qa'eda. All these political currents run against the US, particularly while it supports Israel.

In April 2003, George W Bush tried to overcome the US dilemma and laid out a 'roadmap' to a final settlement of the Palestinian conflict by 2005, based on two states, Israel and Palestine using the Palestine Authority as the basis. However, progress toward a permanent agreement was undermined by Palestinian-Israeli violence between September 2000 and February 2005. Another agreement was then reached at Sharm al-Sheikh in February 2005 and significantly reduced the violence. The election in January 2005 of Mahmud Abbas as the new Palestinian leader following the November 2004 death of Arafat, the formation of a Likud-Labor-United Torah Judaism Israeli coalition government in January 2005, and the successful Israeli disengagement from the Gaza Strip (August-September 2005), presented an opportunity for a renewed peace effort. However, internal Israeli political events between October and December 2005 destabilised the political situation and forced early elections in March 2006.

In 2002 Ariel Sharon's Likud government built a 640 kilometre long West Bank wall to protect Israel from Palestinian suicide bombers and then evacuated 8,000 Israeli settlers from the Gaza Strip. Sharon said the August 2005 pullout was aimed at making Israel safer to revive an international peace plan. Sharon then left Likud in late 2005 and founded a new party, Kadima, saying peace with the Palestinians and Israeli security would be its main goals. The deputy premier, Ehud Olmert, also left Likud and assumed the powers of Prime Minister when Sharon suffered a stroke in January 2006. In elections in March 2006 Likud suffered heavy losses and Kadima effectively won a slim majority in parliament. Olmert then led a four-party coalition government including the centre-left Labour party and the ultra-orthodox Shas party.

Nonetheless, the PA became more difficult to deal with after the former leader, Yasser Arafat, died in November 2004. Mahmoud Abbas, the Fatah candidate, won the January 2005 poll to replace Arafat. But radical Islamist Hamas was the surprise winner of the Palestinian parliamentary elections in January 2006. Hamas was viewed as terrorist by Israel, the US and the EU and its aim was to drive Israeli forces from the occupied territories through attacks on Israeli troops and civilians. It believed that the Israeli withdrawal from Gaza was a victory for this policy. It also had a long-term aim of establishing an Islamic state on all of historic Palestine.

Hamas inflicted many casualties on the Israelis, although it also lost many of its leaders to Israeli assassinations and security sweeps. The decision to stand in the 2006 Palestinian elections was a major departure for Hamas that challenged the Al Fatah-dominated Palestinian Authority that was corrupt, inefficient and lacking popular support. An Arab electorate had used the democratic process to elect Islamists. Hamas' armed wing remained the epitome of the 'terrorist infrastructure' which the PA needed to dismantle under the 'roadmap'. Attempts to form a unity government between Fatah and Hamas in late 2006 failed.

In 2006 Hezbollah supported Hamas with attacks on northern Israel and in July 2006 Israel waged a military campaign against Hezbollah guerrillas in Lebanon. Israel claimed the offensive destroyed much of Hezbollah's weaponry and infrastructure but the operation actually produced a stalemate and Israeli withdrawal.

Policing US Interests in the Middle East

The US pursuit of a liberal world order involved policing its interests in the Middle East with whatever instruments, including force and illiberal regimes, were to hand. It deployed sufficient forces to reverse attacks by any potential Middle East rogue state trying to threaten the US control over Gulf oil. This policy was complicated by the US security guarantee for Israel to which NATO allies were less committed. The key instrument for Israeli security was the US commitment to Israel's technological superiority, accomplished through technology transfer and military aid.

The US military also had to be concerned about two other war scenarios involving the Gulf: a land attack by Iraq or a naval attack by Iran and it continually demonstrated its ability to respond to such actions. The Gulf monarchies could not defend themselves, despite arms deliveries to GCC countries running at about $10 billion a year at the beginning of the twenty first century. So after the 1991 Gulf War the US maintained its own military superiority in the Gulf. Its plans included being able to defend its interests in the Gulf with sufficient air and naval power projection so that little onshore permanently-based, military US presence was needed. Because of Islamic and Arab sensitivities to a permanent US military presence, the demonstration of power projection had to be convincing enough to deter offensives by Iran or Iraq, but without a permanent presence so large as to destabilize local populations into radical anti-US activities.

Thus, the US relied heavily on pre-positioned equipment and a large naval force, including carriers on rotated permanent station, to demonstrate its ability to move quickly into the area. Several thousand airmen were also based in Saudi Arabia to patrol Iraq after Desert Storm, but the US did not construct any permanent facilities. These measures were needed to reassure the major oil-importing liberal democracies, particularly in Europe and East Asia, about access to oil. In the Gulf, the US wanted to show that it would repel aggression but also avoid scaring the locals. The US military also continued to enforce whatever sanctions it could persuade the UN to impose on its adversaries in the Middle East. The US was the main participant in the Multinational Interdiction Force (MW) that monitored ship traffic in and out of Iraq. The US Navy provided on average ten ships dedicated full-time to this mission. But the US also hoped to induce Iran and Iraq to modify their stance by use of economic restrictions.

The principal US military policies in the Middle East during and since the Cold War were to project its own power into the region and arm its allies. The principal instruments were a naval presence in the Gulf and nearby waters, extensive use of pre-positioned but small forces, temporary deployment of units, and arms transfers and reserves of air and land power from its European deployments and ultimately from the US mainland itself. The level of the direct US presence was continuously adjusted to meet the threats to US interests, with the goal being to deter, not just respond to threats. The US military presence was in early 2001 an average of 25,000 personnel. The US military was also involved in large-scale arms sales to the Middle East, mostly to Saudi and GCC states. The US also sold arms to Israel and Egypt after the Camp David peace treaty and in light of the US commitment to maintain Israel's qualitative superiority over Arab states.

Very little of this US activity in the Middle East was couched in terms of liberal values. The post-Second World War liberal international order was built on cheap and accessible oil, much of it from the Middle East. The US persistently sought to ensure this access by whatever means were necessary. Its only democratic ally in the Middle East was Israel which, because it is also a recent settler nation, remains a pariah state among the other states of the region. In the Middle East, the US was a geopolitical superpower with little liberal ideological camouflage.

But, partly because of these US policies, after the Cold War there emerged from the Middle East and West Asia, a new and spreading Jihadist anti-modernisation and anti-US movement determined to expunge the West, led by America, from their societies. It started in Saudi Arabia, was nurtured in Sudan and Afghanistan, and by 2006 it appeared that 'terrorism central' was in northwest Pakistan.[46] A world that hoped for peace and prosperity from the 'peace dividend' at the end of the Cold War faced more, not less, anxiety, disorder and conflict.

46 Stephen Cohen, *The Idea of Pakistan* (Washington DC, 2004).

Chapter 5

Prelude to War

The defining policy of the Bush administration has been its Global War on Terror and its associated invasions of Afghanistan and Iraq. The crucial characteristic of its opponents in these wars has been that they are Muslim, although other competitors have taken advantage of US distractions. Four non-Islamic nations were seriously involved in the invasion of Iraq and the subsequent overthrow of Saddam Hussein's regime – namely, the US, Britain, Australia and Poland, all secular Christian states. Three other nations gave strong diplomatic support to the Coalition in the lead-up to the invasion – Spain, Portugal and Italy – and around forty others made some form of commitment. These initial alignments were determined before 11 September 2001.

Modernisation: Islam, Christianity and Judaism

Many preconditions for modernisation – education, female equality, developed infrastructure, work oriented cultural patterns, democracy, free press, innovative and adaptable institutions and capital markets – all make it difficult for Islamic nations, and other nations with strong traditional religious structures, to modernise. By the twenty first century most of the rich OECD countries were secular Christian, including those of Europe, North America and Australasia although not all developed countries were secular Christian since they included South Korea, Singapore and Japan. Also, many secular Christian nations were not wealthy including most in Africa and many in South America.

Almost all Muslim nations, on the other hand, were poor and underdeveloped. Where they had higher levels of per capita income this was usually drawn from rent on resources, mostly oil, as in Saudi Arabia and the smaller Gulf states. The only Muslim nations to have successfully approached the task of modernisation are Turkey and Malaysia. In Malaysia nearly half the population is non-Muslim and much of its economic success comes mostly from its Chinese entrepreneurial class; even Muslim anti-Western nationalists, such as the former Prime Minister Mahathir, charged that indigenous Muslims in Malaysia have inferior economic skills compared to the Chinese in Malaysia even after decades of favouritism by his government to the Malay Muslim population. The great success of other East Asia cultures rests partly on the absence of a bureaucratic and theocratic religious structures and the capacity of Buddhism, Shinto-ism and Confucianism to adapt to modernisation; adaptation that Islam, in which the civil state is pushed to be coterminous with religious bureaucratic structures, under Koranic law inhibits.[1]

Three religions figure prominently in the GWOT: Islam, Christianity and Judaism. Although many Muslims maintain that Islam and Christianity have ninety per cent of their religious doctrines in common, and strictly speaking this may be true, it is also very misleading. Judaism is the foundation of both and is the religion of a nation of people, the Jews, who settled over three thousand years ago in the area of what is now Israel/Palestine. Now, about half of the world's Jews again live there. Judaism holds there is one God, whose chosen people are the Jews. Their religious authorities transcribed their history in the *Torah* – for Christians effectively the Old Testament of the *Bible* – and their beliefs in the *Talmud* which prescribes appropriate forms of worship, behaviour and laws. The Jews were conquered by the Romans in the first century BCE and revolted against Rome's imperial rule on a number of occasions, often under the leadership of religious mystics. Jesus Christ was, for the Jews, one such minor mystic whose doctrines as now received advocated spiritual emancipation rather than military resistance to Roman rule, for which proselytising he was in any case crucified. For Christians the New Testament of the *Bible,* dealing chiefly with the teachings and life of Christ – the Gospels – forms the basis for their religious beliefs, but has no standing for Jews who were subject to dispersal by the Romans to Asia and Europe after the destruction of Jerusalem in first century CE.[2]

Christianity, having become the official religion of the Roman Empire in 313 CE, survived the Empire and, indeed, according to Gibbon anyway,[3] may have contributed to its downfall by weakening its martial spirit, to become by the Middle Ages the dominant religion of the European area from Ireland to Russia. But it retained at its core the idea of the separation of that which is Caesar's from that which is God's – or the beginnings of the separation of Church and state. It also had a core doctrine of human emancipation and equality devised at a time of resistance to very effective Roman imperial rule and repression. Nonetheless, it was periodically used by secular authorities to justify order, repression and wars until in the twentieth century it rather suddenly experienced a sharp decline in spiritual adherents in most countries of European culture, although its secular impact on them remained strong into the twenty first century. European culture became predominantly 'secular Christianity'. The exception to this pattern was the US which, having been established by refugees

1 For an incisive analysis on the central (but very politically incorrect view) role of culture in economic development see Lawrence E Harrison, *The Central Liberal Truth: How Politics Can Change a Culture and Save It from Itself* (Oxford, 2007). Comprehensive data reveals the difficulties strongly religious societies have in modernizing in general, and Muslim societies in particular, and this can also be seen in the *Failed States Index* published by the Fund for Peace in which the 146 nations surveyed revealed no Muslim nations among the world's top 40 most stable, but among the worst 40 there were 13 Muslim nations: http:www.fundforpeace.org/programs/fsi/fsindex2006.php

2 Neil Faulkner, *Apocalypse: the Great Jewish Revolt Against Rome, AD 66–73* (London, 2004).

3 Edward Gibbon, *The History of the Decline and Fall of the Roman Empire*, London, Volume I, 1776, final volume in 1788.

from England with a powerful religious ideology, remains into the twenty first century strongly Christian.

In their Diaspora, the Jews settled in most of the Roman Empire, and indeed beyond. They were defined by religious practice rather than ethnicity, but their capacity to survive as a cultural and later national entity was truly astonishing.[4] This, together with the compatibility of their religious teachings with commercial operations and the emphasis they placed on education, led to their being an identifiably prosperous, often business-oriented minority in many of the countries from the Atlantic to the Urals and the Indian Ocean by the Middle Ages.

The Islamic religion was founded in the chaos and disorder that characterised the region now known as Saudi Arabia in the seventh century CE. Its Prophet, Muhammad, (570–632CE) was born at Mecca to a family of the declining Quraysh tribe and then worked as a trader. When he was twenty five he married a wealthy widow Khadija, showed an interest in spiritual matters and spent time on retreat in the cave of Hira on 'The Mountain of Light' near Mecca. In 610 Muhammad said he had a vision of the Archangel Gabriel, who told him that he was to be a prophet. These revelations continued over many years during which Muhammad received the text of what became *The Koran.*[5] He claimed that *The Koran* was the last Book of God and that he was the last Prophet. He spread his message and condemned the existing local beliefs and religious customs. By 613 Muhammad had many converts and in 622 Muhammad moved to Medina with seventy followers. This is known as the 'Hijrah' – 'emigration' – and there Muhammad formed a tribe of those who accepted him as the Prophet. Gradually Islam – 'submission' – grew and its armies fought thirty eight battles and greatly expanded Muhammad's power base before he died at Medina.[6]

The Islamic power expanded at the expense of its fellow monotheistic religions Judaism and Christianity at an astonishing speed and within a century had defeated the Christian Byzantine and Sassanid Persian empires and seized much of their territories. The resulting Caliphate, centred on Damascus but extending from Spain to Iraq, was the first model for an Islamic state. The Caliphate was subsequently weakened by internal schisms, mostly caused by the usual divisions of politics and competing interests. This also generated the great Shi'ite-Sunni doctrinal split over the legitimate succession to Muhammad, which later pitted Persians against Arabs. Much of this and subsequent Islamic expansion into Central Asia and northern India, was by military means, followed by a form of rule which privileged Muslims and led to the gradual conversion of the ruled. Islamic expansion created states ruled by Muslims where previously there had been Christians, Jews, Persians, Hindus or people of other religions. Islam often also created order out of chaos and to that extent alone may have offered substantial improvements to the form of life enjoyed within the Levant and then surrounding areas. It may also have been a quite rational improvement on existing beliefs for, say, the lower castes in the very hierarchical

---

4 Paul Johnson, *A History of the Jews* (London, 1988).

5 Thomas Cleary, *The Essential Koran* (San Francisco, 1994).

6 Karen Armstrong, *Muhammad: A Biography of the Prophet* (San Francisco, 1991), provides a balanced account; and see also Bruce Lawrence, *The Qur'an* (New York, 2006).

Hindu world. Islam was spread to Southeast Asia by the fourteenth century mostly by conversion along the Arab trade routes, but there were also some conquests involved. It was stopped in Europe only by force, initially by the army of Charles Martel at Tours in 732 and was contained to the Spanish peninsula where the Al-Andalus Caliphate was created.

The Arab peoples have a particular attachment to Islam since it was in Arabic that Gabriel's message was conveyed, in Arabic that the *Koran* was written, and it was the Arabic language that spread with the early Islamic conquests.[7] Although not all Arabs are Islamic, it is at the heart of their civilisation, and the core of Islam is the Arab arc from Syria, through Palestine to Morocco in the west, Saudi Arabia and Sudan to the south, and Iraq to the east. Its most holy sites are also now in Saudi Arabia, Iraq and Israel. It has been argued that there was greater tolerance of other religions, including Judaism, under Islamic rule than in the Christian states. But this comparison likely depends on time and place. After the initial Islamic expansion both sides of the Christian-Islamic conflict became zealous, and the Christian Crusades were undertaken from the tenth century to retake lands recently lost to Islam by military conquest and by the same military means.[8] The resulting Crusader states in the Levant lasted a similar period to the Al-Andalus Caliphate, a few centuries. But their eviction involved much hostility, doctrinal purifications and military blood letting on both sides.

By the thirteenth century, the initial expansive impulses of Arab Islam had been exhausted and it then only revived under new, Turkish leadership. Migrating from Central Asia to Anatolia, the Ottoman Turks took military service in the Caliphate and converted to Islam. They later established their own state, expanded throughout the Levant, besieged, conquered and sacked Constantinople, the last capital of the Christian Roman Empire, in 1436 renaming it Istanbul, and became an imperial system under some splendidly talented Sultans. Much of their imperial domain was over the Arabs, but they also acquired large portions of southeast Europe where some of the population also converted to Islam.

Interpreting the *Koran* is difficult.[9] It does not mark off specific passages, its 114 chapters (*suras*) are not laid out in chronological order and keys to understanding it are to be found in the Sunnah, the life of Mohammad. The sources for the Sunnah are the traditions (hadiths), of which Sunnis recognise six canonical collections, and biographies of Mohammad (sira literature). This work is mostly available in English, much of it on the internet. It is clear that some Koranic verses encourage violence: 'Fighting is prescribed upon you, and you dislike it. But it may happen that you dislike a thing which is good for you, and it may happen that you love a thing which is bad for you. And Allah knows and you know not'. (2:216) On the other hand, it is equally clear that there are peaceful verses as well, including the famous declaration there is 'no compulsion in religion' (2:256). Muslims do not agree today on how best

7 Albert Hourani, *A History of the Arab Peoples* (New York, 2002).

8 See Geoffrey Hindley, *A Brief History of the Crusades: Islam and Christianity in the Struggle for World Supremacy* (London, 2003); and for the wider context, Andrew Wheatcroft, *Infidels: A History of the Conflict between Christendom and Islam* (New York, 2004).

9 Bruce Lawrence, *The Qur 'an* (New York, 2006) is extremely good on this.

to address these contradictions. Nevertheless, a near consensus developed early in the history of Islam about a doctrine known as abrogation, which states that verses revealed later – when Islam was a secular military power – are generally superior to verses revealed earlier.

The classical approach to violence in the *Koran* was stated by Sheikh Abdullah bin Muhammad bin Hamid, former chief justice of Saudi Arabia: 'So at first "the fighting" was forbidden, then it was permitted and after that it was made obligatory: (1) against those who start "the fighting" against you (Muslims) ... (2) And against all those who worship others along with Allah'. At the beginning, in Mohammad's Meccan period, when he was weaker, passages of the Koran encouraged peaceful relations and avoidance of conflict: 'Invite (all) to the way of your Lord with wisdom and beautiful preaching; and argue with them in ways that are best and most gracious'. (16:125) Later, after surviving persecution and migrating to Medina, authority was given to engage in warfare for defensive purposes only: 'Fight in the path of God those who fight you, but do not transgress limits, for God does not love transgressors'. (2:190) As the Muslim community grew stronger, further revelations expanded the licence for waging war, until in Sura 9, regarded as one of the last revealed, concludes that war against non-Muslims could be waged more or less at any time and in any place to extend the dominance of Islam. Sura 9 distinguished idolators, who were to be fought until they converted – 'When the sacred months are past, kill the idolators wherever you find them, and seize them, and besiege them, and lie in wait for them in every place of ambush' (Sura 9:5) – from 'People of the Book' (Christians and Jews), who were to be given the option of surrendering and living under Islamic rule while keeping their religion: 'Fight ... the People of the Book until they pay the poll tax out of hand, having been humbled' (Sura 9:29).

The resulting doctrine of war was described by the medieval philosopher Ibn Khaldun: 'In the Muslim community, the holy war (Jihad) is a religious duty, because of the universalism of the (Muslim) mission and the (obligation to) convert everybody to Islam either by persuasion or by force'. In the twenty first century most Muslims acknowledge the religious legitimacy of 'defensive Jihad' but others appear to reject the idea of offensive, expansionist Jihad. Most would emphasise the defensive aspects of Mohammad's numerous military campaigns, claiming that his attacks on others were only to pre-empt future aggression against Muslims. However the idea of a purely defensive Jihad hardly describes the phenomenal military expansion of Islam in its first 1000 years when the validity of expansionist Jihad just seemed self-evident, as it was validated by military victories across the greater part of the Christian world, as well as Zoroastrian Persia and Hindu India.

The Ottoman Empire then became the greatest of the Islamic states and menaced Christian Europe for several centuries, besieging Vienna most recently in 1689. At its apogee in the fifteenth century it may have been the most powerful and advanced state in the Eurasian region in terms of culture, science, military prowess and even oceanic trade and navigation. Many of the national boundaries that now exist in the Arab world were, in fact, imperial Turkish administrative divisions. But the Ottomans began a long period of decline in the eighteenth century and were unable to match the rapid technological, economic and military progress of Europe. After two centuries as the Sick Man of Europe, the Ottoman Empire then fatally chose the wrong side in the First World War and was defeated by Arab and European revolts, a British invasion and a coup by Kemil Ataturk. After 1918, it was transformed into a secular national republic with a deeply Islamic population, and its former imperial possessions were chiefly divided by Britain and France.

Between the world wars most Arabs were ruled by the British and French, often under Mandates from the League of Nations which required them to cultivate the creation of independent Arab states. They drew useful state boundaries and established kingdoms that suited their interests. After the Second World War many of these monarchies gave way to the more revolutionary doctrines that had been imbibed: Egypt established a nationalist military regime in 1954; Syria and Iraq passed into Ba'athist (neo-Nazi) rule; a colonel seized Libya; socialist revolutionaries took Algeria from the French; and Yemen became a people's republic. But, like the monarchies that survived in Saudi Arabia, Jordan, Kuwait, Morocco and the Gulf States, these states were often corrupt, usually repressive and rarely brought much improvement in the condition of the mass of the population except briefly during the oil boom of the 1970s before population growth devoured the proceeds.[10] But the repressive state apparatuses often did grow strong. Geo-political competition between the great powers, particularly during the Cold War, enabled the newly sovereign states to look for the best suppliers of arms, aid and doctrines. They had the choice of the US, the Soviet Union, several European powers, and, later, China. What made their choices all the more important was the discovery and development of vast oil fields in the region. Significant reserves of oil had been found by the 1920s in Persia and Iraq, and these were later supplemented by even larger finds in Saudi Arabia and the smaller Gulf states.

Persia was converted to Islam after the Arabs defeated the Sassanid empire in the seventh century but had regained independent statehood in the late Middle Ages. In 1923 a colonel seized the Peacock throne and as Shah claimed heritage to a 2,500 year old dynasty, renaming the country Iran in 1933. He developed pro-German sentiments and the British ousted him in favour of his son in 1941. Using the Anglo-Iranian oil company (later British Petroleum) the British developed the state and its oil resources, until a modest revolution and CIA-sponsored counter coup took Iran into the American orbit in the mid-1950s. Under Shah Pahlavi, Iran then became a major power in the region and by the 1970s the US hoped Iran would be the major guarantor for the flow of oil. Unfortunately for the Americans, the Shah's regime was toppled in 1979 by what was the first successful fundamentalist Islamic movement of the modern era.

The success of the Iranian Mullahs, led by Ayatollah Khomeini, was chiefly due to the alienation of a large proportion of the population from the modernising regime of the Shah. At heart, it was an anti-modernisation revolt. Social and economic change confronted a traditional Islamic society and the clerics led a successful revolt in the name of Islamic stability. At a critical juncture, the Carter administration refused to assist in repressing the rebellion and the Shah fled. A powerful state with a large population, ample military hardware and vast oil reserves fell into hands hostile to

10 Eli Kedourie, *Politics of the Middle East* (New York, 1992).

the US and its protectorates, including Israel, Saudi Arabia, and the smaller Gulf States. It also fell foul of neighbouring Iraq.

Iraq was created during the British mandate out of several Turkish administrative regions often known collectively as Mesopotamia – Kurdish Mosul, Sunni Baghdad and Shi'ite Basra. The British established Feisal as King of the new state and enforced his rule, including by aerial bombardment, when his subjects revolted against him. Oil was discovered and exploited in the region before the Second World War and the British seemed likely to guarantee the monarchy after the mandate expired in 1932. But in 1968 the Ba'athists seized power in a violent coup and established a military regime with both leftist and fascist characteristics, and dependent on the Sunni Muslims who comprised only twenty per cent of the population. There ensued a period of internal conflict until Saddam Hussein killed his rivals and established himself as leader of the Ba'athists and President of the country in 1979. The Iraqi Ba'athist regime moved towards the Soviet Union, acquired a considerable military machine mostly from that source and moved to expand its sphere of influence in the Gulf against its main rival Iran in 1980. The US opposed the Islamist Iranians dominating the Gulf and its oil fields, and so provided assistance to Iraq in the form of intelligence acquired from their satellite systems and some military equipment. This prevented an Iranian victory in the Iraq-Iranian War that ended in stalemate in 1988.

Iraq was, nonetheless, emboldened and two years later invaded and annexed Kuwait in August 1990 in pursuit of the massive oil reserves of Kuwait, improved maritime access, and a staging point for further expansion into Saudi Arabia, whose oil provinces are immediately adjacent to Kuwait. Iraq was only supported by the oil poor states of Jordan and Yemen, and the Palestine Liberation Organisation. Iraq may also have mis-read American signals and expected its neutrality after its recent behaviour over Iran. In fact the US reacted decisively, deployed half a million troops with associated equipment into Saudi-Arabia, organised a diplomatic coalition in opposition to Iraq and got a string of UN resolutions in favour of evicting Iraqi forces from Kuwait. In March 1991 this military coalition led by the US evicted Iraq from Kuwait, and destroyed much of its armed forces in the process.

Nonetheless, the post-war settlement left the defeated Ba'athist regime in power because the UN would not provide for a resolution to seize Baghdad and install another government, since this would have provided a dangerous precedent for many UN member states. Instead, sanctions were imposed which prevented the Iraqi air force from overflying much of the north and south of the country and effectively made the Kurdish north independent. Iraq's trade in oil was then regulated to limited oil exports to be used for buying food and other essential commodities and the UN empowered force comprising mostly Americans was established to police this. The power projection capabilities of the Ba'athist regime gradually eroded under these conditions, although it remained a potent repressive force. In 1991 it put down an internal rebellion that American rhetoric had emboldened but American policy did not support. It also supplied rewards to families of suicide bombers dying while attacking Israel.

Israel and Zionism

The ideas of nationalism that swept Europe in the nineteenth century also had their impact on the Jewish people. The major centres of the Jewish Diaspora were in Europe and the Arab countries and one school of thought among them evolved into Zionism which favoured the creation of a Jewish state in the historic homeland of Israel. At that time the area was Palestine, a province of the Ottoman Empire, mostly peopled by Arabs and encompassing Jerusalem, Judaism's most Holy site. By the early twentieth century Jews were migrating to the region in pursuit of the Zionist goal.

During the First World War, and as the Ottoman Empire was disintegrating, the future of its territories came on to the strategic agenda. In effect, the advancing British power, confident of victory promised the territory to two parties and then arguably delivered to neither. The UK government, desperate for finance to prosecute the war, assured Jewish bankers they would treat their Zionist ambitions for Palestine with sympathy. The British armies, advancing from Egypt towards Damascus and with Colonel Laurence encouraging an Arab insurrection, at the same time promised the creation of independent Arab states. As this was happening, the British also agreed to divide the greater Levant with their French allies on the basis of Britain getting what became mostly Palestine, Israel, Jordan, Iraq and Kuwait, and the French acquiring greater Syria. This Sikes-Picot agreement of 1916 was then endorsed by the League of Nations, which placed these territories under British and French mandates as agreed.

The French then effectively divided their mandate into two states which they took to independence: Syria, an ancient polity in its own right; and Lebanon, a small state contrived to give a numerical majority to the Christian community which had survived thirteen centuries of Islamic regional domination. Even then, a superior Muslim growth rate soon eliminated the Christian advantage. This left both states with little oil and a simmering Syrian claim on Lebanese sovereignty. After the Syrian Ba'athist regime was established by a coup in 1963 this claim was pursued, but like its Iraqi secular counterpart it had to repress Islamism in the process. In 1982 Syrian artillery surrounded Hamah when Muslim Brotherhood rebels seized it, and in the ensuing bombardment killed perhaps twenty thousand people.

The British problem was more difficult to resolve. After 1919 Jewish migrants began to flow into Palestine and the flow increased in the 1930s when the Nazis took over Germany. This migration produced riots among the resident Arab population who feared losing their lands. After 1945 the flow of Jewish migrants became a flood and the British tried to stem the inflow since it was causing deepening unrest among the Arabs. By 1947 this was too much to control for the British, then beset with both Jewish and Arab armed and terrorist hostility towards British rule. They announced they would withdraw from the mandated authority and leave an independent state. The UN voted for a division of the territory of Palestine, effectively between the Jewish populated and the Arab populated areas. This polarized the Arab and Jewish populations and civil conflict ensued with the Palestinians backed by contiguous Arab states. The resulting Arab defeat produced an Arab Diaspora as well as a large Arab population left within the new state of Israel. The Israeli Jewish population was augmented by millions of Jews expelled from neighbouring Arab countries.

After its creation in 1948 Israel was at war with all its extremely hostile Arab and Islamic neighbours. This political hostility was fuelled by the *Koran*'s injunctions to destroy Jews who oppose Islam and to defend Islamic territory against infidels. It was kept alive by millions of Arab Palestinian refugees scattered mostly through the Arab countries but also present in Europe, the US and Australia. It was fired by the continuing geo-political conflict between Israel and neighbouring states. This conflict has broken into open war on six occasions: the Israeli war for independence, 1947–8; the Anglo-French-Israeli attack on Egypt in 1956; the Six Day War of 1967; the Yom Kippur War of 1973; the Israeli invasion and then occupation of southern Lebanon, 1982–2000; and the war against Hezbellah and Hamas in 2006.

In the intervals between these wars, Israel fought a low intensity conflict against Palestinian insurgents supported by some of its neighbours. The Jewish state, heavily armed mostly by the US since 1967, emerged victorious in all these conflicts but it paid a heavy price in terms of its internal security. During that time several of its surrounding neighbours, including Egypt in 1979, Jordan in 1994 and the Palestinian Authority in 1993, but not Syria or Iran, have with great reluctance accepted peace terms with Israel that have usually involved substantial financial aid from Israel's patron, the US. But the Arab populations have not been as ready as their political masters to come to terms, and popular hostility towards Israel is rampant throughout the region.

During the Cold War, the Soviet Union used this hostility to cultivate many of the Arab regimes and to this end turned from being a supporter of the nascent Jewish socialist state in 1948, to being one of its major opponents by the late 1950s. It then armed and supported several of the radical regimes that replaced the monarchies installed and supported by the Europeans, notably in Egypt, Syria, Iraq, Libya, Yemen, briefly Ethiopia and then Somalia and the PLO. In Christmas 1978 it took this policy a stage further when it invaded Afghanistan in support of a pro-Soviet regime threatened by an Islamic insurgency.

The Arc of Crisis

Against this background Washington policy makers began discussing the 'Arc of Crisis', a region stretching from Libya to Afghanistan. Most of the people in this Arc were and are poor and Islamic. The reaction of the Carter administration to the Soviet invasion was pivotal. It moved from pursuing détente with the Soviet Union, to attempting to prevent Moscow's global strategic offensive. Carter said that the invasion had a greater impact on him that any other single event. In 1980 the US moved again to a strategy of containing Soviet power rather than accommodating to it, which had become its major prescription since its defeat in Vietnam. Critical to this was the defence of the Persian Gulf, its oil fields and the trade routes carrying the oil to the world economy. It was in this context that both the neo-conservative movement and the terrorist organisation, Al Qaeda came into being.

In the post Vietnam War period US strategy was to defend the oil trade, protect Israel and prevent the Soviet Union from making further incursions into the Arc of Crisis. At first, it relied heavily on Iran under the Shah to dominate the Gulf. The increased oil revenues allowed the Shah to purchase a vast military arsenal which the US was only too happy to sell to him. This strategy faltered when internal revolution took the Iranian state into extremely hostile hands. This was only exacerbated by the taking of hostages from the US embassy by Islamic terrorists – one of whom in 2005 became President Ahmadinejad – who held them until after the 1980 US election, thereby probably ensuring Carter's defeat. A botched rescue attempt only worsened the matter.

The US then had to depend on an array of local forces including, briefly, Iraq when it waged war on Islamist Iran. It also stepped up the provision of arms to Saudi Arabia, but the Kingdom lacked the population base and its regime the popular support required for being a regional gendarme. The US had to use its own forces to defend the oil. But stationing US forces anywhere in the Arab/Islamic world invited popular hostility. This was only confirmed when 241 US marines were killed by a suicide bombing in Lebanon in 1982. Nonetheless, the situation was dire and the issue urgent. The US pre-positioned troops and military equipment in Saudi Arabia, to undertake a holding operation in the event of hostile incursion until reinforcements could be provided. The first would come from US forces stationed off shore on a fleet of thirty vessels and over twenty thousand personnel with a back up base in Diego Garcia. Finally, a Rapid Deployment Force of air and sea-borne forces was developed in the US. After the Cold War ended, indeed, the entire US military forces were developed with this strategic end in view. Nonetheless, the exposure of US forces to serious casualty rates still risked the kind of domestic upheaval which lost the US the Vietnam War.

The US also attempted to broker deals with the Arab states that involved essentially large US financial bribes in exchange for their recognition of Israel and abandoning the anti-US cause. Such an arrangement was first made with Sadat of Egypt in 1979 and although Sadat was assassinated by Islamic radicals for so acting and the arrangement was not popular, it was sustained under his successor, Hosni Mubarak. Similar arrangements were made with Jordan in 1995, the PLO in 1993, Yemen, and even less successfully Sudan. Although the arrangements often brought peace to the fronts concerned, they were fragile because they were rarely popular and made with authoritarian and corrupt regimes with little popular legitimacy. Finally, the US provided considerable support for the Afghan Islamic insurgency in an attempt to make it into the Soviets' Vietnam. In this, the US succeeded spectacularly well in the short term, but suffered considerably from the results of the policy into the next century. Much of this aid entered through Pakistan.

Pakistan

Pakistan was created as an explicitly Islamic state in 1947–8 when religious violence broke out in British India between Muslims and others, mostly Hindus. India became a secular, reasonably democratic Republic, with over one hundred and fifty million Muslim citizens. Pakistan was predominantly Muslim and only very occasionally democratic. In 1971 its eastern half became independent as Bangladesh. In 2006 Pakistan had a population of over 165 million, ninety seven per cent of whom are

Muslim (Sunni 77 per cent, Shi'ite 20 per cent). It has an area of 803,940 square kilometres with the flat Indus plain in the east, difficult mountains in the north and northwest and the Baluchistan plateau in west. This makes its habitable regions very crowded (and poor), while the mountains are inaccessible and more empty.

The country has been mostly run by the military which declared a constitution in April 1973 that was suspended in July 1977, restored with amendments 30 December 1985, suspended again in October 1999, restored again in stages in 2002 and amended 31 December 2003. Following the military takeover in 1999, the Chief of Army Staff, General Pervez Musharraf suspended the constitution and became Chief Executive. In June 2001, Musharraf named himself president and a referendum in April 2002 extended his presidency by five more years. The military rules the country, but the *ulema* or Muslim clergy, landowners, industrialists and small merchants are also influential.

India and Pakistan also fought two wars – in 1947–48 and 1965 – over the disputed territory of Kashmir. In a third war between these countries in 1971 India effectively created Bangladesh out of East Pakistan. In response to India testing nuclear weapons, Pakistan conducted its own tests in 1998. The dispute over the state of Kashmir continues, and despite decreased tensions since 2002 has fuelled the creation of Islamist terrorist groups in Pakistan. Kashmir remains the site of the world's largest and most militarized territorial dispute with portions under the de facto administration of China, India, and Pakistan. The combination of its Islamic origins, extensive poverty and continuing disputes with secular India has made Pakistan a breeding ground for Muslim extremists, especially through its Madrasahs.

Following the Soviet invasion of Afghanistan in 1979, adjacent Pakistan became a major support centre for the Islamic resistance. Its secret service (ISI) effectively set up what became the Taliban movement and it provided a conduit for arms supplies to the Islamic fighters. This was a vital contribution to their struggle, particularly heat seeking portable missiles that were supplied by the US and used to offset Soviet helicopter gunships. After that war Pakistan retained links with the Taliban regime although Musharraf himself had little interest in the establishment of a similar militant extremist state in Pakistan and suppressed its supporters. They in turn made various attempts on his life. After 9/11 the US wanted to retaliate against the Taliban; Musharraf agreed to align with the US and was rewarded with considerable financial aid. But even after some strong subsequent growth Pakistan's GDP PPP in 2005 was around $400 billion or, at exchange rate, $89.55 billion, and with its per capita income PPP of $2,400, its people remain extremely poor. Radical Islam continued to flourish with wide popular sympathy for Islamic terrorist movements like the Taliban (especially in the northwest) and extreme Islamic Jihadism was nurtured in the madrasahs.

Bangladesh took a similar path with an intermittently democratic state, massive corruption and world leading poverty. By 2006 Islamic extremists were very active and widespread, and there was increasing speculation that the country's military chief was planning a coup d'etat.[11] In April 2007 former prime minister Sheikh

11 Bruce Loudon, 'General looks to grab power in Bangladesh', *The Australian*, 13 April 2007.

Hasina stayed in the US rather than return to face murder charges over the killing of political opponents from Jamaat Islami, the country's biggest Islamic party, during widespread rioting in the capital in October 2006. Bangladesh's army chief, General Moin Ahmed, appeared to be forcing the country's leading politicians into exile as Musharraf forced Benazir Bhutto into exile when he seized power in 1999. The prosecutor of six Islamic terrorists who were hanged was shot dead as he left a mosque. These hangings enraged Islamisists from the growing but outlawed Jamaat-ul-Mujahideen and Siddikul Islam Bangla Bhai groups fighting for shariah law. Bangladesh is governed under emergency rule by technocrats appointed by the leading politicians and in effect backed by the military, but a new poll was unlikely until 2009. This was also a sharp setback for the US, who was trying to resoolve Bangladesh's longstanding crisis.

Madrasahs

In Pakistan, as elsewhere in poor Islamic countries, radical Islam is spread through the madrasahs or private Islamic schools. Although they provide a general education, they also teach the fundamentals of the Islamic religion. A typical madrasah usually offers two courses of study: a 'hifz' course of memorising the *Koran*; and an 'alim' course to become a scholar. The regular curriculum might also include courses in Arabic, Tafsir or interpretation of the Koran, shariah, or Islamic law, Hadith, including the sayings and deeds of Prophet Muhammad, and Muslim History. Some madrasahs also offer additional advanced courses in Arabic literature, English, and other foreign languages as well as science and world history. People of any age can attend although most start young, and some become imams.

There are approximately 10,000 madrasahs in Pakistan, and while only a small percentage of Pakistani school age children are enrolled in traditional madrasahs, this may be as many as one million children. Due to their radical political indoctrination of students and the simple teachings of Islam, the madrasahs are frequently ideological and political training grounds for hatred against the West. In Pakistan, in particular, there is a heavy emphasis on religious teachings. Many of the Taliban cadres were educated in Saudi-financed madrasahs in Pakistan that taught Wahhabism, a particularly austere and rigid form of Islam which is rooted in Saudi Arabia. Around the world, Saudi's new oil wealth and charities contributed to an explosive growth of madrasahs, particularly during the Afghan Jihad against the Soviets. During that war, a new kind of madrasah emerged in the Pakistan-Afghanistan region that was concerned chiefly with making war on infidels. This was perhaps understandable when the near enemy then was the Soviet Union occupying a neighbouring and Islamic country. But more recently the anger has been directed towards America.

One of the aims of the madrasahs has always been to counter heresies within the Islamic faith as well as to resist outside influence which might challenge Islam. Other religions are refuted in the study of 'comparative religions', but there are specific books for heresies within the Islamic world. The earliest madrasahs refuted alien philosophies especially classical Greek philosophy which was seen as intellectually challenging Islam. Since the rise of the West, madrasahs have concentrated on refuting Western philosophies and use books which refute capitalism, socialism and feudalism. They also go to great lengths to make the students aware of Western domination, the exploitative potential of Western political and economic ideas, and the disruptive influence of Western ideas of liberty and individualism on Muslim societies. These are often assisted by western Left literature with which Islamism now shares 'anti-imperialist' ideas.

The madrasahs, then, remain potential centres of Islamic militancy and terrorism in Pakistan and, where radical clerics control them, throughout the world, including in Indonesia, London and Australia. Earlier democratic Pakistan governments wanted to change this by teaching secular subjects in the madrasahs. But it may well be that change will come about only when the level of poverty is reduced so that poor people can afford other systems of schooling and can see gainful employment in a modern economy as the result. It may also require peace between India and Pakistan to take the heat out of religious antagonisms. The larger perception of the US, as well as other Western powers, oppressing Muslims in Palestine, in Iraq, and elsewhere, also plays a role in the reaction within the madrasahs.

But the West's support for Pakistan's military leader, Musharraf, had made the country a 'seedbed' of terrorism, according to a former prime minister, Benazir Bhutto.[12] Pakistan's first and so far only female premier said Musharraf had 'played the West like a fiddle' by offering support in the so-called 'war on terror' to keep the US and Britain 'off his back as he proceeded to arrest and exile opposition leaders, decimate political parties, pressure the press and set back human and women's rights by a generation'.

The Taliban Regime

Afghanistan is even poorer than Pakistan. Ahmad Shah Durrani unified the Pashtun tribes and founded Afghanistan in 1747. The country then served as a buffer between the British and Russian empires until independence from notional British control in 1919. A brief experiment in democracy ended in a 1973 coup and a then in 1978 a Communist counter-coup. The Soviet Union invaded in 1979 to support the collapsing Afghan Communist regime, but it withdrew 10 years later effectively defeated by internationally supported, anti-Communist mujahideen rebels.

In 2006, the country had a population of 31 million with a life expectancy of 43 years indicating of the level of poverty. The country is the world's largest producer of opium and over 80 per cent of the heroin consumed in Europe comes from Afghan opium. The country's population is divided between different ethnic groups including Pashtun 42 per cent, Tajik 27 per cent, Hazara 9 per cent, and Uzbek 9 per cent. Sunni Muslims are 80 per cent and Shi'ite Muslims 19 per cent of the population. A civil war between different mujahideen factions, often ethnically based, erupted following the 1992 fall of the Communist regime. The Taliban, a hardline Pakistani-sponsored movement, emerged in 1994 to try to end the country's

12 Benazir Bhutto, 'Pakistan dictatorship "fomenting terrorism"', *The Guardian*, 23 Aug 2006.

civil war cum anarchy by imposing traditional Islamic law and governance. It seized Kabul in 1996 and then most of the country outside of opposition Northern Alliance strongholds by 1998.

The Taliban's refusal to deal with the existing warlords earned them respect. The Taliban said their aim was to set up the world's most pure Islamic state and ban frivolities like television, music and cinema. They attempted to eradicate crime by the introduction of Islamic law, including public executions and amputations. They stopped girls from going to school and women from working. The Taliban is a Sunni Islamist nationalist pro-Pashtun movement and effectively ruled most of Afghanistan from 1996 until the US invasion in 2001. It gained diplomatic recognition from only three states: the United Arab Emirates, Pakistan, and Saudi Arabia, as well as the (also) unrecognized government of the Chechen Republic. The leaders of the Taliban, including Mullah Mohammed Omar, were village mullahs or junior Islamic religious scholars, and most had studied in madrasahs in Pakistan. The Taliban support derived mainly from Pashtuns of Afghanistan and North-West Frontier Province (NWFP) of Pakistan, but also included many non-Afghan volunteers from the Arab world, as well as Eurasia, South Asia, and Southeast Asia. By 2000 the Taliban controlled all but the far north of the country and refused to hand over Osama Bin Laden who was then accused by the US of plotting the terrorist attacks on US embassies in Africa in 1998.

The Taliban regime demonstrated the kind of society which its ally, Al Qaeda, would like to establish. It imposed Shariah law, restricted women, banned movies and television, destroyed some ancient statues of the Buddha, and permitted the training of Islamic terrorists for world Jihad in camps established by Al Qaeda. But the regime did enjoy a degree of popular support because order was established. It was also an order generally based on ethnic Pashtuns. It is estimated there are 40–45 million Pashtuns, including 28 million in Pakistan and 12 million in Afghanistan who straddle the porous frontier. The efforts of the Pashtuns were pivotal during the Soviet war in Afghanistan when many joined the Mujahideen. The Pashtuns were the main ethnic contingent in the Taliban and in Pakistan they are the second largest ethnic group.

Following the 9/11 2001 terrorist attacks, a US, Allied, and Northern Alliance coalition took military action which toppled the Taliban for sheltering Osama Bin Ladin. In late 2001 a conference in Germany established a process for political reconstruction that included the adoption of a new constitution, a presidential election in 2004, and National Assembly elections in 2005. On 7 December 2004, Hamid Karzai became the first democratically elected president of Afghanistan and the National Assembly was inaugurated on 19 December 2005.

But the Taliban was not finished. In August 2006 three soldiers from the US-led coalition were killed overnight in a 'battle with extremists' in northeast Afghanistan.[13] The same month 400 Australian troops were sent back to the country with the deteriorating situation. Two soldiers were also wounded in the clash with Taliban extremists while conducting operations in Waygal district of Nuristan province. Coalition forces, mainly American, extended their presence in the east and northeast

13 'Troops killed in battle with Taliban', *The Australian*, 12 Aug 2006.

of Afghanistan since the NATO-led International Security Assistance Force took command of military operations in the south in September 2006. Taliban insurgents and other Islamic militants fighting the Afghan authorities enjoyed great freedom of movement in the region which borders northwest Pakistan. During the first nine months of 2006, more than 70 foreign soldiers, the majority of them American, died in action in Afghanistan. In early 2007 the Taliban mounted a very effective offensive in eastern and southeastern provinces of Afghanistan.

Al Qaeda

Al Qaeda co-existed with the Taliban regime in Afghanistan.[14] Al Qaeda (the 'base') was formed by Arab veterans of the Afghan resistance to the Soviet invasion. With US, Saudi and Pakistani support, the local Afghan resistance assisted by many Islamic foreign volunteers defeated the Soviet occupation force which withdrew in 1989. Thereafter, 'Afghanistan replaced the Syrian-controlled Bekaa Valley in Lebanon as the world's premier training centre for about 40 guerrilla and terrorist groups'.[15] In the early 1990s Osama bin Laden, a wealthy Saudi renegade, replaced the murdered Dr Abdullah Azzam, and the Egyptian theoretician, Dr Ayam Muhammad Rabi' al-Zawahiri, as Al Qaeda's leader. Then in 1992 the pro-Soviet regime was overthrown and in 1996 replaced by the Taliban government. Although the Taliban had been trained by the Pakistani ISI and supported by the US, it then set about establishing the late twentieth century version of the medieval Caliphate replete with Sharia law. But as in the Saudi desert of the seventh century, there was a degree of popular support for a force that brought order where chaos and civil war had been the rule for decades.

Al Qaeda was, therefore, an organisation deeply rooted in Islamic tradition that sprang out of two events: the war against the Soviet Union in Afghanistan; and the US military presence in Saudi Arabia, that was designed, initially anyway, to protect the House of Saud. When the Soviets withdrew in 1989 bin Laden returned to Saudi Arabia and was dismayed by the presence of the US forces who were about to free Kuwait from Iraqi occupation. He started to generate opposition to the House of Saud. Bin Laden left Saudi Arabia before he could be arrested and in 1991 started a campaign against the House of Saud from Pakistan. He then moved on to Sudan, under Islamist government, and built the Al Qaeda network from there. In 1994 Saudi intelligence tried to murder him in Khartoum and, partly in response, Al Qaeda blew up the National Guard Building in Riyadh in November 1995. It built up an international network with offices in New York, London and throughout the Islamic world. It also started terrorist activities, including the first attempt to destroy the World Trade Centre Towers in 1993, and in 1996 it was expelled by the Sudanese government that feared US retaliation. Indeed, it was reported that Sudan offered to hand Osama over to the US. But bin Laden relocated Al Qaeda to Taliban-ruled Afghanistan where training camps were established for the international Islamic

---

14 See Rohan Gunaratna, *Inside Al Qaeda: Global Network of Terror* (Melbourne, 2002), for its origins and development to 2002.

15 *Inside Al Qaeda*, page 221.

terrorist movement, and perhaps thirty thousand men were trained before the camps were destroyed in 2001. It also distributed training manuals which it developed in the camps.

Bin Laden's *Declaration of War*[16]on the West was issued in 1996 and included: 'for seven years the United States has been occupying the lands of Islam in the holiest of places the Arabian peninsula, plundering its riches, dictating to its rulers, humiliating its peoples'. In February 1998 bin Laden announced the formation of a World Islamic Front to wage global Jihad. Parts of the Muslim population took an increasingly sympathetic attitude towards him. Bin Laden had become the centre and leader of a Muslim crusade to re-establish the Caliphate. It established cells throughout the world and organised in close cooperation with the Taliban. It also established an extensive financial system to sustain its operations that were estimated to cost about $36million a year by 2000, including credit card fraud, controlling Islamic NGOs, and operating small businesses. 'It is its very broad ideological disposition and targeting of American, Western and Israeli interests that has made Al Qaeda's support and operational infrastructure global and resilient'.[17] The CIA believed in 2001 that Al Qaeda had the support of six to seven million Muslims world wide of whom about 120,000 were willing to take up arms. On 7 October 2001, bin Laden broke with his tradition of silence and claimed responsibility for the 9/11 attacks.

The Al Qaeda movement can trace its theoretical origins from the Wahhabi form of Islam in Saudi Arabia that dates back to the mid-eighteenth century ideas of Muhammad ibn Abdul Wahhab (1703–1787). When his version of Islam was taken up by the House of Al Saud, as they conquered the Arabian Peninsula from the 1740s over the next decade, it emerged as the dominant variant of a xenophobic, ultra-Sunni Islam, that was very hostile to the Shi'ite and all other faiths, in what would become eventually the modern state of Saudi Arabia by 1932.[18] The Salafist thought of the Jihadists was a product of a merger with the political violence espoused by groups like the Egyptian-based Muslim Brotherhood, whose chief ideologue, Sayyid Qutb (1906–1966), was a Wahhabi. But Al Qaeda is also a product of a wider internal crisis within Islam that has been generated over modernisation and terrorism.[19]

Osama bin Laden[20] was a pious product of a wealthy and elite Saudi family that had made large sums of money from the oil boom, mostly from construction. He was offended by the presence of infidel, US forces in the Holy Land of Saudi Arabia, particularly since they were there to protect a corrupt and apostate regime that had been partly installed by the British and now served the Americans and their

16 This and other statements are posted at: http://www.library.cornell.edu/colldev/mideast/histmod.htm. See also, Bruce Lawrence, ed, *Messages of the World: The Statements of Osama bin Laden* (New York, 2005).

17 *Inside Al Qaeda*, page 87.

18 For the apocalyptic strains in Jihadist thought see David Cook, 'Muslim apocalyptic and jihad', *Jerusalem Studies in Arabic and Islam*, 20, 1996, pp. 66–104.

19 See also Ziauddin Sardar, 'Solving the problem from within', *The Australian Financial Review,* 5 Aug 2005, reprinted from the *New Statesman.*

20 Peter Bergen, *Holy War, Inc.: Inside the Secret World of Osama bin Laden* (London, 2002).

oil interests. Using his considerable wealth to bankroll its early growth, bin Laden developed Al Qaeda to wage war on the Saudi regime, its US guarantor and their allies. As it became clear that bin Laden and other Saudi volunteers who returned from the successful campaign in Afghanistan would oppose the Saudi regime, so that government began to repress their activities. Al Qaeda moved to Sudan, set up headquarters in Khartoum, and the leadership developed their Islamist ideas and military strategy. The core of the ideology of Al Qaeda derives from the Islamic religion as interpreted by Sayyid Qutb. It is recognisably medieval Islamic thought, transcribed into a situation of corrupt regimes supported by a foreign Christian/Jewish superpower. Similar ideas had been circulating in the region for some time with the Muslim Brotherhood that was repressed almost everywhere and received some support only, ironically, from the Saudi Princes in their embrace of Wahhabism.

Nonetheless, Al Qaeda gave these existing ideas new impetus by adding a clear strategic purpose, and a knowledge of military weapons and tactics that had been already honed in a successful campaign against another super power in Afghanistan. It also had money from bin Laden's personal fortune and could raise more by levies, extortion and fraud. It began a campaign of attacks on US and Saudi interests that could be clearly identified as amounting to propaganda by deed. The list of successful attacks on US interests included: the killing of marines in Somalia 1991; the attack on the World Trade Centre in 1993; the bombing of the marine barracks in Saudi Arabia in 1994; destroying two US embassies in Africa 1998; and the successful attack on *USS Cole* in 1999. Its affiliates also planned attacks on Los Angeles, on planes flying to the US from the Philippines, and on the Sydney Olympics. Its recruits were typically, 'middle class, well educated, trained in Afghanistan, totally committed and methodical in their plans to bomb Western targets'.[21]

They had six main targets/objectives, the first of which is the removal of US forces from Saudi Arabian peninsula.[22] This was largely accomplished, in fact, at the time of the invasion of Iraq in 2003, when US forces were redeployed there and are now able to offer support to the Saudi regime from vast bases being constructed there. Whether a liberal hegemon should continue to offer regime support for one of the most primitive and unrepresentative autocracies in the world is another question. But the commitment was made by President Roosevelt to King Ibn Saud in February 1945 and has been honoured by all US administrations ever since. It is now, of course, a vital US interest to maintain access to the Saudi oil fields.

The second is the end of aid, particularly from the US, to Israel. The almost unlimited supply of US financial and material aid to Israel since 1967, and more certainly since 1973, is unparalleled in the post-1945 world. It springs almost entirely from domestic political considerations – 'the Jewish lobby' – and is extremely unlikely to be changed by any foreseeable US Cabinet, certainly not a Democrat one led by Hilary Clinton. If the administration of George W Bush, which is deeply embedded into the oil industry, has stuck by Israel so will any conceivable successor. One result has been that Israeli governments have had little constraint placed on their

---

21 *Inside Al Qaeda*, as above, page 193.

22 Michael Scheuer, *Imperial Hubris: Why the West is Losing the War on Terror* (Dulles, VA, 2004).

activities by the limits of their power. Negotiations with surrounding enemies have been in some large part unsuccessful for that reason. The most recent demonstration of this was the July 2006 invasion of Lebanon.

The third is the withdrawal of Western forces from other Islamic countries, including Iraq and Afghanistan. The US commitment to Iraq is now very difficult to abandon if only for reasons of credibility. The lure of what now appears to be the world's second largest oil reserves and a desire to eliminate the Ba'athist regime were enough motivation to invade. But the subsequently revealed desire to construct a 'liberal democratic regime' – in fact a Shi'ite state – was more ambitious.

The fourth is the end of US support for the repression of Muslims in Russia, China, and India. There is not much the US can do about these countries' policies towards their Islamic populations. But it is clear that the common cause of each has brought better relations for the US with these other substantial nations. The Russians have been fighting an anti-Islamist campaign in Chechnya and has experienced terrorist activities there and in Moscow. India has been a target of Islamic hostility since partition with Pakistan in 1947–8 and the resulting mass deaths in sectarian conflict. In 2006 300 people were killed in Bombay. China has been waging a counter insurgency against separatist guerrillas in Central Asia (East Turkestan) since 1949.

The fifth is the end of US support for apostate regimes in Islamic countries like Kuwait, Egypt, Jordan, and now Libya. This is the strategy which the US has pursued in its defence of the Gulf and its resources, and it can not be lightly abandoned. The US is the guarantor of access to Middle East oil and has been since the 1970s and arguably since 1945. If the US were to abandon this role with no prospect of a successor in view, the consequences for the global economy, and so for the US itself, would be extremely severe. Without a long period of adjustment which permitted the European, East Asian and North American capitalist economies to develop alternative energy sources to the oil they presently import, the result would be a world economic depression.

And, finally, Al Qaeda seeks the preservation of Islamic resources, especially oil, and their sale at a much higher price for the benefit of the peoples of these countries. This is, needless to say, a popular cause in countries like Saudi Arabia, where people have seen thirty years of booming oil prices result in per capita incomes going from $24,000 to $8,000 dollars a year. But this campaign puts it directly at odds with US interests and policy which is to ensure open access to the oil fields of the Gulf by the world market.

Al Qaeda is organised to pursue these objectives directly itself, using the tools of asymmetric war, or terror tactics, as Rohan Gunaratna's path breaking study, *Inside Al Qaeda*, made clear in 2002.[23] It has built up its capacity since the end of its campaign against the Soviets in Afghanistan and was able to use camps in that country when it was controlled by the Taliban to train a large number of military personnel. These later dispersed to affiliated organisations in Pakistan, Russia, the Arab countries and Southeast Asia, and pursued similar strategies to Al Qaeda operationally, but independently. Many trained personnel also returned to Western countries like the UK, France, Spain, Canada and Australia, where they tried with

23 *Inside Al Qaeda,* as above, 2002.

some success to establish terrorist cells to operate again independently of the Al Qaeda command structure.

But Al Qaeda also acted as an exemplar and nerve centre. In this capacity it has posted technical information for terrorists on the Internet. It has also proclaimed that Muslims have a duty to follow Islamic principles and attack the enemies of their faith independently where possible. This message has clearly resonated with some Muslims who have had no direct contact with Al Qaeda and its affiliates. The fact that many have taken up the terrorist cause and that many more are planning to do so in countries as diverse as India, Indonesia, the Philippines, Canada, Spain, the UK, Russia, Saudi Arabia, Singapore, New Zealand and Australia, suggests the potency of the message encoded in Islamic teachings and the ability of Al Qaeda to tap into them.

Before September 2001 Islamic extremism was already waging a war on the US and its allies. The main fronts were: attempting to seize state power in states with Islamic populations; campaigning within the Muslim world for support; and acting against those western powers supporting its Muslim enemies. In late 2001 this war was escalated dramatically.

Chapter 6

The Global War on Terror

The terrorist attacks on the US on 11 September 2001 inaugurated the Global War on Terror (GWOT) which President Bush later, perhaps unwisely, described as a 'crusade'. This dramatically changed the way in which many Americans saw the world and pre-occupied its government thereafter. US policy makers believed the unwarranted assault would generate universal support for their policies of retaliation. This proved not to be the case.

The Attacks of 9/11

The most spectacular terrorist action of Al Qaeda was undoubtedly its attacks on New York and Washington on 11 September 2001. This was accomplished by hijacking four planes that had full fuel tanks to maximise the damage. The 19 terrorists – 15 Saudi citizens – involved in the attacks had sufficient pilot training to hit each of the two World Trade Centre towers, which collapsed with nearly three thousand deaths. Another hit the Pentagon building in Virginia near Washington. But a fourth was prevented from hitting, probably, the White House or Congress, by the revolt of its passengers and crashed in a field in Pennsylvania.

The targets were well chosen. The twin towers were not only a symbol of the nerve centre of US and world business, but also a real centre of financial activity and their destruction impacted on New York's business for years after. It also contained many Jewish owned corporations. The financial centre of southern Manhattan was and remains the most important in the world. The Pentagon is, of course, the organisational headquarters of the American military forces. Al Qaeda operatives had done well, even if they missed the White House.

After the initial panic, the US administration began to plan better defensive strategies and its retaliatory measures. The defensive measures included a Department of Homeland Security, the Patriot Act and a range of tighter security measures, particularly involving air transport systems. There were no further successful attacks on US territory. Although arrests were made, in the main the terrorist impulse had not been effectively transmitted to the US Muslim minority by Al Qaeda. Elsewhere, the US undertook a campaign against terrorism by enlisting the assistance of other states and pursuing regimes believed to be aiding Al Qaeda, the two most important of which were the Taliban in Afghanistan and the Ba'athists in Iraq. Other states also supported Islamist organisations that the US regarded as terrorist, including Iran and its relationship to Hezbollah, and Syria with a relationship with Hamas and Hezbollah. But they had no known official relationship with Al Qaeda.

The official US 9/11 Commission later reported: 'The enemy is not just terrorism, some generic evil. The catastrophic threat at this moment in history is more specific. It is the threat posed by Islamist terrorism, especially the Al Qaeda networks, its affiliates and its ideology'.[1] In an interview, bin Laden said,

> The events that happened on 11 September in New York and Washington, that is truly a great event in all measures ... According to their own admissions, the share of the losses on the Wall Street market reached 16 per cent ... a record that has never happened since the opening of the market 230 years ago. ... it reaches $640 billion of losses from stocks, by Allah's grace. .. The daily income of the American nation is $20 billion. The first week they didn't work. ... so it comes out to $140 billion .. and it is increasing thanks to Allah's grace – so watch as the amount reaches no less than $1 trillion .. due to these successful and blessed attacks. We implore Allah to accept those brothers within the ranks of the martyrs, and to admit them to the highest levels of Paradise.[2]

The War in Afghanistan, 2001–7

In 2001 the Al Qaeda leadership was based in Afghanistan, one of the poorest countries in the world with a per capita income of $230 in 2006. Its thirty one million people were ethnically diverse and their political loyalties often crossed national boundaries and related to clan, tribal, religious and linguistic affiliations, as much as to national states. Since 1996 the country had been run by the Pakistani-backed and Pashtun-led Taliban ('Islamic students'), but they had not gained wide diplomatic recognition nor control of the entire country. The Taliban's main remaining opponent was the Tajik-led Northern Alliance in areas adjacent to Tajikistan. Its most effective leader – Ahmad Shah Massoud – was assassinated by Al Qaeda only days before the 9/11 attacks.

The US attacked the Taliban in Afghanistan in late 2001 as quickly as the forces – mostly air force and Special Forces – could be put into the field.[3] It negotiated an arrangement with the Northern Alliance and then undertook extensive aerial bombardment in support of its ground offensive. The combination of US air power and ground forces supported by US and other special forces, including NATO, Australia and New Zealand, evicted the Taliban from Kabul and other cities and installed the Northern Alliance into power.

This invasion was assisted by the cooperation of several surrounding states, including Pakistan, Tajikistan and Uzbekistan. Pakistan's military dictator, General Musharraf, initially received around 3 billion dollars in US aid. Although Pakistan had effectively created the Taliban, it nominally abandoned it in the face of a threat by the US and the offer of a substantial bribe. This was not welcomed by the Pakistani population and opinion polls suggested many preferred the Taliban and Al Qaeda to the US. The Al Qaeda leadership, including Osama bin Laden, escaped capture by

---

1 *The 9/11 Commission Report* (Washington, 2004).

2 Interview with bin Laden, 21 October 2001, quoted in *Inside Al Qaeda*, as above, p. 227.

3 Bob Woodard, *Bush at War* (New York, revised edition, 2003), for an account of Washington decision making.

the US-led forces and probably sought refuge on the Pakistan border, where the mountainous terrain made successful pursuit difficult. In these areas, much of the Islamic Pashtun population was very sympathetic towards both the Taliban and Al Qaeda.

Although the US forces killed thousands of people during the invasion and captured several hundred more, resistance did not end. Some Taliban forces retreated into the Pashtun southeast where hostile mountainous terrain enabled them to escape capture. Others, including foreign Al Qaeda volunteers, dispersed around the world. The occupying forces constructed a government from anti-Taliban forces, and elections were held in 2004 resulting in the election of President Karzai. But the Taliban based insurgency did not expire and after September 2006 when some US forces withdrew and handed over the occupation to NATO command, the insurgency grew in intensity. In August 2006, in response to this, the Australian government announced it was sending 400 more troops to Afghanistan and in April 2007 six hundred more.

The war in Afghanistan started in October 2001 and marked the beginning of the US Global War on Terrorism.[4] In 2004, bin Laden issued a taped statement acknowledging his own and Al Qaeda's involvement in the 9/11 attacks which he said were carried out because 'we are a free people who do not accept injustice, and we want to regain the freedom of our nation'. On 21 May 2006, bin Laden said he had personally directed the 19 hijackers. Further, the *National Commission on Terrorist Attacks upon the United States* (*The 9/11 Commission*)[5] reported on 22 July 2004 that the attacks were conceived and implemented by members of Al Qaeda.

Because the direct link between the 9/11 attacks and the Taliban regime and its Al Qaeda allies was well established, the US was able to get a broad coalition of countries to contribute to its war in Afghanistan. The first wave of attacks was carried out solely by American and British forces. A number of other countries then provided support to the US-led invasion. From the Anglo-Sphere these included Canada with initially about 2,500 troops, six ships and six aircraft; Australia which contributed about 300 SAS troops, air-to-air refueling tankers, Navy frigates, two Orion electronic intelligence gathering aircraft, and F/A-18 fighter aircraft for Diego Garcia; and New Zealand which sent 50 Special Air Service soldiers and two C-130 Hercules.

The NATO European allies of the US also contributed: France with 4,500 troops; Germany sent approximately 2,250 troops, including special forces and naval vessels; Italy contributed naval warships including an aircraft carrier; Netherlands sent ground-attack fighters and Apache gun-ships, as part of the European Participating Air Force with Denmark and Norway. Other contributing countries included: Croatia, 150 military police in the Kabul area; Czech Republic, special forces; Bahrain with Naval vessels; Jordan had a mine clearing team; Japan, in its first military deployment since 1945 contributed naval support for non-combatant reinforcement of the operation; Portugal had 115 Commandos and 37 air traffic

---

4 See Benjamin S Lambeth, *Air Power Against Terror: America's Conduct of Operation Enduring Freedom,* RAND, 2005.

5 *The 9/11 Commission Report* (Washington, 2004).

controllers in Kabul; Lithuania dispatched 40 Special Forces AITVARAS troops, from 2002 to 2004; Poland sent 93 soldiers including GROM special forces; and Romania 25 military police and a C-130 transport aircraft.[6]

Osama bin Laden condemned these attacks against Afghanistan and claimed that the US would fail in Afghanistan and then collapse, just like the Soviet Union. He called for a war of Muslims, a Jihad, against the entire non-Muslim world. Al Qaeda also tried to take retaliatory action against the countries participating in the war. But on the battlefield the Taliban had little anti-aircraft weaponry and US aircraft, helicopter gun-ships and cruise missiles, operated with near impunity. The strikes initially focused in and around the cities of Kabul, Jalalabad, and Kandahar. Within a few days, most Al Qaeda training sites had been severely damaged and the Taliban's few air defenses had been destroyed. The campaign then focused on communications, command and control and the Taliban lost the ability to coordinate battle, but their morale sustained by religious zeal remained high and they did well against the Northern Alliance. Also, thousands of Pashtun militiamen entered the country from Pakistan to fight against the US-led forces.

The UN then organised meetings of Afghan leaders in Germany, although the Taliban was not included. These meetings produced an interim government and an agreement to allow a UN-authorised peacekeeping force to enter Afghanistan. Following a grand council of major Afghan factions, tribal leaders and former exiles, an interim Afghan government was established in Kabul under the Tajik, former Taliban, Hamid Karzai. The number of US-led coalition troops operating in the country grew to over 10,000.

But the Taliban and Al Qaeda had not given up.[7] Al Qaeda forces regrouped in the Shahi-Kot mountains on the border region, and already totalled over one thousand by the beginning by March 2002. They used the region as a base for launching guerrilla attacks like the mujahideen had fought Soviets during the 1980s. The Pakistani armed forces did not seal the border and Al Qaeda fighters established sanctuaries among tribal protectors in Pakistan, from which they began launching cross-border raids on US forces by summer 2002. Taliban forces remained in hiding in the rural regions of the four southern provinces that formed their heartland: Kandahar, Zabul, Helmand, and Uruzgan. The remnants of the Taliban then launched an insurgency in the winter 2002–3, with groups of up to fifty launching attacks on isolated outposts and convoys of Afghan soldiers, police, or militia. These Taliban attacks gradually increased in frequency through 2004 when the US military sustained on average one death and four wounded per week in Afghanistan. In late 2005, Afghan government forces backed by US troops and heavy American aerial bombardment advanced on Taliban positions in the mountain fortresses, but with limited success. Larger operations there were then launched in June and July 2006 and these continued into 2007.

---

6 See *NATO in Afghanistan Factsheet,* at: http://www.nato.int/issues/afghanistan/index.html.

7 See H S Rothstein, *Afghanistan and the Troubled Future of Unconventional Warfare* (Annapolis, MD, 2006).

The US war to remove the Taliban generally received popular support around the world except among hard leftists and extremist Islamist populations. It followed hard on the 9/11 attacks, to which Al Qaeda was linked directly, and the Taliban was, for most people, an odious regime. US opinion supported the war. But much larger protests and general strikes occurred in Pakistan. In some other Islamic nations, protests and rallies against the attack on Afghanistan also took place. There was also a modest anti-US demonstration in London of perhaps 50,000 people. But thereafter support for the US Global War on Terror generally ebbed.

The low level insurgency in Afghanistan continued into 2007. There were three main reasons for this: the Taliban had never been destroyed and it remained a power particularly in the southeast on the frontier with Pakistan relying on ethnic Pashtun support; the Taliban was emboldened by the US handing over control of the occupying forces to NATO, which was rightly regarded by anti-government forces as much less determined and keen to avoid casualties;[8] and some parts of the Pakistani state had never stopped supporting the Taliban. 'All this has created space for the Taliban to surge back, with active Pakistani backing'.[9] Support and reinforcements entered across the Pakistan border: Musharraf continued to run with the foxes and hunt with the hounds.[10]

The US military commander in Afghanistan said in September 2006 that coalition forces were faced with an alliance of foreign-trained enemy forces affiliated to Al Qaeda ideology.[11] He said the alliance comprised the Taliban; Haqqani, led by Jalalludin Haqqani, a former mujahadeen commander and a radical Islamist; and Hizb-I Islami Gulbuddin, run by Gulbuddin Hikmatyar, a warlord and long-time associate of bin Laden. In July 2006, Musharraf struck a deal with religious extremists in the tribal areas of the North West Frontier Province of Pakistan, involving a truce with the army in exchange for their ending armed attacks within the country.[12] In Afghanistan, the Governor of Paktia Province, Hakim Taniwal, warned that 'if they are not being bothered, they will have more time to infiltrate here and do what they want'. Three days later Taniwal was assassinated in a suicide bombing by the Taliban, the first of a number over the next year.[13] Nonetheless, after 2003 the situation in Iraq became so grave that the fragility of the security situation in Afghanistan was overlooked by Washington. The momentum of 'regime transition' was lost in 2002 when the expansion of the UN-endorsed International Security Assistance Force beyond Kabul was blocked by Washington which was mustering airlift assets for use against Saddam Hussein. This was another strategic blunder. Also, after its 2004 campaign against rebels failed, Pakistan unofficially permitted

8 W Maley, 'West has been helping itself, not Afghanistan', *Sydney Morning Herald*, 15 June 2006.

9 *Ibid.*

10 See W Maley, *Rescuing Afghanistan* (Sydney, 2006); and Zahid Hussain, *Frontline Pakistan: The Struggle with Militant Islam* (New York, 2007).

11 Michael Evans, 'Three-headed enemy linked to al-Qa'ida', *The Australian*, 8 Sept 2006.

12 William Maley, 'Fledgling democracy a target', *The Australian*, 12 Sept 2006.

13 Bruce Loudon, 'Minister survives suicide bomb', *The Australian*, 30 April 2007.

the Taliban's renewed campaign to destabilise Afghanistan and Musharraf admitted that the Taliban had been crossing into Afghanistan from their bases in Pakistan.

As the Taliban recovered so NATO casualties in Afghanistan started to mount during 2006, notably among the Americans, British and Canadians. Many of the countries that had pledged support in 2001 ignored urgent requests for more help in fighting the resurgent Taliban and Al Qaeda. In 2006 Turkey, Germany, Spain, Italy and France, rejected the appeal from the US for 2,500 more troops. The 26 nation NATO alliance initially did not volunteer a single extra combat soldier, although Australia did. In Afghanistan the forces were in mid-2006: US 20,000; UK 5,400; Canada 2,500; Germany 2,500; Netherlands 2,300; Italy 1,250; France 1,000; Spain 650; Turkey 580; Romania 560; Australia 500; Norway 380; Poland 100. Later, only the 'New Europe' newcomers to NATO said they would send more soldiers.

The tone was different from 2001 when allies and even some traditional opponents of the US had offered Washington military assistance to destroy Al Qaeda and overthrow the Taliban regime. But in late 2006 the Taliban were more ferocious and more determined than at any time since when they were overthrown in late 2001. As well as carrying out suicide bombings, they were also fighting hand to hand and occupying and controlling towns and districts for days at a time. NATO was thus desperately short of reinforcements for its Afghanistan campaign.[14] By late 2006 NATO forces were locked in their biggest land battles since the alliance was formed.

In late October 2006 the Taliban chief Mullah Mohammad Omar, who had launched the Taliban movement with twenty Islamic students in Pakistan in 1994, announced that international forces would be driven out of the country like Soviet troops in the 1980s. 'It is the fifth consecutive year that Afghanistan, our dear country, is under Crusader colonisation. But this time we also congratulate you on the defeat and the flight of the Crusader'.[15] The one-eyed Mullah Omar had refused to hand over Osama bin Laden to the US after the terrorist attacks of 11 September 2001. A Pashtun, Mullah Omar condemned the Government of Afghan President Hamid Karzai and said a Taliban victory would result in him and other members of his administration being taken before an Islamic court.

The Invasion of Iraq, 2003

The invasion of Iraq took longer for the US to mount than that of Afghanistan.[16] While it was clear from 11 September 2001 that the US would likely overthrow the Ba'athist regime of Saddam Hussein, and Bush discussed this as early as 12 September 2001, this was not entirely a forgone conclusion. After the Taliban was ousted from Kabul, Bush drew up battle plans for the invasion of Iraq. By mid-2002

14 Peter Wilson, 'Poland's forces not enough for NATO', *The Australian*, 15 Sept 2006.

15 Bruce Loudon, 'Taliban leader's threat to the West', *The Australian*, 24 Oct 2006.

16 See Bob Woodward, *Plan of Attack* (New York, reprint, 2004), for a detailed account of the Bush administration's decision to invade Iraq.

it was unlikely these plans would not be implemented although these did not prepare adequately for the post-war reconstruction and government of Iraq.[17]

After the Gulf War of 1991, Iraq's relations with the UN, the US, and the UK remained hostile. But the UN Security Council often could not agree whether Iraq had fully complied with the terms of the Gulf War 1991 ceasefire, and the US and UK independently enforced economic sanctions against Iraq. US and UK warplanes enforced Iraqi no-fly zones to protect Kurds in northern Iraq and Shi'ites in the south. After Iraq terminated its cooperation with the UN in August 1998, the US Congress passed the 'Iraq Liberation Act' in October 1998, which provided $97 million for Iraqi 'democratic opposition organisations' in order to 'establish a program to support a transition to democracy in Iraq'. UN Resolution 687, and others, however, made no mention of enforcing regime change. A substantial US and UK bombardment of Iraq in December 1998, which followed the lack of cooperation by Iraq, substantially degraded its military capability.

The Republican platform in 2000 called for 'full implementation' of the Iraq Liberation Act, the removal of Saddam Hussein and support for the pro-democracy, opposition exile group, the Iraqi National Congress, then headed by Ahmed Chalabi. Later, aides who were with Defense Secretary Donald Rumsfeld on 11 September 2001 claimed that he asked for, 'best info fast. Judge whether good enough hit Saddam Hussein at same time. Not only Osama bin Laden'. They also quoted him as saying, 'Go massive', and 'Sweep it all up. Things related and not'. Shortly thereafter, the Bush administration announced a Global War on Terrorism, accompanied by the doctrine of 'pre-emptive' military action, later termed the 'Bush doctrine'.

In October 2002 the US Congress passed the 'Joint Resolution to Authorize the Use of United States Armed Forces Against Iraq', that granted President Bush the authority to 'use any means necessary' against Iraq. This was largely based on repeated Bush administration statements to Congress and the public, which turned out to be incorrect, that Iraq possessed dangerous Weapons of Mass Destruction (WMDs) – an assessment shared by most analysts at that time. The joint resolution allowed the President to 'defend the national security of the United States against the continuing threat posed by Iraq and enforce all relevant United Nations Security Council Resolutions regarding Iraq'. Overwhelmingly, the Democrats also voted for this resolution, thereby, in contrast to most other countries, limiting domestic US opposition to the war.

In 2003 the US gave several reasons for invading Iraq, which added to the confusion about and indeed the criticisms of US behaviour. But its legal reason, throughout, was that the UN Security Council had passed several motions essentially calling on Iraq to disarm, and that Iraq had been in breach of these motions. The UN Charter permits nations to act to enforce UN decisions. Nonetheless, the US did try in September 2002 to get a further resolution through the UN Security Council explicitly justifying an overthrow of the Ba'athist regime on the grounds of its non-compliance with several UN resolutions concerning, particularly, the development of WMDs. It became clear that the UN Security Council would not pass such further,

---

17 Greg Sheridan, *The Partnership: The Inside Story of the US-Australian Alliance under Bush and Howard* (Sydney, 2006).

enabling resolutions because of the opposition of several members. In particular, the French and Russian delegations would not vote for them. The French had long had relations with the Iraqi regime and clearly aimed at achieving some improved oil access when the situation normalised. It was also reported that French President Chirac's political party had received funding from the Ba'athists. The Russians also had historic links to the Ba'athist state which dated back to the Soviet era.

The US then again took the issue to the UN, and in November 2002 the Security Council unanimously passed Resolution 1441 which led to the resumption of weapons inspections in Iraq. But Resolution 1441 did not itself authorise the use of force. These UN consultations were later forestalled by the US and UK abandoning the Security Council procedure and undertaking their invasion of Iraq. The UK said it abandoned further UN resolutions because of the France announcement that they would veto any further Security Council resolutions on Iraq. The US ambassador Negroponte was recorded as saying, 'one way or another, Mr President, Iraq will be disarmed. If the Security Council fails to act decisively in the event of a further Iraqi violation, this resolution does not constrain any member state from acting to defend itself against the threat posed by Iraq, or to enforce relevant UN resolutions and protect world peace and security'.[18] The US then moved in late 2002 towards an invasion of Iraq.

The British government under Tony Blair had strongly supported the US Global War on Terror and had contributed substantial forces to the suppression of the Taliban. Blair was concerned that the bellicose and unilateralist Bush administration would act alone, rely on existing and rather flimsy UN resolutions for its authority, and alienate much of the world as a result. He proved, of course, to be correct. He persuaded the US to make one more effort to get another, firmer resolution passed by the Security Council, in exchange for his promise to commit British troops alongside the US, even if this UN effort failed. The US went back to the Security Council in early 2003 but, despite strong British support, including a rather unpersuasive dossier purportedly proving Iraq's further development of WMDs, was again rebuffed. US forces, with allied support, including from Britain and Australia, invaded Iraq in March 2003.

By then, a number of US motives beyond non-compliance with UN motions were clear. Several members of the administration regretted the US had not ousted Saddam in 1991. The President himself may have been further motivated by the unsuccessful Iraqi attempt to assassinate his father during a visit to Kuwait in 1993. Blair, in particular, seems to have genuinely believed Iraq was developing WMDs that could be used against Britain, among other states. There were also several attempts made to link the Ba'athist regime to Al Qaeda and its terrorist activities. Although these were never established conclusively, the CIA did report that there were several

---

18 'Explanation of Vote by Ambassador John D. Negroponte, United States Permanent Representative to the United Nations, following the vote on the Iraq Resolution, Security Council, November 8, 2002', US Mission to the United Nations, PRESS RELEASE # 187 (02) (Revised) November 8, 2002.

Al Qaeda training camps in Iraq in 2002 run by Abu Musab al-Zarqawi[19] and Iraq did sponsor terrorists by providing financial assistance to the families of Palestinian suicide bombers. The neo-conservatives led by Paul Wolfowitz, but with much assistance from Richard Perle and sympathetic American intellectuals, then argued that Iraq should and could be democratised and light the way for a new political structure in the Middle East based on Islamic but democratic societies. This view had support from the doyen of Middle East scholars, Bernard Lewis, who became prominent in these discussions in 2002–03.[20]

There were a number of problems with the project to democratise Iraq, and then the wider Middle East, and these became apparent fairly quickly. First, it would involve totally dismantling the Ba'athist regime that, whatever its major shortcomings, had been the effective government of the country for four decades. Secondly, the commitment of the Islamic population to the US version of democracy, bearing in mind that Islam allowed for the ongoing legitimacy of a legal code handed to the Prophet, via Archangel Gabriel, from God thirteen centuries previously, was uncertain. Thirdly, taking power from the Sunni minority and handing it to the Shi'ite majority would likely be resisted, and probably violently so. Fourthly, if the Shi'ites achieved power, they would be more likely to establish a close relationship with the powerful neighbouring Shi'ite theocracy in Iran, than with the liberal democracies. And, finally, if the electorates of the Middle East chose to democratically elect Islamists who were hostile to the US, as they did in Iran and were soon to do in the Palestinian Authority, and try to do in Egypt and Lebanon, the US position might not be improved.

On 11 October 2002, the US Congress had given Bush the authority to attack Iraq if Saddam Hussein did not give up his WMDs – which almost all states wrongly believed he had – and abide by previous UN resolutions on human rights and terrorism.[21] On 9 November 2002, at the urging of the US government, the UN Security Council passed Resolution 1441, offering Iraq 'a final opportunity to comply with its disarmament obligations' that had been set out in several previous resolutions (Resolutions 660, 661, 678, 686, 687, 688, 707, 715, 986, and 1284)', notably to provide 'an accurate full, final, and complete disclosure, as required by Resolution 687 (1991), of all aspects of its programmes to develop weapons of mass destruction and ballistic missiles'. Resolution 1441 threatened 'serious consequences' if these obligations were not met and reasserted demands that UN

19 William Kristol, 'CIA boss tells more than he knows', *The Australian*, 7 May 2007, reviewing the memoires of the former CIA Director under Clinton and Bush, George Tenet, *At the Centre of the Strom* (New York, 2007).

20 James Mann, *Rise of the Vulcans: The History of Bush's War Cabinet* (New York, 2004). During the 2000 presidential campaign, Bush was (correctly) accused of lacking foreign policy experience and responded by surrounding himself with experienced political veterans, consisting of Rumsfeld, Cheney, Powell, Wolfowitz, Armitage, and Rice, who had worked together for a long time, and then called themselves the Vulcans, after the Roman God of Fire. To this group were added Lewis, Henry Kissinger and the long time Saudi Ambassador to the US. See also Woodward, *State of Denial*, *op cit*.

21 *Public Law 107-243 – Oct 16 2002; Authorisation for Use of Military Force Against Iraq Resolution of 2002; US Congressional Record, Vol 148* (2002).

weapons inspectors should have 'immediate, unconditional, and unrestricted access' to sites of their choosing, in order to ascertain compliance.

The US-led invasion of Iraq was, thus, justified on many grounds. But at its geopolitical heart remained the almost unmentioned maintenance of access to oil for the world market without which US forces would be no more interested in the Gulf than they were in the thirty year old Sri Lankan Civil War. US policy on all commodity production and distribution is, in principle, the same as for oil: create a world market in which equal access is provided on the basis of supply and demand. This will ensure stable economic progress in the world of liberal economies it is trying to create. In fact, this usually also involves a better access for the richer American consumer and a major role for US multinational resource companies. Rupert Murdoch famously commented that the liberation of Iraq would create a price of 20 dollars per barrel of oil.

Removing the Ba'athists, therefore, had several advantages for the US. In addition, in the context of post-9/11, the invasion, particularly when it proved initially spectacularly successful, had the further advantage of making the administration more popular in the US. It was seen, particularly in the Republican heartland, as taking the war to the enemy. Most observers anticipated that the military defeat of the Iraqi regime would be undertaken more quickly in 2003 than had occurred in 1991.[22] This proved to be the case, and the US military entered Baghdad in less than three weeks. But the serious difficulties then commenced.

The invasion of Iraq began on 20 March 2003. The US, UK, Australia and Poland supplied the vast majority of the invading forces and co-operated with Kurdish forces. The Iraqi military was quickly defeated and Baghdad fell on 9 April 2003. On 1 May 2003, President Bush declared the end of major combat operations, terminating the Ba'ath Party's rule and removing President Saddam Hussein from office. Coalition forces captured Saddam Hussein on 13 December 2003 and he was later tried and executed. Numerous guerrilla and terrorist groups then became active in the country, including the newly-formed Al Qaeda in Iraq.

In response to the imminent invasion, on 15 February anti-war protests were held in the West, the largest of their kind since the Vietnam War, involving 4–6 million people in over fifty countries. Iraq maintained that it had disarmed as required. The UN weapons inspectors headed by Hans Blix, who were sent by the UN Security Council pursuant to Resolution 1441, requested more time to complete their report on whether Iraq had complied with its obligation to disarm. But the Coalition invasion began without the express approval of the Security Council, and some legal authorities regarded it as a violation of the UN Charter and several countries protested. UN Secretary-General Kofi Annan said in September 2004, 'From our point of view and the UN Charter point of view, it was illegal'.[23]

Approximately 100,000 US soldiers and marines and 26,000 British troops, as well as smaller forces from other nations were deployed prior to the invasion, primarily to several staging areas in Kuwait. In the wider theatre there were 214,000 Americans, 45,000 British, 2,000 Australians and 2,400 Polish troops. Plans for

22 Bob Catley, 'The Second Gulf War', *Quadrant*, April 2002.

23 'Annan says Iraq war was "illegal"', *Boston Globe*, 16 Sept 2004.

opening a second front in the north were abandoned when under Islamic pressure the Turkish government refused the use of its territory. The Coalition Forces were also supported by Iraqi Kurdish militia troops, estimated to number upwards of 50,000. The Coalition conducted parachute operations in the north and dropped the 173rd Airborne Brigade. The number of personnel in the Iraqi military before the war was a poorly-equipped 389,000: army 350,000, navy 2,000, air force 20,000 and air defence 17,000; the paramilitary Fedayeen Saddam 44,000; and with reservists of 650,000. The Coalition had almost total air superiority.

On 20 March 2003 the conventional assault began after Special Forces from the Coalition, including US, British and Australian, crossed into Iraq well before the air war commenced in order to guide air attacks. US plans then envisioned air and ground assaults to seize Baghdad quickly, using a strategy of 'Shock and Awe' and by-passing Iraqi military units and cities in most cases. The plan was that superior Coalition mobility and co-ordination would allow the US-led Coalition to attack the heart of the Iraqi command structure and destroy it quickly. It was expected that the elimination of the leadership would lead to the collapse of the Iraqi Forces and Ba'athist government, and that much of the population would then support the invaders. The Coalition deployed a sufficient numbers of troops to win the battle but not to occupy the country, and the Coalition failed to achieve security and order throughout the country when local popular support failed to meet its expectations.

The invasion produced the collapse of the Iraqi government and military in about three weeks. The oil infrastructure of Iraq was rapidly secured by the Coalition to fund the rebuilding of Iraq. The US 3rd Infantry Division moved west then north through the western desert toward Baghdad; the 1st Marine Expeditionary Force moved along Highway One through the center of the country; and a British Armoured Division moved northward through the eastern marshland. The British fought their way into Iraq's second-largest southern city, Basra, on 6 April. Three weeks into the invasion, US forces moved into Baghdad in strength. On 5 April a 'Thunder Run' of US armoured vehicles tested remaining Iraqi defences by rushing to the Baghdad airport. They met heavy resistance, including suicide attacks, but nonetheless reached the airport. Two days later another thunder run was launched into the Palace of Saddam Hussein, where US forces established a base. Within hours of the palace seizure and television coverage of this spreading throughout Iraq, US forces ordered Iraqi forces in Baghdad to surrender.

Iraqi government officials then either disappeared or conceded defeat, and on 9 April 2003 Baghdad was formally occupied by US forces. Much of Baghdad remained unsecured, however, and fighting continued within the city and its outskirts; indeed it never ended. Saddam himself vanished. Many Iraqis celebrated the downfall of Saddam and one widely televised event was the toppling of a large statue of Saddam in central Baghdad by a US M88 tank retriever, while a crowd of Iraqis cheered. But the fall of Baghdad triggered the outbreak of violence throughout the country, as Iraqis began to fight each other over new power, old grudges or merely loot. Coalition troops then began searching for the key members of Saddam's government. These individuals were identified by a variety of means, most famously through sets of 'most-wanted' Iraqi playing cards and Saddam Hussein was captured in a hole on 13 December 2003.

Extensive looting took place following the Coalition's victory. Most serious was the looting of weaponry and ordinance from military bases which helped fuel the subsequent insurgency. As much as 250,000 tons of explosives were unaccounted for by October 2004. The Coalition forces concentrated on the 938 sites identified as potential WMD facilities, but no WMDs were found. On 1 May 2003 George W. Bush landed on the aircraft carrier *USS Abraham Lincoln* in a fighter aircraft and announced the end of major combat operations in the Iraq war. Clearly visible in the background was a banner stating 'Mission Accomplished'. The banner was made by White House staff and was criticized as premature. It most certainly was. Bush's speech itself noted: 'We have difficult work to do in Iraq. We are bringing order to parts of that country that remain dangerous'. But some of the resistance was already organised.

The decision to invade Iraq produced a fiasco.[24] It diverted resources from the Afghan theatre where they were still needed; it looked like it might fail; it created, at best, a Shi'ite state; it alienated enough Muslims to actually heighten the terrorist threat; it alienated allied states; it degraded popular support for the US throughout the world; it emboldened the Jihadists; and it inflicted many casualties on both the Coalition forces and the Iraqi population. The use of a surgical military strike to remove Saddam's regime with little bloodshed and replace it with a more moderate, perhaps even Ba'athist leadership, was understandable against the backdrop of 9/11 and the successful removal of Serbia's President Milosovich in similar circumstances. The determination to create a democratic state where none had previously existed – or indeed been dreamt of, or aspired to – proved a heroic undertaking. But in 2003 the neo-conservative impulse ran strongly in Washington and its ambitions were extensive.

Fiasco: The US Occupation of Iraq

In 2003 Defence Secretary Donald Rumsfeld, wanted 'regime change', but also wanted to accomplish it with the use of the 'new model army' that he was constructing based on the 'Revolution in Military Affairs'. This army was a very mobile, highly mechanised and extremely lethal force that could patrol US global interests from the US mainland, using pre-positioned material stockpiles and skeleton forces to meanwhile hold the line. The entire US military had become a Rapid Deployment Force. The rapid run through Iraq of armoured columns with air support showed the effectiveness of this concept against conventional forces.

But the neo-conservative agenda had superimposed on this tactical use of military power, the strategic objective of regime change. If this were to involve, as many initially thought to be the case, merely the decapitation of the Ba'athist regime, the removal of, say, 5,000 officials, officers and major torturers, and its gradual liberalisation thereafter, then the US military assault force might be sufficient. But if it were to involve the dismantling of the entire regime and its replacement by a

24 Thomas E Ricks, *Fiasco, The American Military Adventure in Iraq* (New York, 2006).

democratic state, then perhaps the entire US army would be insufficient. Certainly, what was required in April 2003 was a large police force, a sealing of the borders, the imposition of martial law, and the orderly reorganisation of the Ba'athist regime, while some new order was established. General Shinseki, Chief of the Army, told the Senate Armed Services Committee, that 'several hundred thousand' troops would be needed to occupy Iraq after the war was over.[25] The Deputy Secretary of Defense, Paul Wolfowitz, rejected the General's suggestion and said they would not need anything like that number.

Retired Army General, Jay Garner, was the first American placed in charge of post-war reconstruction in Iraq and he drew up a policy for the Coalition occupation.[26] He planned to remove two people from each ministry and major government office, and then let the Iraqis take care of de-Ba'athification. Rumsfeld, Wolfowitz and Feith were most unhappy with this plan. Garner also fell out with the returning exile, Chalabi, whom he regarded as 'a thug, very sleazy'. Chalabi was, however, better connected to the neo-conservatives in the US administration, and wanted the Ba'athists removed and himself installed in power. On 24 April Rumsfeld phoned Garner and told him he would be replaced by a retired diplomat, L Paul Bremer III. Bremer arrived in Baghdad on 12 May 2003 determined to purge the Ba'athists and showed his order to Garner who was appalled. On 16 May the order, 'De-Ba'athification of Iraq Society', was issued by Bremer as Coalition Provisional Authority Order Number One. On 23 May he issued Order Number Two, 'Dissolution of Iraqi Entities', which abolished the Iraqi Armed Forces and the Ministry of the Interior. The neo-conservatives thus destroyed the state apparatus of Iraq and created the insurgency and the new Iraq.

In 2003 the occupation authority made four major mistakes. First, it totally dismantled the Ba'athist power structures, thereby alienating and dispersing up to a million trained and motivated men. Second, it did not seize and control the arms depots that had been dispersed across the country by the Ba'athists. Instead, it looked for the WMDs and feared destroying the arms dumps in case the WMDs were hidden in them. In any case, it lacked sufficient personnel to guard them. Third, it did not seal the borders. Falsely expecting a welcome for liberators, the US did not take action to prevent the hostile part of the population being supplied, reinforced and augmented by international Islamist volunteers from neighbouring states and then elsewhere. And fourth, it dismantled the state controlled economy in the interests of promoting free enterprise, only to see the provision of basic goods and services, including sometimes, electricity, sewerage and water, collapse. The insurgency had already begun in August 2003, when a car bomb hit the Jordanian Embassy. The real war started *after* Bush had declared victory. Saddam Hussein's government (like the Taliban) may have intended some sort of insurgency and stockpiled weapons and laid plans for it. By mid-2004, US forces clearly faced an enlarged and well organised guerrilla war as their allies withdrew and the new Iraqi government proved unable to provide its own security forces.

The previous security force, the Ba'athist army of around half a million quite well trained men plus reservists, was sent out of the barracks, the arms depots

---

25 *New York Times*, 28 Feb 2003.

26 Ricks, *Fiasco*, as above, p. 105.

were looted, and near anarchy hit the streets where, to paraphrase Rumsfeld, 'stuff happened'. A growing army of enthusiastic Islamist foreign terrorists infiltrated into Iraq where they received the support of the old Iraqi army and probably some neighbouring states, like Iran and Syria, the financial support of Al Qaeda and its allies, and the propaganda machine of sympathetic TV stations and Internet sites. In the political classes of Iraq the most influential before (and after) the invasion, were either Ba'athists or sectarian leaders of one or other of the three major communities: Sunni Arab; Shi'ite Arab; or Kurds. To them were then added the Al Qaeda cadres, some led by gangsters like the Jordanian, al-Zarqawi. The Americans bought several politicians from exile with them and some, like Chalabi, enjoyed brief careers in the new Iraq. But the most influential figures emerged as sectarian leaders, like the Shi'ite, Grand Ayatollah Ali al-Sistani.

The difficulties mounted much quicker than the successes. The 'Resistance' in Iraq coalesced into a force of perhaps 15,000–20,000 men comprising Islamist terrorists, the old Ba'athist political structure and military machine, and religious community leaders pursuing political power. Their rival militias were armed from the arsenals that had been looted in mid-2003 and supplemented through borders particularly with Syria and Iran that had not been sealed. This insurgency started in late 2003 and continued to escalate and metamorphosise even after the US eventually managed to get an apparently legitimate Iraqi government into place in April 2006.[27]

The US neo-conservatives appointed Paul Bremer as civil administrator of Iraq on 6 May 2003 and he undertook their work, purging the Iraqi state of all the Ba'athists. The CIA warned that, 'By nightfall, you'll have driven 30,000 to 50,000 Ba'athists underground. And in six months, you'll really regret this'. The CIA proved to be absolutely right. On 22 May 2003 the UN under Resolution 1483 recognised the US and UK as occupying powers – the Coalition Provisional Authority. During 2003 they searched for the WMDs that had been the immediate *casus belli* but failed to find them. The US also asked for more countries to assist in the reconstruction of Iraq and twenty eight including Australia and New Zealand, Japan and several European countries agreed.

The CPA appointed an interim Iraqi Governing Council of twenty five – thirteen Shi'ites, five Sunnis and five Kurds, one Christian and one Turkman – which met on 13 July 2003. By January 2004 a draft constitution was made public with a federal system, Islam as the official religion, and general legal equality. In June 2004 a new Interim Iraqi Government was announced and the CPA handed over sovereignty. On 30 January 2005 elections were held for the 275 person National Assembly and in May 2005 this created the new Cabinet. The Shi'ites, who had 60 per cent of the population, got seventeen positions in the Cabinet and 140 Assembly seats; the Kurds were 20 per cent of the population and got nine Cabinet positions and 75 seats; and the Sunnis who comprised 20 per cent of the population got eight Cabinet positions and only 17 seats in the Assembly. Many of the Sunnis had backed Saddam, resented the new state structure and had, in part, boycotted the elections. A Shi'ite, Ibrahim Jaafari, became Prime Minister and a Kurd, Jalal Talabani, became President. The

27 Thomas E Ricks, 'In Iraq, Military Forgot the Lessons of Vietnam: Early Mis-steps by US Left Troops Unprepared for Guerrilla Warfare', *Washington Post,* 23 July 2006.

main task of this Assembly was to draft a permanent constitution to be approved by referendum, followed by elections in December 2005.

On 15 October 2005 the draft constitution was put to referendum and approved by 79 per cent of voters. It provided for majority rule, but used a two thirds majority check on Shi'ite power. Sunni provinces rejected it, while those with Shi'ite and Kurd majorities expressed approval. Elections were then held on 15 December 2005 for the 275 member Council of Representatives. With a voter turnout of over 70 per cent, The United Iraqi Alliance (Shi'ite) won 128 seats, the Kurdistan Alliance won 53, and all the Sunni groupings won 55. Jaafari tried to continue as Prime Minister but stood down in April 2006, after much wrangling and direct US pressure,[28] to be replaced by another Shi'ite, his aide, Jawad al-Maliki. The President remained a Kurd and the two Vice Presidents were a Sunni and a Shi'ite. This process of rebuilding a government in Iraq was done, in public anyway, by the US much by the book. But it was accompanied by the growth of violence on a massive scale that involved both insurgency against the US and embryonic civil war between Sunnis and Shi'ites. By mid-2006 over 2,500 American personnel and perhaps thirty thousand Iraqis had been killed since the War had officially ended by Bush in May 2003. In 2006 one confidential US government report called Iraq a 'failed state'. By October 2006 three and a half years after the invasion, the US Army was planning on the basis that it might have to maintain current troop levels in Iraq until at least 2010.[29]

Debacle: The Iraq Insurgency, 2003–7

The US administration expected its forces to be greeted as liberators by Iraqis and some may have taken that view initially – but this circumstance evaporated quickly. Many Sunnis were attached to the Ba'athist regime and opposed its overthrow, especially when it became clear that the US really meant to purge all Ba'athists. Sunnis, at first, either boycotted the new state apparatus, joined the resistance, or fled, often to Jordan. By 2007 there were an estimated two million Iraqi refugees. The Kurds were more sympathetic but, by and large, were geographically isolated in the north, as they had been for a decade. The Shi'ites comprised sixty per cent of the population and, although US majoritarian democratic theory and practice would eventually give them state power, other issues were also in play: factionalism, sectarianism and the ambitions of the Shi'ite regime in Iran. Within six months of its declared victory, the Coalition was facing a substantial insurgency. The Coalition headquarters and the site of the new Iraqi government were located in the heavily fortified and defended Green Zone in Baghdad. Outside that zone, chaos soon ruled.

The American army in Iraq was not trained for a counter-insurgency war and did not at first fight one.[30] Between 2003 and 2006, US forces launched major operations to assert and then re-assert control in Fallujah, in Ramadi, in Samarra, and in Mosul, towns that had been supposedly won, though actually by-passed in mid-2003. In mid-2004, General Casey took over as the top US commander in Iraq and had to establish

28 Woodward, *State of Denial,* as above.

29 'Four-year plan to maintain US force', *The Australian*, 13 Oct 2006.

30 A summary of these issues is described in Ricks, *Fiasco,* as above.

an academy to teach counter-insurgency to US officers as they arrived in the country. Casualties among a US force not primarily trained to police these circumstances gradually mounted to two and half thousand dead by mid 2006 and three thousand by January 2007. The number of Iraqi dead is difficult to estimate, but a figure of thirty to fifty thousand dead by late 2006 would not seem excessive, with Bush citing the lower figure. These would include a small number killed by Coalition forces and a majority killed by random and/or selective killings by different components of the insurgency. By late 2006 the violence was looking more like a civil war between Sunni and Shi'ite Iraqis. In the month of July 2006 over 3,000 Iraqis were killed, which gives some indication of the rate of fatalities. In April 2007 up to 200 people were being killed daily, many Shi'ite victims of Sunni suicide bombers.

The CIA assessment of the insurgency in late 2004 believed that it was primarily concentrated in Baghdad and in areas immediately west and north of the capital, and that although it was diverse, it was led principally by Sunni Arabs to evict the Coalition and end US influence in Iraq.[31] Other estimates believed the Iraqi insurgency was composed of at least a dozen major guerrilla organisations, and perhaps as many as forty distinct groups operating as guerrillas. By 2005 they included: Ba'athists, the armed supporters of Saddam Hussein's former regime; Nationalists, mostly Sunni Muslims, who fought for Iraqi self-determination; anti-Shi'ite Sunni Muslims who wanted to regain the power they held under the previous regime; Sunni Islamists, the indigenous armed followers of the Salafi movement; foreign Islamist volunteers, including those often linked to Al Qaeda and largely driven by the Sunni Wahabi doctrine; Communists and other leftists; sometimes the militant followers of the Shi'ite Islamist cleric Muqtada al-Sadr; and criminal insurgents who were fighting simply for money and/or the excitement.

The most intense Sunni insurgent activity was in the cities and countryside along the Euphrates River from the Syrian border town of al-Qaim through Ramadi and Fallujah to Baghdad, as well as along the Tigris river from Baghdad north to Tikrit (Saddam's former home and power base). There was also heavy guerilla activity around the cities of Mosul and Tal Afar in the north, as well as the 'Triangle of Death' south of Baghdad, which included the cities of Iskandariya, Mahmudiya, Latifiya, and Yusufiya. Lesser activity took place in several other areas of the country. The insurgency was assisted by supply lines from Syria through al-Qaim and along the Euphrates to Baghdad and central Iraq, through which foreign terrorists infiltrated. A second route ran from the Syrian border through Tal Afar to Mosul. Iran also provided support for Shi'ite forces, particularly after its change in government in 2005. Assessments in mid-2006 put the number at between 12,000 and 20,000 hardcore fighters, along with numerous supporters, particularly throughout the Sunni Arab community. Guerilla forces also operated in many of the cities and towns of western al-Anbar province, due to mostly ineffective Iraqi security forces in this area. There was extensive guerilla activity in Ramadi, the capital of the province, as well as al-Qaim, the first stop on an insurgent movement route between Syria and Iraq in 2006.

---

31 Douglas Jehl, 'CIA Reports Offer Warnings on Iraq's Path', *New York Times*, 7 Dec 2004.

Baghdad was among the most fiercely contested regions of the country. Insurgents waged intense guerilla warfare in the capital and some Sunni neighborhoods, such as Adhamiya, were often largely under insurgent control. Suicide attacks and car bombs became near daily occurrences in Baghdad by late 2006. The road from Baghdad to the city airport was one of the most dangerous in the country and the world. Nonetheless, Iraqi security and police forces were substantially built up in the capital, despite being constantly targeted. In June 2006 'insurgents launched 700 attacks against US forces... the highest number since the invasion. They are getting more sophisticated, now using shaped charges, which concentrate the blast of a bomb, and infrared lasers, which cannot be easily jammed. They kill enough civilians every week that Iraq remains insecure, and electricity, water and oil are still supplied in starts and stops.'[32]

By July 2006, 2,547 US soldiers, 114 British soldiers and 113 soldiers from other nations had died in Iraq, and 18,777 US soldiers had been wounded. In November 2005 the *Washington Post*,[33] estimated the number of insurgents killed in action in Iraq at between 45,000 and 50,000. Another estimate of insurgency dimensions was attempted in mid 2006:[34]

> Long considered a fragmentary and disorganized collection of groups with varying tactics and aims, Iraq's insurgency is showing signs of increasing coordination, consolidation and confidence, those who study it now say. There is no consensus on the precise number of insurgent fighters, but estimates range from a few thousand to more than 50,000. The vast majority of insurgents, probably more than 90 percent, are believed to be Iraqis from the Sunni minority group that largely ruled the country before the fall of Saddam Hussein. But US commanders say that most of the deadliest attacks, and particularly suicide attacks, are committed by foreigners from a range of neighbouring countries, including Jordan, Syrian, Saudi Arabia, Egypt and Sudan.

It went on to identify some insurgent groups. The *Mujahidin Shura Council* brought together some of the foreign-backed network of Al Qaeda in Iraq, led by the Jordanian terrorist Abu Musab al-Zarqawi – who was later killed on 8 June 2006 by a bombing raid north of Baghdad. *Ansar al-Sunnah*, 'partisans of the law', were Iraqi Sunnis who adhered to the strict, fundamentalist form of Islam, Salafism, and killed 14 US Marines and an interpreter in August 2005, then the deadliest such attack of the war. The *Islamic Army in Iraq* comprised Iraqi Sunnis, including many still loyal to Saddam Hussein's regime and the Ba'ath Party, used improvised bombs and kidnappings but not suicide attacks, against US forces and non-Iraqi contractors.

Iran was involved in starting, mobilising and maintaining the Shi'ite insurgency. Many Shi'ite exiles returned from refuge in Iran when Saddam's regime was toppled. Iran initially supported the new US-installed government in Iraq, which it expected to be dominated by Shi'ites sympathetic to Iran. This policy became more difficult when the US forces fought with some Shi'ite militias in 2004–05, particularly those associated with the radical Shi'ite cleric, bin Sadr. But after the change in government

---

32 Fareed Zakaria, *Newsweek*, 4 July 2006.

33 *Washington Post*, 22 Nov 2005.

34 Jonathan Finer, 'Iraq's Insurgents: Who's Who', *Washington Post*, 19 March 2006.

in Iran in July 2005, a different strategy evolved of creating an Iranian sphere of influence which stretched from India to Palestine and incorporated a Shi'ite Iraq. Integral to this strategy was the eviction of US influence from Iraq, presumably after it had completed its task of constructing a Shi'ite state.

By late 2003 when the insurgency was obviously under way, the early futile demonstrations against the war in the US, Europe and elsewhere, gradually transformed into a less active but much more widespread hostility to US policy and, increasingly, the US itself. This was particularly the case in the Islamic world. Some of the reason for this hostility is to be found in the origins and nature of Islam which clearly instructs its adherents to protect and expand its domain. But the hostility also sprang from the rising tide of violence, death and destruction that the bungled occupation of Iraq was creating. Indeed, the insurgency was severe enough to lead to a reconsideration of US policy by August 2006: 'Senior administration officials have acknowledged to me that they are considering alternatives other than democracy. Everybody in the administration is being quite circumspect, but you can sense their own concern that this is drifting away from democracy'.[35]

The number of civilian casualties in what had become by 2006 Iraq's medium intensity civil war between Sunnis and Shi'ites grew each month. The six thousand Iraqis killed in July–August 2006 easily exceeded the civilian losses in the war in Lebanon and Israel at that time. The attempt by Nouri al-Maliki's Government to then put down sectarian warfare in Baghdad failed, requiring more US troops in the capital, who thus abandoned another heartland of the Sunni insurgency, al Anbar, to the rebels. A Pentagon official told the press in August 2006: 'The insurgency has got worse by almost all measures, with insurgent attacks at historically high levels. The insurgency has more public support and is demonstrably more capable in numbers of people active and in its ability to direct violence than at any point in time'. But US officials pointed optimistically to statistics suggesting that the military focus on the capital had helped to curb sectarian killings between Sunni and Shi'ite groups there.

The official White House position on US troop withdrawals was that they would be 'determined by events on the ground', and that 'as Iraqis stand up, we will stand down'. But there was some scepticism among military experts in Washington. By September 2006 more than 260,000 Iraqis were trained and in uniform and there had been high-profile ceremonies marking the transfer of authority from Coalition to Iraqi troops in small relatively quiet areas. But troop numbers and transfer ceremonies were not an accurate measure of force strength. Replacing the entire Ba'athist state was proving very difficult and slow and, with that time, domestic US opposition to the war grew.

The conservative Republicans had never liked the neo-conservative argument for removing Saddam and did not believe the Iraqis were capable of democracy. They certainly wanted to remove a perceived WMD threat, but most of all, after 9/11 they wanted to show their enemies some US military power. These conservatives wanted to depose Saddam, remove the weapons, install a client dictator and, probably, leave

35 *Andrew Sullivan,* 'Hawkish plan to plant a puppet in Iraq', *The Australian,* 21 Aug 2006.

considerable damage behind. This would deter the Iranians, leave a military victory and show what the US could do, even with a few troops. The plan was probably what Rumsfeld wanted at first, and it helps explain the Bush administration's refusal to add more troops in the first few months after the invasion. This is also certainly what Jay Garner had in mind immediately before the invasion; but his policies were reversed by Bremer.[36] Whatever the merits of Garner's plan, it was abandoned in April/May 2003 and the neo-conservatives must wear much of the blame. Thereafter, the Bush administration was stuck with its Iraq debacle and could not easily extract itself. By 2006, domestic support for Bush was rapidly declining with this apparent failure in Iraq.

By October 2006 the Bush administration was giving some consideration to strategies other than pursuing a democratic state on the one hand, or 'cut and run' on the other.[37] An independent commission was set up by the US Congress, The Iraq Study Group, co-chaired by James Baker, the former US Secretary of State, to report to Bush in late 2006. In October 2006 Bush acknowledged for the first time a parallel between the increased violence in Iraq and the Vietnam War, and Blair conceded, also for the first time, that British troops in Iraq could be a 'provocation'.[38] The Tet Offensive, launched by the North Vietnamese in early 1968, was a military defeat for them, but the scope of the assault shocked Americans and helped turn US public opinion against that war. These comments came with a sharp rise in US deaths in Iraq. Domestic support for the war then collapsed in the November 2006 Congressional elections when the Republicans were heavily defeated.

Nonetheless, by early 2007 the anti-US insurgency was largely Sunni-based and concentrated in Baghdad and the western Al Anbar region. Even more violent was the inter-communal civil war, also concentrated in the capital, which often looked like the ethnic cleansing of suburbs by both sides. The Shi'ite militias appeared to be constrained from attacks on US forces by the Shi'ite politicians who by 2007 controlled the Iraqi government. In January 2007 Bush announced a 'surge' strategy of deploying an additional 26,000 US troops into Iraq mostly into the capital. These would establish stability in the most violent part of the country and enable the Shi'ite-dominated but nominally democratic Iraqi state to establish sufficient security with its own forces for the US to begin a withdrawal in the near future. By April 2007 although there were some signs this strategy was succeeding, suicide attacks on Shi'ite areas increased.[39] Sunni insurgents penetrated the Baghdad security net on 19 April, and hit Shi'ite targets with four bomb attacks that killed 183 people, the bloodiest day since the US troop increase began.

---

36 See Thomas E Ricks, *Fiasco*, as above, pp. 84ff for a detailed account.

37 *Sarah Baxter*, 'US hatches plan to carve up Iraq', *The Australian*, 9 Oct 2006 reprinted from the London *Sunday Times*; the *New York Times* report was less positive, David E Sanger, 'Baker, Presidential Confidant, Hints at Need for New War Plan', *New York Times*, 9 Oct 2006.

38 'Iraq like Vietnam, Bush concedes', *The Australian*, 20 Oct 2006.

39 Steven R Hurst and Lauren Frayer, Associated Press Writers, '4 blasts in Baghdad kill at least 183', 19 April 2007.

The political bloc of Shi'ite cleric Moqtada al-Sadr said it would leave the Iraqi Government as this wave of Sunni bombings left many Shi'ites dead in Baghdad and it demanded a timetabled exit of US-led foreign troops. The Sadr group had six cabinet ministers in Maliki's government and 32 members of the Iraqi Parliament. Sadr strongly opposed the US presence after 2003 and fought two rebellions against US forces in 2004. The US, in turn, accused Sadr's militia of being involved in sectarian killings of Sunnis. The surge and Baghdad security crackdown aimed to rein in his militia and it melted away after the launch of the plan in February. But while militia-based killings were then reduced in Baghdad, insurgent bombings still occurred elsewhere. The inability of the US to contain this violence also fuelled Jihadism elsewhere.

The Islamic Diaspora Front

The number of Muslims world wide is between 1.3 and 1.6 billion. Most Muslims live in Islamic countries in the broad strip from Morocco to Indonesia, but some are in consolidated areas of Islamic society in states ruled by non-Muslims, like southern Thailand and Philippines. For ten centuries Islam expanded by both conquest and conversion but in more modern times Islamic societies were, in their turn, conquered and ruled by non-Islamic states, although their social fabric and legal systems may have remained Muslim. In the twentieth century, however, Muslims started to migrate to other non-Muslim and wealthier societies, particularly the Western developed countries. The most significant Muslim populations among their diaspora in developed countries are: Australia, 300,000 or 1.5 per cent; Canada, 620,000 or two per cent; France, six million or ten per cent; Germany, three million or four per cent; Holland, one million or six per cent; Italy, 1.3 million or 2 per cent; Spain, one million or 2.5 per cent; UK, 1.6 million or 2.5 per cent; and the US, 6 million or 2 per cent. In less developed countries Muslim populations are: China, 39 million or 3 per cent; India, 154 million or 14 per cent; and Russia, 27 million or 19 per cent. There are also substantial Muslim populations in the secular republics of the Philippines and Indonesia and in the Kingdom of Thailand. In all these countries some sections of the Muslim population have responded to the propaganda by deed of Al Qaeda and to the destruction the Coalition has brought to Iraq.

The impact of these events on the Islamic diaspora, particularly among Arabs but also Pakistanis, has obviously been great. The extent of support for Al Qaeda in many Islamic countries is considerable. Polls on this subject show support strongest in Jordan, Pakistan and among Palestinians, but also considerable in Egypt, Syria and Saudi Arabia, where dictatorships make polling less meaningful. But support is also strong in Southeast Asia, including in Malaysia, where former prime minister Mahathir's inflammatory anti-Semitic rhetoric continues to resonate; in Indonesia, where the militant Muslim cleric, Abu Bakar Bashir, was freed in 2006 after a short prison term to be greeted by numerous supporters; and in the southern Philippines, where US troops have been deployed to assist local authorities. But there is also support for the Iraqi 'resistance' in non-Islamic Western countries, particularly among Muslims but also including educated people of the Left like the late Edward

Said, the British incendiary, Tariq Ali, and the celebrated linguistics Professor, Noam Chomsky. The extent of popular support is difficult to gauge, but the British Home Office estimated after a survey that about 13 per cent of the 1.6 million Muslims resident in the UK support terrorism in one way or another – a finding later confirmed in trials of British terrorists.[40] A number of studies have been undertaken of this issue, especially after the terrorist attacks in Europe in Madrid, London, Holland and elsewhere, with not dissimilar results.

In *Eurabia,*[41] Bat Ye'or describes a Europe in which uncontrolled immigration has produced an unintegrated Islamic population which is younger, more fecund and less skilled than the secular Christian majority which is being overwhelmed numerically, culturally and, soon, politically. In these EU countries, the rise of Islamic militancy has often been supported by sections of the political Left. This Red-Green alliance first became apparent in the immediate aftermath of 9/11 when some Leftist icons quickly expressed their qualified support for the attacks.[42] But, more broadly, the academic and intellectual environments had already created a receptive atmosphere by promoting extreme critiques of western civilisation and the non-integrationist values of multiculturalism. The writers most given to excusing or indeed applauding Islamist militancy and terrorism are also those who figure most prominently in academic social science syllabuses including Chomsky, Said, the late Michael Foucault, Tariq Ali, and Robert Fisk, the London *Independent* journalist.

In part, Al Qaeda's actions and propaganda have been designed to incite Muslims in the wider diaspora to undertake terrorist acts against their host societies. This appeal has had some success. A front has clearly been opened by these tactics that has resulted in terrorist activities being undertaken in or against many of the countries that host substantial Islamic communities, including the developed countries of Spain, Holland, France, Germany, Britain, Australia, the US and Canada, and the less developed countries of India, Philippines, Indonesia and Thailand, to take some examples. These numerous intended and actual attacks in vastly different localities were directed chiefly, but not entirely, against states fighting against Al Qaeda and Islamic terrorists. They were not committed or conceived as just mindless acts of terror. This was one front in a global, purposeful Jihad. One of its main targets had long been the democratic state of Israel.

In early 2006, the Palestinians elected a Hamas government, committed to the destruction of Israel, and some Palestinian militia began to bombard Israel with rockets. In support, Lebanese Hezbollah guerrillas crossed into northern Israel and captured two Israeli soldiers.[43] The Israelis retaliated and invaded Lebanon in July 2006 with extended air force strikes as far as Beirut, with naval bombardments, with armoured columns of mobilised reservists, and with commando helicopter attacks as

---

40 'Price of justice was the longest and costliest criminal case ever: With 100 more suspects awaiting trial, Operation Crevice may have set an unwanted precedent', *The Times*, 1 May 2007.

41 Bat Ye'or, *Eurabia: The Euro-Arab Axis* (Madison, NJ, 2005).

42 Greg Melleuish and Imre Saluusinszky, eds, *Blaming Ourselves* (Potts Point NSW, 2002).

43 *The Australian*, 26 Aug 2006.

far as the Bekaa valley. This campaign proved difficult. The Hezbollah was armed by Syria and Iran, including with up to 15,000 missiles on mobile batteries, many dug into bunkers and/or below residential buildings. The Hezbollah fighters were well trained, had planned carefully and were supported by the local population. The Israeli Defence Force was unable to secure a quick or a decisive victory over Hezbollah which fired up to four thousand missiles into northern Israeli towns. Despite re-supply from the US with bunker busting bombs, the redoubts and fortifications, built with Iranian and Syrian help since the Israeli evacuation of Lebanon in 2000, were not entirely overcome.

This strategic stalemate eventually produced a cease fire in mid-August 2006. But Hezbollah was not disarmed and distributed relief throughout devastated regions in the wake of the conflict. Given the performance of Israel in all previous wars with Islamic states and organisations, this was a massive comparative strategic defeat. It was also a tactical victory for the sponsors of Hezbollah – Iran and Syria. Worse still, it was inflicted at a time when the US was bogged down in Iraq and Afghanistan.

Jihadist Retaliation

The Taliban were in control of much of Afghanistan for a decade and hosted a number of Al Qaeda training camps for some of that time. These camps trained perhaps thirty thousand foreign terrorists. After the destruction of the Taliban regime in late 2001, these terrorists dispersed to form the basis for retaliation against those countries that overthrew their government. While the US was fighting the GWOT, its opponents opened new fronts. One of these was among the Islamic diaspora, particularly in the developed countries where enough young Muslims responded to the propaganda of the Jihadists to engage in terrorist attacks and suicide bombings. Among other places, they attacked Westerners, mostly Australians in Bali in October 2002, Madrid in mid-2004, London in July 2005, and the Egyptian resort town of Sharm al Sheik.

The US and its allies pursued the Jihadists, captured many and interrogated them in third countries where often *habeus corpus* and other anti-torture rules did not apply. The US kept hundreds of the 'worst of the worst' captives in Guatanamo Bay detention centre in Cuba. It also, however, sought to try them in military tribunals which the US Supreme Court in 2006 ruled illegal. In September 2006, Bush admitted for the first time that terror suspects had been held in secret CIA prisons outside US borders, saying that they were being transferred to Guantanamo Bay, in Cuba, where he hoped that they would be tried for war crimes.[44] He said that his proposal would mean that the men who 'orchestrated the deaths of nearly 3,000 Americans on September 11, 2001, can face justice'. They had previously been deemed 'illegal enemy combatants', but would be given full rights under Article 3 of the Geneva Conventions.

Human rights groups alleged that the CIA also had 'black sites' or secret prisons in Afghanistan, Iraq, Jordan, Pakistan, Thailand, Uzbekistan, Poland and Romania,

44 *Tom Baldwin,* 'Bush admits to secret CIA prisons', *The Times*, 7 Sept 2006.

and that detainees were moved to these sites through 'extraordinary renditions', that is kidnapping. In December 2005 a Swiss senator reported to the Council of Europe that 14 European countries, including Britain, had colluded with the CIA's renditions, allowing abductions from their soil or acting as stop-off points for flights on the way to prisons. The US claimed that detainees in these prisons were not tortured; but in 2002 Jay Bybee, the Assistant US Attorney-General, suggested that for pain to be defined as torture it should be severe enough potentially to result in organ failure or death. These activities ensured further anti-US campaigns that would further sully its image. The US would not be permitted to fight a total war against the Jihadists if human rights activists, leftists and Islamists could stop it.

Nonetheless, the US publicly claimed to have made progress against Al Qaeda. In September 2006 the White House counter-terrorism strategy was outlined in a twenty three page report that said significant progress had been made against a degraded but still dangerous Al Qaeda network.[45] It stated: 'The enemy we face today in the war on terror is not the same enemy we faced on September 11. Our effective counter-terrorist efforts in part have forced the terrorists to evolve'. It listed the strategy's successes:

> We have deprived al-Qaida of safe haven in Afghanistan and helped a democratic government to rise in its place. Once a terrorist sanctuary ruled by the repressive Taliban regime, Afghanistan is now a full partner in the War on Terror. A multinational coalition joined by the Iraqis is aggressively prosecuting the war against the terrorists in Iraq. Together, we are working to secure a united, stable, and democratic Iraq, now a new War on Terror ally in the heart of the Middle East. We have significantly degraded the al–Qaida network. Most of those in the al–Qaida network responsible for the September 11 attacks, including the plot's mastermind Khalid Shaykh Muhammad, have been captured or killed. We also have killed other key al–Qaida members, such as Abu Musab al-Zarqawi, the group's operational commander in Iraq who led a campaign of terror that took the lives of countless American forces and innocent Iraqis.
>
> We have led an unprecedented international campaign to combat terrorist financing that has made it harder, costlier, and riskier for al-Qaida and related terrorist groups to raise and move money. There is a broad and growing global consensus that the deliberate targeting of innocents is never justified by any calling or cause. Many nations have rallied to fight terrorism, with unprecedented cooperation on law enforcement, intelligence, military, and diplomatic activity.

But, despite high-profile arrests, security operations and upbeat assessments from the White House, many other experts believed that the US was losing its 'global war on terror'.[46] In May 2006 the influential US magazine, *Foreign Policy,* questioned 116 leading US experts, a balanced mix of Republicans and Democrats, including a former secretary of state, two former directors of the CIA and dozens of the country's top security analysts on the progress of the US campaign against terrorism. Eighty-

---

45 *National Strategy for Combating Terrorism*, US State Department, White House, September 2006.

46 Michel Moutot, 'Washington is Losing "War on Terror": Experts', *Agence France Press,* 5 July 2006.

four percent believed the United States was losing the 'war on terror', 86 percent that the world has become a more dangerous place in the last five years, and 80 percent that a major new attack on their country was likely within the next decade.

The US intelligence community came to a similar conclusion. A classified report in April 2006 found that the Iraq war had spawned a new generation of Islamic extremists and that the overall terrorist threat to the West had grown since the 9/11 attacks. The intelligence estimate was the first formal appraisal of global terrorism by US intelligence agencies since the Iraq war began, and represented a consensus view of the sixteen spy services inside the US Government.[47] In the report, *Trends in Global Terrorism: Implications for the United States*, it said Islamic radicalism, rather than being in retreat, had spread across the globe. It concluded that the overall terror threat had increased since the 9/11 2001 attacks. Intelligence officials agreed that the US had seriously damaged Al Qaeda and disrupted its ability to plan and direct major operations, but that radical Islamic networks had spread and decentralised. The intelligence estimate did not offer policy prescriptions. In April 2007 alone, Al Qaeda claimed responsibility for terrorist attacks on the Iraqi parliament in the Green Zone, on a Shi'ite shrine near Karbal, in Somalia, North Waziristan, Afghanistan, Gaza, Algeria, Morocco and Bangladesh. In May 2007 the Deputy leader of Al Qaeda, Ayman al-Zawahiri said, 'we ask Allah that they [the US] only get out (of Iraq) after losing 200,000 to 300,000 killed'. [48]

The US was, unquestionably, the most powerful state in the world, but its writ was not unchallenged. On 7 September 2006 the US-led Coalition handed over control of Iraq's armed forces to the Iraqi Prime Minister. It had to be done five days late and in secret. Hours before, five bomb attacks in Baghdad killed more than eighteen people and earlier a bomb under a mosque killed three others. The Global War on Terror pitted a hegemonic materialist power, with modest messianic inclinations, unable to relinquish its access to oil, against a religious opponent unwilling to give up its religious commitment to God in the wake of the overwhelming forces of modernisation in the twenty first century. By mid-2007 both antagonists remained tenacious and undefeated but the prospects for the US policy seemed problematic.

47 'Iraq war spawns terror', *The Australian*, 25 Sept 2006.

48 'Al-Qa'ida taunts US on 'pullout', *The Australian*, 7 May 2007.

Chapter 7
Allies

Beginning in the 1980s, anti-modernisation forces in the Islamic world began to mobilise seriously. With extreme Jihadist Islam as an ideological base, the hatred of the Jewish Israeli state as a catalyst, and a general rejection of modernisation the larger context, Islamic radicalism declared war on the West. At first the West did not notice. After 9/11 it did, and Bush declared and fought a Global War on Terror. The election contest in 2004 between Senator Kerry and George W Bush rested upon the judgement of the US electorate on how well the GWOT was proceeding, especially in the Iraq theatre. The two candidates, however, did not differ substantially on the need to continue the war against Al Qaeda and to defeat Jihadists and both viewed it as being a struggle between the forces of good and evil. The re-election of Bush in 2004 ensured a sharp ideological edge to the war on terror.

One aspect that emerged in the war on terror was the globalisation of paranoia about and fear of terrorism and the effects this had on civil society. In all the Anglo-Sphere countries, and elsewhere, the political Left either supported the Islamists or resisted policies designed to destroy them. This was deeply rooted in the Left's anti-Americanism, but was extended by the small Left component in the Iraqi insurgency and the adoption of leftist slogans by the Jihadists themselves. The academic Left supported this stance with the terrorists often nominated as a 'significant other', and so therefore always to be preferred to Western powers.[1] In any case, Edward Said supported Hamas and Noam Chomsky, Hezbollah. In Australia, for example, the Australian Research Council was accused of only supporting research that took the narrative of the Jihadists as its starting point.[2] But the majority support generated for the GWOT in the Anglo-Sphere countries was a result of their sharing a common language, culture and structure of representative government. It was also an extension of the core alliance partners with the US during the Cold War who had mostly shared intelligence gathering and distribution since 1948. And, in part,

---

1 David Horowitz, *Unholy Alliance: Radical Islam and the American Left* (New York, 2004); for Australia, David Martin Jones and Carl Ungerer, 'In an Idealist World; Are our researchers into terrorism being appropriately critical or merely hypocritical?', *The Australian*, 21 Oct 2006.

2 David Martin Jones and Carl Ungerer, 'Delusion reigns in terror studies: Academics are using tax dollars to lay the blame on the West for militant Islam', The Australian, 15 Sept 2006, wrote, 'In this Alice in Wonderland world of peer-referenced journals read only by participants in this mutually reinforcing discourse, the focus of study is not Islamist ideology and its propensity to violence, but our own long-repressed responsibility for the cause of Islamist rage. Given the nature of preferment and funding in Australian academe, the imams of critical terror studies will continue to maintain this delusion for the foreseeable future'.

it was a result of sharing a basic world view, historical experience and a common modernised civilisation.

The Anglo-Sphere

Britain, the source of the Anglo-Sphere, is the second largest EU nation at sixty million, with the fifth largest economy in the world, and one of the biggest stock markets outside the US. It also has two super major oil corporations (Shell and BP) in the world's top ten and many more in the top five hundred. The British, like the French, also maintain a substantial armed force and the capacity for a limited global reach. The UK is also a nuclear weapons state capable of mounting an independent nuclear deterrence strategy based on its second strike, nuclear armed submarine fleet. It also has some continuing cultural influence and 'soft power'. This includes a broadcasting system, the BBC, with a world wide reputation for impartiality, not greatly degraded by a recent rather slavish adherence to political correctness. It also has two universities – Oxford and Cambridge – that rate in the world's top ten, a massive tourism industry that leaves many familiar with its institutions, a lead in the structure of law and politics gained in the nineteenth century, and usually the most articulate politicians in the world to state its case, as a result of the adversarial system of Westminster politics.

At the end of the Cold War, Britain stumbled on to an administration of indecision and sleaze under John Major which lost to Blair's New Labour in 1997. New Labour advertised itself as a 'Third Way', but in fact at first simply maintained the liberal economic settings the Tories had established, and rode the newly de-regulated British economy into a high growth era. Britain became the fastest growing of the large EU economies on the basis of its global services, communications and finance sectors. The Labour government then faced the essential choice of becoming a leading European power or pursuing a post-imperial global role, possibly within the NATO alliance, which the US was pressing to assume wider geographical responsibilities. After the attacks of 9/11 Blair believed he could constrain the Americans who were, understandably, baying for blood and revenge. Blair promised a British policy of whole-hearted support if the US went back to the UN for endorsement of an invasion of Iraq. Blair then promoted the possibility of an Iraqi attack on the UK with only forty five minutes warning. The UN gambit failed and Blair – and Britain – was locked into the GWOT essentially on terms laid down by the US.[3]

The British were carried into the war in Iraq almost entirely on the back of Blair's support for Bush, who was widely despised in Labour circles. This was the main reason Blair was forced out of politics despite having won a third successive general election, and on 10 May Blair announced he would resign on 27 June 2007. All other British political leaders distanced themselves from Bush, including the post-2005 Tory leader, David Cameron, Liberal Democrat leader, Menzies Campbell, and Blair's heir apparent, Chancellor Gordon Brown. But Britain remained committed in

3 Martin Walker, ed, *The Iraq War* (Dulles VA, 2003) chapters 1–3.

Iraq and Afghanistan until 2009, although it announced an initial reduction of 1,600 troops in Iraq in February 2007. Canada was more reticent.

At the close of the Second World War, Canada was one of the most powerful states in the world. It had contributed a vast army to the defeat of Hitler and a substantial fleet to the transportation of North American armies to the European theatre. It quickly joined the NATO in 1948 and during the Cold War Canada maintained a high degree of military preparedness and expenditure. In addition, in the 1970s when the global economy required better coordination Canada became a member of the Group of Seven. By the twenty first century Canada was a substantial country of 33 million people with the second largest land mass of any state (after Russia). Its GDP was $1.13 trillion with $35,000 per capita and a healthy growth rate. Even after the post-Cold War run down, it had an army of twenty thousand and air force of 140 aircraft including CF-18s, although the navy was merely for coastal patrol.

But Canada's staunch strategic posture had always been under challenge from that quarter of the Canadian population who were French speaking and influenced by Francophone hostility to the Anglo Saxons in general, and the US in particular. They had been put down by the British in the nineteenth century but, nonetheless, maintained an ambition for independence for their province of Quebec. In the 1970s, to offset this, the Canadians developed the idea of multiculturalism. In 1991, the Quebec government demanded a new constitution or it would secede, but Canadians rejected this in a referendum.

The Liberals in government from 1993 until 2006 then pursued a raft of leftist policies which effectively took Canada out of global strategic considerations. At the end of the Cold War, Canada's substantial contribution to Western security diminished. The primary role of the Canadian armed forces in the post-Cold War world was redesignated as being to contribute to UN security and peacekeeping operations. The right wing opposition was ineffective and lost three consecutive elections until it regrouped and in 2003 became the Conservative Party under Stephen Harper. In 1994 Canada joined the NAFTA with the US and Mexico an act, of course, resisted by the Left in Canada. But it was an accession that ensured the prosperity of the Canadian economy by making it a part of the largest, most dynamic and most productive economy in the world – that of the US. Bush was, of course, extremely unpopular in Canada where the major political issue in 2001 was the funding of health care. Nonetheless, Canada did join the NATO occupation of Afghanistan in 2001 although it avoided Iraq.

In 2004 the Liberal Party was wracked by financial scandals and the resignation of Prime Minister, Francophone Jean Chrétien. In January 2006 the Conservatives won 126 seats in the election and formed a minority government under Prime Minister Stephen Harper. Canada was re-evaluating. Harper, a church going accountant who had worked for an oil company, supported the American invasion of Iraq. Harper met Bush in late March 2006 and Canada moved closer to the US. In 2006, the Conservative government extended the Canadian military mission in Afghanistan by at least two years and in May 2006 the House of Commons voted to extend the mission until 2009 by a slim 149–145 majority. On 3 June 2006 seventeen Muslim men were arrested in Ontario and charged with plotting terrorist acts including decapitating Stephen Harper.

Australia inhabited a less benign environment than Canada. It had two options at the end of the Cold War: align closely with the US or develop a more independent policy and pay the financial price for pursuing it. During the Cold War, Australia was one of the closest allies of the US and fought in the Korean, Vietnam and first Gulf wars, and hosted some of the most important US communications and surveillance facilities. At the end of the Cold War, the Australian Labor government led by Bob Hawke (1983–1991) was closely aligned with the US and heavily supported Israel. Under Prime Minister Paul Keating (1991–1996) it then pursued a more independent policy towards the US, was critical of the British heritage, advocated a republic, and was less aligned in the Middle East. But it was defeated in 1996.

The policy of the incoming Coalition Liberal-led government of Prime Minister John Howard (1996–2007) and Foreign Minister Alexander Downer was from its inception to cement the alliance with the US.[4] Howard was in Washington when the Pentagon was attacked on 9/11 and immediately declared his support for the US. The ANZUS Treaty was then invoked for the first time since 1951 and Australian forces deployed with those of the US to remove the Taliban regime. This policy had popular support in Australia. But when the Howard government agreed to join in the invasion of Iraq, there were large demonstrations against the policy and it did not have popular support.

The Afghanistan policy was mostly supported by the Labor Party leadership of Kim Beazley (leader 1996–2001 and 2005–6). Under the leadership of Simon Crean (2001–3), however, Labor opposed the military commitment to Iraq. In December 2003, Mark Latham took over the leadership and in early 2004 promised to have Australian forces out of Iraq by Christmas. Latham levelled allegations of subservience to the US against John Howard, but provoked angry responses from the White House by sliding into personal abuse, calling Howard 'an arse-licker' and Bush 'the most dangerous and incompetent president in living memory'. Although involvement in Iraq was never popular, it did not emerge as a major election issue in 2004 and Howard won on other issues, including the strong economy and probably national security, Iraq notwithstanding.[5] When Kevin Rudd assumed the Labor leadership in late 2006 he quickly made it clear that he would support the US alliance without qualification, although he then said he would withdraw some troops from Iraq.

The alliance with the US gave Australia access to satellite and electronic reconnaissance intelligence information and access to world's best weaponry. The Australian Defence Force (ADF) was able to train with US forces and this contributed to making the ADF among the best in the world. The alliance itself was always popular, even in the depth of the defeat in Vietnam. Most Australians were prepared to wear the risk and odium of the war in Iraq for the sake of the alliance, particularly when the casualties were light. Howard achieved terms of deployment that kept them light.

4 Sheridan, *The Partnership*, as above.

5 See Catley, *Triumph of Liberalism*, as above.

A much less popular policy of neutrality was advocated from time to time and reached its peak popularity in the early 1970s, when Australia had taken five hundred fatalities in Vietnam and the US was losing the war. Labor was then elected partly on the groundswell of opposition to that war, but never proposed to sever the alliance with the US. A policy of 'go it alone' is occasionally advocated by some Left backbenchers in the Labor Party and by the small Greens Party. Such a policy has never been generally popular in Australia, although New Zealand is a different matter.

New Zealand has a much smaller population, at four million, and territory of 270,000 square kilometres with few mineral resources. It has a GDP PPP of $108 billion and per capita of $26,000. From the First World War New Zealand developed a somewhat different perspective on defence strategy to Australia. In the Second World War its troops stayed in Europe when Australia's were moved to Australia in 1942. It was also not attacked by the Japanese. In the 1970s New Zealanders were very hostile to French nuclear testing in the Pacific. They also became very critical of Reagan's strategy in the 1980s and, with Labour in power, refused access to New Zealand ports by US naval vessels. The alliance between the two countries was severed by 1986, and this policy was generally popular.[6] After this, both Labour and National (conservative) governments adopted a foreign policy independent of the US. The bipartisan policy was supported by the electorate and it seemed likely to remain in the medium term, although the Nationals did reconsider the policy and nearly won the 2005 election.[7]

But relations with the US were not totally severed and, for example, the staging base for US Antarctic operations was in Christchurch. On first being elected in 1999, the Labour government of Prime Minister Helen Clark (1999–) gave indication of strategic disengagement, down graded the armed forces, sold off the air force, and opted out of the joint strategic defence of Australia and New Zealand. Just before the attacks of 9/11Clark declared that the country enjoyed an 'incredibly benign strategic environment'. Then after what must have been an agonising re-appraisal, the Clark government chose to contribute to the GWOT, and sent Special Forces to Afghanistan. It also contributed to the Australian-led operations in East Timor and the Solomon Islands. In July 2004, the New Zealand Labour Prime Minister Helen Clark declared that New Zealand would be open to a visit by a non-nuclear vessel from the US Navy.

The close election win of Helen Clark in 2005 brought into a coalition government the leader of the New Zealand First Party, Winston Peters, as Foreign Minister. He was known for his pro-American views and this possibly signals an end to New

---

6 See James Belich, *The New Zealand Wars* (Auckland, 1986); *Making Peoples* (Auckland, 1996); and *Paradise Reforged* (Auckland, 2001); and Michael King, *The Penguin History of New Zealand* (Auckland, 2003).

7 Catley, *Waltzing with Matilda*, as above; King, *The Penguin History of New Zealand*, as above, p. 445. For both the nuclear ship policy issue and tourist competition with Australia see *The Australian*, 27 July 2004. For an analysis of the crisis see Kevin Kenny, *The ANZUS Crisis: Cold War Diplomacy, 1984–1986*, Flinders University American Studies Honours Thesis, 2005.

Zealand isolation and hostility to US power in the southern Pacific. Further, the Nationals under Don Brash (deposed in 2006) had done well with an openly rightist policy that included rapprochement with the US. Thus it is quite possible that the New Zealand option may be abandoned by New Zealand itself. In any case, in the end, the New Zealand option had only been seriously available because Australia is the dominant power in New Zealand's region.[8] By 2006, New Zealand had been re-integrated into some ANZUS operations, although at a lower order of diplomatic and military commitment than Australia.

It is unlikely Australia will take this more neutralist strategic direction, from which New Zealand has in any case retreated somewhat. The strength of support for the US-Australia alliance in the Australian electorate, although strained by the Iraqi War among the generally Left Australian intelligentsia, would make it unacceptable to the Australian public. It would not be in the Australian national interest, either strategically or in terms of increased defence expenditures, to break with the US. The status quo, therefore, or even closer relations with the US, seems the likely future of Australian military and foreign policy planning. In April 2007 Australia announced its commitment in Afghanistan would be increased to 1,000 troops and this received support from the ALP leader, Kevin Rudd.

East Asian Dilemmas

When Bush was inaugurated the Republicans expected their biggest strategic challenge to be the rising power of China and early in 2001 a stronger US commitment to the defence of Taiwan seemed likely to cause trouble in the bilateral relationship. This was also an issue for Australia, the only regional power to back the US in the 1995 Taiwan Straits crisis. China, indeed, loomed as the major divisive issue in the alliance between Australia and the US. But by 2006, although China was a substantial military and economic power, tensions with the US had been contained. China had become the largest creditor for the large US national debt, to which Bush had substantially added, and had accumulated reserves of over $US176 billion dollars. In spite of US pressure, the PRC made only a small currency revaluation in July 2005. US-China economic relations had become somewhat competitive and there were added difficulties in foreign policy issues such as Taiwan relations, the selling of Chinese nuclear technology to potential US enemies such as Iran, and resolving the Korean impasse.

Tensions over Taiwan periodically intensified. The PRC government became increasingly belligerent towards the Taiwan President Chen Shui-bian of the Democratic Progressive Party who was elected in March 2004 advocating greater independence for Taiwan. The PRC would not accept this and threatened war if necessary to prevent Taiwan gaining independence. In 2005 Major-General Zhu Chenghu, the Dean of China's National Defense University, commented that if the US intervened in a war with Taiwan, the PRC would attack US cities with nuclear

8 Bob Catley, ed, *Australia and New Zealand: Coming Together or Drifting Apart?* (Wellington, 2002).

weapons.[9] In November 2005, Bush appeared to extend the Bush Doctrine of spreading democracy to China.[10] Although during the Cold War Australia shared the view that the PRC should be 'contained', by 2006 Australia had strong trading ties to China and was in a profound dilemma since the US seemed bound to defend the integrity of Taiwan if attacked. Both the US and China applied pressure on Australia to back their position. A shift in public opinion in Australia away from the US and towards China was reflected in the annual Lowy Institute poll in March 2005 which showed more Australians (69 per cent) had a positive attitude toward China, than towards the US (58 per cent). The majority of Australians would not want Australia to back the US in a war against China over Taiwan.[11]

In August 2004, Foreign Minister Downer made it clear that the US could not count on Australian support if it went to war over Taiwan and that the ANZUS Treaty would not necessarily apply. The US was obligated to defend Taiwan, but Australia was under no such obligation. Downer also indicated that it would be unwise for Taiwan to make 'any proclamation of independence [which] would be provocative'.[12] US State Department officials believed Australia's obligations under the ANZUS treaty were 'pretty clear', implying that the US expected continuing Australian support for the US position. The Chinese warned that Australia should not plan to invoke the ANZUS Treaty in case of conflict between the US and China over Taiwan. Downer replied that Australia had no plans to encourage Taiwan independence or to alter the ANZUS treaty whether to suit China or anyone else.[13] Australia was caught in a dilemma about the geopolitics of East Asia. But John Howard did not see an inevitable conflict between China and the US and concluded that 'a strong US presence in the Asia-Pacific will remain vital for stability and security. America's alliance relationships, including with Australia, will be the anchors for that US presence'.[14]

Japan also kept a close eye on Australia and any overt moves toward China on contentious Sino-Japanese issues could jeopardize trading relations with Australia's number one trading partner. Australia had a long rewarding trade relationship with Japan. China's experience of modern Japan has been less benign and was alarmed when Prime Minister Koizumi boosted expenditure to $US46 billion per annum over five years (although in response to the threat to Japan from the DPRK). With PRC spending at least $US 25 billion per annum with some estimates putting the actual figure as high as $US 40 billion, and Taiwan and South Korea another $US 22 billion between them, the total expenditure on defence for northeast Asia, including the sizeable US commitment, was in excess of $US 200 billion by 2005. Japan also had non-combatant armed forces in Iraq, but with very strong domestic opposition, Koizumi withdrew them in 2005. These changes suggested the re-entry of Japan

9 *The Australian,* 18 July 2005.

10 *The Australian,* 17 Nov 2005.

11 *The Australian,* 29 March 2005.

12 *The Australian,* 18 Aug 2004. Adam Cobb, 'Energy the key to regional security', *Australian Financial Review*, 1 Oct 2004.

13 *The Australian,* 8 March 2005.

14 *The Australian,* 13 Sept 2005.

into the world of global strategic players and the end to its self-imposed isolation as Japan viewed the re-emergence of China with suspicion. But in 2007 Koizumi's successor, Zhinzo Abe, tried to improve the bilateral relationship.

Relations with other nations in East Asia also raised serious strategic questions for Japan. The belligerent DPRK presented an extremely difficult issue for Japan in particular. The Six Party Talks, established to resolve the continuing crisis over DPRK's nuclear weapons program, were boycotted by the DPRK in 2005. Japan has raised the possibility of economic sanctions against the DPRK and this threat prompted the DPRK in December 2004, to warn about retaliation against Japan with physical actions if necessary to defend its economic viability.[15] Tensions were further heightened in June 2006 when the DRRK again launched missiles into the western Pacific region, threatening both Japan and the US with the possibility of long-range missile attacks. All parties condemned the exercises and called for urgent resumption of the Six Party Talks. In April 2005, the proposals by the UN Secretary General to enlarge the Security Council, with Japan as a possible new permanent member, brought the opposition of South Korea All of these tensions, and growing trade rivalry between the two East Asian powers, will provide the historical and geopolitical context for interstate relations in the future.[16] Yet, despite these challenges, Japan remained within the US orbit and in a close relationship with Australia.

The strategic relationship with the US presented challenges for Australia. Australian defence expenditures after the Cold War had been reduced. The troop commitments to Afghanistan and Iraq, and the large deployments in East Timor, Solomon Islands and Papua New Guinea stretched the ADF's capacity, the police and troops were withdrawn from Papua New Guinea in May 2005. Nonetheless, this left roughly 3,000 troops to defend the nearly 3,000 square miles of the Australian mainland. With the Defence budget at 1.9 per cent of GDP, the credibility of ADF seemed questionable with the GWOT intensifying in the region to the north of Australia and an 'arc of instability' emerging from the Indonesian archipelago to Vanuatu.[17] In September 2006 the Australian government announced that defence expenditure would be increased and army numbers substantially expanded.

Bush and the Defence of Democracy

The US was attempting to create democracy in Iraq and has historically perceived itself as anti-imperialist promoter of democracy, in spite of having an informal empire and intervening repeatedly in the Americas. The US certainly defeated racist Fascism in Europe and Japanese militarism in Asia; but during the Cold War its

15 *The Australian,* 14 Dec 2004; Paul French, *North Korea: The Paranoid Peninsula, a Modern History* (London, 2005).

16 *The Weekend Australian,* 2–3 April 2005; *The Australian,* 3 March 2005.

17 This situation alarmed even the most ardent government supporters: see *The Australian,* 19 March 2002 and the editorial in *The Australian,* 7 Aug 2003. For a recent historical analysis of Australia's past and future defence strategies see John Birmingham, *A Time for War: Australia as a Military Power* (Melbourne, 2005).

primary strategic interests were to defeat Communism and protect and extend US commercial interests abroad, rather than to promote democracy. The US record after 1945 was, therefore, a mixed one. The US supported dictators including, for example, Syngman Rhee in South Korea in the 1950s, Ngo Dinh Diem in South Vietnam in the 1960s, George Papadopoulos in Greece in the 1960s, Augusto Pinochet in Chile in the 1970s and many others in Latin America. With geo-strategic objectives in mind, it also assisted the overthrow of elected governments like Mohammed Mossadeq in 1953 in Iran, Jacobo Arbenz in Guatemala in 1954, Salvador Allende in Chile in 1973, and was probably involved in the in the deaths of the President of Ecuador Jaime Roldós in 1981, and the President of Panama, Omar Torrijos Herrera, who was also killed in a plane crash in 1981.[18] But it also, however, promoted democracy and anti-Communism, in a reconstructed Europe through the Marshall Plan and by supporting international organisations and the UN.

After the end of the Cold War the US did move towards more clearly and seriously promoting democracy worldwide. But then the Global War on Terror again highlighted US support for non-democratic states, such as Pakistan, Saudi Arabia and Uzbekistan, as allies against Jihadism. The huge trade with the Communist government in China is also maintained usually without much attention to human rights issues. If the US intended to intervene for the neo-conservative agenda to support democracy around the world in, for example, Syria, Iran, Burma, Sudan, Zimbabwe, and many states in Central Asia – to name but a few of the at least fifty states with poor or atrocious human rights records – it would be a serious challenge to US force levels and fiscal probity. It would usher in an era of Orwellian permanent and endless warfare. The rhetoric of Bush's Second Inaugural Address notwithstanding, the prospects for a US-led 'War on Tyranny' around the world is improbable. The US may, at best, become a more serious opportunistic promoter of democratic reform.

On a tour of the Middle East in June 2005, Secretary of State Rice did extend the Bush Doctrine on spreading democracy through US intervention, by admitting that the US had supported dictatorial regimes in the Middle East for the past 60 years and that this was a 'mistake'. She pointed out, in a speech in Egypt under undemocratic President, Mohammed Hosni Mubarak, that the objectives of US policy had been stability in the region but that the consequences too often were neither stability nor democracy. She signaled that the patience of the US with non-democratic systems in the Middle East had worn thin, and that future policy would do more to promote democratic institutions and governments throughout the Arab world.[19]

The pursuit of democracy in Iraq was, in fact, a last minute add-on to the basic agenda of interests that the US was pursing. It was interested in the Gulf region primarily to maintain the flow of oil; and then to defeat Jihadism. It wanted to remove Saddam because the Ba'athist regime he controlled was aggressive, expansionist, supported terrorism and had tried to acquire WMDs. It added democratisation in April 2003 when the neo-conservative impulse in the administration was at its peak.

18 For the actions of the US in overthrowing 'unfriendly' governments, especially in Latin America, see John Perkins, *Confessions of an Economic Hitman* (San Francisco, 2004).

19 *The Australian*, 22 June 2005.

If its occupation of Iraq faltered, the US could comfortably de-list the democratisation objective and revert to a stable, non-aggressive, friendly Iraqi regime which maintained the flow of oil and renounced WMDs as its primary interests. In the circumstances of the contemporary Middle East, this could be counted as a victory.

Allies

In pursuit of its war on terror, the US needed allies. Despite the vast reservoir of sympathy generated by the attacks of 9/11, allies were difficult to find and more difficult to maintain. In the years following these terrorist attacks, opinion in most countries generally drifted away from the US as its policies confirmed preconceived leftist notions that it was merely an imperialist power; have confirmed Muslim beliefs that it is using this convenient excuse to attack them; have generated hostility among those who see its activities as vengeful, disproportionate or illegal; and have persuaded others that it is arrogant in its unilateral wielding of unprecedented power to inflict death and destruction, sometimes indiscriminately, far and wide. This started to be realised in the US as early as 2002, but produced little change in policy other than the creation by Congress on 23 September 2004 of the Office of Policy, Planning and Resources for Public Diplomacy and Public Affairs, designed to undo by propaganda the bad work that other agencies were creating by activities.

The result has been, as with public opinion, a gradual diminution in the support for the US among the two hundred sovereign states of the world. As might be anticipated, support for the US has been strongest, but far from unqualified, among its allies. Its closest allies have been in the Anglo-Sphere, but, even there, government policies have usually been much stronger than popular support; in NATO Europe, support for the US has been reluctant, sporadic and diminishing; among East Asian allies, assistance had been grudging; and in the OAS, movement has been generally away from the US. Perhaps only Israel has been a wholehearted supporter and this has often proven an embarrassment for the US. Despite its leadership of a large and successful alliance structure that won the Cold War, the US has not been able to generate a similar alliance for its Global War on Terror.

The Anglo-Sphere countries had been close strategic allies of the US during much of the Cold War, sharing intelligence information and hosting components of a global reconnaissance system, although New Zealand dropped out of much of this in mid-1980s.[20] These states include the UK, Canada, Australia and New Zealand. The most valuable ally of the US in the GWOT has been Britain, throughout under the Labour Prime Minister, Tony Blair. But he has been opposed in this endeavour by large sections of his own party, often by the Opposition Conservative Party under three different Leaders, and by a majority of the British public.

In August 2006 the British had 7,200 troops in south east Iraq in Operation Telic and were also commanding a number of other Coalition troops. After the invasion, approximately 8,300 troops had been stationed in the south of the country, but 800

---

20 See Bob Catley, ed, *Australia and New Zealand: Coming Together or Drifting Apart?* (Wellington, 2002).

were withdrawn in May 2006. About 1,300 more were stationed in the Gulf region. Blair had rejected an expansion of troop numbers to replace the troops of Spain and other departing nations, but in September 2006 declared that 360 additional soldiers would be sent to Iraq temporarily to reinforce security during the six-monthly rotation, but that they would be then withdrawn. The deployment included infantry, mechanised infantry and armoured units, as well as maritime patrol personnel and a range of aircraft. By September 2006, the UK had lost about 120 soldiers in Iraq, 87 in ambushes, engagements or other attacks. The commitment was not popular in the UK. In February 2007 Blair announced that 4,000 UK troops would be withdrawn from Iraq, including 1600 almost immediately.[21]

In Australia, the tale was a little different. The bombing of the Australian Embassy in Jakarta on 9 September 2004 had sent shockwaves through the Australian electorate, then in an election campaign. Coming on the wake of the bombing in Bali at Kuta on 12 October 2002, and the bombing of the Marriott Hotel in Jakarta on 6 August 2003, this was as close to attacking Australian territory that JI terrorists had attempted. The huge blast blew out all of the windows of the eight-story Embassy and the Jihadist, Jemaah Islamiyah (JI) web site warned that more was to come if Australia did not leave Indonesia and Iraq. This was an attempt to replay the 2004 bombing in Spain which saw the socialist opposition win the election and very quickly withdraw Spanish forces from Iraq. But Prime Minister John Howard declared that Australia would never 'give into the terrorists' and won his fourth consecutive victory in the 2004 election.[22] In October 2005 another bomb in Bali killed twenty four people including four more Australians.

The 2004 federal election victory gave Howard a resounding endorsement of Australia's strategic policies towards the US and the continuing drift of Australia into the American orbit culturally and economically. Howard increased his majority in the House of Representatives and gained control of the Senate (39 of 76) for the first time for any government in twenty five years. In his 2006 book, *The Partnership: The Inside Story of the US-Australian Alliance,* Greg Sheridan, foreign editor of *The Australian,* claimed that Howard had in fact led the Alliance and was far from the compliant subordinate client so often portrayed. Sheridan claimed that 'Howard not George W Bush has made the running in the alliance'. But this assessment seems inconsistent with the record of the Bush administration since 9/11.[23] In fact, Howard had complied with US strategic objectives in the Middle East and in the GWOT because he, personally, believed in them. Australia got the benefits of the alliance without the US casualty rate or the UK domestic political fall out. It also kept the reaction of the Australian Muslims within acceptable limits and used amended security legislation to monitor and arrest terrorist suspects. But under Bush and Howard the US-Australia military alliance has evolved since the 9/11 attacks into a global pact that will very likely, though not inevitably, commit Australia to military action with the US anywhere in the world.

---

21 'Bush urged to follow Blair's lead on troops', *The Australian*, 23 Feb 2007.

22 *The Australian,* 10 Sept 2004; *The Australian,* 11 Oct 2004.

23 Published by New South Books; the quote is from *The Australian,* 3 Aug 2006, p. 10.

The other Anglo-Sphere states were more cautious. In Canada the long standing Liberal government agreed to involvement in Afghanistan under NATO auspices, essentially only after it seemed that hositilities had been concluded. It then took a rather prominent role in the military occupation of that country. Unfortunately, however, the resurgence of the Taliban found the Canadian forces – like those of other NATO countries – dangerously exposed. In 2006 the Canadians took a number of casualties which served to re-ignite the debate about the GWOT and the reationship with the US. But this occurred after the formation of Norman Harper's Conservative government, so the dynamics were rather unique. The uncovering of the plot in mid 2006 by Muslims to wage terror in Canada and kill Harper somewhat disarmed his critics. The birth place of multiculturalism was feeling some reason to re-assess the doctrine.

New Zealand had encountered the GWOT with its most left wing government of the previous half century led by Helen Clark, who had made her career by anti-Americanism, including by being criticially instrumental in destroying the New Zealand alliance with the US in the 1980s. Nonetheless, 9/11 had delivered an epiphany for the feminist socialist. New Zealand deployed in the Afghan campaign but kept some distance from Iraq. This was generally justified by a small population, an even smaller defence force, and other pressing regional obligations, including in Timor and the Soloman Islands. Given the previous ideological dispostion of the government, this was a firm resolve to support the US.

Despite these qualifications, the Anglo-Sphere states were, by some considerable margin, the staunchest group of allies that the US could muster. In view of the considerable errors made by the US in Iraq, this was considerable testimony to the strength of the civilisational ties that bound them together.[24]

NATO and East Asian Allies

The old Europe NATO states were divided, but in the main less inclined to support the US than the Anglo-Sphere states. Nonetheless, NATO deployed into the Afghan theatre and took over command of it on 31 August 2006. But, as time has gone on, there has been some movement towards the US position on the GWOT, except on the issue of the occupation of Iraq. In general, with the exception of the UK, the contribution of the NATO allies to the GWOT has been limited and their contribution to the conflict in Iraq has been extremely limited in the number of states involved, the size of the contributions they have made, and the duration of their commitments. Indeed, several have opposed the war from the outset. These postures were a fair reflection of European popular sentiments on these matters.

After 9/11, *Le Monde* declared: 'We are all Americans now'. The French government was led by the rightist, former Gaullist, President Jacques Chirac. Chirac maintained the basic tenets of Gaullism including national and European independence from the US. In December 1974, Saddam Hussein then Vice President

24 James C. Bennett, *The Anglosphere Challenge: Why the English-Speaking Nations Will Lead the Way in the Twenty-First Century* (New York, 2004).

of Iraq, hosted Chirac in Baghdad and approved a deal granting French oil companies a number of concessions including a 23 per cent share of Iraqi oil. France also sold a nuclear reactor to Iraq. Chirac was initially very sympathetic to the US after 9/11 and France agreed to assist in the GWOT and provide forces to Afghanistan and by 2006 more than 4,200 French military personnel were operating in Afghanistan.

The differences between France and the US were principally over the invasion of Iraq. France opposed the US plans for the invasion of Iraq from early 2002. The French government was more closely connected to the Iraqi Ba'athists and traded with Iraq, importing oil and providing value added product. Chirac's party may also have received covert Ba'athist financial assistance. This also coincided with an independent diplomacy in the Middle East which had been a part of French geo-political strategy since the Gaullist ambition of creating a 'third force' in global politics with the EU. This ambition had popular support in France, and was buttressed by mass anti-Americanism.

Throughout 2002, therefore, Chirac tried to organize a European coalition in opposition to the US plan to invade Iraq. It was mainly this coalition that prevented the US from getting a further enabling resolution from the UN Security Council in September 2002, which the French made it clear they would veto. In any case, the Russians or the Chinese may well have done so. The French then continued to oppose US policy in Iraq but with progressively less determination and effect after the occupation and reconstruction was underway. In any case, Chirac's government tended to lose domestic authority after extensive riots by Muslim youths in late 2005, by opponents of labour law reforms in early 2006, and as the administration limped through several scandals towards it final days and election of a new President in May 2007. That election was won by Nicolas Sarkozy, who was more pro-US, more liberal and less inclined to tread cautiously with Islam that Chirac.

But after 2003 the French continued their contribution to Afghanistan and the pursuit, arrest and interrogation of terrorists caught elsewhere. Paris then in 2005 significantly boosted its military presence in Central Asia and Afghanistan as both it and Washington mended fences after their bitter falling out over the Iraq War.[25] A French Defence Ministry official said Paris was determined to keep battling terrorism in the wake of the 9/11 attacks and was increasing its military cooperation in Afghanistan to support the 2005 landmark elections. 'We had a very clear position when it comes to Iraq … That has nothing to do with our fight against terrorism, with France working with our American colleagues'.[26] By 2007 France's deployment was its largest since the start of the Afghan campaign and included 500 French pilots. But France had not diluted its opposition to the US-led invasion of Iraq.

The German government of Gerhard Schroeder was the major French EU ally in the efforts to forestall the US invasion of Iraq. Like the French, however, the Germans contributed to the Afghan campaign under NATO auspices. The US had been trying to make NATO into a global alliance since the mid-1990s and its intervention in the Balkans. The Schroeder government was a coalition of left wing parties led by the Social Democrats including the Greens, thus combining old style Marxists with

---

25 'France Steps Up Role in War on Terror', *NewsMax.com Wires*, 29 Aug 2005.

26 *Ibid.*

environmentalists. Both parties were anti-American and one Minister compared Bush with Hitler during the course of the diplomatic hostilities in 2002–03. In opposing the war in Iraq, Schroeder undoubtedly tapped into contemporary German pacifism and isolationism. Indeed, during the 2003 election campaign, Schroeder successfully stepped up his anti-American rhetoric to improve his vote.

But Germany's flagging economy and the unpopularity of Schroeder's liberal reform program resulted in a series of SPD electoral defeats in 2004 and 2005. Schroeder called an early election in September 2005, which resulted in a protracted period of political stalemate. In October 2005 a deal created a left-right 'grand coalition' led by the new Christian Democratic Union Chancellor, Angela Merkel, who was much more sympathetic to the US, but not keen on joining Bush in Iraq. Nonetheless, in late 2006 the German contribution to the GWOT included 2,800 German personnel currently operating in Afghanistan including police trainers and Special Forces and the German Navy operating out of Djibouti, in the Gulf of Aden area.

In April 2003 Spain under the Popular Party centre-right government of Prime Minister Jose Aznar offered support for the US in Iraq. In November 2003 seven Spaniards were killed in Iraq and opinion polls estimated eighty five per cent of the Spanish people opposed the commitment of 1,300 troops. Aznar called an election for 14 March 2004. On 11 March four bombs went off simultaneously in the Madrid railway system killing 191 and wounding many more. The government initially blamed Basque separatists, but it was soon linked to Al Qaeda and opposition to Spanish involvement in Iraq. Later, 21 Muslims from North Africa were arrested and others killed. Despite having a good lead in earlier polls, the PP lost 35 seats and the Socialists won the election. The new Prime Minister, Jose Zapatero, ordered the withdrawal of Spanish forces from Iraq as he had promised to do during the campaign. The Spanish people had overwhelmingly opposed the war, and noted Al Qaeda's statement that the Madrid attack was 'a response to your collaboration with the criminals Bush and his allies'.[27]

In Italy, in May 2001 the House of Freedom Alliance won the Italian elections led by media and business magnate, Silvio Berlusconi. In April 2003 it announced Italy would contribute to the 'coalition of the willing' in Iraq. There followed some controversies involving the CIA's kidnapping suspected terrorists in Italy to take them elsewhere for torture or interrogation, and some kidnappings of Italians in Iraq. In early 2006 the government announced all Italian forces would withdraw from Iraq by year's end. In any case, Berlusconi lost the elections of April 2006 and a former communist, Roman Prodi, became Prime Minister. Italy had a contingent of 1,600 troops in Iraq and the 'Garibaldi Brigade', including mechanised infantry, helicopters and Carabinieri in South Central Iraq, around Nasiriyah was serving a four month tour of duty from May 2006. Prodi pledged to withdraw the troops in his first speech to the senate and called the war 'a grave mistake that has complicated rather than solved the problem of security'.

27 Marjorie Cohn, ' Spain, EU and US: War on Terror or War on Liberties?', *The Jurist*, 17 March 2004.

The Netherlands had sent a contingent of 1,345 troops, including 650 Dutch Marines, three Chinook helicopters, military police, a logistics team, a commando squad, and a field hospital and Royal Netherlands Air Force AH-64 attack helicopters in support, based in Samawah (Southern Iraq) that left Iraq in June 2005. The Netherlands lost two soldiers in separate insurgent attacks. In Holland, in November 2004 the film maker Theo van Gough was spectacularly murdered by a Muslim, thereby probably transforming Dutch liberalism.[28] Nonetheless, the Dutch Government turned down an Iraqi Government request to extend the Dutch contingent's stay and by late 2005 the Netherlands had only half a dozen liaison officers in Iraq.

Denmark sent 515 troops under UK command to South-East Iraq, including infantry, medics and military police in South East Iraq near Basra at 'Camp Danevang'. This was in addition to 35 troops operating under UNAMI. Denmark lost four soldiers in Iraq. From 2003 till 2006 Denmark extended its Iraqi forces by biannually parliamentary decisions. However, in May 2006 the Danish parliament voted to extend the Danish military force in Iraq for a full year, until at least July 2007, or for so long as the Iraqi government wanted it.

Turkey was the only Muslim member state of NATO and its secular government remained a close ally of the US, supporting it in the war on terror in the post 9/11 climate. However, the Iraq war faced strong popular domestic opposition in Turkey and the Turkish parliament voted against allowing US troops to attack Iraq in 2003 from its south-eastern border. This led to a period of cooler relations, but they soon recovered through diplomatic, humanitarian and indirect military support. Turkey was concerned about an independent Kurdish state arising from a destabilised Iraq since it has fought an insurgent war against the Kurdistan Workers Party (PKK) that wants Kurdish independence and in which an estimated 30,000 people have lost their lives. This has led Ankara to pressure the US to clamp down on guerrilla training camps in northern Iraq, though the US remains reluctant due to its relative stability compared to the rest of Iraq. Turkey must therefore balance domestic pressures with commitments to its strongest ally.

The 'New Europe' states of eastern Europe that had recently joined NATO and/or the EU, had previously been in the Soviet bloc and were influenced by the gratitude they had for the US that freed them from communism. They were also less susceptible to the anti-American ideology that was then rampant in Western Europe. They were persuaded to deploy forces to Iraq in 2003 and some have stayed longer.

Poland deployed 900 troops into Iraq and then augmented them. The number of troops was then reduced from 2,500 to 1,500 during the second half of 2005. Poland's former leftist government had planned to withdraw the remaining 1,500 troops in January 2006 but lost the 25 September 2005 elections. The new Prime Minister, Kazimierz Marcinkiewicz, visited Washington in December 2005 and announced that he had asked President Lech Kaczynski to keep Polish troops in Iraq for another year, calling it 'a very difficult decision' since Poland had lost 17 soldiers

28 See Ian Buruma, *Murder in Amsterdam: The Death of Theo van Gogh and the Limits of Tolerance* (New York, 2006).

in Iraq. The contingent was cut from 1,500 troops to 900 troops in March 2006 and Polish forces shifted toward the training of Iraqi security forces.

Romania deployed 628 troops under British command in Southeastern Iraq. The Romanian President, Traian Basescu, announced on the 30 August 2006 that Romania would withdraw its troops from Iraq. He said: 'The Iraqi Government announced today that in 45–60 days at the most, the Dhi-Qar province where a Romanian battalion is deployed will be transferred under the control of the Iraqi army', and that the presence of Romanian troops in Iraq is 'no longer necessary'.

Many other former communist states of eastern Europe were persuaded by the Americans to send more modest contingents often of less than one hundred to Iraq, although these were later progressively reduced. These countries included the Czech Republic, Slovakia, Lithuania, Armenia, Bosnia and Herzegovina, Estonia, Macedonia, Kazakhstan, Ukraine, Moldava and Bulgaria and it would not be entirely accurate to describe these forces as token contributions. But nonetheless in April 2007 Georgia, in pursuit of membership and the protection of NATO announced it would deploy 2,000 troops to Iraq.

It would be fair to say that the vast majority of the fighting and then occupation was undertaken by US forces with strong British support and some lesser assistance from Australia and Poland. By December 2006 even this support was diminishing.[29] British Defence Secretary Des Browne said it expected to withdraw thousands of its 7,100 troops from Iraq by the end of 2007. The US then had about 136,000 military personnel posted around the country. Browne outlined an accelerated exit strategy in which British troops train Iraqi forces, gradually transfer security responsibilities to them, and pull back forces while keeping rapid response teams ready if needed.

Several East Asian US allies also contributed to the Iraq occupation. Japan provided some non-military forces in Iraq, but these were withdrawn by July 2006. This reconstruction mission in Samawa had been limited to 'non-combat zones'. The Japanese Cabinet decided on 8 December 2005 to extend their stay despite a poll by the *Asahi* newspaper which found that 69 per cent of respondents were against renewing the mandate. Three Japanese hostages were captured in Iraq in early 2004 but were released unharmed a week later. In July 2004, al-Zarqawi threatened Japan, Poland and Bulgaria over their troop deployments saying that 'lines of cars laden with explosives are awaiting you'.

After April 2003 The Republic of Korea deployed 3,300 troops to the Iraqi occupation, but 1,000 troops were withdrawn in the first half of 2006 and 2,300 South Korean troops were deployed by July 2006. The main task of the troops was to offer medical services and build and repair roads, power lines, schools and other infrastructure. South Korea had the third-largest military presence in Iraq after the United States and Britain.[30]

The Thai government was faced with a long festering Muslim secessionist movement in the south of the country and sided with the US in the GWOT. It had also taken an extremely hard line with its own southern Muslims – one cause of the

29 'British pledge Iraqi pullout', *The Australian*, 28 Nov 2006.

30 Jim Garamone, 'Korea to Deploy 3,000 More Soldiers to Northern Iraq', *American Forces Press Service*, 2 April 2004.

September 2006 coup. Thailand's 423-strong humanitarian contingent was deployed in 2003 but then withdrawn by September 2004. Prime Minister Thaksin Shinawatra had previously announced early withdrawal if the situation became too dangerous. Thailand lost two soldiers in Iraq.

In 2003 49 countires contributed to the original Operation Iraqi Freedom and another four later joined. By February 2007 twenty two countries still had forces in Iraq.[31]

Israel

One of the objectives of Al Qaeda and other Jihadists organisations, and some Islamic states, was to stop US support for Israel and destroy the Jewish state. But Israel has the same right to survival and security as any other member of the international community and the United Nations. Nonetheless, this does not, in itself, explain why the US has provided over one hundred and forty billion dollars worth of assistance to protect Israel, and each year provides a further ten billion dollars worth of aid. The US has also guaranteed the survival of Israel on three known occasions: 1967, 1974 and 1991. It continues to do so when providing front line weaponry to Israel which it would deny to most other states, particularly were they to build nuclear weapons, engage in pre-emptive war against neighbouring states and on-sell some of the military technology to other embargoed states like China.

Some strategist have agued that the basis for such overwhelming US support for Israel has been its providing a strategic alliance in the Middle East for the US that allows it to carry out its regional ambitions more cheaply. But US and Israeli objectives are divergent in many respects and Israeli policies are sometimes in conflict with those of the US. A 2006 study argued that the policy was largely a result of the strength of the Israeli lobby in the US.[32] Although there are only six or seven million American Jews among the 300 million Americans, their political strength has been concentrated in the ownership of the media, including Hollywood, in business generally, among intellectuals and in the strategic location of Jewish voters in the key states of New York, Florida and California. A combination of these instruments has been able to maintain US policy as a guarantor of Israel since the late 1950s.

Other issues have no doubt served to consolidate this support into a popular consensus, including Israel's reputation as a liberal democracy, Israel's support for the US in general, the strength of the pro-Israel Christian right in US culture, and the odious nature of the Arab powers and states seeking to destroy Israel. But it seems unlikely that this would have produced US support to the level where Israel has been able to ignore the requirements of accommodation and negotiation that would have been necessary if it had not maintained the overwhelming power that its US connection provided. The extent of US support for Israel periodically comes in to question within the US. It did in the 1980s, for example, when Israel occupied southern Lebanon. It did again after 9/11, when one of the administration's first

31 'Bush urged to follow Blair's lead on troops', *The Australian*, 23 Feb 2007.

32 John Mearsheimer and Stephen Walt, 'The Israel Lobby and US Foreign Policy', *London Review of Books*, 23 March 2006.

reactions was to try to force a negotiated settlement of the Palestinian issue, in order to clear the decks for the principal item, the destruction of Al Qaeda. But this was quickly rebuffed by a combination of Israeli recalcitrance and the Israeli lobby in Washington.

The neo-conservatives may, indeed, have attached too much priority to the strategic aims of the Israeli rather than the US state. Many of the early neo-conservatives of the 1970s were Jewish intellectuals centred around the journal, *Commentary,* and its then editor, Norman Podhoretz, and Irving Kristol. They advocated a tougher position on the Soviet Union, became influential in the Reagan administration and took some credit for the defeat and destruction of the Soviet Union by confrontational means. A similar loose neo-conservative grouping did re-emerge after 9/11 advocating a tough War on Terror, the uncompromising defence of Israel, and regime change in Iraq. People associated with this position included the prominent sons of Podhoretz and Kristol, Paul Wolfowitz, John Bolton, Richard Perle, and the Fox TV network and its affiliated beltway policy journal, also owned by NewsCorp, *The Weekly Standard.* It was also frequently claimed that Vice President Dick Cheney was the coordinator of this line of approach, with which Donald Rumsfeld accommodated but not Colin Powell who was replaced by Condoleezza Rice, who did. Many of these people were, of course, Jewish and were also connected to the Israeli Likud party and its influential leader, 'Bibi' Netanyahu, who was also, in turn, well connected, known and respected in the US where he had been Israeli Ambassador to the UN.

But to see a united American Jewish community behind this process would be very misleading, since many of the prominent opponents of neo-conservatism were also Jewish, including most famously Noam Chomsky, most of the New York Jewish electorate, and many prominent academics throughout the university system. The majority of American Jews also vote for Democrats, particularly when, like the Clintons, they are unbending in their support for Israel. Nonetheless, these leftists had little say in the administration of George W Bush and the neo-conservative impulse acquired some momentum in Washington after 9/11.

But for Islamists this information, casually canvassed and assessed in common discourse provides overwhelming evidence for the Al Qaeda case that US policy is determined by Jews bent on annexing Islamic territory for Israel, and oil men determined to extract the natural resources of the Muslim world while simultaneously impoverishing its population. This argument is, of course, daily disseminated and updated on websites easily accessed. It acquires the more force from the repeated identification of Jews as enemies of the Prophet in the *Koran* itself.

Israel is a staunch supporter of US policy, but not a client state. The US has provided Israel with the means to be the dominant economic and military power in its region since the mid-1960s. But Israel has usually pursued an independent strategy sometimes to the embarrassment of the US that finds itself dragged along behind its often bellicose ally. The situation in the Middle East was made worse for the US by the Israeli invasion of the Lebanon in 2006 which only worsened when it failed in its immediate military objectives. The US had to then expend more diplomatic reserves in delaying a settlement until the Israelis could make some real military headway, which they failed to do. Israel is a questionable strategic asset for the US, but one that it can not abandon for sound political and peripheral moral reasons.

The Organisation of American States

The OAS was founded in 1948 in Bogata, Colombia, with 21 member states and now includes all the nation states of the Americas, including North America and the Caribbean. It was chartered to promote peace, trade and good relations between the nations of the Americas. The US intended it to be an instrument for its own regional hegemony and the modern manifestation of the Monroe Doctrine. But during the period of globalisation, many OAS states have developed rapidly into middle income economies with ambitions independent of the US. With the US distracted to the GWOT, several of them have used this opportunity to become even more independent. This has prompted many South American states, led by rebel and new number one regional critic of the US, Hugo Chavez of Venezuela (the alleged leader of the 'Chavez-Castro Axis' and major source of oil for the US and China) and the less vocal President of Brazil Luiz Ignácio Lula da Silva, to join with China to produce a counterbalance to the traditional regional hegemonic power of the US.[33]

The involvement of South America in the GWOT has been extremely limited. The region has been considered as an American sphere of influence, at least by the US, since the Monroe Doctrine. When the US is distracted elsewhere, often regional states take the opportunity to pursue more independent policies, and since 1960 Castro's Cuba has encouraged such developments. Several elections in South America since 2003 have shown a swing to the Left: Uruguay (Taboré Vásquez), Venezuela (Hugo Chavez), Bolivia (Evo Morales), Chile (Michelle Bachelet), Brazil (Luiz Inácio da Silva), Argentina (Néstor Kirchner), and Ecuador (Rafael Correa) have all elected left-leaning, social democratic governments, with Venezuela and Bolivia being the most radical. Colombia (Álvarollribe Vélez), Peru (won by the centre-right candidate Alan Garcia) and most recently Mexico, however, have produced narrow victories for conservative candidates. After months of wrangling, the Mexican courts declared the centre-right candidate Felipe Calderon elected as President of Mexico, thus checking a general trend toward the Left in Central and South America.

On closer inspection, in any case, some of these elections do not represent a strong swing to the Left, nor pose a real threat to US interests. Although Hugo Chavez in Venezuela and Evo Morales in Bolivia are Left populists using strongly anti-US rhetoric, others, such as Michelle Bachelet, have a more cautious approach to government. Overall, therefore, this Left trend does not overtly threaten US interests in Latin American or indicate a sharp lurch to the Left for the region as a whole. The US remains the dominant force in Latin America and the Chavez-Morales axis appears more tame when examined closely within the larger continental context. In early August 2006, for example, Evo Morales announced that his plan to nationalize gas and oil resources in Bolivia was suspended because he was unable to raise the money from the banks to finance the process. The long-term consequences for the US, therefore, remain to be tested. Bush's visit to South America in mid-2007 and

33 See Isabel Hilton, 'South America looks east', *The Australian Financial Review,* 24 June 2005, reprinted from the *New Statesman.*

the Brazilian President da Silva's return visit to the US, indicated bilateral relations between the US and South America have not been permanently strained.

Some threats to US economic interests may come from emerging internal and external trade patterns in Latin America. The Mercosur Group represents some 700 million Latin Americans, threatens to present a trading challenge to the US. In international trade the Chinese have also been very active in Latin America, especially in negotiating oil and gas contracts, and the EU has given notice of a desire to increase its trade profile in the historically American sphere. This all promises to release historical and economic forces which indicate the US will not have the free run it has enjoyed in the region for the past two hundred years. But this is all occurring within the chosen US configuration of a globalised economy and there is no immediate challenge to US strategic preponderance.

Apart from the long standing Castro regime, whose leader's death seems imminent, the only likely exception to this is presented by Venezuelan President Hugo Chavez. He spent six days in China in August 2006, during which time he steadily increased the amount of oil he said he would sell to that energy-hungry country.[34] Chavez said on his arrival: 'This will be my most important visit to China, with whom we will build a strategic alliance. Our plans are to create a multipolar world, and to challenge the hegemony of the United States'. His attempts to enmesh China in his high-stakes diplomatic efforts to create a global alliance opposed to the US, with the 'axis of evil' states to the fore, were deflected by courteous Chinese formalities. Chavez praised communist China as an economic model for the world, saying: 'One of the greatest events of the 20th century was the Chinese revolution'. During his visit, Chavez also signed letters of intent that could trigger a major engagement by China in Venezuela from railway building to tanker construction, iron ore processing to oil rigs.

A more serious problem would be presented to the US if one of the larger South American states, like Brazil, broke entirely free of its orbit. Independent since 1822 and by far the largest and most populous country in South America, Brazil overcame more than half a century of military government in 1985 when the military regime peacefully ceded power to civilian rulers. Brazil has successfully pursued industrial and agricultural growth and the development of its interior. Exploiting vast natural resources and a large labour pool, it is today South America's leading economic power and a regional leader. It has a population of nearly 200 million with one per cent annual growth, a territory only slightly smaller than the US containing vast natural resources, and large and well-developed agricultural, mining, manufacturing, and service sectors. Brazil's economy outweighs that of all other South American countries and it is expanding its presence in world markets. It has a GDP PPP of \$1.6 trillion (at exchange rate \$620 billion) with \$8,400 per capita. But Brazil does not have a radical regime and is most concerned to develop the country within the established order that the US has done much to create.

The collateral damage of the GWOT has thus included a serious weakening of the ties that bound the US to the vast alliance system that had been constructed during

34 *Rowan Callick,* 'Anti-American Chavez trying to oil China's palms', *The Australian*, 28 Aug 2006.

the Cold War. That alliance system was, if anything, strengthened in the 1990s by the US pursuit of globalisation and the resulting period of considerable economic growth and prosperity. Since 9/11 the US has had a hard task keeping its alliance system together. Nonetheless, the Jihadists might well recruit more to the US cause by continuing their campaign of indiscriminate terror.

Chapter 8

Foundations of American Power

Realist theory of inter state politics reduces power to the three kinds identified by E H Carr in his classic, *The Twenty Years Crisis:*[1] military power; economic power; and power over opinion. More recently, theorists dealing with the US have tended to use the two categories of hard power and soft power. This analysis follows that distinction. The US entered the twenty first century as undoubtedly the most powerful state in the world. But its power was not unlimited. From a realist perspective one issue for any state is whether its ambitions have outreached its capabilities.

Bush and the Home Front

In the US, the Democrats were locked in to the invasion of Iraq by the 2002 Congressional motion passed in the heated aftermath of the 9/11 killings. This mood lasted into the 2004 Presidential elections. Thereafter support for the invasion and occupation of Iraq began to wane and Democrat politicians tried to pick the time that opposition to the war would yield better results than maintaining a national patriotic front. It was certainly not appropriate before the November 2004 Presidential elections; but then change set in.

An ABC/*Washington Post* poll in December 2004 showed a majority thought Rumsfeld should resign and that for the first time a majority (56 per cent) of Americans thought the war in Iraq was a mistake and 57 per cent disapproved of Bush's handling of the war.[2] In 2005 Bush's approval rating dropped to 32 per cent and support for his domestic programs also collapsed. Polls for Bush, in general and on Iraq, reached new lows in June 2005: 60 per cent thought Iraq was a mistake and wanted US troops withdrawn and only 42 per cent believed Bush was doing a good job as president. Even some Republicans in Congress were breaking ranks and one, Walter Jones from a North Carolina area with a number of military bases, wanted US troops brought home. Support for Bush's administration and Iraq policy declined during mid-2005 when in August his poll ratings were 43 per cent approval with a majority wanting to pull out of Iraq. Even the Right was falling out and Fox's Bill O'Reilly attacked Rumsfeld as incompetent. In early 2005 Wolfowitz moved from the administration to head the World Bank (from which he resigned in mid-2007 due to scandal) and in August 2005 Feith returned to academic life.

1 E H Carr, *The Twenty Years Crisis* (New York, 2001).

2 *The Australian,* 23 Dec 2004.

By May 2006 approval for Bush's war was down to 29 per cent. Nonetheless, in August 2006 he maintained that the 'US is at war with Islamic fascists'. In August 2006 the Pew poll found 63 per cent of Americans believed the US was 'losing ground' in preventing a civil war in Iraq. A clear majority then believed Bush was not a 'strong leader' and 'not trustworthy', two qualities on which he once had commanding support. Anti-incumbent feeling was stronger than at any time since the Republican takeover of Congress in 1994. In August 2006 one poll had Bush's public rating at a new low of 34 per cent. Pessimism about Iraq deepened even after the killing of leading Al Qaeda terrorist in Iraq, Abu Musab al-Zarqawi.[3] By August 2006 Americans saw the war in Iraq as distinct from the fight against terrorism, and nearly half believed Bush had focused too much on Iraq to the exclusion of other threats, according to *New York Times*/CBS News poll. The finding that 51 percent of those surveyed saw no link between the war in Iraq and the broader anti-terror effort was a jump of 10 percentage points since June. It came despite the regular insistence of Bush and Congressional Republicans that the two were intertwined and should be seen as complementary elements of an overall strategy to prevent terrorist attacks on the US.

By August 2006 the increased scepticism presented a real political obstacle for Bush and his allies on Capitol Hill, who made their record on terrorism a central element of the mid-term election campaign for November. The Republicans hoped the public's desire for forceful action against terrorists would offset unease with the Iraq war and blunt the political appeal of growing Democrat calls to establish a timeline to withdraw American troops. Public sentiment about the war became increasingly negative and threatened to erode the Republican advantage on national security. Fifty-three percent of those polled said that going to war in the first place was a mistake, up from 48 percent in July; 62 percent said events were going 'somewhat or very badly' in Iraq. Bush recorded a gain of four per cent in how the public viewed his handling of terrorism, rising to 55 percent approval from 51 percent a week earlier, but the figure was his highest on the issue since the summer, and followed the arrests in Britain in a suspected plot to blow up airliners heading for the US.

Bush's overall standing was nevertheless unchanged from the previous week and rested at 36 percent approval to 57 percent disapproval, threatening Republicans in Congress who faced the voters in November. Compounding the political problems of majority Republicans, the August survey reflected significant dissatisfaction with the way the Republican Congress was doing its job and those polled indicated a strong preference for Democrat candidates in November. The *Times*/CBS News poll differed somewhat from other surveys and showed somewhat higher approval ratings for the president. In surveys for *USA Today* and CNN, which were conducted in August 2006, 42 percent approved of how Bush was handling his job and this gave Democrat Congressional candidates less of an edge. According to that poll, terrorism and the war in Iraq held about equal importance in the minds of Americans. Forty-six percent said the Bush administration had concentrated too heavily on Iraq and not

3 Carl Hulse and Marjorie Connelly, '51% in Poll See No Link Between Iraq and Terror Fight', *New York Times*, 22 Aug 2006.

enough on terrorists elsewhere, while 42 percent considered the balance just about right.

Bush's problems were compounded by the release in September 2006, by the *New York Times*, of the *National Intelligence Estimate* (*NIE*), prepared for the National Intelligence Council, the peak body of the top sixteen US spy agencies. The fifty page document, among other gloomy conclusions, indicated that the war in Iraq had greatly increased the numbers of insurgents and Al Qaeda membership, and was a magnet for Jihadists from around the world. This was not the message promoted by the Bush administration which argued that the war was making America safer and that the GWOT was being won by the US. The election was becoming almost a referendum on the Iraq war and much rested on its outcome for the last two years of the Bush administration.

Bush went into the mid-term elections with support for his administration's policies in Iraq in a state of collapse and numerous other domestic crises adding to the image of an administration in early lame duck form. Adding to Bush's image of weak crisis management, was the announcement by the DPRK in early October, 2006, that it had tested a nuclear device underground, eliciting the strong antagonism of virtually the entire world. The incapacity of the US to act as the world hegemon in this era of disorder was thus further eroded and Bush's credibility as a world leader further diminished. The Republicans' campaign to retain control of Congress weakened through October 2006 as the death toll in Iraq of civilians and US forces continued to rise, forcing Bush to call a special meeting of his war cabinet and the leaders of US forces in Iraq.

In late October, Bush held a crisis meeting with Cheney, Rumsfeld, Rice, the National Security Adviser, Stephen Hadley, General Casey and Ambassador Khalilzad, and canvassed the need for a change in policy towards the war. One option clearly considered was reducing the commitment of US troops and increasing the role of the Iraqi security forces then reported to number over 300,000. This would be like a replay of the policy of Vietnamisation introduced by Nixon in similar circumstances in 1969. It had then had some success; but it did not win the war.[4] The Bush administration moved partly in this direction and also towards negotiating local amnesties with sectarian militias in Iraq to try to defuse the nascent civil war and pave the way for the disarmament of Shi'ite militias.[5] The tactic marked a reversal of policy by the US military, which had blocked attempts to pardon insurgents with American blood on their hands after handing over sovereignty to a secular Iraqi Government in June 2004. The U-turn came during the bloodiest fighting for two years and growing domestic opposition to the war. Amnesty proponents hoped that once the threat from Sunni terrorist bombs had diminished, Shi'ite militias would have less cause to remain under arms. Prime Minister al-Maliki, whose two main Shi'ite partners in government ran the two largest militias, might then be able to negotiate a disarmament program. US troops could deploy to neighbouring countries, leaving military advisers with Iraqi government troops, but they would return if necessary.

4 'Rising Iraq Toll Forces Exit Talks', *The Australian*, 23 Oct 2006.

5 *James Hider,* 'US makes U-turn on offer of amnesty', *The Australian*, 24 Oct 2006.

Bob Woodward's book, *State of Denial,* then rocked the Bush administration and raised crucial issues concerning Bush's comprehension of the complexes in the Iraq War and the possibilities of bringing it to a satisfactory conclusion. The release of the book on the eve of the November 2006 elections greatly increased its coverage and forced both Congressional and Senatorial Republican candidates to distance themselves further from Bush. For example, California Governor Arnold Schwarzenegger, did not even meet with Bush when he came to the state for a campaign visit in October.

In the election there was a strong national swing against Bush and to Democrats mostly attributed in exit polling to the administration's policies on the war in Iraq. The Democrats gained control of the House with a majority of 31 (233–202), by winning seats spread across red and blue states and narrowly gained control of the Senate with a 51–49 majority. They also regained the majority of Governorships, 28–22, which was important for positioning for the 2008 presidential poll. This meant that Bush would face hostile inquiries from House and Senate committees who would try to produce a lame duck period of two years in the final phase of his presidency. The result also indicated a very strong Democratic challenge in the presidential election in 2008.

The fallout from the defeat was immediate and the first victim was the architect of the Iraq War Secretary of Defense, Donald Rumsfeld, who was replaced by the subdued President Bush with the former Director of the CIA, Robert Gates. The swing to the Christian Right, so pronounced since 1998, also appeared to be halted. Some observers viewed this election swing as an adumbration of the shift in America to a quasi-isolationist position and even the possibility of a repeat of the post-Vietnam reaction ('the Vietnam Syndrome') into a kind of 'Iraq Syndrome'. This would help create a multi-polar world in which regional powers – such as China, Russia, Iran and Brazil – would have greater influence in regional conflicts and trade, as America went through a phase of exercising less direct power around the world. But such an option was not really open to the US whose economy was by that time effectively globalised.

The new Congress, however, divided along partisan, factional and ideological lines even before it convened for its first session in January 2007, suggesting it might not be a formidable check to Bush's strategies. In elections to leadership positions in the House and Senate the Democrats split on the election of a new majority leader with the new Speaker to-be Nancy Pelosi's endorsed candidate and outspoken war opponent, John Murtha, defeated by a large margin (149–86) by her former rival for Democratic party leadership positions, Steny Hoyer. Politics as usual then resumed within the Washington Beltway as the parties and candidates positioned themselves for both Congressional positions and the 2008 presidential contest. In 2007 the Democratic attack on Bush, led by Speaker Pelosi, was consistent but relatively ineffective on most major policy fronts, including Iraq. Congressional resolutions could, after all, be vetoed by the President who retained executive power.

On 10 January President Bush finally announced the new strategy of a 'surge' in US forces, and named General David Petraeus as overall commander of Coalition military forces in Iraq to supervise it. His primary mission was to establish security and only secondarily to transition to full Iraqi control and responsibility. At that time it was believed that the eight southern Provinces were under the influence of the Shi'ite dominated government – which enabled the British to start withdrawing their forces from that region – and three or four northern provinces were controlled by the Kurds. Only two Provinces were largely under insurgent control – Al Anbar and Diyala – although areas of Baghdad were often controlled by the dominant sect. In the other four central and northwestern Provinces authority was contested. The plan was to devote the new US forces to establishing order in areas controlled by the insurgents and then spreading this throughout.

In late January 2007, five new Army brigade combat teams started reaching Iraq at the rate of one a month and this was showing some results by mid-April 2007 with control established over much of Al Anbar province and reduced insurgent attacks in Baghdad. But the Jihadists soon rallied, counter-surged, and retaliated in late April launching a wave of insurgent violence designed to thwart the joint US and Iraqi security plan. The US Defense Secretary, Robert Gates, then held talks with his top generals and Iraqi leaders in Baghdad and said that American patience with its Iraqi allies was wearing thin and urged faster work on political reconciliation.[6] Gates wanted Iraq's beleaguered coalition Government to find ways to bridge the Shi'ite and Sunni divisions that was feeding the sectarian war. He wanted new laws that could reintegrate former Ba'athists into public life and distribute revenues from oil – mostly located in Shi'ite and Kurd regions – more equally. But now the Democrat controlled US Congress wanted to tie funding for the wars in Iraq and Afghanistan to a timetable to withdraw US troops from Iraq in 2008. Bush warned he would veto any such bill and he did so in early May 2007.

The massive fatalities in Baghdad and to a lesser extent elsewhere by the Jihadist counter-surge dealt a blow to the White House's plan to quell sectarian unrest, particularly in Baghdad, with the surge deployment of 30,000 extra troops across the country to be completed by June 2007. In a series of mostly car bombings from 18 April, more than 200 people were killed in Baghdad including especially in the Shi'ite dominated al-Sadriyah district where over 140 people were slaughtered in the single biggest attack in the country since the March 2003 invasion. Al Qaeda and other Sunni Jihadists carried out such high-profile bombings to both keep the anti-US insurgency alive and to exacerbate the bitter Shi'ite-Sunni divide. Shi'ite militia soon retaliated and killed about one hundred Sunni in a few days. The US would clearly find the new strategy difficult to impose and within two weeks General Petraeus conceded that the surge of US and Iraqi troops into Baghdad had not reduced overall violence in the country and that the situation was 'exceedingly complex'.[7] In May 2007 President Bush appeared to indicate that he would maintain troop levels until the end of the year at the prescribed surge number of 146,000 in spite of Congressional opposition.

---

6 'Maliki told to hasten peace efforts', *The Australian*, 21 April 2007.

7 'US surge fails to stem Baghdad violence: commander', *The Australian*, 27 April 2007.

Is America in Decline?

For several decades academic analysts have pronounced the decline of America as a world power and the end of American hegemony. But in 2007 the American behemoth was still there, even if stalemated in Iraq. The first wave of this interpretive stream on the decline of America came in the early 1970s with the disillusionment caused by the failures of the US in the Vietnam conflict (1960-1975), the Watergate scandal that led to Nixon's resignation in 1974, economic stagflation in the late 1970s, the expansion of Soviet power, 1975–81, and the two oil shocks of 1973 and 1979. In 1970 Andrew Hacker published *The End of the American Era,* which predicted that the US was in a terminal decline, crippled by excessive individualism, badly damaged by Lyndon's Johnson's ill-fated fiscal policies of 'guns and butter', with domestic institutions in crisis, and pursuing futile attempts to defend an increasingly costly world empire of political and economic networks. The decade of the 1970s, with the weak presidencies of Gerald Ford and Jimmy Carter, reinforced these views and the decade ended with the humiliating seizure of American embassy personnel as hostages in Tehran.

The Reagan era of the 1980s, in contrast, took its cue from the unbridled optimism of Middle America represented by 'the gipper', a role Reagan played as George Gipp, a Notre Dame football player who died prematurely in the 1940 film *Knute Rockne – All American.* These positive views played well with the general public, but not in the academy. Nonetheless, with the 1991 victory in the Cold War and the 1990s economic recovery, the best days of America, as Reagan had confidently predicted, seemed still to be realised. But the warnings about American decline, the 'declinist view', had been revived in the academy by the publication of Paul Kennedy's *The Rise and Fall of the Great Powers* in 1987, and the strong antagonism in the academy towards Reaganism in all its manifestations. This sparked off renewed debate when Kennedy's chief antagonist, the conservative Reaganite, Francis Fukuyama, answered these arguments in views dubbed 'revivalist' or 'renewalist' or even 'triumphalist', with his optimistic prediction of impending universal, Americanised liberal capitalism and the 'end of history', in *The End of History and the Last Man* in 1992.[8]

By the turn of the twenty first century this debate appeared exhausted by the economic boom of the Clinton years, the dotcom revolution and the increasing technological gap between the military might of America and the rest of the world. However, the stock market decline and the attacks of 9/11 in the early years of the new millennium, began another cycle of debate on the future of the US with

8 The paradigm of declinism in the modern era employed by historians to depict Western Civilization dates back at least to the early twentieth century with macro-historians such as the Englishman Arnold Toynbee, *A Study of History*, 12 vols., 1934–61, and the German Oswald Spengler, *The Decline of the West,* 1926–28, in their analyses of the alleged rise and decline of the West as a civilisation. This was a premature prediction as it turned out. But they expressed the deep despair of both sides in the aftermath of the carnage of the First World War. With the great post-1945 economic boom these views went completely out of fashion. Fukuyama first expressed his views in opposition to Kennedy in 'The End of History?', *National Interest,* 16,1989, but the 1992 book developed his argument more fully.

virtually dozens of books such as Chalmers Johnson's *Blowback* in 2000, Samuel P, Huntington's *Who Are We?*, and Niall Ferguson's *Colossus: the Price of America's Empire* both in 2004. These books had their analogues in films by ideologues such as Mike Moore's *Fahrenheit 9/11* (2004) and journalism from Left writers such as John Pilger, Noam Chomsky and Tariq Ali. These anti-American writers again pursued the argument that America, particularly with Bush's doctrine of pre-emptive miliary action, had overstretched its imperial capacities and would go the way of other previously overcommitted empires, such as Persia, Greece, Rome, Spain, Britain and the Soviet Union. The US, bogged down in Iraq and Afghanistan, had committed the classic errors of empire: arrogance has led it into overseas adventures which overstretched its armed forces, demoralized its people and would eventually bankrupt its domestic economy. Excessive military spending would send its budget, external trade and national debt into massive deficits. America, in short, would not be exempt from the laws of history.

The overarching strategy of an empire is to make it profitable by avoiding undertakings whose benefits exceed their costs. The expansion of the oil industry had clearly made America strong; waging war in Vietnam weakened it. At the beginning of the second term of the Bush Administration in 2005, there were indeed many new danger signs for America. In Iraq, there was still an active insurgency in spite of the success of the national elections in late January 2006. Both Iran and North Korea were pressing ahead with nuclear weapons programs, in spite of warnings from Bush and his new Secretary of State, Rice. The US budget deficit and trade deficit were large and continuing to grow, and the Bush administration budget for 2005 showed a deficit, including the war and social security costs, close to $US600 billion, against Clinton's surplus. While Bush then led a party in total control of the political system, it was increasingly divided on fiscal and cultural issues. Arguments once more appeared about the imminent decline of US power when confronted by the growing economic power of the EU, the emerging economic giants of India and China, and the simultaneous GWOT.[9]

In late 2005 a new chorus arose that America was on the ropes: bogged down in Iraq; troubled by rising oil prises; deficits blowing out in both fiscal areas and in foreign trade; its national debt financed by China and Japan; humiliated by Hurricane Katrina before the world by governmental ineptitude and revealing a huge poor underclass of African-Americans left to fend for themselves in New Orleans; and frustrated by intractable conflicts with Iran, North Korea and China. Yet the underlying dimensions of US power remained: the gap between the militarily capacities of the US and the rest of the world was still growing; its basic legal and educational institutions were rock solid; its inflation and unemployment rates revealed a strong and still growing economy; and its corporations and stock markets still dominated the world economy. In short, the US was not about to implode. Historians and commentators are prone to bandwagon when history appears to be shifting, and too quickly conform to what appears to make sense of short to medium term global change. On present evidence the substantial decline of American hegemony remains at the level of low probability

9 See, by a Reaganite conservative, Clyde Prestowitz, *Three Billion New Capitalists: the Great Shift of Wealth and Power to the East* (New York, 2005).

over the next decade.[10] Nonetheless, this does not necessarily mean that the US can always apply that enormous power which it has, to resolve all the problems that it may choose to pursue. If a problem proves too intractable, the wise policy option may be to abandon attempts to resolve it, particularly if this does not threaten to damage prime interests.

Hard Power

The US has one of the largest territories of any country in the world, and almost ninety per cent of US territory is habitable, in the sense of having productive land, adequate rainfall, moderate climate and ease of access. It acquired this by conquest and subsequent settlement. Of course, this does not mean that it will now permit similar expansion by other states. Its own occupation it regards as heroic and sometimes even God given; its repetition would be unacceptable aggression because it is now a *status quo* power. Its territory has large resources and the capacity to produce others, including food, timber, coal, iron, hydroelectric power, oil, shale, natural gas, and so on. During the Cold War, however, it became a net importer of many of these commodities including, perhaps most importantly, oil. After the Cold War it imported capital. It used its own resources and those of European foreign investors, particularly the British, to develop the country but by the twenty first century was addicted to importing resources produced by the rest of the world and importing capital, much of which in 2007 took the form of purchases of Treasury bonds, but also of US companies. If only for these reasons, the US must now have an expansive foreign policy to ensure such access to resources, markets and finance.

Generally, US policy towards resources has been to pursue the establishment of a world market in the resource.[11] This entails the producing or possessing country agreeing to free access by investors to exploit the resource. It then needs to permit the resource to be traded freely on the international market. The US then assumes that, in accord with liberal economic theory, the most efficient and productive consumers will be able to pay the market price for the commodity. In general, of course, this means the US, where productivity and purchasing power is highest. As a result of this policy being successfully applied to many of the world's commodity markets, the US is the largest consumer of many of the commodities traded internationally, including oil. It is also, along with Australia, the most reluctant of the developed countries to establish any binding regime on the manner in which this consumption affects the global environment and, again along with Australia, rejected the Kyoto agreements on climate change, pretty well out of hand.

This large territory with extensive resources permitted the creation of a large nation of three hundred million people. When the Soviet Union collapsed in 1991, the US became the third most populous nation in the world, after China and India. It

10 For discussions on the alleged decline of America, see Owen Harries, 'The parochialism of the present', *The Australian Financial Review,* 16 Sept 2005; and John Fortier, 'Do not write off America', *The Australian*, 16 Sept 2005.

11 Stephen D Krasner, *Defending the National Interest; Raw Material Investments and US Foreign Policy* (Princeton, 1978).

has the largest single middle class; the most productive workforce; the best educated citizenry; and, although it is culturally and ethnically diverse, its population has strong loyalties to the central state. The US population has among the highest life expectancy of any in the world, criticisms of its health system notwithstanding. It is also growing at over one per cent a year as a result of continuing natural growth and buoyant immigration, much of which it can choose from among the millions of skilled persons who want to live in the US. It amounts to four and a half per cent of world population, a proportion that may be declining but only slowly. On the other hand, it is growing as a per cent of developed or rich world population because many other developed countries have stable or declining populations, particularly in Europe and Japan. This large US population has been able to sustain simultaneously both large wars – by 2007 the Iraq War has cost between $500 and $700 billion – and a high productivity, high growth economy.

The American economy is the largest single national economy in the world. It has enjoyed this status uninterrupted for the last hundred years. When it emerged victorious from the Second World War, the US economy accounted for perhaps half of global production. This unusually high proportion then declined, chiefly because the other developed countries recovered from wartime devastation, but later because many Third World countries enjoyed rapid development as they joined the world market which the US was creating. As a result, the US proportion of global output sank to just over thirty per cent by the end of the Cold War. But it maintained approximately this proportion until 2001, when it slipped a bit more relatively while remaining impressive absolutely. In 2004, the World Bank estimate of the world's economic output was $US41,365.8 billion; of which, for Japan, $4,622.8 billion; for Germany, $2,740.6 billion; for UK, $2,124.4 billion; for France, $2,046.6 billion; for PRC, $1,931.7 billion; for Italy, $1,677.8 billion; for Canada, $978.0 billion; for India, $694.7 billion; and for Australia, $637.3 billion. The total output of the European Monetary Union was $9,500.9 billion; of the whole of Europe and Central Asia, was $17,950.9 billion; and of the whole Middle East and North Africa was $550.0 billion. In the same year the GDP of the US alone was $11,711.8 billion.

After the US under Clinton cut its military spending to three per cent GDP, from over double that of most of its allies in the late Cold War – six per cent of GDP as against most of NATO Europe at 3 per cent, Australia at two per cent and Japan at one per cent – it regained a growth rate among the highest of developed countries. Of countries over twenty million people, the US has the highest real per capita income – and Australia is second and the other Anglo-Sphere countries very close. The US economy is not growing as quickly as that of China or India, and several other poor, developing countries for that matter, and this has led to predictions that these countries' GDPs will overtake the US GDP at some time in the future. Similar projections were made about the European countries and Japan at earlier times. None of these has yet proven to be correct and the US maintains a sizeable gap in its capacity to innovate and capture large world markets through technological advances (presently in aerospace, computers, life sciences and transport).

The quintessentially American form of economic organisation is the joint stock company or modern corporation. These were invented by the US (or conceivably the UK, and then improved by the US) in the late nineteenth century. The legal intention was to give individual legal rights and obligations to a business organisation partly separated from its owners. The financial consequence was to enable people to buy into business ventures run by other people and benefit from the profits, thereby allowing vast sums of money to be concentrated and deployed to productive operations. The economic result was to separate ownership from management and create modern management practices and theory. The US corporations then emerged triumphant from the victory in the Cold War with a much extended market in which to operate, as the Soviet bloc deregulated, China liberalised, and former Soviet clients, like India and Arab socialist regimes, had to rethink their economic strategy.

These corporations became very powerful adjuncts to the policies of the US state, where indeed they did not direct it. In 2006, six of the world's top ten corporations were headquartered in the US. These included Exxon/Mobile (first), Chevron (sixth) and ConocoPhilips (tenth), which are primarily oil companies. Wal-Mart, a retailer increasingly dependent on selling cheap imported products, was second. At fifth and ninth were the US motor companies, GM and Ford. Daimler Chrysler (Germany) was seventh and Japan's Toyota company was eighth. The final two were the oil companies, Royal Dutch Shell at third and British Petroleum at fourth. It is worth noting that nine of the top ten were directly dependent on oil and so dependent on US strategy to sustain access to it. Also, General Motors may face bankruptcy as a result of its overly generous compensation packaging for employees and a declining market share. Among the 2006 top five hundred corporations, the US had 170 companies, Japan had 70, Britain had 38, France also had 38, Germany 35, Canada 12, Italy had ten, and Australia had eight. Interestingly, China had emerged with twenty, South Korea with 12, the same as Switzerland, and India had developed six.

In terms of market capitalisation the American stock exchange in Wall Street, South Manhattan, New York, a few hundred meters from the very large hole where the Twin Towers once were, is the largest in the world, and so remains the very heart of world capitalism.

Rankings of Stock Exchanges by Market Capitalisation
(in trillions of US dollars)

New York Stock Exchange	$22.7
Tokyo Stock Exchange	$4.65
NASDAQ	$3.76
London Stock Exchange (LSE)	$3.25
Euronext	$2.96
Toronto Stock Exchange	$1.62
Frankfurt Stock Exchange (Deutsche Börse)	$1.38
Hong Kong Stock Exchange	$1.30
Milan Stock Exchange (Borsa Italiana)	$0.89

The third largest exchange is also American, NASDAQ, originally an acronym for National Association of Securities Dealers Automated Quotations. It was founded in 1971 by the National Association of Securities Dealers (NASD), who sold it off in

2001. It is owned and operated by The Nasdaq Stock Market, Inc, which was listed on its own stock exchange in 2002. NASDAQ has become the largest electronic screen-based equity securities market in the United States. With approximately 3,300 companies, it lists more companies and, on average, trades more shares per day than any other US market.

But these stock markets have also become a vital component in the sustained generation of capital to pay for US fiscal and external deficits. The US balance of payments deficit increased substantially in the early twenty first century. This was mostly paid for by foreigners holding US dollars as payment, which they will continue to do while they have confidence in the value of the US currency. Prolonged national deficits usually lead to currency devaluations. But at the start of 2006, 66.3 per cent of the identified official foreign exchange reserves in the world were held in US dollars, 24.8 per cent in Euros, 3.4 per cent in Japanese yen, and 4.0 per cent in pounds sterling. Although the EU and Japan might try to change these ratios, which would among other things weaken the USD, in the short term the US dollar's status as a reserve currency – the world's money – sustains strong demand for it and underpins its value.

US Balance of Payments
Millions of US dollars

1994	-98,493
1995	-96,384
1996	-104,065
1997	-107,949
1998	-164,606
1999	-263,286
2000	-377,559
2001	-362,795
2002	-421,067
2003	-494,897
2004	-611,296
2005	-716,730

The growth of US national debt has contributed to this contradiction of a deficit currency largely sustaining its value. Under President Clinton the growth in debt ceased, but after the Republicans' radical change in fiscal policy, debt has taken off under Bush. It increased from just six trillion dollars to eight in 2006, and is projected to increase to over ten trillion by 2009 when Bush leaves office. The debt was in 2006 already at an all time record high. As a proportion of GDP, however, the record is not quite as bad. National debt grew hugely in the Second World War and was then gradually run down from 120 per cent of GDP to less than 40 per cent when Reagan took office. He then ran it up to around seventy per cent of GDP where it stayed until Clinton took it down in his last four years to near sixty per cent GDP. Bush is pushing it back to seventy per cent of GDP by running large deficit budgets, caused chiefly by increased military expenditure married to tax cuts in 2001 and 2004 targetted at corporations and the well off, as part of his election strategy. US defence expenditure has gone up to four per cent of GDP, or 47 per cent of world defence expenditure, but this is an understatement since the Iraq and Afghan wars have been funded by special allocations.

During the post-Cold War years, the US has also remained the primary locus of technological innovation in the world economy. The most important sectors of technological innovation have been in Information Technology and health/biotechnology. In IT, US corporations have led the world in the development of the Internet and the associated technologies and commercial applications. The largest corporations directly involved have included Bill Gates' Microsoft and Larry Ellison's Oracle, and US companies have taken up the commercial applications of the Internet quicker than those of other countries. In the field of health, most of the scientific innovations that have fuelled the recent extensions of life expectancy and improvements to health while living, have been developed in the US, including key hole surgery, drug development and cancer treatment. Seven of the largest pharmaceutical companies in the world are US, led by top two, Pfizer and Johnson and Johnson, and their achievements are clear despite denigration as 'Big Pharma' in UK novels and films like *The Constant Gardener*. Harvard Medical School is the navel in the body of the medical world. This advanced level of technological development has been applied to military matters with considerable results.

The US accounts for about half of total global military spending and is fully equipped to defeat any state power, likely combination of powers, or conventional enemy ranged against it. In the post-Cold War period the US military forces were designed to be able to fight two wars in either the Middle East, or Europe, or East Asia simultaneously and win them. These three regions contained the resources vital for the maintenance of the international economy on which the current level of US prosperity and consumption ultimately rested: the major developed economies and trading partners of the EU and Japan, South Korea and, increasingly, China; and the energy fields of the Middle East. The US was able to contemplate such an expansive strategic posture, precisely because it was able to deploy such superior technology.

By 2000 the US order of battle was determined by these objectives, and less by the need to deter or defeat a threat to the survival of the US itself, as had been the case in the Cold War. To that end, relatively small numbers of US forces and/or equipment were stationed or stockpiled in those three strategic zones identified. US Cold War bases in Germany and the UK, and in Japan and South Korea, were scaled down to meet new requirements other than meeting large Soviet bloc armies in open conflict. They were now to be pre-positioned to hold ground against lower level assaults, while reinforcements were rushed in from the US. Allies were then recruited to assist in the protection of these areas against hostile incursions or political realignments.

At the same time, the Revolution in Military Affairs (RMA) – termed 'transformation' by Rumsfeld – was designed to give these US forces greater lethality, by introducing a new range of weaponry and communications systems. The RMA included making US ground forces more effective by re-equipping them with new automatic weapons, body armour, field rations, GPS navigation, and night fighting and radio communications equipment. They were then made more mobile with the provision of more helicopters, humvees and armoured transport vehicles. Long flight, heavy lift military air transports were then developed to shorten transportation times from US bases to other locations. As the US defence forces became in effect a large rapid deployment force for global power projection, so new naval and air force technologies were developed for their support. Much of the naval fleet that had been mothballed was re-commissioned and several additional carrier task forces re-deployed to meet the needs of the new GWOT. A new, multi-purpose fighter plane was contracted and hundreds would be purchased to supplement the Stealth bomber. More attention was paid to the production of unmanned drones and Cruise missiles for use against ground forces. And, of course, the large fleet of upgraded B52s remained in service and saw extensive and early duty in Afghanistan.

In August 2004 Bush announced that the US would also adjust the structure of its overseas military bases and forces, in order to better fight the GWOT. America's European bases were home to over 116,000 troops, 125,000 dependents, and 45,000 support personnel. Because troops were stationed at these bases for years rather then on a rotational basis, this large civilian complement was necessary. But it meant that the US government had to provide support services for thousands of non-military personnel. New style bases would likely be smaller and maintain rotational forces. As the Army developed self-deployable and modular brigades and lessened its reliance on much larger divisions, these bases would likely be geared more toward brigade-size forces. Deployments would demonstrate America's ability to move at least three brigades from the US to Europe very quickly. These smaller bases would also foster the mobility and strategic agility of America's forces and facilitate the lighter and more mobile force that the GWOT required. South Korea would also be a model for future bases. Equipment and infrastructure there would remain on base, while troops rotated in and out on year-long assignments. Families could stay in the US because of these quick rotations. The 37,000 troops stationed in South Korea were accompanied by just over 4,000 dependents and 25,000 civilian support personnel. The new bases, however, would look more like the deployment in Bosnia-Herzegovina, where the US maintained over 3,000 troops on six-month rotations with virtually no dependents. In either case, the US would have the flexibility to ramp up capabilities as needed.[12]

The effect of these changes was designed to give the US defence forces a lower level of personnel while retaining their lethality, mobility and financial efficiency. Although these RMA changes were begun during the Clinton administration, their greatest advocates were among the Republican Party that, while out of office, drew up plans to increase American military capacities without increasing the taxes needed to pay for them.[13] Two of the main protagonists of this position were Dick Cheney and Donald Rumsfeld. After the Republicans returned to power Rumsfeld, as Defense Secretary, began to accelerate the application of the RMA, in which he was a true believer. As a result, the US defence forces maintained their lead over

---

12 For the general strategy, *Military Transformation: A Strategic Approach*, US Dept of Defense, Fall, 2003.

13 See Bob Catley, 'The Bush Administration and the Changing Geo-politics of the Asia Pacific region', *Contemporary Southeast Asia,* April 2001.

other national defence forces where they did not, indeed, extend it. But in 2001 this was still an armed force equipped to defeat any other armed force in the field. When it entered Iraq in March 2003, although heavily outnumbered at 130,000 to perhaps one million, it quickly defeated the Iraqi army in precisely the manner for which it had been trained and equipped. Two mighty armoured columns punched through south Iraq to capture the capital in three weeks, while a slightly lesser British version seized Basra. It then faced an insurgency. It had little training to deal with this contingency and, essentially, failed to contain it and, indeed, by late 2006 faced the possibility of what amounted to a politico/military defeat. In part, this resulted from the untrammelled powers of the US executive formulating an ill-considered policy.

The US state was designed, after extended debate by its founding fathers, to be highly democratic, and for the political factions that would be thereby generated to be neutralised by the separation of powers.[14] This did not apply, however, to the executive power. The executive power was deliberately concentrated in the Presidency, who was also Commander in Chief and appointed the Cabinet, giving it the capacity to mobilise resources and sentiment in the event of the young Republic being threatened by the major predatory powers of the time, notably Britain or France. But as the US developed from a small, chiefly agricultural (and earlier slave holding) society, so the new industrial and commercial concentrations of wealth acquired political power in Washington. This power could, at least in theory and often in practice, be offset by other influences. For example, Standard Oil was dismantled as was Bell Telephones. More recently, the US state has tried to control the monopoly power of Microsoft and the Clinton Democrats tried (but failed) to reduce the power of the private medicine industry.

But in external relations, the power of the executive is not readily offset by any other – except, in the longer run, the voting public. This is not usually enough to prevent the US government from pursuing its strategic objectives, or indeed from waging war, provided it is of short duration. It also often means the executive exercises external power without a thoroughgoing democratic debate about the decision and the lengthy consideration of other options, as would usually happen, for example, in a Westminster system. The GWOT was initially popular among an American population traumatised by the attacks of 9/11 and anxious to wreak revenge. Anti-war demonstrations took place, but these were limited in size and consequence. The easy apparent defeat of the Taliban, mostly by air power, in 2001, followed by the quick defeat of the Iraqi conventional forces and the capture and arrest of many terrorists world wide, only added to this support.

The first test of this popular resolve came in November 2004 at the Presidential elections. At that time, the dimensions and character of the Iraqi insurgency were not apparent and US casualties remained relatively low. In any case, the Democrat candidate, John Kerry, had supported the initiation of the war and had only minor criticisms to make about the manner in which the war was being prosecuted. Bush was re-elected with an enhanced majority but a similar support base. The US state was able to continue into 2005 applying its hard power in prosecuting the GWOT. The

---

14 Bob Catley and Wayne Cristaudo, *This Great Beast: Progress and the Modern State* (Aldershot, 1997), Chapter nine, 'The extension of Representation'.

US system enabled a very small number of people to determine its strategy towards the GWOT, and an even smaller number to determine the disastrous occupation policy for Iraq in April-May 2003 as the detailed accounts of decision making by Bob Woodward[15] and Thomas E Ricks[16] make clear.

Soft Power

The US has also been able to use its extensive soft power, chiefly for influencing opinion. As argued above, usually domestic US opinion can be relied on to support the executive if only for well established reasons of patriotism. Only in the rarest of cases – notably the Vietnam War – has this not been sufficient. This was an exceptional case when battlefield losses, including 50,000 dead, combined with a lengthy war for uncertain objectives produced unwanted economic results and business opposition to a degree that after seven years of battle, 1965–72, the US withdrew from the field. But since its victory in the Cold War, much of the US media has been supportive of US foreign policy. During the initial phases of the GWOT, the main TV networks were in support of the administration, although they continued to carry hard news where it ran against the administration, including US casualty rates and the mounting insurgency in Iraq and, more recently, Afghanistan. In this cause, Foxtel was clearly the most supportive of the main media outlets, and the *New York Times* the most critical. Although Foxtel originated as an Australian company, it was Americanised in 2004 when it was incorporated in the US (Delaware). It was the most strongly supportive of Bush of all the large US media companies. It also had a strong media presence in both the UK and Australia, where it backed the invasion of Iraq and – until 2006 – neo-conservative causes more generally. Nonetheless, even in these countries, opinion ran against the US intervention in Iraq, although not as strongly as elsewhere.

Foreign opinion has been more difficult for the US to manipulate, since neither US patriotism nor direct US government supervision has been normally present. And many countries, including the US, limit the amount of media ownership of foreigners. News management in other countries by the US has been particularly difficult in the last decade or so when, typically, the generation who were alienated by US policy in Vietnam, has come to acquire the reins of power in many states and views the US with great suspicion. This has been made worse since 1991, when the US hegemony has not been excused by reference to a credible Soviet threat as a 'clear and present danger' although Clinton's low intensity intervention policy calmed this growth of anti-Americanism.

Much of the soft power that the US is said to exert through 'low culture' is fairly illusory. While it is true that the US corporations have a large slice of the international low culture market, in areas that range from Hollywood movies through popular music in its various guises – rap to rock – and sells literature from novels to comics, these media are rarely politically influential. The same point can be made about its

15 Bob Woodward, *Bush at War* (New York, 2002), *Plan of Attack* (New York, 2004), and *State of Denial* (New York, 2006).

16 Thomas E Ricks, *Fiasco* (London, 2006).

fast food franchise systems, clothing fashions and even designs for houses and cars. Indeed, some of this product may even be counterproductive in generating support for US state policy. While there has not been a sympathetic treatment of an Arab character in a Hollywood movie since Rudolph Valentino – the notable exceptions are not Hollywood made, like *Laurence of Arabia, Black Hawk Down, Kingdom of Heaven,* all with British directors – Hollywood has often been critical of right wing corporations – as in *Syriana* – and the Republicans – *American Dreams* and Mike Moore's *Fahrenheit 9/11* – but entertaining and sympathetic on the Democrats, like *Air Force One* and *Primary Colours.* Hollywood's political take in the post-Cold War world, is generally multi-cultural, pro-Jewish, pro-Democrat and anti-War. American TV programs which are sold world wide also tend to be produced in New York or Hollywood, both bastions of the Democrats, including in the 2000 and 2004 Presidential elections. In short, US low culture products are made for sale and profit, not for propaganda.

'High culture' is a little different. Many educated Europeans tend to be anti-American while at the same time recognising that the US leads the world in many areas of high culture including painting, classical music, museums and literature. Even more clearly, the leading US universities are usually taken to be the best in the world in areas as diverse as economics, medicine and engineering. The world's top universities are also in the US and in 2006 these were, in one survey, in order, (American unless specified): Harvard, Stanford, Cambridge (UK), California, MIT, CIT, Princeton, Oxford (UK), Colombia, Chicago, Yale, Cornell, Tokyo (Japan), University of Pennsylvania, Uni.Cal, Wisconsin, Michigan and Washington. But in the fields examining subjects where the US state is seeking to projects its power, like international relations, cultural studies or political science, critics of US policy and structures are more common than supporters. The anti-Americanism so common in universities throughout the world is often generated or certainly fanned by the American universities, where hostility to the American government's foreign policy is commonplace if not universal. This has only intensified during the Bush presidency. In part, this stems from the fact that up to ninety per cent of social scientists in the US vote Democrat, but also from an academic hostility to all war, even against terrorism.

The US economy's superior performance for over a century has involved a combination of a substantial domestic resource base, a large, growing and well educated population, large efficient and globalised corporations, the world's strongest research sector, and huge stock exchanges to mobilise capital. But none of these accomplishments will make its state's foreign policy popular.

World Opinion

At the time of the attacks on New York and Washington, sympathy for the United States was widespread worldwide, and domestic support for US retaliatory measures was very high. By late 2002 and after the invasion of Afghanistan, this had shifted and world opinion was moving against the US. Following the invasion of Iraq, which was widely viewed as a unilateral and unnecessary action, opinion in the rest of the world moved more sharply against the US government and policy. Even in the UK and Australia, majority opinion was against the invasion, although in both countries other factors ran sufficiently strongly for both governments, led by Blair and Howard respectively, to be returned at elections in 2005 and 2004. During the waging of the GWOT the number of people holding a favourable view of the US has fairly steadily declined although there may have been a slight recovery in 2005.[17]

The per centage of different countries' populations expressing a favourable view of the US in the five years from 2000 to 2005 were as follows: Canada, 71, 72, 63, n/a, 59; UK, 83,75 70, 58, 55; France, 62, 63, 43, 37, 43; Germany, 78, 61, 45, 38, 41; Russia, 37, 61, 36, 47, 52; Indonesia, 75,61, 15, n/a, 38; Turkey, 52, 30, 15, 30, 23; Pakistan, 23, 10, 13, 21, 23; Lebanon, n/a, 35,27, n/a, 42; Morocco, 77, n/a, 27,27, n/a. Anti-Americanism in Europe, the Middle East and Asia, which surged as a result of the US war in Iraq, showed some modest signs of abating by 2005. But the US remained broadly disliked in most countries surveyed by Pew, and the opinion of the American people is not as positive as it once was. The magnitude of America's image problem is such that even popular US policies have done little to repair it. President Bush's calls for greater democracy in the Middle East and US aid for tsunami victims in Asia have been well-received in many countries, but only in Indonesia, India and Russia has there been significant improvement in overall opinions of the US. Attitudes toward the US remained very negative in the Muslim world, although hostility toward America eased in some countries in 2006. Many Muslims who see the US supporting democracy in their countries, and many of those who are optimists about the prospects for democracy in the Middle East, give at least some credit to US policies. But the improvement in America's image in these countries was very small, and solid majorities in the five predominantly Muslim countries surveyed still expressed unfavorable views of the United States.

People were also asked in 2005 whether they favourably viewed the US, Germany, France, Japan and China, and the following positive per centages were recorded respectively: Canadians, 59, 77, 78, 75 and 58; British, 55, 75, 71, 69 and 65; French, 43, 89, 74, 76, 58; Germans, 41, 64, 78, 64, 46; Spanish, 41, 77, 74, 66, 57; Dutch, 45,88, 69, 68, 56; Russians, 52,79, 83, 75, 60; Poles, 62, 64, 66, 60, 36; and Americans themselves, 83, 60, 46, 63, 43. Even among allies of the US, China was more favourably regarded than the US. The polling in Western Europe, conducted in the weeks leading up to the decisive rejection of the EU constitution by voters in France and the Netherlands, found pockets of deep public dissatisfaction with national conditions and also concern in several countries over immigration from the Middle East, North Africa and Eastern Europe. There were

17 This section has used the Pew Global Attitudes Project, a series of worldwide public opinion surveys on subjects ranging from people's assessments of their own lives to their views about the current state of the world and important issues of the day. It is co-chaired by former US Secretary of State, Madeleine K. Albright, and by former Senator John C Danforth, currently partner, Bryan Cave LLP. The Pew Research Center is a non-partisan 'fact tank' in Washington. After 9/11 September 2001, the scope of the project was broadened to probe attitudes toward the US more deeply in all countries. Recent surveys have gauged worldwide opinion about international news developments, including the war in Iraq. The project has surveyed more than 90,000 people in 50 countries.

no signs, however, that Euro-scepticism about the EU has fuelled a desire for a closer trans-Atlantic partnership. On the contrary, most Europeans surveyed wanted to take a more independent approach from the US on security and diplomatic affairs. Indeed, opinion of the US continued to be mostly unfavourable among the publics of America's traditional Atlantic allies, except Britain and Canada. Even in those two Anglo-Sphere countries, however, favourable views of the US have slipped 2003–05 and China was better regarded. Moreover, support for the US-led war on terror plummeted in Spain and eroded elsewhere in Europe. Japan, France and Germany were all more highly regarded than the US among the countries of Europe; even the British and Canadians had a more favourable view of these three nations than they did of America. Strikingly, China had a better image than the US in most of the European nations surveyed. Attitudes toward the US in the former Soviet bloc nations of Poland and Russia were much more positive than in most of Western Europe. In Russia, also beset by terrorists, favourable opinion of its former Cold War adversary rose from 36 per cent in 2002 to 52 per cent in 2006. Opinions of the US in Poland declined since 2002, but still remained relatively positive at 62 per cent.

The Pew Project also asked people whether they thought US foreign policy considered the interests of others in 2003, 2004 and 2005, and then measured the changes over that period. The results were, respectively: US, 73, 70, 67 with a six per cent drop; Canada, 28, n/a, 19, nine per cent down; UK, 44, 36, 32, twelve per cent drop; France, 14, 14, 18, four per cent up; Germany, 32, 29, 38, up six per cent; Spain, 22, n/a, 19 or three per cent drop; Russia, 22, 20, 21 or one per cent down; Turkey, 9, 14, 14 or up five per cent; Pakistan, 23, 18, 39 or up 16 per cent; Indonesia 25, n/a 59 or up 34 per cent (after Tsunami aid); and India 63 China 53, both 2005. Yet there was modest optimism among Muslims that the Middle East would become more democratic, and even in countries like Jordan and Pakistan, where people have a low regard for the US, many believed the region would become more democratic and gave some credit to US policies for making this possible. Roughly half of respondents in Jordan and nearly two-thirds of Indonesians thought the US favoured democracy in their countries. About half of the public in Lebanon also took that view. But on this question, and others relating to opinions of the US, Lebanon's Muslim majority, which is about 60 per cent of the population, was far more negative than its minority Christian population.

The survey found that while China was well-regarded in both Europe and Asia, its growing economic power got some hostile reactions. Majorities or pluralities in France and Spain, believed that China's growing economy has a negative impact on their countries. Respondents in the Netherlands and Britain had much more positive reactions to China's economic growth. Public opinion in the US on this issue was divided and 49 per cent viewed China's economic emergence as a good thing, while 40 per cent said it has a negative impact on the US. Whatever their views on China's increasing economic power, European publics were opposed to the idea of China becoming a military rival to the US, despite their deep reservations over American policies and hegemony. Solid majorities in every European nation, except Turkey, believed that China's emergence as a military superpower would be a bad thing. In Turkey, and most other predominantly Muslim countries, where antagonism toward the US runs much deeper, most people think a Chinese challenge to American military power would be a good thing – and they may, of course, get the chance to support it.

There was also considerable support across every country surveyed, with the notable exception of the US, for some other country or group of countries to rival the US militarily. In France, 85 per cent of respondents believed it would be good if the EU or another country emerged as military rivals to the US. Most West Europeans wanted their countries to take a more independent approach from the US on diplomatic and security affairs than it had in the past. The European desire for greater autonomy from the US was increasingly shared by the Canadian public, and 57 per cent of Canadians favoured Canada taking a more independent approach from the US, up from 43 per cent two years previously in 2004. The American public, by contrast, increasingly favoured closer ties with US allies in Western Europe, probably in reaction to Bush's unilateralism. The perception that the US conducted a unilateralist foreign policy was widely shared across the surveyed countries. Overwhelming percentages of people in Europe and the Middle East believed that the US does not take their countries' interests into account when making foreign policy. Yet there are a few notable exceptions, and a majorities in both India of 63 per cent and China of 53 per cent believed the US took their respective countries' interests into account. The percentage in Indonesia expressing that view more than doubled from 2003 from 25 per cent to 59 per cent probably reflecting the overwhelmingly positive reaction in response to US tsunami relief in that country.

The war in Iraq continued to generate broad international opposition, and there was little optimism that the elections in Iraq in January 2006 would foster stability. Even the American public had diminished expectations that the January elections held in Iraq will lead to a more stable situation there. The US and India were the only countries surveyed in which pluralities believed Saddam Hussein's removal from power had made the world a safer place. While the war in Iraq was as unpopular in Europe in 2005 as it was in 2003 and 2004, there was still majority support for the general US-led war on terrorism among Western publics that were otherwise highly critical of the US, notably in Germany and France. But support for the war on terrorism all but evaporated in Spain after 2003, and, notably, Canadian opinion on the American-led war on terror was in 2006 evenly divided. The 2006 poll found Canadians held increasingly negative views of both the US and the American people. In most Western countries surveyed, majorities associate Americans with the positive characteristics 'honest', 'inventive' and 'hardworking'. At the same time, substantial numbers also associated Americans with the negative traits, 'greedy' and 'violent'. Canadians, who presumably have the greatest contact with Americans, agree with Europeans on the negatives, but are less likely to view Americans as honest. And Canada is the only Western nation in which a majority, of 53 per cent, regards Americans as rude.

Muslim publics, including Indonesians, are highly critical of Americans in many respects. In particular, they are much more likely than others to view the American people as immoral. Yet people in predominantly Muslim countries also see Americans as hardworking and inventive. The Chinese are also largely critical of Americans. They were the least likely of the sixteen publics surveyed to consider Americans hardworking at 44 per cent, and just over a third or 35 per cent saw Americans as honest. A majority of Chinese, or 61 per cent, associated Americans with being violent and 57 per cent thought them greedy. The one positive trait most Chinese, or 70 per cent, associated with Americans is inventive. By contrast, Indians held largely positive views of the American people. Clear majorities see Americans as inventive, hardworking and honest (86 per cent, 81 per cent and 58 per cent respectively). None of the negative traits were linked with Americans by a majority in India.

America's international image problem was not lost on its own people. Only 26 per cent of the US public deludes itself that the country is well-liked by people around the world. Only the Turks and Russians come close in seeing their country as internationally unpopular with only 30 per cent and 32 per cent believing themselves well-liked, respectively. Canadians stand out for their nearly universal belief, of 94 per cent, that other nations had a positive view of Canada. The American public also looks at US conduct in the world much differently than do publics in Europe, the Middle East and Asia. In response to a hypothetical question, Americans overwhelmingly, at 73 per cent, saw the US as the major power most likely to come to the aid of people threatened by genocide. Only Poles, Canadians and Germans see the US in this way in any significant numbers. America evoked even less confidence with respect to the global environment. Fewer than one in ten West Europeans surveyed most trust the US in this regard. But 59 per cent of Americans say they most trust the US to do the right thing in protecting the world's environment.

Anti-Americanism in the Modern World

The anti-Americanism of the modern era, clearly intensified during the GWOT, has many roots, some indigenous to America and some from outside sources that in the twenty first century have become globalised, especially among Left and Islamic intellectuals. They include particularly the anti-materialist tradition and the left Marxist tradition. Both picture America as an unreformable, predatory society imposing its imperialist hegemony on the world with its vulgar and degenerate popular culture. These two apparently contradictory views cohabit the international Left. Adherents to this view have included the poet Walt Whitman, the socialist Eugene V Debs and dozens of literary figures and social critics, such as Theodore Dreiser through to Noam Chomsky and Gore Vidal.[18]

In England the long Tory anti-American tradition which always doubted the viability of American democracy, goes back at least to the widely held mid-nineteenth century English view of Abraham Lincoln as an ineffective dolt, and Charles Dickens' view of American culture, formed after his tour of America, as shallow and fragile. These views also dominated conservative circles in Australia, until the American alliance in the Second World War saved Australia from the Japanese Empire and the Cold War shifted them to America-philia. Today the Conservative Party's hatred of Tony Blair has spilled over to hostility towards Bush to the extent that when Michael Howard visited the US in 2004, he was not invited to the White House.

---

18 For an analysis of this in the Australian Left see Paul Kelly, 'Gulf debacle an excuse for terror denial', *The Australian*, 13 Sept 2006.

As a result, even in that close ally of the US in the GWOT, Britain, opinions were not close to President Bush. Although a majority of British people wanted the Government to adopt an even more 'aggressive' foreign policy to combat international terrorism, according to an opinion poll conducted after the arrests of 24 terrorism suspects in August 2006, by a margin of more than five to one, the public wanted Tony Blair to split from Bush and either go it alone in the 'war on terror', or work more closely with Europe.[19] Only eight per cent of those questioned by You Gov said Bush and Blair were winning the battle against Muslim fundamentalism.

In Europe, the anti-American tradition has been dominated by France, from de Tocqueville in the 1830s, to Sartre in the mid-twentieth century, to the post-modernists who picked up the Marxist and existential hatred of everything American from foreign policy to all aspects of culture. This is largely a reaction to the spectacular decline of French power and influence in the world that is now accelerating in almost all fields of human endeavour, and equally applies to the anti-Americanism of the Right from the Gaullists, including President Chirac. The virulent, long lasting and understandable reaction against the US war in Vietnam, three and four decades ago, created a generation around the world hostile to US foreign policy and in many ways to US 'cultural imperialism' in spite of accepting continued world leadership in higher education and technology where it could be objectively tested. When the Cold War ended, and with it the requirement for alliance with the Anglo-Sphere countries, particularly the US, to protect Western Europe, anti-Americanism flourished, especially in France.[20] This has deepened enormously in opposition to the US Middle East policy and joined forces with a growing left anti-Zionist movement and the broader growth of anti-Semitism.[21]

The Ideology of American Liberalism

The American people believe, with some justification, that they espouse and support the principles of liberal democracy. They generally think that at its core, the very ideology of liberalism can be transposed into economic, political, cultural and social dimensions elsewhere and that America, in the main, represents them. It is often, then, something of a surprise when they discover that many others in the world do not share these views, and that, indeed, many do not even share their support for liberal values in the first place. While liberalism may be a major source of strength for the US in some parts of the world, it is exactly the opposite in others.

In the US the ideology or beliefs of liberalism are taken to mean: in economics a form of free trade or market economy but corporatism in fact; in the political sphere, a representative system of government, but one in which only the rich get elected in fact; in the cultural domain, a great toleration is praised but only of chosen persons, like gays, assertive women and integrated blacks in fact; and in the social

19 Toby Helm and Philip Johnston, 'Ditch US in terror war, say 80pc of Britons', *Daily Telegraph* (UK) 17 Aug 2006.

20 Jean-Francois Revel, *L'Obsession Anti-Americaine* (Paris, 2002); and Philippe Roger, *L'Ennemi. Genealogie de l'antiamericainisme francois* (Paris, 2002).

21 Mervyn Bendle, 'Ties that should bind', *The Australian*, 2 Aug 2006.

arena, a form of non racist, secular Christianity is in fact the dominant form. The US version of liberalism is very specific and hugely successful, when judged by its own standards. But there are critics.

In the first place, the US academy recognises that the external behaviour of states should be examined by realist methodologies. It then invents a theory of 'American exceptionalism', to permit its own behaviour to be examined according to the dictates of its own specific form of nationalist liberalism. It then usually, as realism would predict, uses the cloak of liberal rhetoric to justify behaviour more readily explicable by realism. In the Middle East, this dichotomy is clearly attributable to the need to retain access to oil and to protect Israel, both interests arrived at by the logic of political realism. The one is an economic interest; the other one determined by domestic political pressures. The rest of the world tends to see this as hypocrisy, particularly when the chosen object of the US to democratise the Middle East was the Iraqi Ba'athist regime, when the House of Saud was closer to hand, as it had been for nearly sixty years.

In the economic sphere, the dictates of liberal economic theory – or neo-liberalism if preferred – with their emphasis on freedom and competition are continually transgressed by a giant US economy whose quintessentially typical organisational form is and has been for a century the giant, and often monopolistic or oligopolistic corporation. It is the corporation that dictates the parameters of US state policy in its pursuit of markets, investment opportunities and resources. Further, having imposed the Washington Consensus with its inhibitions on fiscal profligacy, the US runs the largest domestic and external deficits in world history, to finance tax cuts for the wealthy and its corporate sector, and to run a very lethal war in the pursuit, ultimately, of oil.

Politically, the US supports the most illiberal regimes in the world when it suits its strategic interests. These include the House of Saud that it has guaranteed since 1945. As a result, that state is one of the worst transgressors of human rights in the world, and, moreover, exports its Islamist product. But, more significantly, it has spawned both internal opposition in the form of Al Qaeda and an international support system for the most reactionary doctrines of Islam in the form of Wahhabism. The same could be said, with some variation about Pakistan, the Gulf states and, soon, no doubt, of Iraq. In terms of the culture of liberalism, the United States itself is a fractured society in which health care is expensive to the point of being prohibitive to many, while jails are readily accessible to the 50 per cent of young Black males who find their way into them.

Nonetheless, the ideology of liberalism is the best cloak that the US has to mask its pursuit of strategic, economic and political interests. It is not, however, the best methodology to use when analysing it behaviour. It is also not the necessarily its own best means for determining how to sustain its interests. Its liberals, led by John F Kennedy, launched it into Vietnam in pursuit of freedom and delivered defeat; its neo-conservatives, forty years later, led it into Iraq in pursuit of democracy and delivered a debacle. Realist theory would have provided a better road map on both occasions.

Chapter 9

Competitors

One of the basic realist theories about international relations concerns the balance of power.[1] It essentially argues that states will adjust their diplomatic relations to prevent any single state (or any combination of states) from completely dominating the international system. For each individual state, such domination would eventually threaten its own interests, and possibly its very existence as a sovereign power. Historically, alliances of countervailing power have usually come into existence to resist dominant powers, like Hapsburg Spain, Bourbon and then Revolutionary France, and Imperial and then again Nazi Germany. During the Cold War, US theorists often depicted the Western alliance system as such a means for containing Soviet power. This process does not depend on ideological affinities or enmities; indeed it specifically assumes that states would not be guided by such considerations since it requires great flexibility in alliances, which would shift to accommodate to power and not to belief systems.

After the Cold War was won, the US clearly became the dominant power in the international system, having the largest economy, richest people, most powerful military machine, and with reserves of soft power. Yet for a decade no countervailing alliance system sprang into being. In part, as we argued in *Global America*, this was because of the dimensions of America's preponderance. But it was also because the US, under President Clinton, was relatively unassertive, particularly for a hegemonic power. Its main strategic project was globalisation, a benign aspiration which could provide benefits for most states.

During the Bush administration this changed and the US became more assertive and unilateralist for two reasons. The Republican administration on coming to office made a point of declaring that it would pursue US interests more determinedly and with less emphasis on multilateral institutions. Further, the US was attacked in September 2001, and it began to pursue the Global War on Terror rather than global economic outcomes as its major strategic objective, and did so, when necessary, on its own terms. This was most clearly the case when it invaded Iraq, although for a while it mustered the support of some often reluctant allies and the majority of its own population. Balance of power theory would suggest that this would throw up a countervailing alignment of powers.

Since the Cold War ended, different states have indeed tried to construct groupings designed to check US dominance. The Russians in the early 1990s tried to rescue a Commonwealth of Independent States from the Soviet system, but failed to prevent

1 Edward V Gullick, *Europe's Classical Balance of Power* (Ithaca, NY, 1955); and Hans J Morgenthau, *Politics Among Nations* (New York, 1960) part four, 'Limitations of National Power: The Balance of Power'.

the drift towards the West by many of their former satellites, particularly since the Russian economy itself depended so heavily on the US in the 1990s. There was some attempt by ASEAN in the mid-1990s to construct, with China, an East Asian grouping to deal with Europe and exclude the regional Anglo-Sphere states like the US and Australia, but this foundered, particularly after the regional financial crisis of 1997 and the retirement of Malaysia's Prime Minister Mahathir. At the time of the US efforts to rally UN support for its invasion of Iraq, France tried to construct a loose pan-European alliance against the Bush administration centred on France, Germany and Russia, but this failed in the face of British policy in Europe, a change of government in Germany, declining French morale with internal crises, and US determination. A serious attempt to construct such a diplomatic alliance was also made by China.

The Peoples Republic of China

The PRC was initially identified by the Bush administration as the most serious threat to US hegemony. With a population of 1.3 billion, China is the most populous nation on earth, although with a modest growth rate of 0.59 per cent, it will soon be overtaken by India. It is ethnically homogeneous with Han Chinese comprising 92 per cent, and other nationalities only eight per cent of its people. It is officially atheist and Muslims are less than 2 per cent of the population.

For centuries China was East Asia's dominant state, but in the nineteenth century it was defeated repeatedly by the Europeans, particularly the British, French and Russians, and ceded its sovereignty and much territory. In the early twentieth century the country was beset by rebellions, civil unrest, major famines, military defeats, and foreign occupation, notably by the Japanese. After the Second World War, the Communist Party under Mao Ze Dong established in the PRC an autocratic socialist system that, while re-instating China's sovereignty, imposed strict controls and cost the lives of tens of millions of people. After 1978, under Mao's successor, Deng Xiaoping, the PRC focused on market-oriented, more liberal economic development, and by 2000 output had quadrupled. For much of the population, living standards improved dramatically, yet political control remained tight and autocratic especially after a minor student revolt at Tiananmen Square in 1989.

Despite these economic reforms the PRC remained a communist political state with Hu Jintao President and Wen Jiabao Premier after March 2003, both assuming power in orderly and peaceful succession. China has a stable communist regime with extensive popular legitimacy, the support of the armed forces, some muted remaining territorial ambitions but a voracious economic appetite which requires growing resource imports and consumption despite its own considerable resources.

China's economy during the last quarter century has changed from a centrally planned system largely closed to international trade, to a more market-oriented economy that has a rapidly growing private sector and is a major participant in the global economy. Reforms started in the late 1970s with the phasing out of collectivised agriculture, and expanded to include the gradual liberalisation of prices, fiscal decentralisation, increased autonomy for state enterprises, the foundation of a diversified banking system, the development of stock markets, the rapid growth of the non-state sector, and the opening to foreign trade and investment. China, unlike the Soviet Union under Gorbachev, generally implemented reforms in a gradualist or piecemeal fashion. This process is continuing with more important reforms made in 2005, including the sale of equity in China's largest state banks to foreign investors and adjustments to foreign exchange and bond markets. The restructuring of the economy and resulting efficiency gains have contributed to a more than tenfold increase in GDP since 1978 while population growth has been slowed enabling per capita incomes to rise considerably. Measured by PPP, China in 2005 was the second-largest economy in the world after the US, although in per capita terms the country was still a lower middle-income nation and 150 million Chinese fall below international poverty lines. China's GDP at PPP is around $8.8 trillion, but nonetheless only $2.2 trillion at the official exchange rate (at which rate the PRC buys resources), with a GDP per capita at $6,800 PPP. In 2005 its growth rate was 9.9 per cent, around its recent average.

The US is still the only megapower, but China might seriously aspire to a similar status within the next 15 years. Its annual rate of economic growth is likely to be at least double that of the US until it approaches maturity, while its population is already over four times that of the US. These trends would make China the second-largest economy in the world by 2020 and the main trading partner for a wide range of countries. With this will come political influence and a steady rise in its already substantial military expenditure. China already has a permanent seat on the UN Security Council and the ability to exercise a veto.[2] Unlike the US which subscribes to values like human rights, China strongly supports the principles of national sovereignty and non-interference, as in Sudan over the Dafur issue, fearing that anything else might set a precedent to be used against itself in the future. Particularly in Asia and the Pacific, China will try to use its economic strength to reduce US influence in the regions closest to its borders. The Shanghai Cooperation Organisation, at China's behest, has called for an end to US bases in Central Asia. By 2020 China will have accumulated a great deal of 'soft' power, allowing it to strengthen commercial ties with friendly countries.

China's rise may prove difficult for the US to manage. Its one-party system is likely to be still intact in 2020, but nationalism cum Great Han Chauvinism will likely replace communism as the prevailing ideology. The US has called for China to become a 'responsible stakeholder' in the international system, but under unilateralist Bush the US has not set a good example and China is no more likely than the US to commit to international treaties that restrict its freedom to pursue interests. Containment of China is not an option for the US which it is trying to integrate the PRC into globalism.

In the 2000s China has made considerable efforts to end the disputes over its borders with several neighbours. In 2005 China and India began drafting principles to resolve all aspects of their extensive boundary and territorial disputes and started a security and foreign policy dialogue including over regional nuclear proliferation. China also started talks and confidence-building measures designed to defuse tensions

2 Victor Bulmer-Thomas, '2020 VISION', *The Age*, 21 Aug 2006.

over Kashmir, site of the world's largest and most militarized territorial dispute with portions under the de facto administration of China, India and Pakistan. The PRC had asserted its sovereignty over the Spratly Islands in the South China Sea,[3] but the 2002 *Declaration on the Conduct of Parties in the South China Sea* eased tensions over the islands and in March 2005, the national oil companies of China, the Philippines, and Vietnam signed a joint accord on marine seismic activities in the Spratly Islands. China also occupies some of the Paracel Islands also claimed by Vietnam and Taiwan, and rejects both Japan's claims to the uninhabited islands of Senkaku-shoto (Diaoyu Tai) and Japan's unilaterally declared equidistance line in the East China Sea. There is also a boundary dispute with North Korea over islands in the Yalu and Tumen rivers and a section of boundary around Mount Paektu. China and Russia seem to have agreed in October 2004 over the long-disputed islands at the Amur and Ussuri. The PRC appears to have resolved to settle all these border problems in order to diminish its neighbours' suspicions about Great Han Chauvinism.

The continuing rise of Chinese power must be expected although it has made the calculation that it is not yet strong enough to directly challenge the military power of the US. This assessment sprang from the late 1990s when it briefly and unsuccessfully challenged the US in the Taiwan Strait, and then observed the use of American power against Serbia in the Balkans and took a direct hit on its embassy in Belgrade. It can only have been impressed with the rapid advance of US forces through Iraq in early 2003 – and then, mightily relieved at the subsequent fiasco. In September 2006, for example, the Chinese Prime Minister, Wen Jiabao, voiced confidence in the strength of the booming PRC economy, but ruled out any swift advance towards greater democracy:[4]

> China's progress towards democracy would be a very gradual process, and the Prime Minister avoided giving a timetable. He cited the country's huge size, its enormous population and the large gaps between rich and poor, educated and uneducated, as reasons for the Communist Party's decision to delay change. He said that China would steadily improve the system of nomination of candidates to enable the people to have a greater say and more choice. He was referring to direct elections for leaders of 680,000 villages – the lowest administrative area in China, where sometimes more than one candidate is allowed to contest. Elections higher up the chain would not come without greater evidence that the system was effective. The absence of democracy posed no obstacle to the advance of economic reform, in his view. Mr Wen voiced confidence in the Government's ability to sustain the current boom, although he took care to calm the anxieties of those who feared that China's rapid rise might prove a threat to other nations. China, helped by a huge population, a high level of education, a strong savings ratio and a commitment to capitalist-style market reforms, could overcome obstacles in the way of development.

The PRC government would retain its popular legitimacy while it could sustain economic growth and broaden prosperity, although even then there were 87,000 civil disturbances in the country in 2005. Yet it has contained Islamist extremism and while the US struggles to grapple with Al Qaeda, China has succeeded in countering

3 Bob Catley and Makmur Keliat, *Spratlys,* as above.

4 Jane Macartney, 'Democracy can wait, declares Chinese PM', *The Times*, 7 Sept 2006.

the terrorist network despite the vulnerability of its vast northwestern region of Xinjiang.

China can afford to wait politically and has the cultural patience to do so, but it requires expanding resource imports. It has a rapidly growing economy, well supported government and already impressive military power that it is augmenting with space technology, ICBMs and nuclear weapons every year. Nonetheless, its chief objective is to grow its economy within a liberal trading order that has been created mostly by the US. The only serious and unavoidable difference between the US and China is the issue of Taiwan, and this can in fact be deferred indefinitely with good will. Nonetheless, US hegemony will be diminished by its accommodation to the rise of China.[5]

The PRC has also been active diplomatically in expanding its influence and acquiring economic partners. The Shanghai Group, for example, was established in 1996 by China, Russia, Kazakhstan, Kyrgyzstan, Tajikistan, and Uzbekistan. It started more to create better relations between Russia and China and resolve border issues in Central Asia, than to confront the US. Nonetheless, and particularly as the US encroached on the Central Asian region in pursuit of its GWOT and the resources the region held, the Group moved somewhat away from the US. Then in May 2006 it was announced that Iran planned to join the Shanghai Group, thereby complicating US efforts to curb Tehran's nuclear ambitions. In 2006 Iran gained observer status at the SCO (Shanghai Cooperation Organisation), although SCO membership was not a foregone conclusion and does not involve mutual defence commitments. But being in the Shanghai grouping could bring Tehran extra support from its two key members, Russia and China. Membership of the SCO could also offer Iran shelter from the intense US-led international pressure on Tehran to end its uranium enrichment and presumed pursuit of nuclear weaponry. The Iranian Deputy Foreign Minister, Manuchehr Mohammadi, said in April 2006: 'What we are seeing is really a tectonic shift of diplomatic and every other kind of activity into Western and Central Asia.' Russia and China gave Tehran some support in the UN debate over its nuclear program. Both also resisted pressure from the US and its European allies to formulate a UN draft resolution that could open the way for economic sanctions or even military intervention unless Iran stopped work on the nuclear fuel cycle.

But after 2005, President Ahmadinejad's more radical government believed that Iran needed to cultivate much wider diplomatic relations including with China, the SCO and the South-East Asian nations. For instance, Ahmadinejad received a warm reception during his mid-2006 visit to Indonesia, as part of the non-Arab Islamic states grouping, and wanted Iran to pursue good relations with similar states. But not all the SCO foreign ministers welcomed Iran, since many Central Asians shared a suspicion of long standing Persian regional ambitions. Tajikistan's Minister, Talbak Nazarov, said the question of Iranian membership was not being considered, at least for the time being. Nazarov said the SCO could not extend its membership indefinitely, and that there was presently no document to regulate the process for taking on new members. However, Russian Foreign Minister Sergei Lavrov told

5 Rowan Callick, 'Beijing targets hearts, minds to beat al-Qa'ida's push', *The Australian*, 26 Feb 2007.

reporters after the May 2006 meeting in Shanghai that the SCO was in the process of negotiating possible membership with Tehran, along with prospectively India, Pakistan, and Mongolia – all of which had observer status in the SCO.

The SCO is seen by the Russians as very much a Chinese initiative that they chose to join, but they remain wary of China's actions towards Central Asia. West and Central Asia are once more focal points of international competition. India may also join the SCO group, together with Pakistan, if the group wanted to enhance its security role in Central Asia. PRC misgivings about Pakistan were reduced after it became clear that Pakistan's involvement in SCO could help reduce the leverage the US had acquired in Islamabad. The SCO may develop no further, but it brings together a number of powerful states with different reasons for opposing the dominance of the US in Mackinder's Eurasian heartland: China, Russia, India, Pakistan and Iran. Each already has smaller allies which can also be brought to the table of anti-hegemonic activity.

The PRC has also been actively courting friends in other parts of the world. It has hosted a number of multilateral meetings with African regimes among whom its disregard for human rights in its diplomatic activities is an advantage which makes its search for resources easier. It has produced a high profile foreign aid program in developing countries made affordable by its large trade surpluses. And it has won recognition from states previously committed to Taiwan, particularly in central and south America, the Caribbean and the Pacific by generous grants. The PRC also collaborates with the Russians when their interests coincide.

The Russian Federation

After the collapse of the Soviet Union, the Russian Federation re-emerged with essentially its historic identity. The Principality of Muscovy was founded in the twelfth century, and gradually conquered surrounding states. In the early seventeenth century, the new Romanov Dynasty continued this policy of expansion across Siberia to the Pacific, which was reached under Peter the Great (1682–1725), and its territory was extended to the Baltic Sea. The country was renamed the Russian Empire. During the nineteenth century, more territory was acquired in Europe and Asia and it became the largest state in the world. But devastating defeats of the Russian army in the First World War led to widespread insurrection, the overthrow of the Tsar in 1917 and contraction of Russia's territory. The Communists under Vladimir Lenin seized power soon after, formed the Soviet Union and began a new cycle of expansion. The brutal rule of Joseph Stalin (1928–53) strengthened communist rule and Russian dominance at a cost of tens of millions of lives.

The Soviet economy and society grew until the mid-1970s and then stagnated until General Secretary Mikhail Gorbachev (1985–91) introduced *glasnost* (openness) and *perestroika* (restructuring) in an attempt to modernize Communism. But his initiatives inadvertently released forces that by December 1991 splintered the USSR into the Russian Federation and fourteen other independent republics. After that, the Russian Federation struggled under Boris Yeltsin (1991–2000) in its efforts to build a democratic political system and market economy to replace the totalitarian social, political and economic controls of the Communist period. While initially some progress was made on the economic front, after the financial collapse of 1998 there was a recentralization of power and the erosion of nascent democratic institutions under Vladimir Putin (2000–2007). A separatist Islamic conflict also broke out in Chechnya giving Putin some sympathy for the US GWOT.

Gorbachev transformed the powerful Soviet imperial dictatorship into a ramshackle Commonwealth of Independent States. Boris Yeltsin then turned Russia into a stumbling, poor democracy. Vladimir Putin remade Russia into an ambitious autocracy floating on resource wealth. But despite losing many Soviet 'colonies', Russia was still about 1.8 times the size of the US with an area of 17 million square kilometres. Its population is still substantial at 142.8 million, but has a negative growth rate of -0.37 per cent and has shrunk since the Soviet era. Among its great advantages are its natural resources base that includes major deposits of oil, natural gas, coal, many strategic minerals, and timber. But it does face formidable obstacles of climate, terrain, and distance that hinder their exploitation. Despite its size, much of the country lacks good soils and the climate is either too cold or too dry for agriculture. The Russian people have also been traumatised by the Soviet collapse, the war in Chechnya and terrorism in Russia, including a massacre of several hundred people, mostly children, in an attack on a school in Beslan, in September 2004 by Chechen rebels.

Russia is unlikely to evolve into a liberal democratic state. Marshal Goldman[6] concludes that 'under Putin, Russia is reversing some of the most important economic and political reforms it adopted after freeing itself from the yoke of communism'. Nonetheless, Russia ended 2005 with its seventh straight year of growth, averaging 6.4 per cent annually, and had largely recovered since the financial crisis of 1998. Although high oil prices and a relatively cheap rouble were important drivers of this economic recovery, since 2000 investment and consumer driven demand played an increasing role. Real fixed capital investment grew at 10 per cent annually, and real personal incomes increased over 12 per cent. During this time, poverty declined steadily and the middle class continued to expand. Russia has also improved its international financial position since the 1998 financial crisis, with its foreign debt declining from 90 per cent of GDP to around 31 per cent. Strong oil export earnings allowed Russia to increase its foreign reserves from only $12 billion to $180 billion at year end 2005, and in April 2007 it had $356 billion in gold and foreign exchange reserves (the world's third biggest). Government efforts to advance structural reforms had also raised business and investor confidence in Russia's economic prospects despite its authoritarian political drift. Although Russia has an economy of only $750 billion at official exchange rates, a GDP of $1.6tril at PPP, and a middling per capita income GDP PPP of $11,000, this did constitute progress since Soviet times. But it was neither a liberal nor modernised society and serious problems persisted.

Russia's manufacturing base inherited from the Soviets was dilapidated and must be replaced or modernized if the country were to achieve broad-based economic growth. Other problems include a weak banking system, an uneven business climate

---

6 Marshal Goldman, 'Return of the statists: Putin takes on the oligarchs', *The Australian Financial Review,* reprinted from *Foreign Affairs,* 3 Dec 2004.

that discourages both domestic and foreign investors, and widespread corruption and lack of trust in institutions. President Putin is also re-asserting state control over the economy and it did indeed increase in 2005–07 with a number of large acquisitions. Most fundamentally, Russia has made little progress in building the rule of law, the bedrock of a modern market economy. Russia's is a statist, resource-based economy under the control of a modestly despotic regime.

Putin is, however, clearing up international disputes. In 2005, China and Russia ratified the treaty to divide the islands in the Amur, Ussuri, and Argun Rivers, thereby resolving the final part of their centuries-long border disputes. The sovereignty dispute with Japan over the islands group, known in Japan as the 'Northern Territories' and in Russia as the 'Southern Kurils', occupied by the Soviet Union in 1945, now administered by Russia, and claimed by Japan, remains the only real obstacle to signing a peace treaty formally ending of the Second World War. Russia and Georgia agreed on delimiting all but small, strategic segments of the land boundary, and the maritime boundary and most other boundary issues have been resolved or quietly shelved.

Russians were shocked politically by the Soviet Union's disintegration, and Boris Yeltsin's administration had a difficult time running the Russian Federation, with the President often vodka addled, and only survived with substantial US assistance (which did not readily translate into Moscow's support for US foreign policy). Yeltsin's was almost a client regime of the Clinton administration. Vladimir Putin introduced a measure of competence after taking over in 2000. But at first he too was weak, and lurched from one disaster to the next. Chechen terrorists took over a theatre in Moscow and one hundred and thirty hostages died when Special Forces stormed the building. The 'oligarchs' who – with more US assistance – rigged the privatisations of the 1990s were busy spending conspicuously overseas and the economy languished. 'Democracy is a messy process', the former US ambassador, Alexander Vershbow, said, 'You have to give Russia time'.[7] Others were less charitable, including the famous and later assassinated author, Anna Politkovskaya, who claimed that Putin was moving Russia back to a Soviet style dictatorship.[8] It has certainly reversed whatever trend towards liberalism that was evident under Yeltsin (died 2007).

But by 2007 Russia was stronger, richer and more stable than at any time since 1991. In 2006 it hosted the G8 summit, listed its state oil company on the London stock exchange, and finally killed Shamil Basayev, its most wanted Islamic terrorist. But Russia is not a democracy and Putin has deliberately dismantled the political freedoms that Russians won through the 1980s and 1990s. It is also renewing its earlier geopolitical strategy of expanding its regional influence. In general, the Russian public appear willing to ignore, excuse or support Putin's campaign to re-assert central and Russian authority. Putin has considerable power with almost total control over the executive, legislative and judicial branches of government, as well as the national media and the oil and gas industries. A 2006 poll showed 40 per

7 Jeremy Page, 'Putin cannot tame the beast', *The Times*, 21 Aug 2006.

8 Anna Politkovskaya, *Putin's Russia (London, 2004);* Mark Franchetti, 'Anti-Putin journalist killed in hit', *The Australian*, 9 Oct 2006.

cent of the people would vote for whoever he nominates as his successor. Most Russians may not want democracy after their experiences with Yeltsin's version. But Russia's newfound prosperity is less the result of sound economic management and modernisation than of the record oil and other resource prices. Russia's population also falls by 700,000 each year.

In September 2006 Russia put the world's largest oil and gas venture in doubt, by cancelling an environmental permit for the energy giant Royal Dutch Shell. A Shell-led consortium was developing a massive oil and gas field under the ocean off Russia's far eastern coast near the island of Sakhalin, which is estimated to have reserves of one billion barrels of oil. It began operating in 1999 but the $25 billion project came to a stand still. Russia's Resources Ministry withdrew its ecological approval for the site as part of a campaign by the Kremlin to gain more control over Russia's energy resources. Russia joined many international agreements and institutions in the 1990s, including the Council of Europe, the Organisation for Security and Co-operation in Europe, and the G8, on the understanding it was becoming a liberal democracy. Russia continued to pretend it was a democracy, but it was not, although this may not detract from the popular support for the regime.[9]

Russia has a growing but fragile economy, a vast resource base, a large but shrinking population, large military forces, including a nuclear armoury second only to the US, and some geo-strategic ambitions. But these are mostly regional and confined to the Balkans, eastern Europe, Central Asia, parts of the Middle East and East Asia. It is most unlikely again to challenge directly US power, in any region vital to US interests. But it can bring military muscle and geographic strength to any combination of powers wishing to check the projection of US power into the Eurasian heartland.

The Republic of India

India might be a partner in such an enterprise. It has a confident national state and the experience of a long close relationship with Moscow during the Soviet period. The Indus Valley core Indian civilisation dates back at least 5,000 years. Aryan tribes from the northwest entered the area three thousand years ago and, with the earlier Dravidian inhabitants, created modern Indian culture. During the nineteenth century, Britain assumed political control of virtually all of India creating the 'Raj' which politically unified the sub-continent. Non-violent resistance to British colonialism, led by the mystic Mohatma Gandhi and politician Jawaharlal Nehru, brought independence in 1947. The subcontinent was then divided amid inter-communal rioting and mass migrations into the large secular state of India, the smaller Muslim state of Pakistan, and several other states including Burma and Sri Lanka. Several wars were then fought over the boundaries, particularly in Kashmir. A third such war between India and Pakistan in 1971 resulted in East Pakistan becoming the separate nation of Bangladesh.

9 Jeremy Page, 'Putin cannot tame the beast', *The Times*, 21 Aug 2006.

Despite some recent impressive gains in gross economic investment and output since the liberal reforms beginning 1991, India faces considerable problems including ongoing disputes with Pakistan, massive overpopulation, environmental degradation, extensive poverty, and ethnic and religious strife. But it is, nonetheless, a potential Great Power[10] with a population of 1.1 billion growing at 1.38 per cent annually. Its composition is Indo-Aryan 72 per cent and Dravidian 25 per cent. The major religions are Hindu at 80.5 per cent, Islam at 13.4 per cent, Christian at 2.3 per cent, and Sikh at 1.9 per cent. The English language enjoys only associate status, but is the most important language for national, political, and commercial communication giving the country great advantages in a globalisation era. The Indian state is reasonably liberal democratic, with a federal republic version of the Westminster model. Cabinet is appointed by the president on the recommendation of the very powerful prime minister after parliamentary elections. The prime minister is chosen, as elsewhere, by parliamentary members of the majority party following legislative elections which were last held April – May 2004 with the next to be held May 2009. The head of government since May 2004 has been the reformist liberal, and first Sikh, Prime Minister Manmohan Singh.

India's diverse economy ranges from traditional village farming and handicrafts, to modern agriculture and a wide range of modern industries. It has many globalised services which are now the major source of economic growth, accounting for half of India's output with less than one quarter of its labour force. But about three-fifths of the work-force remains in generally low productivity traditional agriculture. Government controls on foreign trade and investment have been reduced since liberal reform began in 1991, but there are still high tariffs and controls on foreign direct investment. The government in 2005 liberalised investment in the civil aviation, telecom, and construction sectors, but privatisation of government-owned industries essentially came to a halt in 2005. Nonetheless, although the economy has grown by more than seven per cent annually since 1994, the huge and growing population is the fundamental social, economic, and environmental problem. While GDP at PPP is $3.611 trillion, at official exchange rate it is only $719.8 billion, and the per capita income, even at PPP, is a modest $3,300.

India's military expenditure is estimated at about $20 billion which accounts for 2.5 per cent of its GDP. It has a large and well equipped voluntary army of over one million, including 5,600 tanks, a missile force and nine squadrons of helicopters. Its air force is equipped mostly with Russian MIGs, but also some French Mirages. It has a substantial naval fleet which patrols the India Ocean with some aircraft carriers. It also has nuclear weapons. India has fought four wars with Pakistan; has had some border clashes with China; and has intervened in the affairs of all its neighbours, and occupied a few of them. India is a serious regional power with wider aspirations. But for some time it will be consumed with its own development which lags a generation behind China which began its liberal reforms in 1978. Within the sub-continent, however, it is dominant although impeded by the resistance of Pakistan. This rivalry has a strong religious dimension which ensures that even if India had not been the

10 Jann Einfeld, *India* (San Diego, 2003); and Henmann Kulke and Dietmar Rothermund, *A History of India* (New York, 2004).

subject of terrorist attacks, most recently in Mumbai in July 2006 when 200 people were killed, it would side with the US in the GWOT.

In early March 2006, George Bush made the first visit to India of an American President since Richard Nixon in order to gain support for America's role in South and East Asia. It was agreed the US would supply uranium for India's nuclear energy. In his next stop, in Pakistan, President Bush hoped to reduce tensions with the Muslim world and offered the help of the US in continuing negotiations between India and Pakistan on Kashmir, as well as to shore up the War on Terror on Pakistan's border region with Afghanistan.[11]

India, like the PRC, is trying to resolve its international boundary disputes. India and China launched a security and foreign policy dialogue in 2005 and subsequently discussions related to: the dispute over most of their rugged, militarized boundary; regional nuclear proliferation; Indian claims that China transferred missiles to Pakistan; and other matters including confidence-building measures to defuse tensions over Kashmir. In 2004 India and Pakistan instituted a cease fire in Kashmir and in 2005 and restored bus service across the highly militarized Line of Control. Pakistan has taken its dispute on the impact and benefits of India's building the Baglihar Dam on the Chenab River in Jammu and Kashmir to the World Bank for arbitration.

Nonetheless, India faces a growing battle with terrorism and continuing sectarian conflict between Hindus and Muslims. In late 2006 Sonia Gandhi, the Italian-born widow who effectively runs the ruling coalition, planned to fire the key cabinet minister in charge of national security[12] – Home Minister Shivraj Patil, one of the most powerful figures in the UPA coalition Government, dominated by the Congress Party. Ms Gandhi was forced to abandon a meeting of bombing victims because of the hostility of local people near Mumbai, after a series of blasts outside a mosque killed more than 30 people and injured 300. The security forces continually failed to prevent terrorist bombings, including the devastating attacks on the Mumbai train system in July 2006. There was mounting concern about the terrorist threat in India, and when Prime Minister Singh met Pakistani President Musharraf in Havana in September 2006 Singh demanded that Islamabad do much more to curb Jihadist terrorist groups based in Pakistan. Meanwhile, a court in Mumbai convicted four members of a family over 13 terror bomb blasts in the city in 1993 that killed 257 people and injured over seven hundred. The case, involving 123 defendants, had taken thirteen years to progress through the judicial system. The blasts were planned by a leading Muslim underworld figure in Mumbai, allegedly at the behest of Pakistan's intelligence agency, the ISI, to avenge demolition of a mosque in Ayodhya in December 1992, and the killing of Muslims in the religious rioting that followed.

India has a very good relationship with more distant Iran based on trading Indian manufacturers for Iranian oil. It imports 70 per cent of the crude oil it consumes and its energy demands, both in oil and gas, are expected to double by 2020 as the country's economy grows rapidly. In 2005, Iran and India signed a $22 billion

11 See Kishore Mahbubani, 'The Asian Challenge', *The Australian Financial Review*, 3 March 2006.

12 Bruce Loudon, 'Gandhi to sack security minister', *The Australian*, 14 Sept 2006.

deal for Tehran to supply five million tonnes of gas a year to India. The proposed gas pipeline link is expected to come through Pakistan. Washington urged India to rethink such ambitious projects with Iran, but Delhi resisted. India-Iran relations steadily evolved and a declaration in January 2003 clearly stated the intention of the two countries to enter a strategic partnership which goes beyond the proposed gas pipeline. India has the second largest Shi'ite population (after Iran) in the world and improving ties with Iran could send encouraging signals for the nearly 20 million Shi'ites in the country. The two countries have also been stepping up their military co-operation and Delhi is keen to have a foothold in Afghanistan using Iran as an entry point.

Nonetheless, the US has pursued a policy of assisting India become a major presence in the international community, including the possible future sales of uranium, and under the Bush administration this has proven to be very successful.[13] In 2007 the possibility of a US-India-Australia-Japan arrangement was canvassed with clear implications for the containment of rising Chinese power. But India and the US would differ over Iran.

The Islamic Republic of Iran

The Persian Empire was one of the dominant states of antiquity and left a clear cultural legacy in Iran. It was defeated by Alexander the Great in the fourth century BCE but then re-constituted under the Sassanid dynasty to dominate territory that spread from modern Pakistan to Egypt. The Islamic Republic of Iran is a very ancient state within more or less its present boundaries containing a substantial territory of 1,648 million square kilometres, slightly larger than Alaska. It has a population of 69 million with a growth rate of 1.1 per cent. Fifty one per cent of these are Persian, and Azeri comprise 24 per cent, while there are several small minorities. But religiously, they are mostly Shi'ite Muslims at 89 per cent, with Sunni Muslims 9 per cent, and small Zoroastrian, Jewish, Christian and Baha'i minorities. The country has extensive natural resources, particularly oil, natural gas and coal. Iran has emerged in the last several years as a serious regional contender in the Middle East. The Islamic regime since 1979 has harboured quite expansive ambitions but these have been difficult to achieve in the face of the regional balance of power and US containment policy. At first it was attacked by Iraq and then effectively contained by US power operating in conjunction with its regional Arab allies. This has changed substantially since the US invasion of Iraq.

After 1979 the victorious fundamentalist clerics established a theocratic system of government with ultimate political authority nominally vested in a learned religious scholar – at first the leader of the revolution, Ayotollah Khomeini. Although elections are held, candidates are vetted by the clerics and the results deeply affected by the religious authorities. This is probably the form of Islamic democracy most likely to occur in Middle Eastern Islamic states, whereby people may vote but within confines

13 Sharif Shuja, 'The United States and India', *National Observer*, Melbourne, Winter 2006.

determined by the clerics' interpretation of the *Koran.* The present Head of State is Ayatollah Ali Khamenei. He is The Supreme Leader and so Commander-in-Chief of the armed forces, controls the military intelligence and security operations, and has sole power to declare war. The heads of the judiciary, state radio and television networks, the commanders of the police and military forces, and six of the twelve members of the Guardian Council of the Constitution, are appointed by the Supreme Leader. The Assembly of Experts elects and dismisses the Supreme Leader on the basis of qualifications and popular esteem.

The Guardian Council has the authority to interpret the constitution and to determine if the laws passed by the parliament are constitutional. As such, the Council itself is not a legislative body, but it has veto power over the Iranian parliament (Majlis). Its members are composed of clerics and lawyers. Six members of the Council are clerics selected by the Supreme Leader. The other six members are lawyers proposed by Iran's head of judicial branch (selected in turn by the Supreme Leader), and voted in by the Majlis. Members are elected for six years on a phased basis, so that half the membership changes every three years. The Council also holds veto power over all legislation approved by the Majlis and can veto a law for being against Islamic law. This gives the state an organisational totalitarian coherence, yet it may still be more representative than the neighbouring Arab states and, consequently, more capable of seriously mobilising popular support.

In addition, Iran has substantial military forces. In 2002, its total active armed forces numbered approximately 520,000 with reserves of 350,000. The army had 325,000 soldiers including four armoured divisions with 1,565 main battle tanks and about 890 multiple rocket launchers. The air force had personnel numbering 52,000 and 306 combat aircraft. The navy had 3 frigates, 6 submarines, and 56 smaller patrol and coastal combatants. The Revolutionary Guards (Pasdaran) had an estimated 125,000-man army and 20,000 sailors and marines. The paramilitary had 40,000 active members of law enforcement forces including border guards. There was a reserve of the Popular Mobilization Army of around 300,000 peacetime volunteers, mostly youths. This number can swell up to 1,000,000 and was used successfully in the war against Iraq. Iran is also, of course, developing nuclear weapons. The official military budget in 2000 was $9.7 billion or 3.1 per cent of GDP. From its inception, the Islamic Republic of Iran has been committed to the destruction of Israel as its new President re-stated in November 2005.

The Iranian regime represents the Shi'ite strand of Islamic extremism, claims to be the centre of a global Islamic revolution, and supports Shi'ite parties and religious leaders throughout the Arab world, most notably the Hezbollah in Lebanon, which Iranian agents created in 1982. Hezbollah's leader, Hassan Nasrallah, has declared that Jews invented the legend of the Nazi atrocities and that Israel is a cancerous body in the region that must be uprooted. Hezbollah has carried out numerous bombings and political assassinations abroad on Iran's behalf. The most spectacular were a suicide bomber's massacre of 241 US marine peacekeepers in Lebanon in 1983, and the bombing of the Israeli embassy and Jewish cultural centre in Buenos Aires in 1994, slaughtering more than 100 Argentinian Jews. Hezbollah also kidnapped scores of Western journalists in Lebanon during the 1980s, torturing and murdering many of them, and has assassinated Iranian opposition politicians in France and elsewhere.

Iranian-US relations have been extremely strained and diplomatic relations non-existent since Iranian students seized the US Embassy in Tehran on 4 November 1979 and held it until 20 January 1981. During 1980–88, the war with Iraq expanded into the Persian Gulf and led to clashes between US Navy and Iranian military forces 1987–1988. Iran has been designated by the US as a state sponsor of terrorism for its activities in Lebanon and elsewhere, and remains subject to US economic sanctions and export controls because of this. Following the elections of a reformist more liberal president and parliament (Majlis) in the late 1990s, there were attempts to foster political reform in response to popular dissatisfaction. But this foundered as conservative politicians prevented reform measures from being enacted, increased repressive measures, and then made electoral gains against the reformers. After Parliamentary elections in 2004 and the August 2005 inauguration of the conservative Islamist, Mahmud Ahmadinejad, as president, the conservative clerics effectively resumed power in Iran's government.

Iran has substantial military forces some inherited from the ambitious Shah, augmented by purchase from various sources, including missiles from North Korea, and has a nuclear weapons program which will probably produce nuclear bombs by about 2010. President Ahmadinejad has stalled in responding to international demands, led by the US and its major NATO/Europe allies, that Iran stop enriching uranium for nuclear use.[14] The messianic Shi'ite President will not retreat. 'Nuclear power is our right. No one can take this away from us ... Our main task is to develop and build the Iranian nation. No one will stop us'. The most serious challenge to the West is not a resurgent Hezbollah but Iran, the guerrilla organisation's oil-rich patron. The European Union represented by Britain, France and Germany, spent three years, 2004–06, trying to talk Iran out of its nuclear program but to little effect. Inspectors from the International Atomic Energy Agency (IAEA) were evaded, and in April 2006 the Iranian President laid on a ceremony with dancers and doves of peace to celebrate the glorious news, as he put it, that 'Iran has joined the countries with nuclear technology'.

The Bush administration, once impatient with the EU's unsuccessful diplomacy in Iran, was chastened and divided by its own failure to pacify Iraq. The war there has, so far, been a strategic disaster as far as containing Iran is concerned. Power in Iraq has reverted to the majority Shi'ite, including factions close to the Iranian mullahs; Iranian agents poured into Iraq from the moment Saddam Hussein fell; and, after its experiences of the past three years, the US military has little desire to take on the well-armed and nationalistic Iranians. Israel's brief 2006 war in southern Lebanon – a proxy conflict in which the US backed Israel to destroy Iran's client, Hezbollah – also failed to fulfil its aims and suggested the worth of Iranian bunker technology.

When the US invaded Iraq the Iranian government, then dominated by the reformists who wanted to re-enter the international community, at first appeared to

---

14 Sarah Baxter, 'Apocalyptic Ahmadinejad rattles sabre', *The Australian*, 21 Aug 2006.

welcome the overthrow of its old adversary, Saddam Hussein, and the creation of a democratic state that would be dominated by its co-religionist Shi'ites. It would also likely have some influence over the new government. In 2004 there was a re-evaluation and at the 2005 Presidential election the clerics backed the more radical firebrand Ahmadinejad. His election as a fairly young radical was a surprise to the region. He blocked further liberalisation within Iran, and started to move to a more assertive global diplomacy and a regional strategy to reclaim Persia's historical domination of the region between Pakistan and Syria. Ahmadinejad is the son of an ironworker and hero-worshipped Ayatollah Khomeini as a student and was in the vanguard of the 1979 revolution. He went on to join Iran's Revolutionary Guards, where he became known as a persecutor of dissidents. In 2005 he was pushed into the presidency by the mullahs as a trusty hardliner who had impressed working-class Iranians with his simple lifestyle as Mayor of Tehran. He is a millenarian who believes in the coming of the twelfth imam, the mahdi (or messiah) of Shi'ite theology. In his first speech to the UN in 2005, he begged: 'O mighty Lord', 'hasten the emergence of your last repository, the promised one, that perfect and pure human being, the one that will fill this world with justice and peace'. But Ahmadinejad is also a shrewd political opportunist who has consolidated his power by being a devout Muslim. One expert believes: 'The leaders of Iran are hardline, revolutionary militants and men of power, but they are not crazy'.[15] Iran's growing regional superpower status poses a secular, geopolitical challenge to America. The Iranians believe that the Israeli failure in Lebanon 2006 showed that shock and awe does not always work. US defence officials came to the same conclusion. 'Hezbollah has really empowered the Iranians. If Hezbollah is a surrogate for Iran, and you can not bomb it successfully, you are not going to be able to bomb Iran'.

At that time Rumsfeld rightly believed he had his hands full in Iraq, where 130,000 American troops were vulnerable to Iranian interventions. Further, US intelligence has not located all of Iran's nuclear installations and the US lacked the weaponry to penetrate the deep bunkers in granite mountains. Iran, moreover, could retaliate to such an attack by closing the Strait of Hormuz through which 40 per cent of the world's oil trade passes. The damage inflicted by Hezbollah on an Israeli ship with a C-802 missile, an Iranian version of the Chinese Silkworm, was a reminder of the level of Iranian military technology.

The US might well have to bargain with Iran, because the US can do nothing else. 'The "international community" is now powerless in its nuclear confrontation with Iran, even more so than with North Korea. Pyongyang needs food and fuel to survive and is therefore susceptible to pressure from China. Iran, with its oil wealth, needs nothing and is not dependent on anyone'.[16] Economic sanctions have been debated by the UN Security Council and include cutting investment in Iran's oil industry or banning exports to Iran but they would likely be ineffective. Oil prices have gone up because of rising demand, especially from China. If Iran, which is the world's

---

15 Vali Nasr, *The Shia Revival* (New York, 2006).

16 Anatole Kaletsky, 'Stop issuing threats and bring Tehran back into the civilised world', from *The Times, reprinted in The Australian*, 29 Aug 2006.

third-largest oil producer after Russia and Saudi Arabia, had its exports removed by sanctions from world markets, the oil price would only increase further.

Some neo-conservatives, such as Edward Luttwak, believed military action might be necessary and feasible and argued for a short, sharp US bombing strike on Iran. In mid 2006, before the Congressional elections, his views seemed influential. Neo-conservatives then wanted to foster regime change in Iran, but that prospect was more difficult even than in Iraq. It seemed that by the time Bush leaves office at the beginning of 2009, Iran will be close to having WMDs. If Bush sticks to his promise that Iran will not go nuclear on his watch, he seems likely follow the UN route and try to impose sanctions if Ahmadinejad refuses to give up his nuclear ambitions. But the UN is probably not capable of imposing meaningful sanctions.

On 27 August 2006, in a show of defiance against US-led Western efforts to curb Iran's nuclear program, President Ahmadinejad inaugurated a new phase of a heavy-water power reactor, prompting an Israeli warning that Tehran had taken another step towards making an atom bomb.[17] The Arak nuclear plant in central Iran can make eight tonnes of heavy water a year, with output expected to rise tenfold. Heavy water aids nuclear fission, and the plutonium by-product could be used to make bombs, but the reactor to produce plutonium is still under construction. Still Ahmadinejad insisted the plant was for peaceful power purposes: 'We are not a threat to anybody … There is no talk of nuclear weapons'. He said Israel had nothing to fear, although he had, of course, repeatedly called for Israel's destruction. 'There is no discussion of nuclear weapons, even for the Zionist regime, which is a definite enemy', he said. The US continued to contemplate merely sanctions.

Iran's economy has been greatly strengthened by the rise in oil prices 2002–7, although it still had a large, inefficient state sector and statist policies that created major distortions throughout. Most economic activity remains controlled by the state. Private sector activity is typically small-scale and includes workshops, farming, and services. President Ahmadinejad continued the modest market reform plans of former President Rafsanjani with limited progress. Nonetheless, relatively high oil prices enabled Iran to amass some $40 billion in foreign exchange reserves, amidst high unemployment and inflation and little real modernisation. The proportion of the economy devoted to the development of weapons of mass destruction remains a contentious issue. Iran's GDP at PPP in 2005 was around $561 billion or, at official exchange rate, $181 billion. Its growth rate has recently been around 6.1 per cent which has left a middle level per capita of PPP $8,300. These figures may now be improving more sharply with recent rises in the price of oil, since it accounts for around eighty per cent of Iran's exports, and goes to Japan, China, Italy, South Africa, South Korea, France, Turkey and Taiwan. These countries might not want sanctions imposed on their energy provider.

By 2007 it was clear that the US-led GWOT and occupation of Iraq had significantly bolstered Iran's power and influence in the Middle East.[18] A report published by Chatham House said the wars in Iraq and Afghanistan had removed Iran's main (Sunni) rival regimes in the region. Israel's conflict with the Palestinians

---

17 Sarah Baxter, 'Defiant Iran boosts N-reactor', *The Australian, 28* Aug 2006.

18 'US interventions have boosted Iran, says report', *Guardian,* 23 Aug 2006.

and its invasion of Lebanon had also put Iran 'in a position of considerable strength' in the Middle East. Unless stability could be restored to the region, Iran's power would continue to grow. The study said Iran had been swift to fill the political vacuum created by the removal of the Taliban in Afghanistan and Saddam Hussein in Iraq. The Islamic Republic now had a level of influence in the region that could not be ignored. In particular, Iran had superseded the US as the most influential power in Iraq, regarding its former adversary as its 'own backyard'. It was also a 'prominent presence' in its other war-torn neighbour, Afghanistan.[19] The report concluded: 'There is little doubt that Iran has been the chief beneficiary of the war on terror in the Middle East'. The US, with Coalition support, had eliminated two of Iran's Sunni regional rival governments – the Taliban in Afghanistan and Saddam Hussein's regime in Iraq – but failed to replace either with coherent and stable political structures. The West needed to understand better Iran's links with its neighbours to see why the country felt able to resist Western pressure. Iran had been able to use the insurgency in Iraq to advance its own cause against the Americans and had used the Hezbollah to inflict damage on the Israelis. It had also been able to widen its diplomatic leverage by more extensive contacts including the Shanghai Group.

Iran may also be fanning the Iraq insurgency, although one of Iraq's most powerful Shi'ite politicians dismissed claims by US officials that Iran was interfering in Baghdad's affairs. Abdul-Azziz al-Hakim said that despite repeated requests from him and other Iraqi politicians, American officials failed to show any reliable evidence of Tehran's interference. '[The US] has been making such claims for a long time', he said, 'and for three years we've told them, "Show us proof". But they never have'.[20] Hakim headed the Supreme Council for the Islamic Revolution in Iraq, or SCIRI, the largest of Iraq's political parties which had close ties to Tehran, and many of its leaders – including Hakim – spent many years in exile in Iraq during the Saddam Hussein era. Shi'ite politicians dismissed US statements that Iran was actively arming and training Shi'ite militias in Iraq. 'They are looking for somebody to blame for the failure [of the US military to halt the sectarian killings in Iraq] and it is easy to blame Iran', said Hadi al-Amiri, the head of the Iraqi parliament's security and defence committee, while also helped run the Badr Organization, a Shi'ite militia.

Brigadier General Michael Barbero claimed that there was 'irrefutable' evidence of Iranian collusion with Iraqi militias. But that was not what US military officials in Baghdad said. The top US military spokesman in Iraq, Major General William Caldwell, told journalists that there 'is nothing that we definitively have found to say that there are any Iranians operating within the country of Iraq'. He added that although 'some Shi'ite elements have been in Iran receiving training ... the degree to which this is known and endorsed by the government of Iran is uncertain'. There was some irony in Barbero's claim that Iran was helping the militias with technology to make improvised explosive devices (IEDs), since in 2004 US officials

19 R Lowe and C Spencer, eds, *Iran, Its Neighbours and the Regional Crisis* (London, 2006).

20 A Gosh, 'Is Iran Really Controlling Militias in Iraq?', *Time*, 25 Aug 2006.

said Tehran was supplying IED technology to Iraq's Sunni insurgents. Several Sunni insurgent leaders – whose hatred of Iran compares with their animosity toward the US – told *Time* magazine they had no need of such outside help since they had many explosives experts from Saddam's military. As sectarian violence grew in Iraq, each side accused the other of getting outside help. Sunni leaders claimed Shi'ite militias were trained by Iran and Shi'ite leaders say Sunni terrorists were funded by Saudi Arabia and Syria. US officials have frequently accused Damascus of aiding and abetting the Sunni insurgency. All these accusations were likely to be true.

Many Iraqi Shi'ite politicians, who made up the majority in parliament, like Hakim and al-Amiri, and many leading figures in the Iraqi government owed Iran for its support of the anti-Saddam movement. Even Shi'ite leaders who did not live in Iran have close ties there and some condemned US efforts to pressure Tehran into abandoning its nuclear program. The radical young Shi'ite cleric, Muqtada al-Sadr, warned that if the US launched a military campaign against Iran, his Mahdi Army would fight with the Iranians. Leaders like Hakim say that rather than blame Iran or the Shi'ite militias, the US military – and Iraqi security forces – should focus on defeating the mainly Sunni insurgent and terrorist groups. 'The main cause of the violence in Iraq are the Saddamists and [Jihadist terrorists]', Hakim said.

As one commentator accurately observed

> Despite America's military superiority in the Middle East, the balance of power in the region is turning against both the US and Israel ... The magnitude of Iran's strategic gains in the five years since the 9/11 attack on America is still not grasped. Iran, in fact, is the major winner from President Bush's war on terrorism, a dramatic and unintended consequence. Given that the US and Israel regard Iran as the single most dangerous terrorist threat in the world today, this is an astonishing outcome – almost difficult to comprehend. ... The Bush Administration has changed the power balance in the region decisively in favour of Iran. Tehran is the winner from the Iraq war. It was a winner from the removal of the Taliban in Afghanistan. It is a winner from the radicalisation of the Israeli-Palestinian conflict with the election victory of Hamas. It is a winner from Israel's unsuccessful war against Hezbollah. Indeed, it is probably only a matter of time before Iran replaces America as the major external influence in Iraq, exercising a controlling say in the south or a veto on the fate of a Shia-dominated Iraq. [21]

It seems, nonetheless, most likely that the Iranians are supporting elements of the insurgency that will help move the Shi'ite state, that the US has created, closer to Iran in the longer run. And they may well succeed.

In late 2006, the tone of relations between the US and Iran was made clear when Bush compared Ahmadinejad with Lenin and Hitler, and declared him to be a new bin Laden who could not be allowed to develop nuclear weapons. In retaliation, the Iranian President said that the US President was 'nothing' compared to the will of God.[22] 'I am telling (Bush) that all the world is threatening you since the general path that the world is taking is towards worshipping God and divinity', he told a conference ahead of a festival marking the birth of the 'hidden' twelfth Shi'ite Imam

21 Paul Kelly, 'US policy makes Iran the winner', *The Australi*an, 1 Sept 2006.

22 'Iran leader a new Osama, says Bush', *The Australian*, 7 Sept 2006.

Mahdi. 'This massive stream is moving and you are nothing in comparison to God's will'. As if to demonstrate this, Iran seized fifteen British sailors and marines in March 2007 and then released them at will.

The Syrian Arab Republic

Syria dominated much of the Levant at different times in antiquity. After the break up of the Ottoman Empire, France administered Syria until its independence without Christian Lebanon in 1946. The country then experienced a series of military coups until it united with Egypt in 1958 to form the United Arab Republic. In September 1961 the two separated and the Syrian Arab Republic was re-established. In November 1970, Hafiz al-Asad, a member of the Ba'ath Party and the minority Alawite sect, seized power in a coup and brought authoritarian political stability to the country. In the 1967 Arab-Israeli War, defeated Syria lost the Golan Heights to Israel, although in the 1990s Syria and Israel held occasional peace talks over its return. Following the death of President al-Asad in July 2000, his son, Bashar al-Asad, became president after a rigged popular referendum. Syrian troops that had been stationed in Lebanon since 1976, ostensibly in a peace-keeping role but where it has irredentist ambitions, were pulled out in April 2005 after Syrian agents killed the Lebanese President and mass demonstrations demanded they withdraw.

Syria had pursued anti-Israeli and anti-US policies since it was close to the Soviet Union during the Cold War. Although Syria is much smaller and poorer than Iran, it is strategically located and hence very influential. It has a territory of 185,180 sq km and a population of nineteen million with a rapid growth rate of about 2.3 per cent. It is 90 per cent Arab but with Kurdish, Armenian, and other minorities. It is 74 per cent Sunni Muslim with other minority Muslim sects comprising 16 per cent. The minority Alawites comprise much of the regime. The country has some natural resources including limited oil, phosphates, chrome and manganese ores, asphalt, iron ore, rock salt, marble, gypsum, hydropower, but it is not generously endowed.

Syria has been a Ba'athist republic under an authoritarian, military-dominated regime since March 1963 and is now a hereditary military dictatorship. The Syrian economy grew by 4.5 percent in real terms in 2005, led by the oil and agricultural sectors, which together account for about half of GDP. The Government recently implemented modest liberal economic reforms including cutting interest rates, opening private banks, consolidating some of the multiple exchange rates, and raising prices on some subsidised foodstuffs. Nevertheless, the economy remains highly controlled by the government. Long-run economic constraints include declining oil production and exports, increasing pressure on water supplies caused by rapid population growth, industrial expansion and water pollution. It has a small GDP PPP of $72 billion, GDP at exchange rate of $26 billion, and a modest PPP per capita of $3,900. But it has regional ambitions.

The Syrian armed forces are impressive and have performed well against Israel in past wars. In 2002 the active armed forces numbered 319,000, plus 354,000 reservists. The army had an estimated 215,000 regular troops, including seven armoured divisions, three mechanized infantry divisions, three SCUD missile brigades, two artillery brigades, nine special forces battalions and one border guard brigade. It also had more than 4,700 heavy and medium tanks and sophisticated anti-tank and anti-aircraft weapons. In the Mediterranean the navy had 4,000 personnel with vessels including two frigates and 18 patrol and coastal combatant vessels. Naval aviation included 16 armed helicopters. The air force had 40,000 personnel, 611 combat aircraft, and 90 armed helicopters. The air defence had approximately 60,000 personnel with 25 air defence brigades and two SAM regiments. Paramilitary forces included a gendarmerie of 8,000 and a workers' militia with an estimated 100,000 members. Military expenditures were reported to be $921 million in 2000, but that may underestimate actual spending. Syria had 18,000 troops in Lebanon before they were withdrawn in 2005, and still employs 150 Russian advisors.

Syria forms an important part of an emerging Iran-Iraq-Syria-Hezbollah-Hamas axis that is competing with the US and its Israeli ally for influence in the Middle East. While the other more pro-US Arab countries may resent this grouping, they may be unable to resist it. In 2006 it became clear that Syria would align with Iran rather than the other Arab states. This was a potentially powerful combination in regional terms, however, there is some indication of US diplomatic efforts to involve both Syria and Iran in a regional settlement of both the Palestinian and Iraq issues in 2007.

Conclusion

During the 1990s when the central objective of US foreign policy was the pursuit of a globalised liberal economy with multilateral institutions, many of its competitors were eased into its fold and effectively supported its strategy. It did, after all, hold the promise of widespread prosperity and a place in the system for those countries willing to access it. The almost unilateral pursuit of the second phase of the GWOT, which the US launched when it invaded Iraq, has substantially altered this circumstance. The resolve of its allies has been degraded; the ambitions of its rivals have been emboldened; and more opportunities for its competitors have been opened.

Chapter 10

Contested Zones

There are a number of other states hostile to the US, who might be recruited to a countervailing power alignment but who remain of nuisance value rather than significant obstacles to US power. Nonetheless, they create, collectively, substantial checks to the application US power, particularly at a time when the US is bogged down in a real military conflict ten thousand miles from its shores with limited allied support, little international sympathy and dwindling domestic approval. These states mostly run in the strip from Morocco in North Africa to the island of Sulu in the Philippines – the Islamic world. In this zone the general population is mostly impoverished, the states are illiberal and mostly dictatorial and modernisation has rarely been accomplished. The only two exceptions are Turkey and Malaysia; Pakistan is more typical.

The Islamic Republic of Pakistan: Pashtun-istan

Pakistan was one of the first modern states established on the Islamic principle when it was separated from secular India in 1947.[1] The Pakistani population is a major source of terrorist support and recruitment, although its state is officially in alliance with the US in the GWOT. Most of the young men in the UK involved in the terrorist plots in 2005–06 were of Pakistani origin and co-ordinated with terrorist groups in Pakistan, as did many charged with planning similar activities in Australia. Al Qaeda itself established its terrorist training camps, and plotted and controlled the 9/11 attacks under the patronage of the Pakistan-backed Taliban government in Afghanistan. Lashkar-e-Toiba (LeT) the Al Qaeda-affiliated terrorist group is Pakistan-based.[2] Yet it was intelligence co-operation from Pakistani authorities that enabled the British to foil the August 2006 terrorist plot.

Pakistan is pivotal in the GWOT and the only Muslim nation that possesses nuclear weapons. After 9/11 Pakistan's Government officially abandoned the Taliban and then assisted the US military in removing that regime. It has also undoubtedly taken some real actions against terrorists: in the first half of 2006 alone, it arrested more than 1,000 extremists. It also sent its army into remote northern tribal provinces, as in 2004, to try to re-establish government control in areas that had long given sanctuary to both Taliban and Al Qaeda – although it has not always succeeded.

But the Pakistani Government has also hedged its bets on terrorism. Musharraf rose under a previous dictator, General Zia ul Haq (1977–88), and then in 1999

1 'Stan' is an old Persian word meaning 'land'.

2 Greg Sheridan, 'Islamabad key to deadly puzzle', *The Australian*, 12 Aug 2006.

staged a coup. His government then supported Kashmiri and other Islamist terrorism against India. LeT began as such a Kashmiri group but became one of the most violent of the Islamic global terrorist groups. Pakistan did outlaw LeT, but few LeT leaders were arrested and LeT still operates in Pakistan. LeT is also active among the Pakistani emigrant communities in the UK and Australia. While Musharraf's state has made a strategic alliance with the US, he either cannot or will not pull his nation in that direction. The Pakistani education curriculum continues to attack the West, Jews, Hindus and Christians. Musharraf has nearly destroyed the traditional, secular, democratic parties of Pakistan, and he relies on the overtly Islamist parties in Pakistan's weak parliament.

Since 9/11, Pakistani society has become more radically Islamist, while its Government has apparently moved towards the West. The Pakistani army exercises state power but among the junior ranks there is increasing Islamisation. Terrorists have tried to assassinate Musharraf, yet he was powerful in the army when it created the Taliban and sponsored murderous terrorists in India. Musharraf is driven solely by the need to retain power. If the US withdraws in defeat from Iraq, the Pakistani regime will align with the rising powers in the region, notably Iran, and perhaps take Afghanistan with it. In 2001 Musharraf's regime might even have collapsed under tribal Islamist insurgency and in August 2006 another uprising broke out followed the army's killing of the fugitive tribal leader, Nawab Akbar Bugti.[3] The army was badly demoralised by the long, unsuccessful campaign against the Taliban in the tribal lands of Waziristan on the Afghan border. This campaign was only waged after strong demands (and bribes) by the US for Pakistan to help police the border. This strained Musharraf's control of the army and helped push the religious parties, with whom Musharraf had allied, to try to stop him remaining president beyond 2007.

Pakistan is both a major US ally and a major breeding centre for the terrorist opposition. As part of its role in the coalition fighting global terrorism, Pakistan deployed about 80,000 soldiers in Waziristan and, repeatedly, Musharraf has said he is determined to capture Al Qaeda fighters there. In August 2006 he told his hosts in Kabul they should stop blaming Pakistan for attacks by the Taliban and rejected claims that Islamabad was playing a subversive role in the insurgency. 'This is not sponsored by Pakistan. The Pakistan Government or the ISI (Inter Services Intelligence agency) are not – I repeat not – behind anything happening in Afghanistan'; but on the ground Pakistani commanders had made deals with the Taliban. In September 2006 hundreds of Pakistani troops were withdrawn from the crucial battleground of North Waziristan after it seemed an agreement was reached between Islamabad and Taliban militants.[4] Waziristan is nominally part of Islamabad's Northwest Frontier Province, but Pakistan's soldiers had to retreat from what had become a major centre of global terrorism. From there, the Taliban staged their 2006 offensive on Afghanistan and by April 2007 Al Qaeda had re-established

3 Bronwen Maddox, 'Musharraf losing grip after chief's killing', *The Australian*, 1 Sept 2006.

4 Bruce Loudon, 'Pakistanis give up on lair of Osama', *The Australian*, 9 Sept 2006.

and strengthened its base.[5] By that time the NATO-led forces in Afghanistan were in combat against the predominantly Pashtun tribesmen who had long supported the Taliban. NATO demanded that Pakistan provide more assistance but it would not allow foreign forces to enter its territory in search of Osama bin Laden or hot pursuit of Taliban terrorists.

India also put pressure on Musharraf, particularly after the 11 July 2006 terrorist bombings in Mumbai which killed over 200 people were clearly linked to Al Qaeda and LeT. Afghan President Karzai said coalition forces in Afghanistan could not end the Taliban onslaught unless 'terrorist sanctuaries' outside the country were destroyed, a clear reference to Pakistan. The top US commander in Afghanistan, General John Abizaid, also said Taliban military activity was being organised from and supported by Pakistan. In October 2006 NATO complained that Pakistan was allowing the former Taliban Leader, Mullah Omar, to live openly in Quetta, while its military intelligence continued to train Taliban fighters to attack NATO troops.[6] By 2007 NATO had 31,000 troops, from 37 countries fighting in Afghanistan against a resurgent Taliban aided from within Pakistan. Several agreements between Karzai and Musharraf failed to deal with the problem.[7]

In his 2006 memoir, *In the Line of Fire*, Musharraf claimed the CIA secretly paid his Government millions of dollars for handing over hundreds of Al Qaeda suspects to the US, although the US bans such payments to foreign powers involved in the war on terror. He also claimed the Bush administration had threatened to bomb Pakistan 'back to the Stone Age' if it did not co-operate with the US after the 9/11 terror attacks, which might account for his unenthusiastic shift. Among the suspects surrendered to the US was Khalid Shaikh Mohammed, the alleged architect of the 9/11 operation and many terror plots in Britain, including a failed attack on Heathrow airport in 2002.[8] In mid-2006, Musharraf claimed his country had captured 689 suspects since 9/11, to counter claims that Pakistan has not done enough to combat Al Qaeda. Nonetheless, liberalism has made little headway in Pakistan and Musharraf no doubt has contingency plans for a US withdrawal.

The Central Asian Front: Gangster States

Turkey is the only predominantly Islamic society that can stake any serious claim to have undertaken modernisation – and this to a modest degree. Huntington nominates it as a potential leader of the Islamic civilisational zone.[9] A former imperial power in its own right Turkey is a secular state with a strong military and a large population of 72 million Sunni Muslims, at a middle annual income level of $US5,000. It has a

5 *Bruce Loudon,* 'Heat on Pakistan, "terrorism central"', *The Australian*, 16 Sept 2006; 'US hopes fade of smashing al-Qa'ida', *The Australian* , 3 April 2007.

6 Christina Lamb, 'NATO chief to front Musharraf over Taliban', *The Australian*, 9 Oct 2006.

7 'Musharraf and Karzai in anti-Taliban pact', *The Australian*, 1 May 2007.

8 Daniel McGory, 'CIA paid Pakistan for terror suspects', *The Australian*, 26 Sept 2006.

9 Huntington, *Clash of Civilisations*, as above.

diversified economy that has been somewhat liberalised in the last three decades and is growing strongly. Against this, its military regularly interferes in politics and it has continuing disputes with the EU that appear to preclude its membership. In addition the Islamic nature of its population has prevented its serious participation in the GWOT – which has damaged its relationship with the US – and sustains the unlikely possibility of a successful local Jihadist movement. It is a pivotal state because of its location adjacent to the Arab world and Central Asia from where the Ottoman Turks originated and political instability in mid-2007 has thus alarmed the entire region.

Central Asia was under the control of the Russian and then Soviet empires from the mid nineteenth century until the collapse of the USSR. It was then broken up into five sovereign states each based on its dominant ethnic group that had previously been constituent Soviet Republics: Kazakhstan, Kyrgyzstan, Tajikistan, Turkmenistan and Uzbekistan. About eighty million people live in the region, the northernmost extension of Islam. In the Soviet period there was some attempt at communist modernisation, but also attempted suppression of local cultures, hundreds of thousands of deaths from failed collectivization programs, and a legacy of ethnic tensions. In all the new states, former Communist Party officials retained power and many observers regard them as 'gangster states', ruled and looted by former Soviet strongmen.

Russia, Turkey, Iran, China, Pakistan, India and the US are all now attempting to project influence into the area. In the context of the US GWOT and global competition for resources, Central Asia has once again become the center of geostrategic calculations – the old 'Great Game'. US military bases were established in Uzbekistan and Kyrgyzstan in 2001–02, causing both Russian and the PRC concern over a permanent US military presence in the region. Russia, China and the former SSRs, on the other hand, took advantage of the GWOT to increase oppression of separatist ethnic minorities.

Kazakhstan is the largest state, with fifteen million people on a large territory of 2.7 million square kiliometeres, or the size of western Europe. Nursultan Nazarbayev has ruled since Kazakhstan became independent in 1991, won a 7-year term in the 1999 election and was re-elected in December 2005 in rigged elections. A sixty per cent majority of Kazakhstanis are ethnic Kazakhs, and about 26 per cent are Russians. The main religions are Sunni Islam and Russian Orthodox; Kazakh, the 'state' language is spoken by 64.4 per cent while Russian is the 'official' language and is used in business. Kazakhstan pursues a 'multidimensional' foreign policy, seeking equally good relations with Russia and China, and the US and the West generally. The policy has yielded results in the oil and gas sector, where companies from the US, Russia, China, and Europe are active and several pipelines export oil out of Kazakhstan. Kazakhstan's GDP is $130 billion, or a healthy $8,300 per capita, and growing at around 9 per cent, almost entirely as a result of high world oil prices. Kazakhstan also has uranium, coal, iron and other valuable reources and has attracted over $40 billion in foreign investement since 1993.

Kyrgyzstan is a poor, small, mountainous, landlocked country, bordering China with 5.3 million people on almost 200,000 square kilometres, with a GDP of about $10billion and a low $2,000 per capita. The Kyrgyz semi-nomadic herders, living in yurts and tending sheep comprise 69.5 per cent of the population. Ethnic Russians are 9 per cent concentrated in the North, and Uzbeks at 14.5 per cent live in the South. Islam is the religion of 75 per cent of the population, and most of the Kyrgyz are Sunni Muslims. The dictatorial President Askar Akayev declared independence from the USSR on 31 August 1991and lasted until the 'Tulip Revolution' forced his resignation on 4 April 2005. Kurmanbek Bakiyav formed a new government and Akayev fled the country. Since then, various groups linked to organized crime have competed for power while popular support for Bakiyav rapidly declined amid corruption and violence. Kyrgyzstan has significant deposits of coal, oil and natural gas, but despite the backing of major Western donors, the Kyrgyz Republic has great economic difficulties as a result of the breakup of the Soviet trading bloc despite economic reforms which led to membership of the WTO in 1998.

Tajikistan is the smallest of the five states with a population of about seven million on 143,000 square kilometres, slightly smaller than Wisconsin, with a GDP of only $8 billion, yielding a meagre $1,300 per capita. Most of the population is Sunni Muslim. The Soviets did little to modernise Tajikistan and in the 1980s dissident Islamic parties formed. When the Soviet Union collapsed, Tajikistan declared its independence and went through a devastating civil war between Muslim factions from 1992 to 1997. Non-Muslims, particularly Russians and Jews, fled the country. The dictator and former communist, Emomali Rahmonov, came to power in 1992 and was re-elected in 1999. Since the end of the civil war, newly-established political stability, foreign aid and oil and gas have allowed the country's economy to grow a little. Russian troops were stationed in southern Tajikistan to guard the border with Afghanistan until summer 2005. Since 9/11, some US and French have also been stationed in the country.

Turkmenistan is a sparsely populated dictatorship with substantial resources. It has around five million people on nearly 500,000 square kilometers of territory, much of it desert. Nonetheless it has a GDP of $40 billion, giving a healthy but uneven $8,000 per capita. As a Soviet republic, Turkmenistan went through a process of limited Europeanisation. When the Soviet Union began to collapse, Turkmenistan needing Soviet markets and at first favoured maintaining links. Turkmenistan was one of the last FSRs to declare its independence. The former Soviet leader, Saparmurat Niyazov, remained in power but changed his economic policies and became friendly to foreign corporations. He was a dictator who promoted traditional Muslim, Turkmen culture, ran a Cult of Personality and crushed political dissent, until December 2006 when he died of heart attack. His son, Gurbanguly Berdymukhamedov, became president after a rigged election with 89 per cent of the vote and 95 per cent turnout. About sixty per cent of the population is unemployed and lives in poverty. But the country has the world's fifth-largest reserves of natural gas as well as substantial oil resources. The regime plans to use gas and oil to sustain its inefficient economy, and the value its exports have risen sharply because of higher oil and gas prices. But economic prospects in the near future are for little modernisation, widespread corruption and poverty and large foreign debt.

Uzbekistan is Central Asia's largest nation with 27 million people who are nearly ninety per cent Sunni Muslim, on an area of 447,400 square kilometres, slightly larger than California. Uzbekistan was one of the poorest republics of the Soviet Union with cotton farming in small collective farms. Uzbeks comprise 80 per cent of the total population. In 2002 a national referendum extended the term of the dictator, President, Islom Karimov, to December 2007. Its oil and gas industry may increase its economic growth prospects and in 2005, Russian President Putin and Karimov signed an 'alliance' treaty. Russian businesses have become involved in Uzbekistan, especially in oil and gas. Although the GDP is only $48 billion and $1,800 per capita, annual growth has lifted to seven per cent. Uzbekistan was initially an active supporter of US efforts against worldwide terrorism and joined the coalitions that intervened in both Afghanistan and Iraq. But relations with the US deteriorated following the so-called 'colour revolutions' in Georgia, Ukraine and Kyrgyzstan and after the US called for an independent international investigation of some bloody events in Uzbekistan. Karimov then moved closer to Russia and China, countries which refused to criticize the Uzbekistan (or other) regime for its behaviour. In 2005, Uzbekistan ordered the US to vacate the air base in Karshi-Kanabad near the Uzbek border with Afghanistan.

US policy in Central Asia was officially described by the Assistant Secretary of State for Central Asian Affairs, Richard A Boucher:[10]

> Our strategy rests on three integrated pillars: security cooperation; our commercial and energy interests; and political and economic reform.... Central Asia faces numerous threats to its stability, including Islamic extremism, a population that remains poor and has little economic opportunity, the post-Soviet legacy of authoritarianism, public perceptions of injustice, and high levels of corruption. As a consequence, nurturing both economic and democratic reform in the region is difficult, even daunting. ... The second set of our policy priorities ... involves our energy and commercial interests. ... we want to help build new links among the countries of the broader region and connect them more closely to the rest of the world. ... The third key pillar of our strategy for Central Asia is to promote freedom through democratic and economic reform, because long-term stability comes from democratic governments that enjoy the trust of their people and that are accountable to them. To paraphrase President Bush, all people, given a free choice, will choose democracy over tyranny. We actively support democracy and civil society in the region not only because it is the right thing to do, but because it creates conditions that lead to greater political and economic opportunity.

But these positive initiatives have now been so overshadowed by the military agenda, where a readiness to provide air bases and other facilities is the key to improving relations with the US, that regional governments have largely ignored reforms and continued with dictatorial policies. In pursuit of its GWOT the US has in fact ignored the needs of modernisation and the gangster regimes have used US involvement to help legitimize their rule. US influence in Central Asia is unlikely to be enduring since the Russians have the proximity, ethnic affinities and historical ties, and the PRC the neighbouring strategic weight to resist US influence. Washington might well treat such expanded commitments with more care than it did Afghanistan and Iraq.

10 'US Policy in Central Asia: Balancing Priorities', Richard A. Boucher, Assistant Secretary of State for South and Central Asian Affairs, Statement to the House International Relations Committee, Subcommittee on the Middle East and Central Asia, 26 April 2006.

The African Front: Failed and Terrorist

Islam dominates in the north of Africa but the reforming monarchy in Morocco and the one party state in Tunisia have contained the Jihadists. In Algeria, the Islamists have been essentially defeated by the military regime after 100,000 deaths during their earlier assault on state power. But there are also some limited opportunities for Jihadists in several sub-Saharan African countries, including Nigeria and South Africa, and terrorist bombings occurred in Kenya and Tanzania in the 1990s. But in three African states forms of Islamism already have achieved state power: in Sudan, in Somalia until early 2007, and in Libya until 2005.

After Sudan gained independence from the UK in 1956, military regimes favouring Islamic-oriented governments dominated national politics. The Islamist regime harboured the Al Qaeda leadership until it left for Afghanistan in the mid-1990s. The country has also had two prolonged civil wars rooted in the Arab Islamic north's economic, political, and social domination of the largely non-Muslim, non-Arab southern Sudanese. The first civil war ended in 1972, but it re-opened in 1983. The second war and famine-related effects resulted in more than 4 million people being displaced and more than 2 million deaths over two decades. The Naivasha peace treaty of January 2005 granted the southern rebels autonomy for six years, when a referendum for independence would be held.

But in 2003 a separate conflict broke out in the western region of Darfur that resulted in 200,000 deaths and two million displaced. Sudan also has faced large refugee influxes from neighbouring countries, primarily Ethiopia and Chad. Sudan has a population of 41 million mostly around the Nile River growing annually at 2.5 per cent, 52 per cent of which are black, 39 per cent Arab, and six per cent Beja. The northern Arabs are Sunni Muslim. The country is the largest in Africa with 2,505,810 sq km, slightly more than one-quarter the size of the US. It contains oil, and small reserves of iron ore, copper, chromium ore, zinc, tungsten, mica, silver, gold, and hydropower. The government has been dominated by the Islamist National Congress Party (NCP), since its military coup in 1989, and Sharia law applies to all residents of the northern states regardless of their religion. Although after 1997 Sudan implemented IMF macroeconomic reforms and began exporting crude oil agriculture remains Sudan's most important sector, employing 80 per cent of the work force. The chronic political instability ensured that much of the population remains below the poverty line. Sudan has a GDP PPP of $85 billion, or at official exchange rate $22.75 billion, and a low per capita income of $2,100.

Nonetheless, Sudan vowed to defy a UN takeover of peacekeeping forces in the war- torn Darfur region, although the US declared Khartoum's agreement was not needed. The UN Security Council voted on 1 September 2006 to approve the deployment of up to 17,000 UN troops to the Sudanese region to take over from the African Union force.[11] The AU mission was unable to stop the conflict in the region. The then US ambassador to the UN, John Bolton, urged stronger action. 'It is imperative we move immediately to implement (the vote) to stop the tragic events unfolding in Darfur'. But in Darfur, Sudanese Vice-President, Ali Osman, vowed

11 'We'll resist UN force, warns Sudan', *The Australian*, 2 Sept 2006.

to resist the UN force, describing Hezbollah as a model. He said Hezbollah had 'exacted on the army of the Zionist enemy' a severe price in the conflict in Lebanon 'due to the determination, patience and political will the party enjoys'. Twelve of the Security Council's fifteen members voted in favour of the resolution, which stated that the deployment of UN forces would take place 'on the basis of the acceptance of the (Sudanese) Government'. Russia, Qatar and the PRC, which has become a major market for Sudan's oil, abstained.

Somalia was formed in July 1960 from a merger of British Somaliland and Italian Somaliland. The pro-Soviet regime of Mohamed Siad Barre was ousted in January 1991 and factional fighting and civil anarchy followed. It has an area of 637,657 sq km, slightly smaller than Texas and a mostly Sunni Muslim population estimated at nine million, growing at 2.85 per cent. It is extremely poor with a GDP PPP of $4.809 billion and a per capita income of $600. After decades of internal conflict, Islamists took over the capital, Mogadishu in June 2006 and declared Sharia law. They then moved to control the entire country and drive out the US-backed warlords who had declared an independent Republic of Somaliland not recognized by any government. The regions of Bari, Nugaal, and northern Mudug also comprised a self-declared autonomous state of Puntland. In 1993, a two-year UN humanitarian program tried to alleviate famine conditions, but the UN withdrew in 1995, after the US suffered significant casualties, made famous in the movie *Black Hawk Down*, and order still had not been restored. There are significant Somali links with global terrorism, particularly with Al Qaeda. Somalia's economic failures are driven by its deep political divisions. Agriculture is the most important sector, and nomads and semi-nomads who depend on livestock, make up a large portion of the population. The near anarchy, ongoing civil disturbances and clan rivalries, have prevented broad-based economic development, modernisation and even international aid arrangements. Statistics on Somalia's GDP, growth and per capita income are likely optimistic. This is a state with pervasive civil in which the US has little reason to be involved although it backed Ethiopian intervention to subdue the Islamists in 2006–07.

Libya has a mostly flat, barren, desert territory of 1,759,540 sq km, slightly larger than Alaska. It has a population of nearly six million growing at 2.3 per cent, 97 per cent Berber and Arab Sunni Muslims, who live quite well off oil and natural gas. Libya's GDP PPP was $66 billion in 2005, at GDP official exchange rate $31.49 billion, with growth at 8.5 percent, and a healthy per capita income of $11,400. The Libyan economy depends primarily on revenues from the oil sector, which contribute about 95 per cent of export earnings. These export revenues coupled with a small population, give Libyans one of the highest incomes in Africa.

After his 1969 military coup, Libya's dictator, Colonel Muammar Abu Minyar al-Qadhafi created his own political system, the Third Universal Theory – a combination of Islam, socialism and tribal practices. Qadhafi at first saw himself as a revolutionary and visionary leader and he used oil revenues during the 1970s and 1980s to promote his ideology outside Libya, supporting subversives and terrorists abroad to bring an end to both Marxism and capitalism. In 1973, he attacked northern Chad to gain access to its minerals, but retreated in 1987. In 1986 Libyan agents bombed US servicemen in Berlin and the USAF bombed Tripoli in retaliation. In 1988 Libyan agents destroyed the PanAm Flight 103 over Lockerbie, Scotland, and the resulting UN sanctions in 1992 isolated Qadhafi politically, although Libyan support for terrorism did then appear to decrease somewhat. During the 1990s, Qadhafi also began to rebuild his relations with Europe. UN sanctions were suspended in April 1999 and finally lifted in September 2003 after Libya resolved the Lockerbie case.

In December 2003, worried that Libya would be treated like Iraq, Libya announced that it would end its programs to develop weapons of mass destruction. Qadhafi then made efforts to normalize relations with the West and several European leaders visited Libya and he made his first trip to Western Europe in 15 years in April 2004. In 2004 Qadhafi finally resolved several outstanding cases against his government for its terrorist activities in the 1980s by compensating the families of victims of bombings. Washington removed Libya from its list of terror-sponsoring states in May 2006.[12] While Libya remains an anti-democratic and backward regime, it appears to have genuinely turned away from terror and WMDs. Since 2003 Libya has made progress on economic reform as part of a broader campaign to reintegrate the country into the international order. Libya has been an undoubted win for the Bush administration, but an unusual one in the Islamic world.

The Southeast Asia Front: A New Caliphate?

Several of the nations of Southeast Asia are also contested terrain.[13] Islam was spread to the region by Arab traders in the fourteenth century, and then expanded by force and conversion to dominate much of the Malay Archipelago and some of the mainland, including what are now Indonesia, Malaysia, southern Philippines, Brunei and southern Thailand. In Singapore, Islam was overwhelmed by Chinese immigrants during the British colonial period. Al Qaeda's principal ally in the region is Jemaah Islamiah (JI or 'Islamic Community'), a radical Islamist terrorist organisation dedicated to the establishment of a Caliphate in southeast Asia, in particular Indonesia, Malaysia, Philippines, Brunei, Singapore and southern Thailand. JI has killed hundreds of civilians and probably executed the Bali nightclub bombing on 12 October 2002, in which suicide bombers killed 202 people, including 88 Australian tourists, and wounded many more. JI also carried out the Zamboanga bombings, the Metro Manila bombings, the 2004 Australian Jakarta embassy bombing, and the 2005 Bali terrorist bombings.

JI was established as a loose confederation of several Islamic groups. In the late 1960s Abu Bakar Bashir and Abdullah Sungkar began to propagate the Darul Islam Islamist movement that had been almost destroyed in the 1950s after it tried to create an Islamic state in Indonesia. Both Bashir and Sungkar were imprisoned by Indonesian dictator Suharto (1966–98). Bashir escaped to Malaysia in 1982 and set up JI. In the 1980s, many members of JI, including Sungkar and the terrorist

12 Michael Hirsh, 'The Real Libya Model: The main lesson of the deal with Tripoli is that it's time for Washington to be drop the pretenses in dealing North Korea and Iran', *Newsweek*, 11 May 2006.

13 International Crisis Group, *Jemaah Islamiyah in South East Asia: Damaged But Still Dangerous*, August 2003.

Hambali joined the resistance in Afghanistan and the connections between Al Qaeda and JI were then established. JI changed in the 1990s when Bashir met Hambali who became its military leader. Hambali wanted a Caliphate to be established across Southeast Asia, with its population of 420 million. JI then formed into a group of terrorist cells. Hambali formed a front company, Konsojaya, to launder money for such plans in 1995. In 1998, when Suharto's dictatorship collapsed, the leaders of JI went back to Indonesia. Hambali went underground while Bashir openly preached Jihadism and set up a string of Madrasahs, or Pesantren, for this purpose. In January 2000, Nawaf Alhazmi and Khalid al-Midhar, two of the 9/11 hijackers were hosted by JI in Malaysia.

In the twenty first century JI has engaged in regular terrorist acts in the region: in August 2000 it blew up the Philippines Ambassador to Indonesia, killing two; in September 2000 a car bomb exploded in a car park beneath the Jakarta Stock Exchange building, killing 15 and injuring 20; in December 2000 JI co-ordinated the 'Christmas Bombings' terror strikes; in March 2002 three JI members were arrested in Manila carrying explosives and one was later jailed for 17 years; in June 2002, the Kuwaiti, Omar al-Faruq, was arrested while planning terrorist attacks; in September 2002 a bomb in Jakarta killed one of the bombers; in October 2002 people were killed in the Philipinnes by a mail bomb in Zamboanga, and six were killed in Kidapawan; in October 2002 202 were killed in Bali; in 2003, the Hotel Marriot was bombed in Jakarta; in September 2004, the Australian embassy in Jakarta was bombed; and in October 2005 another twenty four were killed in Bali. Bashir was convicted of being involved in this campaign and sentenced to brief imprisonment but released in 2006. An Australian, Jack Roche, got eight years jail for plotting to bomb the Israeli embassy in Canberra. On 5 August 2006, Al Qaeda's Al Zawahiri announced that JI and Al Qaeda had joined forces. There is little likelihood of these terorists achieving state power in any state in this region, but there is some sympathy for their actions among a minority of the region's Muslims.

Indonesia is the largest Muslim country in the world and the successor state to the Netherlands East Indies. It has an archipelagic and porous land area of 1,919,440 sq km, about three times the size of Texas. The diverse population is the fourth largest in the world at 245.4 million, growing at 1.4 per cent, and is 88 per cent Muslim. There have recently been several terrorist attacks on Western interests and attacks by Muslims on Christians, and there is also an extensive system of radical Madrasahs led by Bashir. It has oil fields that provided the origins of Royal Dutch Shell, tin, natural gas, nickel, timber, bauxite, copper, fertile soils, coal, gold, and silver. Indonesia was the nation worst hit by the December 2004 tsunami, which caused over 100,000 deaths and over $4 billion in damage. Since 1998 Indonesia has become a secular, fairly democratic republic with Susilo Bambang Yudhoyono (SBY) directly elected President in October 2004 for a five-year term.

Indonesia has high unemployment, a fragile banking sector, endemic corruption, an inadequate infrastructure, a poor investment climate, and very unequal resource distribution among regions and classes. The GDP at PPP is $865.6 billion, at exchange rate is $270 billion, giving a modest and uneven per capita PPP income of $3,600. Indonesia has considerable ethnic tensions, particularly involving the small Chinese community, often Christian, which is considered too rich relative to the

Pribumis who are considered natives of Indonesia and are mostly Muslim. Power and influence in the business sphere is held by relatively few, very wealthy ethnic Chinese Indonesians. Some of the resentment is directed against the shopkeepers and small-time creditors who constitute much of the Chinese Indonesian community. The Indonesian government has attempted to remedy these problems which have helped trigger ethnic/religious riots but, due to widespread corruption and the discontent experienced by poorer Indonesians, ethnic harmony has been slow in coming, and JI feeds off this. The major problem for Indonesia is to establish a democratic regime based on a growth economy. Militant Islam is a low level but continuing threat to this process. Nonetheless, the SBY government had cracked down on terror, broken up JI, killed its bomb maker, Azahari Husin, and imprisoned Hambali and many other terrorists. But its success is not assured.[14]

The Federation of Malaysia is effectively the successor state to most of the British colonies in Southeast Asia,[15] although Singapore seceded from the Federation in 1965 and the oil rich, Brunei Sultanate never joined. It has an area of 329,750 sq km, making it slightly larger than New Mexico, and extensive raw materials including oil, tin, timber, copper, iron ore, natural gas, and bauxite. It has a population of 24.5 million growing at 1.7 per cent. Only just over half the population are Malays, who are Muslims, with Chinese at 23.7 per cent, indigenous Borneans at 11, Indians at 7.1, and others at 7.8 per cent. The state is an effective constitutional monarchy with a bicameral Parliament. Abdullah bin Ahmad Badawi who heads the ruling-coalition National Front (Barisan Nasional or BN) has been Prime Minister since October 2003. The BN embraces political parties of all the major ethnic groupings but is controlled by Malays, and in the 2004 elections won 91 per cent of the vote. Badawi has greatly moderated the anti-Western Islamist rhetoric of his predecessor, Mohamet Mahathir.

After ethnic riots in 1971, Malaysia transformed itself into a middle-income country with an emerging modern economy. Growth was driven by exports, particularly of electronics and oil. As an oil and gas exporter, Malaysia has profited from higher world energy prices but used them to diversify its economy. Healthy foreign exchange reserves, low inflation, and a small external debt make it unlikely that Malaysia will experience a financial crisis over the near term similar to the one in 1997. It has a GDP at PPP of $290 billion, and at official exchange rate of $122 billion, giving a prosperous per capita income of $12,100. Malaysia is a very successful multi-ethnic society that is an effective democracy under Malay leadership, with a prosperous economy mostly run by Chinese and Indians. But there are opportunities, although limited, for Islamic extremists, and Mahathir often appeared to encourage such sentiments. But he is now merely an ageing irritant. While Malaysia propers, it is not only part of the solution to the war on terror, it is also an exemplar of how a prosperous Islamic democracy might evolve elsewhere.

---

14 See International Crisis Group, *Indonesia: Jemaah Islamiyah's Current Status*, Asia Briefing Number 63, 3 May 2007.

15 Barbara Watson Andaya and Leonard Andaya, *A History of Malaysia* (Honolulu, 2001).

The Philippines has a land area 300,000 sq km, slightly larger than Arizona. The Philippine Islands became a Spanish colony during the sixteenth century, were seized by the US in 1898 and became independent in 1946. The population of ninety million is mainly Roman Catholic at 80.9 per cent, and other Christian (4.5 per cent). Economic growth accelerated to about 5 per cent after 2002 but poverty is widespread, with a high population growth rate of 1.8 per cent and a very unequal distribution of income. It has a GDP at PPP of $451.3 billion, at official exchange rate $91.36 billion, and a modest but growing PPP per capita income of $5,100. Although Muslims are only 5 per cent of the people, these are concentrated in the southern islands, particularly Mindanao, where Islam expanded until it met with Spanish Catholicism.

The Moro Islamic Liberation Front (MILF) is a militant Islamic secessionist group concentrated in Mindanao. There are approximately 4.5 million Muslims in the Philippines and the majority live in this area. The MILF was founded by Salamat Hashim, who studied in Saudi Arabia and Egypt. The MILF calls for 'jihad in the Moroland' against 'the colonial Philippine occupation armies'. Salamat died in 2003, and was replaced by Al Haj Murad Ebrahim. The MILF's military wing consists of a guerilla army of about 12,500 personnel. With the outbreak of the GWOT, US forces returned to assist the government in its war against the MILF. There have been divisions among the Muslims about strategy and a two year cease-fire broke down in January 2005 when MILF attacked government troops and a new round of fighting occurred after June 2006. Although the MILF denies ties with Jemaah Islamiyah, JI has provided training facilities in areas it controls. The MILF also denies connections with Al Qaeda, though it has admitted to sending around 600 volunteers to Al Qaeda training camps in Afghanistan. This low level and regional, but serious insurgency is many decades old, is likely to continue and could conceivably lead to secession.

A unified Thai kingdom was established in the fourteenth century and was formerly known as Siam. A bloodless revolution in 1932 led to a constitutional monarchy. An ally of Japan during the Second World War, Thailand then became a staunch US ally. It has an area of 514,000 square kilometres, or twice the size of Wyoming, with 65 million people growing at a modest 0.6 per cent, of whom 75 per cent are ethnic Thai and 14 per cent Chinese. It has natural resources including tin, rubber, natural gas, but relies on its industry. The country had a democratically elected parliament until September 2006. It has a well-developed infrastructure, a free-enterprise economy, and pro-investment policies. The economy is one of East Asia's best performers and has recently grown at over six per cent and is export-oriented. The GDP at PPP is over $560 billion, at exchange rate, $184billion and GDP per capita is a healthy $8,000.

Thais are 95 per cent Buddhist, but the nearly five per cent who are Muslim are concentrated in the southern Malay-populated provinces. There, Thailand is currently facing an armed insurrection. On 25 October 2004 Thai army soldiers killed at least 85 people – 78 of them suffocated in trucks – while suppressing a riot by Muslims in Tak Bai. Anger at this 'Tak Bai massacre' served to intensify a small existing rebellion by radicalized Muslim villagers in southern Thailand. Years of economic backwardness and Islamist liberation theologies imported from the Middle East, coupled with perceived discrimination against Thailand's Muslim minority, fuelled a regional civil war that killed more than 600 people in 2004–05.[16] The rebellion posed a regional challenge to Thailand's US-aligned government and could give Al Qaeda and its allies a new foothold in Southeast Asia.

On 20 September 2006 there was a military coup in Thailand. Two issues fuelled it: claims of corruption against Prime Minister Thaksin Shinawatra; and the Muslim rebellion in the southern provinces. Thaksin's handling of both was lamentable.[17] In the south the grassroots insurgency was claiming 60 lives a month. In 2001, there were thought to be no more than 200 active separatists, but by 2006 there were thousands of young Muslim militants among the Malay Muslim population. The region of the old Pattani sultanate, only annexed by Siam in 1909, was put under martial law in April 2004 and from July 2005 administered by emergency decree. Thaksin fell out with the military by appointing his own loyalists to senior positions, but his failures in handling the Islamist insurgency proved decisive. The military, apparently with the approval of the King, removed Thaksin when he was in the US.

The insurgency undoubtedly grew, and between the beginning of 2004 and the coup about 1,700 people died in the conflict. In September 2006, renewed terrorist bombings in southern Thailand killed four people and injured sixty, seemed to target tourists, and occurred outside the three provinces that had been the centre of insurgent activity. The Thai army led by General Sondhi Boonyaratkalin – a Muslim himself – wanted to re-create a political dialogue with the insurgents and try to address any legitimate grievances that the insurgents have exploited. Thaksin, in contrast, was determined to pursue a forceful, military approach that proved ineffective and was making things worse.[18] It was not clear whether the coup would improve matters. The longer the insurgency goes on, the more will outside terrorists get involved. The rebellion is centred in the farmlands, rubber plantations and mountains of three provinces on Thailand's border with Malaysia. While Thailand's national identity is based on its ethnic Thai culture, language, monarchy and the Buddhist faith, people in the far south are ethnic Malays and Muslims. These provinces were ruled for centuries by the independent Muslim sultanate of Pattani. After the Thai monarchy conquered Pattani in 1786, the region rebelled repeatedly and kept a degree of autonomy until formal annexation.

From the 1960s to the 1980s, a few alienated Muslims tried to revive the Pattani state. Then in the 1990s Islamic militancy emerged through Arab satellite channels and Malay networks. Militant versions of Islam have been brought home by students who studied in Egypt, Iraq, Sudan, Syria and other Middle Eastern countries. Arab donors have founded mosques, schools and an Islamic college. The Thai government supported the US GWOT and in 2004 handed Hambali, the mastermind behind the 2002 Bali bombing, to the US. He was later transferred to Guantanamo Bay.[19] President Bush admitted in September 2006 that Hambali had been held in a secret CIA detention system outside the US, along with thirteen other high-level terrorist operatives. Myanmar has not been so cooperative.

16 James Rupert, 'An insurgency in Thailand', *Newsday*, 4 May 2005.

17 'Strife in the south takes a national toll', *The Australian*, 21 Sept 2006.

18 Greg Sheridan, 'A coup for the better', *The Australian*, 21 Sept 2006.

19 *Geoff Elliott,* 'Hambali taken to Cuba for trial', *The Australian*, 8 Sept 2006.

Myanmar, a former British colony, has a population of 51 million people. Immediately after independence in 1948, a number of ethnic based secessionist revolts broke out, plus a communist insurgency. The continuing military rule has been in some measure a response to these revolts. It has isloated itself from the outside world since a military coup in 1960 made General Ne Win a dictator. Since then the country has been run by the military. The economy has been isolated and has not developed. It has a GDP of $94 billion, very low growth and a very poor per capita income of $1,500, despite vast natural resources including timber and natural gas and petroleum. Its population is 89 per cent Buddhist, Christian 4 per cent, and Muslim 4 per cent. Its political system has been under the tight control of the military government led by Senior General Than Swe since 1992. Legislative elections in 1990 resulted in the main opposition party, the National League for Democracy (NLD), winning a landslide victory, but the ruling junta refused to hand over power. NLD leader and Nobel Peace Prize recipient Aung San Suu Kyi, was under house arrest from 1989 to 1995 and 2000 to 2002, was imprisoned in May 2003 and subsequently transferred back to house arrest, where she remains virtually incommunicado. Her supporters, as well as all those who promote democracy and improved human rights, are routinely harassed or jailed.

The government also perceives a threat from the largest religious minority in Myanmar. Myanmar's Muslims, two million people, comprise 4 percent of the overwhelmingly Theravada Buddhist state – a percentage as large as in neighbouring Thailand. There are at least four distinct ethnic Muslim communities in Myanmar all of whom are Sunni. The government in Myanmar has never recognized the Rohingyas as a native population and it sent hundreds of thousands of them fleeing into Bangladesh in 1978 during a cleansing campaign. Similar pogroms erupted again in the early 1990s, resulting in similarly massive migrations of refugees. Most of the Rohingyas have since repatriated to Myanmar, but over 100,000 remain inside Bangladesh. From these refugee camps have sprung several generations of resistance groups which have operated a low-level insurgency along the north-western border where a few have demanded the creation of a separate Muslim state. But they have been mostly ineffective against Myanmar's large military, battle hardened by 50 years of counter-insurgency warfare.

The Rohingya Solidarity Organisation (RSO) is one of these groups. Founded in the early 1980s, the RSO has copied movements like the Taliban and the Kashmir-based Hizb-ul-Mujahideen. The RSO has split into several factions, but at least one has got financial and technical support from pan-Islamist organisations throughout South and Southeast Asia, including the Bangladeshi/Pakistani Jamaat-e-Islami, Afghan warlord Gulbuddin Hekmatyar's Hizb-e-Islami, and most importantly, Bangladesh's Harakat-ul-Jihad-ul-Islami (HuJI), all of whom are unquestionably linked with Al Qaeda. The Burmese junta is very close to the PRC which arms it and wants to use Burma as a route to the Indian Ocean and Middle East and as a source of raw materials. Clinton did try some leverage against the regime to reform it, but Bush largely gave up. Myanmar's military forces can be expected to try to crush ruthlessly any Islamic revolt, but not in concert with the US. Indeed, the junta moved the capital inland in 2005 in fear of a US Iraq-style assault and it could be a candidate for any anti-US coalition in the east Asia-Pacific.

Thus, in parts of Indonesia, Thailand, and the Philippines, and to a lesser extent, Malaysia and Myanmar, conflicts involving Muslim communities have become recruiting and training grounds for Al Qaeda and its affiliate, JI. Fortunately, the regional regimes will mostly provide useful partners for the US. Progress has been made against Al Qaeda's terrorist affiliates in the region, and in November 2005 Indonesian police killed master bomb maker Azahari bin Husin. But JI probably has the capacity to strike again.[20] Indonesia has arrested 330 JI members and more than 250 were successfully prosecuted, but it has not targeted JI's social networks. JI is still not criminalised, so membership is not a crime. But Indonesia has launched successful counter-terrorism efforts at a time of difficult democratic transition. Counter-terrorism has not come at the expense of civil liberties or brought Indonesia back to the repression of Suharto's New Order. And often this is done in collaboration with Australian authorities.[21]

Korean Peninsula and DPRK: Stalinism Revisited

The North Korean (DPRK) regime is a legacy of the Cold War. After the Korean War it survived as an odious Stalinist dictatorship, and satellite regime of the Soviets who subsidised it with large shipments of cheap energy, under Kim Il Sung (1946–94) and then his son Kim Jong Il (1994–). The subsidies were withdrawn by Gorbachev and as the consequences flowed through the DPRK's economy, it came to near collapse and mass starvation. The regime resorted to any means for generating revenue, including drug smuggling, currency forgery, kidnappings, terrorism, arms sales and assassinations. It also accelerated its nuclear program and provided the Iranians with missile technology.

In 1994 the US tried to offset this by a deal that allowed the DPRK access to uranium for peaceful purposes in exchange for weapons inspections and effectively financial aid. This arrangement collapsed in 2003 as the regime continued to develop missiles and, probably, nuclear weapons. But there seemed little the US could do despite having over 20,000 troops in South Korea. The US then tried to use the leverage the PRC had on the DPRK to inhibit its nuclear program, and initiated six power talks from which the DPRK withdrew in 2005.In 2002 Bush linked the DPRK into the 'Axis of Evil' with Iraq and Iran. In August 2006, Rumsfeld warned of the threat that North Korea posed as a supplier of weapons to terrorist groups: 'I think the real threat that North Korea poses in the immediate future is more proliferation than a danger to South Korea'. Kim visited China four times 2000–06. In January 2006 Kim travelled to Shanghai, Guangdong and finally Beijing for talks with Chinese leaders and 'agreed to maintain the stand of seeking a negotiated peaceful solution to the issue' of WMDs.

20 Zachary Abuza, 'Killer network spreads: A leading scholar on terrorism in Southeast Asia, warns that the threat posed by al-Qa'ida affiliate Jemaah Islamiah is rising', The Australian, 9 Oct 2006.

21 Martin Chulov, *Australian Jihad* (Sydney, 2006); and 'Bomber on the line', *The Australian,* 9 Oct 2006.

For China, the DPRK had become a disruptive irritant to its long term plans of economic growth. On 5 July 2006, North Korea test-fired six short and medium range missiles and one long-range missile, the Taepodong-2, which all fell harmlessly in the Sea of Japan.[22] Nonetheless, China was growing impatient with its erratic client and PRC government officials said Kim Jung Il would again visit China in August 2006.[23] The reports came after China had invited Kim to visit 'as soon as possible' amid reports that Pyongyang was preparing for a nuclear bomb test. Beijing was the chief drafter of the UN Security Council resolution that demanded Pyongyang suspend its missile program. The People's Bank of China responded to North Korean counterfeiting of China's currency and froze all of North Korea's accounts. In September 2006 US Assistant Secretary of State Christopher Hill flew to Beijing to throw American weight behind new efforts, led by China, to bring North Korea back to the table. But in August 2006, Chinese Foreign Ministry spokesman Liu Jianchao said that Pyongyang 'doesn't listen to Beijing'. In the year to July 2006, China's imports from North Korea fell 15.9 per cent, following a 14.8 per cent fall in 2005. North Korea's access to international banking was severely hampered by first the US, then China closing down bank accounts linked to dubious activities including money laundering.[24]

But US-South Korean relations had also deteriorated since the Cold War. They got even worse after President Roh was inaugurated in February 2003 and insisted on pursuing an independent and conciliatory strategy – 'Sunshine diplomacy' – towards the DPRK.[25] Roh urged the Americans to open direct negotiations with Pyongyang and to withdraw the threat of sanctions over Kim Jong Il's July 2006 ballistic missile tests. But the US believed that the Kim regime's bad behaviour should not be rewarded with the direct access to Washington: the US wanted concerted trade and economic sanctions against the DPRK. This opened the question of the future disposition of US military forces in South Korea (USFK). Although anti-American feeling was strong among Roh's supporters, he still viewed the US military presence as essential to deterring the DPRK. He wanted American forces to stay, but less visibly. Roh was assisted by Rumsfeld's 'global military transformation' under which the US military in the ROK fell from 37,000 in 2001, to 29,500 in 2006, with a target of 25,000 for 2008. But South Korea refused to discuss allowing USFK to deploy elsewhere in the region and there were also annual squabbles over Seoul's contribution to the cost of the USFK. Roh's officials also made much of the fact they were negotiating to end the long-standing arrangement of the US command taking control of Korean forces under wartime conditions which South Korea wanted to end by 2012. The

22 'Russia wary of US missile plan', *The Australian*, 29 Aug 2006.

23 'N Korea leader "on covert China visit"', *The Australian*, 31 Aug 2006.

24 Rowan Callick, 'N Korea leader on slow train to China', *The Australian*, 6 Sept 2006.

25 Peter Alford, 'US-Korea summit in the usual barren field', *The Australian*, 14 Sept 2006.

distraction of the GWOT appeared to be making US policy objectives on the Korean peninsula more difficult to achieve.[26]

From 1953 until the collapse of the Soviet Union the major deterrence for the DPRK against US attack was perceived to be the Soviet nuclear umbrella. Thereafter, it was the capacity of DPRK forces to strike at Seoul. But in 2006 it apparently achieved a nuclear capacity itself, without which it calculated it was open to US attack.[27] The DPRK nuclear test on 9 October 2006 was met by a US-Japan push to impose a total economic embargo on the already isolated regime, but the regime's sense of increasing isolation has been exacerbated in the by the prospect of its most hated neighbour, Japan, moving to stabilise relations with China and South Korea.

Nonetheless, in an agreement was reached on 13 February 2007. The DPRK said it would 'shut down and seal' its main nuclear reactor at Yongbyon within 60 days. In return it would receive 50,000 tonnes of heavy fuel oil, to be supplied by the five other countries involved in the nuclear negotiations – the US, China, South Korea, Japan and Russia. The DPRK would then declare and disable all its existing nuclear facilities, and in return receive a further 950,000 tonnes of heavy fuel oil. The DPRK would also invite the UN's nuclear inspectors to return to the country to monitor the agreement and would begin talks to normalise its diplomatic relations with the US and Japan. These initial steps were meant to implement the earlier 2005 agreement under which the DPRK committed to abandoning all its nuclear weapons and nuclear programmes and returning to the treaty on the non-proliferation of nuclear weapons (NPT). This looked like a clear win for US diplomacy, one which was essentially overlooked by an Iraq-obsessed world press.

Latin America

The Venezuelan President, Hugo Chavez, addressed the UN General Assembly in 2006 while holding Noam Chomsky's latest anti-US book, *Hegemony or Survival: America's Quest for Global Dominance,* in his hand. The opposition to US policy in the Americas was being justified by the criticisms of a US Professor of Linguistics, just as the views of the American Left had been incorporated into Jihadist theory.

The Caribbean rim has been the region of America's most long-standing history of intervention and economic control, dating from the earliest years of the Republic and the Monroe Doctrine of 1823. The US has always perceived this as its own 'backyard' to be maintained free of other outside influence whether from Europe, Britain or, in the Cold War era, the Soviet Union. It has not, therefore, hesitated to intervene to protect its perceived security and economic interests, and Mexico, Nicaragua, Cuba, Haiti and many other nations of the Caribbean and Central America have experienced American intervention, sometimes enduring for decades, 'to maintain peace', 'to ensure security of American property', or 'to guarantee American national security'. Overtly and covertly the US has aggressively pursued

26 John B Judis, *The Folly of Empire, What George W Bush Could Learn from Theodore Roosevelt and Woodrow Wilson* (New York, 2004); Michele Cunningham, *Mexico and the Foreign Policy of Napoleon III* (New York, 2000).

27 Peter Alford, 'North Korea risks total isolation', *The Australian*, 9 Oct 2006.

its interests in the Western Hemisphere for most of its 200 years of interaction with the region.

The oil supplies of the Caribbean have long been a key determinant in US policy and have become even more crucial as the twenty first century moves into an era of global oil scarcity. Oil – and events such as the 1930s nationalization of US oil assets in Mexico, the development of oil in the Gulf of Mexico throughout the twentieth century, and the large oil supplies exported to the US from Venezuela – have dominated US strategic policy in the region for close to a century. Recent events, such as the effect of Hurricane Katrina on US refinery capacity (coupled with problems with oil production in BP's northern Alaska oil fields), the radicalization of the Chávez regime in Venezuela (1998–) and its proselytizing a Left anti-American message in Latin America, and the rise in world oil prices driven by rising global demand, have all focused US strategic thinking on Central America and the Caribbean into the future. It has never been more important in US hemispheric strategy.

The US has always been keenly sensitive of the need to secure its southern border with Mexico and maintain its hegemony in the region. President James Monroe warned off outside intervention from Britain and Europe in the Monroe Doctrine in 1823, while relying on the British fleet to back this up against Europe. The US seized all of northern Mexico in the Mexican War (1846–1848) that gave the US its entire modern Southwest, with the states of Texas, New Mexico, Arizona, California, Nevada, Utah and Colorado, at the conclusion of hostilities. In 1863 the US was tied up with the Civil War and had to wait until its conclusion in 1865 to respond to the attempt of Napoleon III to gain control of Mexico. The threat of an invasion by one million troops was then enough to persuade the French to back off and abandon their puppet Maximilian in Mexico to face a firing squad in 1867. Theodore Roosevelt extended the Monroe Doctrine in 1904 with the bellicose Roosevelt Corollary (adumbrating George W Bush) that proclaimed that the US would exercise virtually unlimited interventionism in the Western Hemisphere when needed to protect US interests (as defined by Roosevelt and subsequent Presidents).

US forces under General John J Pershing intervened in Mexico under Democrat Woodrow Wilson in the Mexican Civil War in 1916–1917 in order to punish the cross-border raids and killings by bandit leader cum nationalist Pancho Villa. Only the exigencies of the First World War and Pershing's command of US forces in Europe prompted their withdrawal after an ineffectual campaign. The Zimmerman Telegram in 1917, a suggestion by the German Foreign Secretary Zimmerman that Mexico join Germany in an alliance with the irredentist promise of regaining Texas, New Mexico and Arizona, led directly to the US entrance into the First World War shortly thereafter. Franklin Roosevelt came under great pressure to intervene in Mexico in 1938 when the Mexican government nationalized US oil assets, a temptation, however, which he resisted, after having declared in 1933 a policy of non-intervention in Latin America. Throughout much of the late twentieth century, and into the twenty first century, the issue of illegal immigration from south of the Rio Grande River, has bedevilled US governments with the Hispanic population in the US, that is now some 50 million and growing to be the largest minority in the US, soon to be the majority in several South-western states.

Cuba became a semi-dependent state of the US in the aftermath of the Spanish-American War (1898) in which the US gained part of a global empire from the Spanish in the Philippines, Guam, Puerto Rico, and thus became a Pacific and Caribbean colonial power. The US troops left Cuba in 1902 but only after agreement was reached on the Platt Amendment which give the US a permanent lease for a naval base at Guantanamo Bay (used for detentions in the GWOT) and the right to intervene if Cuba could not maintain internal order or was threatened by an external agent. This de facto control of Cuba was not altered until Franklin Roosevelt's administration, when under the Good Neighbour Policy the US rejected interventionism in Latin America in 1933 at the Pan-American Conference in Montevideo. But this did not, of course, end US interventionism in Latin America and the Caribbean. The Platt Amendment was repealed in 1934.

In the dislocation of the Great Depression an armed revolution took place in Cuba by an army sergeant, Fulgencio Batista, whose government had some economic success but evolved into a typically corrupt and venal Latin American government. In 1959 forces led by Fidel Castro swept Batista from power when they entered Havana and President Batista fled. The Cuban Revolution, and Castro's hold on power, dominated US-Cuban relations from Eisenhower to George W Bush. The Cuban question has haunted presidents of the US for almost 50 years, as the venerable dictator, Fidel, has watched nine US presidents in office. The existence of now millions of Cuban exiles living in Florida, and their crucial vote in a swing state, has complicated the thinking of US policy makers, juggling the often contradictory needs of US domestic politics and strategic policy in the region. Isolating Fidel's Cuba forever may not have been in the best interests of US Latin American policy in the twenty first century. Castro, ailing in late 2007, will not live forever and the results of his demise in Cuba and in the larger Caribbean region are not predictable, although they may well involve an east Europe style democratisation. The US must now face these issues in the world of global terrorism and the growing alliance of rogue states throughout the world, sometimes including Castro and Venezuela's long-time Castro supporter, Hugo Chávez.

Venezuela declared independence in 1811 as one of the first South American nations to rebel against Spanish colonial rule. In 1821, led by the greatest of the South American patriot leaders Simón Bolivar (born in Caracas in 1783), Venezuela triumphed in battle and became one of the many free South American states. Like virtually all new Latin American states Venezuela went through seemingly endless cycles of civil war, corrupt and ineffectual governments and unfulfilled promises of better government and more equitable societies in a continent replete with natural wealth. In the twentieth century it gained great wealth through its oil resources in the Gulf of Mexico, but by the 1990s it still had not stabilized civil conflict nor eliminated widespread poverty. The 1990s was characterized by severe civil conflict and social unrest and resulted in an attempted coup by army officer Hugo Chávez in 1992.

In spite of his failed coup Chávez entered legitimate politics and was elected President in 1998. His self-styled program, called grandly the 'Bolivarian Revolution', was directed at a new social policy for Venezuela which he intended to export to the rest of Latin America. The core stated objectives were to combat disease, illiteracy, malnutrition and poverty, that is, the historic goals of countless Latin American reformers. His government survived numerous counter-coups (some possibly US supported) and political setbacks. The foreign policy of his administration has challenged the Washington Consensus for Latin America and Venezuela has forged ties with US foes in Cuba, Syria, and Iran.

Chávez generated fierce domestic critics who charged him with corruption and fraud in domestic policy and foolhardy anti-Americanism in foreign affairs. Left groups, such as Amnesty International and Human Rights Watch, have recorded human rights abuses, especially by the police and armed forces within Venezuela. Some US commentators, such as the TV evangelist Pat Robertson, have even called for his assassination, but generally the US has been cautious in its policies toward Chávez' government, although defenders of his polices have frequently charged the US with complicity in the plots against him. He has often opposed US interests over trade, foreign policy, Cuba and in international affairs but he has continued to send oil exports to the US at the quite substantial rate of 1.3–1.5 million barrels per day, around 10 per cent of US oil imports. As a focal point for the Left in Latin America, and still with a good deal of domestic support in Venezuela, he has become a key opponent of US hegemony in its own hemisphere and globally. The Caribbean littoral has always been replete with unstable island states (such as Haiti and Jamaica) and the small states of Central America, with weak monocultural economies, will continue to be an unstable region in the future. Chávez, however, now flush with oil revenues from high world oil prices for the indefinite future, and determined to move the Mercosur Group, in which Venezuela has the third largest economy behind only Brazil and Argentina, in an anti-American direction, will certainly seek to increase his influence over regional affairs.

Chávez attacked George W Bush at the UN General Assembly in September 2006, labelling the US President 'the devil himself' who acts like 'he owned the world'. 'The devil was here yesterday. It still smells of sulphur around here. ... The President of the United States, the gentleman to whom I refer as the devil, came here, talking as if he owned the world – truly, as the owner of the world'.[28] Chavez's taunts came a day after Iran's President Mahmoud Ahmadinejad railed against Bush. Chavez' performance was one of the most outrageous at the UN since Yasser Arafat, the late head of the PLO, wore a pistol into the General Assembly, and Russian leader, Nikita Khrushchev, banged his shoe on a desk. Chavez brandished a Spanish-language copy of the US left-wing intellectual, Noam Chomsky's, 2004 book, *Hegemony* or *Survival*, and recommended all read it. Vying to become the de facto leader of a growing anti-American clique in the Third World, he attacked Bush for everything from imposing US 'imperialism' on the Third World, to an 'immoral veto' at the UN that he said would have ended Israel's war with Hezbollah weeks earlier than it did. Washington considered Chavez, a close ally of communist Cuba, to be a destabilising influence in Latin America – even as the US is a major consumer of Venezuelan oil.

Nonetheless, in October 2006 Chávez failed to persuade the world body he deserved a seat on the UN Security Council. Venezuela was unable to overcome

28 'Bush is the devil, Chavez tells UN', *The Australian*, 22 Sept 2006.

the challenge of the more pro-US Guatemala for the seat in four rounds of voting for Latin America's regional, non-permanent seat being vacated by Argentina. The fourth round went to Guatemala, 110 votes to 75. But Guatemala still failed to capture the council seat: to win, a country must get two-thirds of the votes from those member countries taking part in the polling, which meant at least 124 votes. The losses were a rebuke for Chávez, who has repeatedly said the United States wields too much power.

Conclusion

The Global War on Terror has opened a number of new fronts for the United States and has weakened its power to deal with many of them. Potential strategic competitors have been emboldened by its difficulties in Iraq, Iran has taken the opportunity to strike a claim as a regional hegemon, Islamist rebellions are active in fronts that stretch from west Africa to Southeast Asia, domestic opposition to Bush's policies has risen, and support among US allies has declined. It had not been an auspicious start to the Global War on Terror and President Bush promised to become one of the weakest lame duck presidents in American history before he steps down in January 2009.

Conclusion

Balance Sheet

The US won the Cold War because it had a superior economy, a higher level of technology, including military technology, and a sound strategic posture. In the end, the claim by Marxists that they had unravelled the problems of development and progress and had solutions to them was false. As this became apparent in the 1980s, so the ideological glue that held America's adversaries together fell apart. It is hardly surprising that the US emerged from that conflict in a mood of quiet triumphalism. Indeed, in retrospect, this relative modesty is somewhat surprising. This is not to say that the US made no strategic errors in the Cold War, and the Vietnam War must rank among the worse of them. But for two decades after that defeat it played to its own strengths of financial, economic and technical superiority which enabled it to win many minor conflicts and the Cold War.

In the late twentieth century and after this victory, the US embarked on the extremely ambitious project of creating a liberal world order. But it generally eschewed the use of direct military force, the Balkans wars being an exception to that rule and one that was carefully calibrated. At the onset of the twenty first century it was having some success with its globalisation project. There were more liberal states, and others aiming to create the conditions of liberal representative democracy, than had been the case during the late Cold War. The international economy had been liberalised to the extent that it had been given a new name: globalisation. And the US had maintained its position as the most powerful and, arguably, most widely popularly supported of the Great Powers. Less than a decade later and much of this has changed, and much for the worse.

Military Power

In terms of conventional military power, the US is still clearly the most powerful state in the world. It spends the most, is technically the most advanced, and it can project its power further than any other state. The US still has the most powerful nuclear arsenal, and it has reached agreements with the Russian Federation that have stabilised their relationship of Mutual Assured Destruction. Since the US has a clear lead in technology it may also be the case that during the upgrading and improving processes that have continued, together with the development of related satellite, guidance, and Communications, Command and Control systems, the US may have actually advanced its lead. It may be doubted that this amounts to very much in the post-Cold War World. Indeed in recognition of this the Pentagon is considering a plan to replace nuclear warheads on some intercontinental ballistic missiles with conventional weapons for pre-emptive strikes against terrorists.[1] In the same arena the PRC has also been able to make up little or any leeway, and the US strategic superiority may well rest at the same margin as in the 1990s. But these are not now the major concerns of US nuclear strategy.

In the late twentieth century a number of new nuclear-armed states emerged to challenge US power. Pakistan tested its first nuclear weapon in the 1990s and quickly passed the technology to Iran and, possibly, North Korea.[2] This has made the nuclear non-proliferation regime difficult if not impossible to police. Since all three of these states have sponsored terrorism in the past – and probably continue to do so – the main issue they pose is passing their nuclear technology on to terrorist organisations that challenge the US. This is very hard to defend against and may have greatly increased the vulnerability of the US during the last decade.

Pakistan is a major sponsor of terrorist organisations, and has been unwilling to control their spread. It has also disseminated nuclear technology. Because it is itself nuclear armed, none of the states alarmed by this development has been able to stop it. In addition, Iran may decide to use nuclear weaponry in its pursuit of its regional power ambitions, to expand its control over the oil fields, and/or to pursue the destruction of Israel. This is a new challenge to US power that it has been unable to prevent. The same is the case with North Korea that has already developed the missiles to deliver nuclear weapons at quite long range, which suggests an inter-continental capacity may not be long off. Again, and despite PRC cooperation, the US has been unable to prevent the evolution of this serious threat to its interests although there are high hopes for the Six Party Agreement in 2007. The deployment of anti-missile defence systems may help offset this most unwelcome development for US policy.

In conventional non-nuclear terms, the US has persisted with the two main strategic directions it undertook during the 1990s: the two and a half war strategy and the Revolution in Military Affairs. It has continued with its plans to make the entire US defence force an extremely mobile reserve capable of deploying to its three major regions of interest in support of pre-deployed formations. It has also continued the RMA which is supposed to permit it to successfully wage two conventional and one asymmetrical war simultaneously in different theatres. This entire strategy must now be adjudged to be in tatters. It has run into three major problems.

First, the US armed forces have been proven unable to defeat quickly a serious asymmetric military threat in the form of the Iraqi insurgency. Indeed, it may also yet face effective defeat in Afghanistan. That same armed force is not able to undertake conventional military action against Iran and/or North Korea, neither of whom is one of the major powers the US military was planning to be able to confront successfully and simultaneously in the 1990s.

Secondly, the US strategy relied on allies to provide logistics, personnel and territory in support. This policy has been seriously thrown into question by the recent behaviour of allied powers. They have been reluctant to declare or act in

1 'Russia wary of US missile plan', *The Australian*, 29 Aug 2006.

2 See International Institute for Strategic Studies, *Nuclear Black Markets: Pakistan, A Q Khan and the Rise of Proliferation Networks* (London, 2007).

support of the US- led GWOT. The Europe NATO allies and the East Asian bilateral allies have shrunk from the task, from France, Germany and Spain, to Korea and Japan. Reliable contributors in this respect have been reduced to the Anglo-Sphere states. Even here the British government has acted despite British opinion and its support may not outlive Prime Minster Blair. New Zealand and Canadian support has been little more than nominal. And while Australia has been a partial exception, its regional commitments dictate that its global contributions will be limited. In any case, popular acquiescence likely rests on the low casualties which, in turn, have resulted from a low commitment.

Thirdly, it may be reasonably doubted that any further serious projection of US power will be supported by US popular opinion. The commitment to Iraq was, like the commitment to Vietnam, initially popular. It was also made against a backdrop of recent, short, low casualty, interventions in the Balkans. This popularity even outlasted the failure to find WMDs and the extension of the commitment to democratisation. But it did not long outlast the rising casualties against an insurgency, whatever its goals. By 2006, opinion was running strongly against the war. Another serious projection of US power had become extremely problematic.

These limitations will place constraints on the mobilisation and application of America's considerable military power into the medium term future.

Economy

The US has had the largest economy in the world since the beginning of the twentieth century. It has maintained this situation into the 2000s. It still has the largest number of corporations in the world's top five hundred; it still has the most productive work force in the world, reflecting its overall lead in productivity against other major economies; and it still leads in technological innovation in many sectors from information technology, through aerospace to bio-technology. It is not easy to calculate whether this lead has eroded, but the dispersal of these technologies suggests it no longer has exclusive access to any. Nonetheless, its margin of economic superiority has begun to erode for a number of reasons.

The successful pursuit of globalisation has enabled the US to introduce the principles of a liberal economy to many states that had, for a number of different reasons, resisted this social formation. The combination of internal market mechanisms, the utilisation of comparative advantage in international trade, technology transfers and a global market in capital has enabled those states skilful enough to access them to grow and develop more quickly that the US itself. These states have included the giant nations of China and India, several countries of East Asia and South America, and, recently, a few resource rich countries like Australia, Iran and Russia. More surprisingly, the US also seems to have lost some of its edge in running capital markets, including to London.

The US economy in the twentieth century has, meanwhile, run into three major bottlenecks. The first has been the erosion of the fiscal discipline which was paying off some of the national debt at the end of the twentieth century. It has greatly increased its military spending during the GWOT, while the administration has reduced taxes on the wealthy and corporations as part of its electoral strategy. The result has been a considerable increase in its budget deficits which have, so far, been funded by foreign investors, many of them from East Asia. This will be difficult to sustain without incurring increased inflation or currency devaluation, or both. The US share of world output had fallen to just over a quarter by 2004.

The second has been the renewed growth of external deficits. This has, in turn, come from two major processes. As the US policy of globalisation has opened more low-wage countries to world trade, they have soaked up previous American sectors like labour intensive manufacturing and, increasingly, lower wage service sector occupations like call centres which are moving to India, and movie production which is moving to nations such as Canada, New Zealand and Australia. Yet, at the same time, the US has found it hard to offset this by exporting commodities or importing corporate profits. The US ran up giant domestic budget deficits in the 1980s from military spending by Ronald Reagan, which were extended by George H W Bush in the early 1990s, reduced by Clinton during the late 1990s, but then exploded under George W Bush and the GWOT and the Second Gulf War. The US economy was running record fiscal and external deficits and a record national debt level. For any other country this would, eventually, produce sharp currency devaluation. If this occurs, as remains likely, US relative economic power will decline with it, commensurately.

And thirdly, the US has become an increasing importer of energy. It is, of course, the leading consumer of energy in the world both absolutely and in per capita terms. Its Middle East strategy is a reflection of this. But the price of energy is now rising steadily as new demand for energy from emerging countries kicks into a market already dominated by American demand. The US national economy – as opposed to US energy corporations – may be a major loser from this process if it fails to adjust quickly by reducing demand for energy. As a net importer of resources the US is vulnerable to resource wars.

By the turn of the twenty first century, and especially after the attacks of 9/11 on the US, hope had turned to despair and the optimistic prognostications of historians like Francis Fukuyama about the 'end of history' and the triumph of a benign global liberal capitalism in a uni-polar world seemed naïve and even absurd.[3]

Demography

The distribution of world population has changed dramatically during the last half century as the 'demographic transition' has unevenly impacted on states. The developed countries are at the tail end of this process and experiencing, to varying

3 See, *The End of History and the Last Man* (London, 1992); *Our Post-human Future* (London, 2002); and *State-Building: Governance and World Order in the 21st Century* (Ithaca, New York, 2004). Not only did the US run huge domestic budget deficits under George W Bush but there were also dangerous blowouts in the national debt, foreign debt and trade deficits which alarmed even conservative economists and supporters of the Bush Republican administration: see by former Bush Secretary of Treasury Paul O'Neill (with Ron Suskind), *The Price of Loyalty: George W Bush, the White House, and the Education of Paul O'Neill* (New York, 2004).

degrees, declining or even negative rates of population growth as birth rates fall and populations age. The developing countries are, again to varying degrees, experiencing growing populations with increasing life expectancy set against still high birth rates. In some developing states, like China, population growth has already slowed considerably, while in others, mostly Muslim, growth rates remain high.

Among the developed countries life expectancy has risen but birth rates fallen – partly due to declining religious affiliation – and population contraction is faced in most of them including notably, Italy, Japan, Russia and much of the EU. To offset this, some, including Germany and France, have imported large numbers of fecund developing country migrants. This has altered their demographic structure and had an impact on their foreign policy capabilities, particularly with respect to the Muslim world where the migrants are predominantly Islamic and will actively resist anti-Islamic policies. This has had less impact on the US, where the natural growth rate is higher than Europe, and a large number of its immigrants have been Hispanic rather than Islamic. It is estimated that nearly twelve million of these immigrants are illegal, and, therefore, of unknown value to the US state. Some believe, however, that they will contribute to a diminution of national cohesion,[4] which may well itself, diminish US national power.

The low population growth has also made young persons an even more precious emotional commodity for families, who have fewer of them, and can now all vote. In contrast to the nineteenth and early twentieth centuries, this combination of low fertility, declining religiosity and increased democracy has often generated a widespread popular reluctance to participate in violent conflict that might generate considerable casualties. The religious impulses which produced a climate of sacrifice disappeared from most developed secular societies in the late Cold War. This perspective is less the case in the US, the most religious of developed countries, but is nonetheless discernable. Modern democracies find it hard to fight serious wars.

The US has sought to offset this problem, in part, by recruiting its armed forces from rural areas where religious and patriotic sentiment is highest. It has also designed armed forces in which fire power and technology have replaced personnel (the RMA). The result was the army that it deployed in Iraq, which could destroy any other similar conventional force, but had neither the training, nor disposition, nor popular support to fight the war of attrition which it then faced. Its opponents on the other hand could. It seems extremely unlikely that a US population that is increasingly Hispanic in background, urbanised in disposition and educated to university level, is going to be better disposed to that purpose in future. This is particularly the case after its experience in the GWOT, and Iraq in particular.

Culture

Most of the developed states have reacted to recent immigration from Third World countries by adopting a form of multiculturalism. This has had the effect of diluting

4 Samuel P Huntington, *Who are We?: the Challenges to America's National Identity* (New York, 2004).

popular commitment to the national value structure, which appears to be (and is depicted as) but one among many of equal worth. They have also thereby diluted their commitment to enforce a legal code based historically on traditional, usually secular Christian values. In the end this has impeded their capacity to pursue their own strategic objectives and impose a unique values structure on citizens. The experience of the GWOT is likely to lead to a diminution of the commitment to this form of multiculturalism.

The US in particular has also not found it easy to generate popular global support for its purposes. During the Cold War there was a genuine and identifiable threat to free societies. During the period of globalisation there was a clear goal with benefits to be identified and pursued. These threats and promises mobilised populations, even when the particular culture of the US was not to their taste. The GWOT has not served this purpose.

American culture is now a two edged sword because the US breeds and generates its own best critics. While much of Islamist terrorist ideology is generated by the *Koran*, much too is augmented by the standard fare of US college students: Noam Chomsky, Edward Said and *The New York Times* op eds. The sullen hostility of the US cultural elite towards the Bush administration and the GWOT will not be offset by a diet of patriotic Hollywood blockbusters, however well produced. And in those countries where US culture barely reaches, including much of the Islamic world, China and India, its soft power remains irrelevant.

The dominant paradigms of public policy over the past two generations have for the US become more difficult to sustain: unlimited economic expansion, cheap oil, available water resources, viable nation states and the hope for a world GDP expanding indefinitely. Control of civil conflict, containing pandemic disease, effective use of water resources, poverty eradication and the prudent use of a finite environment may be the new dominant determinants of public policy if the world's civilisations are to survive in their present form.

Yet, alternatives to US hegemony still do not appear to be part of the short to medium projections for the world balance of power. The new giants of Asia, China and India, both have catastrophic problems of population, poverty and pollution with enormous potential for civil disorder. In spite of some commentators predicting that they will pose both an economic and military counterbalance to the US, it seems unlikely given their limitations from overpopulation and the immense complexities of modernisation. Europe has yet to show the high level of unity that it would require in order to challenge the world hegemony of the US, especially in military and geopolitical spheres. Judging by the votes in France and the Netherlands against the EU constitution in 2005, this has not emerged. Other contenders, such as Brazil or Russia, have neither the social cohesion, military capacity nor the economic strength to present a threat to the hegemonic position of the US. The US, therefore, in spite of its intractable Global War on Terror and its Iraq quagmire, is likely to retain its position as the world's leading power in the short-to-medium term and possibly in the long-term as well. But its hegemony is at serious risk.[5]

5 For a most perceptive analysis by Oxford Europeanist, Timothy Garton Ash, see the pessimistic 'Twenty-seven countries looking for a purpose', *Australian Financial Review*, 23

The Anglo-Sphere may well also decide to set a distance from the US. The British are clearly sceptical about Blair's level of support for Bush. Canada and New Zealand have been somewhat reluctant and intermittent allies. Only Australia, therefore, as a medium sized patch of Anglo-Saxon culture in a sea of nearly three billion Asians will continue to align itself with the US. This, of course, does not preclude good relations between Australia and Asia but the geo-strategic needs of Australia living in the Arc of Instability in the Southwest Pacific indicate it should maintain and extend the US alliance. Australia pays a small price for a large dividend for the alliance and is unlikely to move away from this historical arrangement whether judged by geopolitical, trade, nationalist or cultural criteria, even under a Labor government.

Opinion and Ideas

The standing of the US in world opinion has declined as a result of the spread of sovereignty, the end of the Cold War, the rise of opposition to liberal modernisation, and resistance to the Bush administration's GWOT. This is shown by the polling cited in chapter eight and the orientation of state regimes. The Anglo-Sphere has been the most pro-US of groupings, but even its governments and peoples have been cautious, like the Australian and New Zealand governments, not to contribute too heavily. Canada has been unwilling to be involved in Iraq and Tony Blair is paying the price for doing so. Other states have left the Anglo-Sphere entirely, and the Commonwealth has no collective policy on the GWOT.

The main great power rivals of the US – Russia, China and Iran – have used its distractions in Iraq and Afghanistan to forge better positions and have taken their peoples with them. The popular standing of the US in Western Europe is very low, and the prestige it won in Eastern Europe by liberating those peoples from the Soviets, has been decidedly diminished. In the Islamic world reaction against the US GWOT has been severely hostile, to the point of threatening the survival of pro-US regimes in states as diverse as Pakistan, the Palestinian Authority, Afghanistan, and perhaps Saudi Arabia. Only Libya has moved decisively in the opposite direction.

It cannot be said that the US position has improved in the Third World. Although India shows some signs of congruence with US thinking and has recently opened its economy, in South America the trend is, if anything, in the opposite direction.

The Cold War and the GWOT

The GWOT and the Cold war have similarities that deserve enumeration, particularly since the latter was the last strategic conflict won by the US and its allies.

The most obvious similarity is that the GWOT also pits the ideology of American liberalism against a Manichean ideology. American liberalism has its great strengths as a thought system that recommends equality before the law, a representative system

---

March 2007, pp. 3–4. The possibility of an imminent EU challenge to hegemonic America, according to Ash, seems slim indeed.

of government and a private economy that encourages initiative and innovation. It can provide benign government and a wealthy economy. But in the world of realist power politics, US liberalism also comes attached to the particularities of the American experience and culture, and is often used to justify or pursue US interests that have little to do with liberalism – access to the Saudi oil fields being one such prominent example. In the Cold War, among the population occupied by communist states the message was, nonetheless, clear enough to produce rapid results in the late 1980s. It was also sustained by the American people with very few defectors.

In addition, the US was clearly the dominant single power during the Cold War. It is true that, as a result of the prolonged defeat in Vietnam, Henry Kissinger devised a picture of a five pointed star in which the US was challenged by four other clusters of power: the Soviet Union, China, Japan and Europe. He argued that a declining US had to accommodate to these challengers. But, in the event, the Reagan administration rejected this strategy and in a demonstration of its belief in the US system, effectively confronted all four rivals and opponents. The result was a resurgent US leading the world into globalisation by the onset of the twenty first century.

Moreover, it has been popular sport, particularly among the Left, to see the debacle in Iraq as the Vietnam quagmire of this century: the US, attempting to impose a regime on a people, is resisted by a diverse coalition which attracts international and popular support, and leads to the defeat of the US and its withdrawal from further imperial ambitions – at least for a while. The US is unable to win militarily, and its electorate will not sustain a long war against determined popular opposition in the field.

The target of these blandishments to oppose the US was, in the Soviet case, organised workers and the Left intelligentsia, and in both strata it had its successes. It used financial assistance, political literature openly sold in book shops, newspapers and trips to successful Soviet societies, to sustain support. Islam operates in much the same way, using Saudi money, prayer rooms and literature, internet sites and training visits to Pakistan. It has a ready made target group in the Islamic Diaspora, and a few others, like the Australian David Hicks, that may be drawn into its web. Not surprisingly, the US and allied states are trying to devise policing methods for dealing with such subversion and potential terrorism. In this, it is also opposed by the same alliance of human rights advocates and the Left, in this case allied with Muslims, who would, like the communists before them, not themselves tolerate the freedoms they so advocate.

The Islamic doctrine may be, however, more difficult to defeat than Soviet Marxism for two main reasons. In the first place, it is the belief system of over 1.3 billion people world wide. It has sustained people, societies and states for the last thirteen centuries and will not be as easily refuted as Soviet Marxism whose theoretical origins were in 1848, and thus only one and a half centuries years old, and whose societies lasted only two or three generations. Islamic scholars have worked hard at developing a hermetically closed philosophical system against encroachments, including particularly those of Western liberalism. Islamic societies are obviously durable and their deficiencies more evident to non-believers than to Muslims, Bernard Lewis' arguments not withstanding. And in certain circumstances, including much of contemporary Pakistan, Afghanistan and even Iraq, its promise of order from chaos could be most attractive.

But the Iraq War is not the Vietnam War. Those that are eagerly proclaiming it is, are drawing analogies form their youth, including Chomsky, Pilger, Tariq Ali and all the ageing professors and deans of Western universities. There is no great state at the centre of the world Islamic movement bristling with nuclear weapons, although the theocratic oligarchy of Iran and the dictatorship of Pakistan may both be testing for the role. The primitive, poor, theocratic societies of Pakistan and Afghanistan offer no beacon of hope for most of humanity. There is no promise of a better political and economic system that will attract converts in their millions in the Western countries. And there is little sympathy for the Jihadist cause in the other great centres of world power – China, Japan, Europe, Russia, India. For Western societies the problem of dealing with the Islamists within them, is in the end merely a major policing issue.

Nonetheless, the Iraq invasion has produced a profound strategic error; one that has compounded the problems just mentioned. The decision to remove the regime of Saddam Hussein may have been appropriate: he was a monster; had attacked his neighbours; and he threatened access to the oil fields. His removal and replacement by a more compliant authority together with the trial of the most odious of his followers – say one thousand – may well have paid dividends. This may have been followed by a progressive liberalisation of the successor regime under US patronage. Instead, the US undertook the most ambitious of projects: the de-Ba'athification and the democratisation of Iraq. What it has created is an insurgency, leading to a civil war, and a Shi'ite state. This is, as Thomas Ricks rightly notes, a fiasco. The US has no clear exit strategy and is creating a carcass on which Iran and the Jihadists may well feed. It has few allies left in this project and the only other contributor of substantial forces, Britain, will likely withdraw under Gordon Brown. Australia and others can only sustain their effort at a minimal level. Nonetheless, even at this late stage a solution may be produced.

The growing critique of America and the belief that it may be entering a period in its history of rapidly declining power is based on two almost false assumptions: an overestimation of its weaknesses; and an underestimation of the weaknesses of its opponents. Historically, the great strength of the US has been its underlying institutional base in Anglo-Saxon legal institutions, its powerful education system, its culture based upon innovation and adaptation to modernisation, its huge domestic market, a culture of innovation and consumption, and a social policy of inclusion welcoming energetic migrants from virtually every nation in the world. In spite of the well-known problems of crime and alienation, these crucial social characteristics remain and in many ways have allowed the US to increase the gap between itself and the rest of the world. In recent world survey of higher education institutions, 17 out of 20 of the world's top universities were American (the other three being Oxford, Cambridge and Tokyo) and the technological superiority of the US in military, aerospace and communications areas is growing every year. In short, the US is not about to implode in spite of the growing costs of its foreign policy and massive deficits.

Concomitantly, critics overestimate its opponents. China and India have enormous social tensions and in spite of their huge economies they are poor societies, fragile and not about to soon supersede the US either economically or geo-strategically. The EU cannot even reach consensus on its budget let alone replace the US as a world hegemon. Russia has great wealth in energy resources but its internal weaknesses make it unlikely to come back as a superpower. Consequently, the US is likely to remain the world's hegemon in the near-to-medium future. Many of its critics are merely restating a position learned and established in the dying days of the US commitment to Vietnam. But the Cold War was still won.

The Vietnam analogy dominated much of the critical reasoning about US policy in Iraq which by 2007 had superseded the Global War on Terror as the principal focus of US foreign policy and its critics. Idealism dominated both sides of the debate. But in fact US primary interests could be achieved without the additional burden of trying to democratise a nation that had only been created in the 1920s and had no known history of or, for that matter, aspirations for democratic processes. US interests were created by oil and geopolitics and could have been reasonably and quickly achieved in 2003. The idealist and neo-conservative impulse made the task more difficult and the price much higher. But the primary goals could still be attained, although in 2007 an unsatisfactory result appears more likely.

A final point should be made. The decline in relative US power and its ability to advance its liberal cause during the period following 9/11 has resulted largely from errors of policy, not from a decline in capability. A new and successful strategy might easily be constructed on the massive base of US power that remains.

Bibliography

The Australian, published six times a week by NewsCorp, was used as the newspaper of record with others consulted and cited where appropriate.

Agoncillo, Teodoro, *A Short History of the Philippines* (New York, 1969).

Andaya, Barbara Watson, and Andaya, Leonard, *A History of Malaysia* (Honolulu, 2001).

Anderson, Fred, and Clayton, Andrew, *The Dominion of War: Empire and Conflict in North America, 1500–2000* (New York, 2005).

Armstrong, Karen, *Muhammad: A Biography of the Prophet*, (San Francisco, 1991).

Barnhart, Michael, *Japan in the World Since 1868* (London, 1995).

Beasley, W G, *Japanese Imperialism, 1894–1945* (Oxford, 1987).

Belich, James, *The New Zealand Wars* (Auckland, 1986).

Belich, James, *Making Peoples* (Auckland, 1996).

Belich, James, *Paradise Reforged* (Auckland, 2001).

Bennett, James C., *The Anglosphere Challenge: Why the English-Speaking Nations Will Lead the Way in the Twenty-First Century* (New York, 2004).

Bergen, Peter, *Holy War, Inc.: Inside the Secret World of Osama bin Laden* (London, 2002).

Birmingham, John, *A Time for War: Australia as a Military Power* (Melbourne, 2005).

Black, Edwin, *Banking on Baghdad: Inside Iraq's 7,000-Year History of War, Profit and Conflict,* (Hoboken, New Jersey, 2004).

Bromley, Simon, *American Hegemony and World Oil: The Industry, the State System, and the World Economy* (University Park, PA, 1991).

Brune, Peter, *A Bastard of a Place, the Australians in Papua* (Sydney, 2003).

Brzezinski, Z, Scowcroft, Brent, and Murphy, Richard, 'Differentiated Containment', *Foreign Affairs,* 76, May/June 1997.

Buruma, Ian, and Margalit, Avishai, *Occidentalism: the West in the Eyes of its Enemies* (New York, 2004).

Buruma, Ian, *Murder in Amsterdam: The Death of Theo van Gogh and the Limits of Tolerance* (New York, 2006).

Byman, Daniel, Pollack, Kenneth, and Rose, Gideon, 'The Rollback Fantasy', *Foreign Affairs,* 78, January/February 1999, pp. 24–41.

Carr, E H, *The Twenty Years Crisis* (New York, 2001).

Catley, Bob, and Cristaudo, Wayne, *This Great Beast: Progress and the Modern State* (Aldershot, 1997).

Catley, Bob, and Keliat, Makmur, *Spratlys* (Aldershot, 1997).

Catley, Bob, *Waltzing with Matilda: Should New Zealand Join Australia?* (Wellington, 2001).

Catley, Bob, 'The Bush Administration and Changing Geo-Politics in the Asia Pacific Region', *Contemporary Southeast Asia*, Singapore, April 2001.

Catley, Bob, ed, *Australia and New Zealand: Coming Together or Drifting Apart?* (Wellington, 2002).
Chang, Jung, and Halliday, Jon, *Mao: the Unknown Story* (London, 2006).
Chulov, Martin, *Australian Jihad* (Sydney, 2006).
Churchill, Winston, *A History of the English Speaking Peoples* (New York, 1965).
Cleary, Thomas, *The Essential Koran* (San Francisco, 1994).
Cockburn, Andrew, and Cockburn, Patrick, *Out of the Ashes: The Resurrection of Saddam Hussein* (New York, 1999).
Cohen, Stephen, *The Idea of Pakistan* (Washington DC, 2004).
Cohn, Marjorie, 'Spain, EU and US: War on Terror or War on Liberties?', *The Jurist*, 17 March 2004.
Collier, Paul, and Dollar, David, *Globalization, Growth, and Poverty: Building an Inclusive World Economy,* World Bank, 2001.
Cook, David, 'Muslim apocalyptic and jihad', *Jerusalem Studies in Arabic and Islam*, 20, 1996, pp. 66–104.
Costello, John, *The Pacific War, 1941*–1945 (New York, 2002).
Cunningham, Michele, *Mexico and the Foreign Policy of Napoleon III* (New York, 2000).
Daniel, E., and Potts, Annette, *Yanks Down Under, 1941–1945: the American Impact on Australia* (Melbourne, 1984).
Davies, Norman, *The Isles* (Oxford, 1999).
Denoon, Donald, *et al, A History of Australia, New Zealand and the Pacific* (Oxford, 2000).
Downing, Brian, *The Military Revolution and Political Change* (Princeton, NJ, 1991).
Drucker, Peter F, 'The Global Economy and the Nation-State', *Foreign Affairs,* 107, Sept/Oct 1997, pp. 159–171.
Dunn, John, 'Introduction: Crisis of the Nation State?', *Political Studies,* 42, 1994.
Ehrlich, Paul R, *Population, Resources, Environments: Issues in Human Ecology* (San Francisco, 1972).
Einfeld, Jann, *India* (San Diego, 2003).
'Exceptionalism', Volume 102, No. 3, *The American Historical Review* (1997).
Faulkner, Neil *Apocalypse: the Great Jewish Revolt Against Rome, AD 66–73* (London, 2004).
Ferguson, Niall, *Colossus: the Price of America's Empire* (New York, 2004).
Ferrell, Robert, *American Diplomacy, a History* (New York, 1969).
Foner, Eric, 'The Lie that Empire Tells Itself', *London Review of Books,* 19 May 2005.
Francis, Richard, *Judge Sewall's Apology: the Salem Witch Trials and the Forming of an American Conscience* (New York, 2005).
Freedman, L, and Karsh, E, *The Gulf Conflict 1990–1991: Diplomacy and War in the New World Order* (London, 1993).
French, Paul, *North Korea: The Paranoid Peninsula, a Modern History* (London, 2005).
Friedman, Thomas, *The Lexus and the Olive Tree* (London, 1999).
Friedman, Thomas, *The World is Flat: a Brief History of the Twenty-First Century* (New York, 2005).

Fukuyama, Francis, 'The End of History?', *National Interest,* 16, 1989.

Fukuyama, Francis, *The End of History and the Last Man* (London, 1992).

Fukuyama, Francis, *Our Post-human Future* (London, 2002).

Fukuyama, Francis, *State-Building: Governance and World Order in the 21st Century* (Ithaca, New York, 2004).

Gabler, Neal, *An Empire of Their Own: How the Jews Invented Hollywood* (New York, 1989).

Gibbon, Edward, *The History of The Decline and Fall of the Roman Empire* (London, 1776–1788).

Goldberg, David Howard, *Foreign Policy and Ethnic Interest Groups: American and Canadian Jews Lobby For Israel* (New York, 1990).

Gullick, Edward V., *Europe's Classical Balance of Power* (Ithaca, NY, 1955).

Gunaratna, Rohan, *Inside Al Qaeda: Global Network of Terror* (Melbourne, 2002).

Halliday, Fred, *Soviet Policy in the Arc of Crisis* (Washington DC, 1981).

Ham, Paul, *Kokoda* (Sydney, 2004).

Harrison, Lawrence E., *The Central Liberal Truth: How Politics Can Change a Culture and Save It from Itself* (Oxford, 2007).

Haynes, Sam W, *James K Polk and the Expansionist Impulse* (New York, 2002).

Hindley, Geoffrey, *A Brief History of the Crusades: Islam and Christianity in the Struggle for World Supremacy* (London, 2003).

Hiro, Dilip, *Desert Shield to Desert Storm* (London, 1992).

Hitchens, Christopher *The Trial of Henry Kissinger* (New York, 2001).

Horowitz, David, *Unholy Alliance: Radical Islam and the American Left* (New York, 2004).

Hourani, Albert, *A History of the Arab Peoples* (New York, 2002).

Huntington, Samuel P, *The Clash of Civilisations and the Remaking of World Order,* Simon and Schuster (New York, 1996).

Huntington, Samuel P, *Who are We? The Challenges to America's National Identity* (New York, 2004).

Hussain, Zahid, *Frontline Pakistan: The Struggle with Militant Islam* (New York, 2007).

Indyk, Martin S, Assistant Secretary for Near Eastern Affairs: remarks at the Council on Foreign Relations New York City, NY, 22 April 1999.

International Crisis Group, *Jemaah Islamiyah in South East Asia: Damaged But Still Dangerous*, August 2003.

International Crisis Group, *Indonesia: Jemaah Islamiyah's Current Status*, Asia Briefing, Number 63, 3 May 2007.

International Institute for Strategic Studies, *Nuclear Black Markets: Pakistan, A Q Khan and the Rise of Proliferation Networks* (London, 2007).

Irving, Helen, *To Constitute a Nation* (Cambridge, 1999).

Johnson, Paul, *A History of the Jews*, (London, 1988).

Judis, John B, *The Folly of Empire, What George W Bush Could Learn from Theodore Roosevelt and Woodrow Wilson* (New York, 2004).

Kagan, Robert, *Of Paradise and Power: America and Europe in the New World Order* (New York, 2003).

Kedourie, Eli, *Politics of the Middle East* (New York, 1992).

Kennedy, David M., *Freedom from Fear, the American People in Depression and War, 1929*–1945 (New York, 1999).
Kennedy, David M, 'What "W" Owes to "WW"', *The Atlantic Monthly* (March, 2005).
Kenny, Kevin, *The ANZUS Crisis: Cold War Diplomacy, 1984–1986,* Flinders University American Studies Honours Thesis, 2005.
King, Michael, *The Penguin History of New Zealand* (Auckland, 2003).
Klare, Michael, *Blood and Oil* (New York, 2004).
Kolko, Gabriel, *The Politics of War: The World and United States Foreign Policy, 1943–1945* (New York, 1968).
Krasner, Stephen D, *Defending the National Interest; Raw Material Investments and US Foreign Policy* (Princeton, 1978).
Krauthammer, Charles, 'The Unipolar Moment', *Foreign Affairs*, No 70, 1990–91.
Kulke, Henmann, and Rothermund, Dietmar, *A History of India* (New York, 2004).
Lach, Donald F, *Japan in the Eyes of Europe* (Chicago, 1968).
LaFeber, Walter, *The Clash: a History of US-Japanese Relations* (New York, 1997).
Lambeth, Benjamin S, *Air Power Against Terror, America's Conduct of Operation Enduring Freedom,* RAND, 2005.
Lawrence, Bruce, *The Qur'an* (New York, 2006).
Lawrence, Bruce, ed, *Messages of the World: The Statements of Osama bin Laden*, (New York, 2005).
Layne, C, 'The Unipolar Illusion: Why New Great Powers Will Rise', *International Security*, Spring 1993.
Lewis, Bernard, *The Middle East: Two Thousand Years of History from the Rise of Christianity to the Present Day* (London, 1996).
Lewis, Bernard, *What Went Wrong? The Clash between Islam and Modernity in the Middle East* (London, 2002).
Lim, Robyn, *The Geopolitics of East Asia: Search for Equilibrium* (New York, 2003).
Linklater, Andro, *Measuring America, How the United States was Shaped by the Greatest Land Sale in History* (London, 2002).
Lipset, Seymour Martin, *American Exceptionalism: a Double-Edged Sword* (New York, 1996).
Long, David E, *The United States and Saudi Arabia* (Boulder, 1985).
Lowe, R, and Spencer, C, eds, *Iran, Its Neighbours and the Regional Crisis,* (London, 2006).
Lustik, Ian, ed, *Arab-Israeli Relations in World Politics* (New York, 1994).
Mahan, Alfred Thayer, *The Influence of Sea Power upon History* (Boston, 1898).
Maley, W, *Rescuing Afghanistan* (Sydney, 2006).
Mann, James, *Rise of the Vulcans: The History of Bush's War Cabinet* (New York, 2004).
Melleuish, Greg, and Saluusinszky, Imre, eds, *Blaming Ourselves* (Potts Point NSW, 2002).
Merry, Robert, *Taking on the World, Joseph and Stewart Alsop – Guardians of the American Century* (New York, 1996).

Mearsheimer, John, and Walt, Stephen, 'The Israel Lobby and U.S. Foreign Policy', *London Review of Books*, 23 March 2006.
Meadows, Dennis L, *et al*, *The Limits to Growth* (New York, 1972).
Micklethwait, John, and Wooldridge, Adrian, *The Right Nation: Why America is Different* (New York, 2005).
Micklethwait, John, and Woolridge, Adrian, *A Future Perfect: the Challenge and Hidden Promise of Globalization* (New York, 2000).
Morgenthau, Hans J, *Politics Among Nations* (New York, 1960).
Morris, Edmund, *Theodore Rex* (London, 2002).
Mosler, David and Catley, Bob, *Global America: Imposing Liberalism on a Recalcitrant World* (Westport, Conn, 2000).
Mosler, David, *Australia, The Recreational Society* (Westport, Conn, 2002).
Moore, John, *Over-sexed, Over-paid and Over Here, Americans in Australia, 1941–45* (St Lucia, Queensland, 1981).
Napoleoni, Loretta, 'The most wanted man in Iraq', *Foreign Policy,* No. 151.
Nasr, Vali, *The Shia Revival* (New York, 2006).
National Strategy for Combating Terrorism, US State Department, White House, September 2006.
NATO in Afghanistan Factsheet, at: http://www.nato.int/issues/afghanistan/index.html
Odell, P R, *Oil and World Power*, 8th ed (New York, 1986).
O'Neill, Paul, (with Ron Suskind), *The Price of Loyalty: George W. Bush, the White House, and the Education of Paul O'Neill* (New York, 2004).
Organsky, A, *The $36 Billion Bargain: Strategy and Politics in US Assistance to Israel* (New York, 1991).
Osborne, Milton, *Southeast Asia, an Introductory History* (St Leonards, NSW, 2000).
Painter, David S, 'Oil', in A DeConde, R D Burns and F Logevall, eds, *Encyclopedia of American Foreign Policy* (New York, 2002).
Parker, Geoffrey, *The Military Revolution: Military Innovation and the Rise of West* (New York, 1996).
Perkins, John, *Confessions of an Economic Hitman* (San Francisco, 2004).
Phillips, Kevin, *American Dynasty, Aristocracy, Fortune and the Politics of Deceit on the House of Bush* (New York, 2004).
Podhoretz, Norman, 'World War IV: how it started, what it means, and why we have to win', *Commentary*, September 2004.
Politkovskaya, Anna, *Putin's Russia* (London, 2004).
Preston, Diana, *A Brief History of the Boxer Rebellion, China's War on Foreigners, 1900* (London, 2002).
Prestowitz, Clyde, *Three Billion New Capitalists: the Great Shift of Wealth and Power to the East* (New York, 2005).
Ralph, Barry, *They Passed this Way: the United States of America, the States of Australia and World War II* (East Roseville, NSW, 2000).
Reischauer, Edwin O, *Japan, the Story of a* Nation (New York, 1981).
Revel, Jean-Francois, *L'Obsession Anti-Americaine* (Paris, 2002).
Ricks,Thomas E, *Fiasco, The American Military Adventure in Iraq* (New York, 2006).

Ritzer, George, *The McDonaldization of Society* (Thousand Oaks, CA, 2004).
Roberts, Andrew, *A History of the English-Speaking Peoples Since 1900* (New York, 2006).
Roger, Philippe, *L'Ennemi. Genealogie de l'antiamericainisme francois* (Paris, 2002).
Rothstein, H S, *Afghanistan and the Troubled Future of Unconventional Warfare* (Annapolis, MD, 2006).
Sampson, Anthony, *The Seven Sisters: The Great Oil Companies and the World They Made* (London, 1975).
Sawer, Marian, and Hindess, Barry, eds, *Us and Them: Anti-elitism in Australia* (Perth, 2004).
Scheuer, Michael, *Imperial Hubris: Why the West is Losing the War on Terror* (Dulles, VA, 2004).
Schrecker, Ellen, *Many are the Crimes: McCarthyism in America* (Princeton, NJ, 1999).
Schwartz, Herman M, *States Versus Markets: History, Geography and the Development of the International Political Economy* (New York, 1994).
Schoenbaum, D, *The United States and the State of Israel* (Oxford, 1993).
Sharp, Andrew, *Ancient Voyagers in the Pacific* (Mitcham, Victoria, 1957).
Shawcross, William, *Sideshow* (New York, 1979).
Sheridan, Greg, *The Partnership: The Inside Story of the US-Australian Alliance under Bush and Howard* (Sydney, 2006).
Shuja, Sharif, 'The United States and India', *National Observer*, Melbourne, Winter 2006.
Simmons, Matthew R, *Twilight in the Desert: The Coming Saudi Oil Shock and the World Economy* (Hoboken, New Jersey, 2005).
Simmons, R C, *The American Colonies, from Settlement to Independence* (London, 1976).
Smith, Gaddis, *The Last Years of the Monroe Doctrine, 1945–1993* (New York, 1994).
Smith, Joseph Wayne, *Global Meltdown* (New York, 1998).
Spengler, Oswald, *The Decline of the West,* [1926–28] (New York,1939).
Stephan, John, *Sakhalin: a History* (Oxford, 1971).
Stephan, John, *The Kurile Islands: Russo-Japanese Frontier in the* Pacific (Oxford, 1974).
Stephan, John, *The Russian Far East: a History* (Oxford, 1994).
Stelzer, Irwin, ed, *The Neo-Con Reader* (New York, 2004).
Taylor, A J P, *English History, 1914–45* (Oxford, 1965).
The 9/11 Commission Report (Washington, 2004).
Thompson, Peter, and Macklin, Robert, *The Battle of Brisbane* (Sydney, 2000).
Thorne, Alan, 'Australia's Oldest Human Remains: Age of the Lake Mungo 3 Skeleton', *Journal of Human Evolution,* Vol. 36.
Tindall, George, and Shi, David, *America, A Narrative History* (New York, 1992).
Tivnan, Edward, *The Lobby: Jewish Political Power and American Foreign Policy* (New York, 1987).
Toynbee, Arnold, *A Study of History*, 12 volumes, 1934–61.

Tyrrell, Ian, 'American Exceptionalism in an Age of International History', *The American Historical Review*, Vol. 96, No. 4 (1991), pp. 1031–72.

Unger, Craig, *House of Bush, House of Saud* (New York, 2004).

US Dept of Defense, *Military Transformation: A Strategic Approach*, Fall, 2003.

US Department of Energy, *International Energy Outlook* (New York, 2003).

US Department of Energy, Energy Information Administration, web site: http://www.eia.doe.gov/emeu/international/contents.html

Van Alstyne, Richard W, *The United States and East Asia* (New York, 1973).

Von Clausewitz, Carl, *On War* (Princeton, NJ, 1989).

Walker, Martin, ed, *The Iraq War: As Witnessed by the Correspondents and Photographers of United Press International* (Dulles VA, 2003).

Wheatcroft, Andrew, *Infidels: A History of the Conflict between Christendom and Islam,* (New York, 2004).

Woodward, Bob, *Bush at War* (New York, 2002).

Woodward, Bob, *Plan of Attack* (New York, 2004).

Woodward, Bob, *State of Denial* (New York, 2006).

'X' (George Kennan), 'The Sources of Soviet Conduct', *Foreign Affairs*, July 1947.

Yergin, Daniel, *The Prize* (New York, 1991).

Ye'or, Bat, *Eurabia: The Euro-Arab Axis* (Madison, NJ, 2005).

Index

Note: Numbers in brackets preceded by *n* refer to footnotes.